THE WORLD'S CLASSICS

THE POLITICS

ARISTOTLE (384–322 BC), with Plato one of the two greatest philosophers of antiquity, and in the view of many the greatest philosopher of all time, lived and taught in Athens for most of his career. He began as a student in Plato's Academy and may for some time have acted as tutor to Alexander the Great. He left writings on a prodigious variety of subjects, covering the whole field of knowledge from biology and astronomy to rhetoric and literary criticism, from political theory to the most abstract reaches of philosophy. The *Politics* was probably written towards the end of his career when he was head of the Lyceum and draws on Aristotle's own extensive research into the constitutional affairs of the Greek cities. It is possibly the most influential book on political theory ever to be written.

Sir ERNEST BARKER (1874–1960) held fellowships at several Oxford Colleges before becoming Principal of Kings College London in 1920 and Professor of Political Science at Cambridge in 1928. He retired in 1939. He was one of the most distinguished scholars of his day and had a lifelong love for Aristotle's *Politics*. His many publications included *The Political Thought of Plato and Aristotle* (London, 1906). His translation of the *Politics* was first published in 1946.

R. F. STALLEY studied Classics and Philosophy at Oxford and spent a year at Harvard as Frank Knox Memorial Fellow. Since 1968 he has taught Philosophy at the University of Glasgow. His main interest has been in the political philosophy of Plato and Aristotle. His publications in this field include *An Introduction to Plato's Laws* (Oxford, 1983).

THE WORLD'S CLASSICS

ARISTOTLE
The Politics

Translated by
ERNEST BARKER

Revised with an Introduction and Notes by
R. F. STALLEY

Oxford   New York
OXFORD UNIVERSITY PRESS

Oxford University Press, Walton Street, Oxford OX2 6DP

Oxford New York
Athens Auckland Bangkok Bombay
Calcutta Cape Town Dar es Salaam Delhi
Florence Hong Kong Istanbul Karachi
Kuala Lumpur Madras Madrid Melbourne
Mexico City Nairobi Paris Singapore
Taipei Tokyo Toronto

and associated companies in
Berlin Ibadan

Oxford is a trade mark of Oxford University Press

British Library Cataloguing in Publication Data
Data available

Library of Congress Cataloging in Publication Data
Aristotle.
[Politics. English]
The politics / Aristotle: translated by Sir Ernest Barker:
revised with an introduction and notes by R. F. Stalley.
p.   cm.—(World's classics)
Includes bibliographical references and index.
1. Political science—Early works to 1800.   I. Barker, Sir
Ernest, 1874–1960.   II. Stalley, R. F.   III. Title.   IV. Series.
320'.01'1 – dc20   JC71.A41B3   1995   94-15287

ISBN 0–19–283109–7

3 5 7 9 10 8 6 4

Printed in Great Britain by
BPC Paperbacks Ltd., Aylesbury, Bucks

INTRODUCTION

ARISTOTLE'S *Politics* raises more clearly than any other text some of the most fundamental issues which confront anyone who attempts to think seriously about the ways in which human societies are organized and governed. These issues are as pressing now as they were in the fourth century BC when the *Politics* was first written. But although the *Politics* can still speak to us with a powerful voice there are a number of ways in which it is unlike any modern text and in which it can appear puzzling to the modern reader. First, it is not the work of a narrow specialist but is part of what is probably the most comprehensive system of thought ever devised. We need therefore to relate the *Politics* to the general principles and methods of Aristotle's philosophy. Secondly, the world in which Aristotle lived was very different from our own. So, although the fundamental issues may be the same as those which concern us, the context in which Aristotle raises them may seem very unfamiliar. We have therefore to study the *Politics* against the background of the Greek world as it was in the fourth century BC—a world in which the basic unit of political organization was not the nation state but the small independent city-state or *polis*. Thirdly, there are, as one might expect, difficulties in the style, organization, and vocabulary of Aristotle's writing which have to be addressed if we are to read it with any understanding.

Aristotle on the Nature of Society

Aristotle was not only a great philosopher but also what we would now call a scientist. In particular he wrote extensively on biological topics and his study of biology clearly exercised a powerful influence on his thought in other areas. It makes sense therefore to begin a study of the *Politics* by thinking about Aristotle's conception of nature (*phusis*) in its bearing on political matters.

During the fifth century the Greeks had evidently become

particularly conscious that laws and customs varied from people to people and from place to place. According to a story told by Herodotus (III. 8), the Greeks were shocked to hear that some Indian peoples ate their dead. The Indians were equally shocked to hear that the Greeks burned theirs. Thus what seemed right to one people seemed wrong to another. To understand such phenomena many Greek thinkers used the two contrasting terms *phusis* or 'nature' and *nomos*, which is commonly translated as 'law', 'custom', or 'convention'. Examples like the burial practices described by Herodotus demonstrate that *nomos*, convention, varies from place to place. But nature, *phusis*, is the same everywhere. We must therefore distinguish between what holds by *phusis* and what holds by *nomos*. This distinction between *phusis* and *nomos* could be used in different ways. One could, on the one hand, argue that there are some beliefs about right and wrong which are universally accepted and which may thus be attributed to *phusis*, even though many particular practices are based simply on a *nomos* accepted by a particular community. But, on the other hand, one could also use the distinction in more radical ways. In particular it could be argued that *all* beliefs about right and wrong are a matter of *nomos* and thus depend purely on human convention. Thus in Plato's *Republic* (358e–359b), Glaucon refers to the view that we would all really like the freedom to do whatever harm we want to others but do not, of course, want others to have the same freedom to harm us. We therefore make 'laws and mutual agreements'. In other words we forgo the freedom to harm other people in return for a guarantee that we will not suffer harm from them. On this view, morality and law have their basis in human convention and the state too is an artificial creation constructed by human beings to protect themselves from one another.

In the *Republic*, Plato opposes this conventionalist view by arguing that there are what he calls Forms, which cannot be perceived through the senses but can be grasped by the reason. One function of the Forms is to serve as ideal standards. The views of the ordinary man about right and wrong embody a dim recollection of the Form of justice, but a true philosopher would be able to grasp the Form in full clarity. Thus only a society ruled by philosophers could be perfectly just. In his later work, the *Laws*, Plato says nothing of the Forms but offers instead a picture of law as the deliverance of reason—the same divine reason which governs the universe as a whole and whose operations are beautifully displayed in the movements of the heavens. Thus Plato seeks to answer those who see morality as an artificial creation by appealing to eternal standards which are outside the changing world of ordinary experience, and are grasped by reason rather than by observation.

Aristotle shares Plato's antipathy to the conventionalist view and the conception of nature and society which he offers has much more in common with Plato's than is often supposed, but the route by which he gets there is very different. Rather than turning away from the world of perception, Aristotle's method is to start with the data of experience—what he calls the phenomena. In a natural science, like biology, this means that one must study the various facts of observation in order to achieve a grasp of the underlying principles. Observation of different animals may, for example, enable one to grasp the underlying general truths about their nature. In the case of ethics and politics the phenomena include laws and customs of different communities, but they also include the different opinions of men at large and in particular of those deemed to be wise. The fact that Aristotle starts from this kind of data does not mean that he is committed to seeing all institutions as equally valuable or to accepting as true every opinion that has popular support. What it does mean is that he examines and sifts these data in order to discover the truths that lie within. It is characteristic of him not to reject an opinion outright but to see it as involving a partial truth—that is as being true in one way but not in another.

The concept of form may be as important for the understanding of Aristotle's political philosophy as it is for Plato's, but to explain its significance requires a digression. We can begin by thinking about artefacts, such as a statue or a house. A sculptor who creates a statue imposes a form on a certain quantity of matter. He may, for example, impose on a lump of stone a form like that of a man. The stone here occupies the role of matter, so the statue is a combination of matter and form; it is in-formed matter. Aristotle in fact sees the form as entering into the process of creating the sculpture in three different ways. The sculptor conceives the form in his mind before he sets to work; the sculpture he creates has that form; and the form is also the goal or end of the sculptor's activity, i.e. he seeks to produce something of that form. The process of building a house can be analysed in the same way. The builder conceives the house in his mind; he then sets to work to create that house by imposing the form on his materials; and the house is the end or goal of his activity. The house is not simply a pile of bricks and planks. In creating the house the bricks and planks are given a form—that is a structure or organization. If they cease to have that organization, the house no longer exists. If the materials are rearranged in a different form we have a different building.

Aristotle recognizes a parallel between artefacts and things such as animals or plants which exist by nature. A tree is not just a collection of roots, trunk, and branches but has a definite form. When it loses that form it ceases to be a tree. Similarly an animal is not just a heap of flesh and bone. The difference between the artefact and the plant or the animal is, of course, that plants and animals are not produced by a craftsman. In the case of an oak tree, to use a favourite example of modern commentators, an already existent tree produces an acorn which, in turn, has a natural tendency to grow into a tree. Of course, not all acorns grow into trees. Some rot or are eaten by pigs, but the nature of the acorn is to grow into a tree, provided that it encounters the right conditions. In this sense the end or goal of the acorn is to become a tree and one can grasp what an acorn is only by seeing that this is its end. The same pattern of analysis applies to human beings and other animals. A man produces a 'seed' or sperm whose nature is to grow into a man if it encounters the right conditions (in the womb). Thus living things have within them a principle of growth which impels them not to sprout randomly but to develop towards an end, i.e. to instantiate a particular form. Aristotle's conception of nature is thus thoroughly teleological. Everything which exists by nature exists for an end and one cannot grasp its nature without understanding that end.

In the *Politics* Aristotle clearly means to use an analysis of this kind. He argues that the *polis* is a compound and a whole rather than a mere aggregation (1258ª18, 1274ᵇ39). In other words the *polis* is not simply a collection of human beings. Nor, for that matter, is it a geographical area. Rather, as Aristotle suggests in Book III, its identity consists in its organization and structure. This organization is its constitution. So the constitution stands in the role of form to the *polis*. If the constitution ceases to be in force then the *polis* ceases to exist. This view would, of course, be compatible with the view that the *polis* is an artefact, like a house. Some of Aristotle's phrases may seem to suggest this view. He talks, for example, of the statesman as a master-craftsman (*architektōn*) and speaks on one occasion of the man who first constructed a *polis* (1253ª30). But Aristotle also sees the *polis* as natural. Human beings naturally form families, the village is a natural outgrowth of the family, and the *polis* is an outgrowth of the village (I. 2). He argues too, in one of his most famous phrases, that man is a political animal: that is, man is made by nature to live in a *polis*, or more briefly he is a *polis*-animal (1253ª2–5). These claims may not be so difficult to reconcile as it might seem. Art and nature compliment rather than contradict one another. For example, we might think of the gardener whose skill enables the rose bush to fulfil its nature by producing beautiful flowers. So the man who creates a *polis* works with nature, not against it. Furthermore, man is naturally endowed with powers of practical reason, so that in creating a *polis* he is fulfilling his nature. Aristotle could well argue that man is as much a *polis*-creating as a *polis*-inhabiting animal. A more serious source of difficulty is the claim that the *polis* is prior to the individual, so that the man without a *polis* is like a hand without a body (1253ª18–23). Aristotle could argue that the *polis* is prior to man in the sense that one cannot really understand what human nature is without referring to the *polis*. He could also argue that a man without a *polis* cannot fulfil his nature and is therefore like a stunted oak tree. But the analogy with the hand suggests the stronger view that one could not be a man at all without being part of the *polis*. This seems to be incompatible with Aristotle's own apparent belief that there was a time when the *polis* did not exist and human beings lived in scattered families.

Aristotle's teleological conception of nature also underpins his moral philosophy. In the *Ethics* Aristotle seeks to discover what he calls the 'good for man'. Everyone, he thinks, will agree that this consists in what he calls *eudaimonia* (*Nicomachean Ethics* 1095ª18–20). This term is generally translated 'happiness' but really means rather more than that. *Eudaimonia* is a general condition of well-being or the condition of one who is living well. The view that the good for man is *eudaimonia* is supported, Aristotle believes, by two considerations: (*a*) *eudaimonia* has, above everything else, the character of an end—i.e. we seek other things for the sake of *eudaimonia* but seek *eudaimonia* purely for its own sake; and (*b*) it is self-sufficient—i.e. *eudaimonia* is not only desirable in itself but there is nothing which could be added to it to make it more desirable.

To say that the good for man is *eudaimonia* is clearly not very informative unless one can say what this consists in, and the main project of the *Ethics*, in both its versions, is accordingly to discover the nature of *eudaimonia*. Here Aristotle relies heavily on his conception of nature. Since nature does nothing in vain (i.e. does everything for a purpose), man must have a purpose or function (*Nicomachean Ethics* I. 7; *Eudemian Ethics* II. 1). Just as a good flute-player is one who performs well his function of playing the flute, so a human being will achieve his good by performing well his function whatever that is. To discover man's function we need to consider what it is that distinguishes man from other creatures. We share with both plants and animals the capacity for nutrition and growth and with animals the capacity for movement and perception. What is unique to us is reason. Thus, Aristotle argues, man's purpose or function is to be found in the active life of the rational part of the soul (*Nicomachean Ethics* 1098ª3). The good life is one in which we perform this function well, i.e. in accordance with the appropriate standards of excellence or virtue. Thus *eudaimonia*, or *happiness*, can be defined as 'activity in accordance with excellence, and if there is more than one kind of excellence in accordance with the best and most perfect of these'. But rational activity takes two forms. There is practical reason, which one shows primarily in deliberating on behalf of oneself or one's city, but there is also theoretical reason, which one displays particularly in philosophical contemplation. There is thus an ambiguity in Aristotle's account of the good life. Is it to be sought in the life of practical reason, or of theoretical reason, or both? One might expect Aristotle to argue that the best life involves both forms of reason, but, in fact, in the closing pages of the *Nicomachean Ethics* he seems to give priority to theoretical reason and the life of contemplation. The difficulty for Aristotle is that while he sees man as a political animal, that is as a being which cannot flourish outside society, he also believes that man's highest element is the reason and that this is most perfectly exercised in a god-like life of pure contemplation. It is reasonably clear that he would wish to integrate both these points into his account of the best life, but it is much less easy to see quite how he means to do so.

On Aristotle's understanding, the city or *polis* exists for the sake of the good life. It is he claims a form of association or partnership (*koinōnia*); all associations exist for the sake of some good; the city is the most sovereign of all associations and must be directed to the most sovereign of all goods (I. I). The purpose of the city is thus to enable its citizens to live a life of virtue or excellencé. It has to furnish not only the physical means for this life but also the necessary leisure and the kind of education and upbringing which will render its citizens virtuous. This does not, of course, mean that all cities do in practice promote a life of virtue. It may even be that no existing city does so. But the life of virtue is the goal of the city's existence and the closer a city comes to achieving that goal, the better it is. This, of course, immediately differentiates Aristotle's position from that of those, like the sophist Lycophron (1280ᵇ10), who see the city as simply a device for mutual self-protection or as a kind of commercial alliance. It has a positive moral purpose. This conception informs Aristotle's discussions in the *Politics* in at least two ways. In the first place, it underpins his accounts of existing and possible constitutions. Aristotle is well aware that any state needs to provide security and stability for its inhabitants and much of his discussion, particularly in Books v and vi, is directed to these points. But, in his eyes, security and stability are not enough. A good constitution must be directed to the good of its citizens, and this means that it must not only have well-meaning rulers but must be based on the right conception of the good. In other words, it must be directed to the life of goodness or virtue as Aristotle understands it. In the second place, Aristotle's conception of the moral purpose of the *polis* quite obviously provides the framework for the incomplete account of an ideal *polis* which occupies Books VII and VIII. That account is explicitly founded on the assumption that the purpose of the *polis* is to make possible a life of Aristotelian virtue. Thus a major concern for Aristotle is to describe how, given conditions that are not totally unrealistic, one might construct a community in which the citizens have the leisure for the kinds of activity which he regards as truly worth while. Disturbingly, however, he does not disguise the fact that only a limited section of the population will be able to achieve such a life. Many people lack the appropriate capacities, but, in any case, the existence of a city requires that a substantial number of its inhabitants engage in occupations which are inconsistent with a good life. Manual labour and trade not only take up time but they also render people unfit for the activities which Aristotle sees as worth while. Thus those engaged in such occupations are necessary for the existence of the *polis* but cannot strictly be members of it. It is implicit in Aristotle's conception of the good life that not everyone can achieve it, and that the rest of us are best off serving those who can.

Aristotle in the Greek World

The Greek world which Aristotle took for granted comprised well over a thousand independent city-states. These were located not only on the Greek mainland and on the islands of the Aegean Sea but on the coast of what we now call Turkey, in Italy, on the Adriatic and Black Sea coasts, and even as far afield as Spain. More marginally the Greek world also included the growing power of Macedon, whose kings at least were recognized as Greeks and allowed to compete in the Olympic Games. Aristotle's political theory is based on an extensive knowledge of the affairs of these communities—something like a hundred of them are mentioned in the *Politics*.

The Greeks believed that they shared a common ancestry. They also shared a loose cluster of beliefs and myths about the gods and heroes which could accommodate local traditions and practice while also allowing them to recognize certain common religious shrines and festivals. But clearly what contributed most to their sense of unity was the possession of a common language (albeit with significant variation of dialect). The world as seen by the average Greek (the Greek whose views are largely echoed and justified by Aristotle) consisted of two kinds of people, Greeks and barbarians. The term 'barbarian' was applied to all those who did not speak Greek (even to those like the Egyptians who were acknowledged to have achieved a high level of civilization). It may originally have meant 'those who say "ba-ba"' i.e. people who make unintelligible noises. According to this way of thought the Greeks were not just different but better—more intelligent and inventive and more competent in military and other matters. This sense of superiority was clearly strengthened by the defeat of the Persian invasions of 490 and 480–479 and the consequent liberation of the Greek cities of Ionia (the coast and adjacent islands of modern Turkey) which had been under Persian control. Although only a small minority of the Greek cities had fought against the Persians, the fact that they had defeated the most powerful empire of their day strengthened the Greeks' sense that they were intrinsically better than the rest of the world. This sense of superiority did not prevent individual politicians or cities looking for Persian support (particularly support of a financial nature) when it suited them and it survived the 'King's Peace' of 386 which enabled the Persians to reassert their authority over the Ionian cities.

Aristotle shows little sign of recognizing the arbitrariness of the distinction between Greeks and barbarians. He believes that while Greeks are intrinsically capable of ruling as well as being ruled and are thus fitted for freedom, barbarians lack a 'ruling element' in their souls and are thus fitted to be ruled in the manner of slaves (1252^{b}5–10). Characteristically Aristotle finds a justification for this claim in the supposed facts of Biology and Geography. 'The peoples of cold countries generally, and particularly those of Europe, are full of spirit but deficient in skill and intelligence.' For this reason they are comparatively free but have no capacity for governing others. 'The peoples of Asia are endowed with skill and intelligence, but are deficient in spirit.' For this reason they continue in a condition of servility. The Greeks come between the two. They therefore combine spirit with intelligence. They can live in freedom and achieve a high level of political development. If only they could attain unity, they could govern every other people (VII. 7. 1327^{b}23–33).

The basic unit of society as Aristotle sees it is the *oikia* or household, which is constituted by the relations of husband and wife, father and sons, and master and slave (1253^{b}1–4). The household is an economic as well as a social unit (indeed our 'economics' is derived from Aristotle's word for household management). Aristotle clearly envisages that the household will produce most of what it needs by agriculture and domestic crafts such as spinning and weaving. It must also produce a sufficient surplus to purchase whatever else it needs, but Aristotle disapproves strongly of activities which are designed purely to make a profit (I. 8–10). He regards trade and most kinds of manual labour as unfit for a free man. They should be left to slave or non-citizen foreigners (1328^{b}33–1329^{a}32).

Aristotle sees the institution of slavery as essential. A slave is for him a 'living tool' or 'instrument' without which there would be no leisure for the activities which really make life worth while (1253^{b}23–33). He justifies the institution by arguing that some human beings lack the kind of rational power that is necessary for ruling or giving directions and are thus fitted by nature to be slaves, but he has to admit that, in practice, those who are enslaved may not be those who are intended by nature for that role ($1255^b16-1256^a2$). In one sense Aristotle's attitude here is understandable, if not excusable. Greek society depended heavily on slavery. Without it most of what we admire in Greek civilization and most of what Aristotle thought really valuable in life would have been impossible. Given this background it is perhaps not surprising that Aristotle could convince himself that some people are born to be slaves. But Aristotle's treatment of slavery is not just a concession to contemporary prejudices. It follows naturally from his views (a) that the good life requires leisure from manual labour and (b) that nature is hierarchically organized so that the lower elements within it exist for the sake of the higher. Given these assumptions it is a natural step to the claim that some inferior kinds of men are born to enable the better kind to live a life of leisure.

It is equally unsurprising that Aristotle accepts the general Greek view that women are fitted only for a domestic role. He criticizes at some length what he takes to be Plato's suggestion that women and children should be held in common (i.e. that the family should be abolished) (II. 2–4), but gives no serious attention to the associated idea that women should be rulers. He assumes that the position assigned to women in Greek society is justified by nature, i.e. that women are fitted by nature to exercise control only in a limited domestic sphere. He argues that women, unlike natural slaves, do have the power of deliberation, but says that in them it 'lacks authority' (1260^a10-14). Perhaps the thought is that a woman's emotional character makes her unfitted for being ultimately in charge of anything.

The typical Greek city-state was by modern standards tiny. Athens in Aristotle's day had a territory of around 1,000 square miles and may have had a population, including women, children, slaves, and aliens, of over 200,000, but most other cities were much smaller, comprising no more than a small town and the surrounding countryside. Aristotle is certain that the city should not exceed a certain rather modest size. He notes that while it would be possible to build a wall all the way round the Peloponnese, that would not turn it into a single *polis*. Equally a huge city like Babylon or a state which consisted of a whole race of people could not be *polis* (1276ª25–30). A *polis* must be large enough to be self-sufficient —that is, it must provide all that is necessary for human flourishing—but it must not be allowed to grow out of proportion. The citizens, for example, must know each other if they are to choose the right candidates for office, or if they are to decide lawsuits correctly, and it must be possible for the whole citizen body to be addressed by a single herald (VII. 4). So the *polis*, as Aristotle understands it, is a face-to-face society which presupposes that the citizens know one another and can all take part in a single assembly.

Many commentators have pointed out that the Greek *polis* evidently meant much more to its citizens than the modern state does to its inhabitants, though it is difficult to express the difference with any precision. We, for example, are accustomed to draw a distinction between the state and its citizens. We may distinguish between spheres of life which are properly the concern of the state and those which are not. We may worry that the state is growing too powerful and is restricting the liberties of the citizens. It would have been difficult for the Greeks to grasp this contrast between state and citizen. When we would refer to the state of Athens or of Sparta, the Greeks would speak simply of the Athenians or the Spartans. Similarly there was no sharp distinction between law and morality. The single word *nomos* is used not only of laws incorporated in the legal code of a particular city, but of unwritten rules which are supposed to be binding on all men and of social customs which are unique to a particular community. This wide scope of *nomos* is reflected in the practice of the Greek courts. The forensic speeches of the orators, for example, often appeal to what we would think of as extra-legal considerations—that is to considerations of morality or public interest. Again we are apt to conceive of religion as a private matter—or at least as one for the Church rather than the state. But the Greeks had no conception of a Church—the cult of the gods was a public matter which was the responsibility of the *polis*. Priests were generally public officials and the temples which served as symbols of the identity and prosperity of the *polis* were erected at public expense.

Barker wrote of the *polis* as conceived by Aristotle and by

Greek thought generally that 'it is a small and intimate society: it is a church as well as a state: it makes no distinction between the province of the state and that of society: it is in a word an integrated system of social ethics, which realises to the full the capacities of its members, and therefore claims their full allegiance' (lxvii). There is a danger here of idealizing the *polis*. Greek cities were often ridden with strife. Political quarrels were often fought out with a ferocity which would match any conflict of our own day and it was clearly possible for whole sections of the population to feel thoroughly alienated. As is evident in *Politics* v, which deals with the problems of civil disorder and constitutional change, Aristotle is only too aware of such conflicts. But at the same time he has high aspirations for the *polis* and does see it in much the way that Barker describes. These aspirations are implicit in the definition at the beginning of the *Politics* of the *polis* as a *koinōnia,* an association or partnership. It is in fact the most inclusive association and the one which exists for the highest goal—the living of a good life. The Greek term *koinōnia* is connected with the idea of sharing or holding something in common, so Aristotle sees the *polis* as a shared enterprise—almost like a club—in which the participants pool their resources in order to achieve a common goal—that of living a good life. This is in many ways an immensely attractive picture, but it has its unattractive side. Aristotle recognizes that, even where conditions are as favourable as ever they could be, it is not possible for everyone in the city to live what he sees as a good life. People are needed to carry out tasks which are necessary but, in Aristotle's eyes, demeaning. These people cannot be part of the *polis* because they are incapable of participating in the end to which it is directed, but they are, nevertheless, necessary for its existence. Thus Aristotle's conception of the *polis* as a common undertaking depends on the presence of slaves and resident foreigners who are not members and do not share its privileges.

Aristotle on Greek Politics

Through the fourth and fifth centuries BC a dominant theme in the politics of many Greek cities was the struggle between

democracy and oligarchy. Democracy, which means literally
'the rule of the people', is commonly supposed to have originated at Athens with the reforms of Cleisthenes in 508/7. The
process of democratization was carried forward by Pericles
and Ephialtes, so that Athenian democracy reached its most
developed form in the latter part of the fifth century. Under
this form of constitution the most powerful body was the
ekklēsia or assembly. All adult male citizens had a right to
take part in the deliberations of this body and it took all
major decisions. Day-to-day business was carried out by the
council or *boulē*, which had 500 members chosen by lot. Most
other public officials were also chosen by lot, so that every
citizen had an equal chance of finding himself in one of the
major offices—the most notable exception was the office of
polemarchos, or general, which was always chosen by election.

The obvious alternative to democracy was what the Greeks
called 'oligarchy' or 'the rule of the few'. Under this form of
constitution participation in political affairs was restricted to
those who possessed a fixed property qualification. The level
of qualification could vary—quite low in the more moderate
oligarchies and quite high in the more extreme ones. The
normal method of choosing public officials was by election
(with only those who satisfied the property qualification
taking part). The quarrels between oligarchs and democrats
were fought out within and between cities. In the fifth century
when Athens was at the height of her power she fostered and
sometimes imposed democratic regimes on other cities. Oligarchic cities tended to look for leadership to Sparta. So the
Peloponnesian War, which broke out in 431 and lasted inter-
mittently until Sparta defeated Athens in 404, was in some
respects a war between democracy and oligarchy. In the
fourth century no city in Greece succeeded in establishing a
dominant position for long and many cities were torn apart
by faction fighting. One of Aristotle's avowed aims in the
Politics is to address this situation. In Books v and vi he
investigates the causes of disorder and change and discusses
the ways in which constitutions can be made more stable.

As one would expect, Aristotle is much concerned with the
problems of oligarchies and democracies, but he recognizes,

of course, that cities may be governed in other ways. The Greeks believed, no doubt rightly, that they had once been governed by kings. In the more recent past aristocracy had been the norm—that is political power had been in the hands of a small group of families who thought of themselves as the *aristoi*, the best people. Many cities had also experienced periods of 'tyrannical' government. A tyrant was what we should call a 'dictator', an individual who had managed to seize power for himself and establish a form of extra-legal monarchy. In Book III Aristotle provides himself with an analytical framework with which to understand these different forms of government. Constitutions, he claims, can be classified according to whether power is in the hands of one man, of a few, or of many. In each case we can distinguish a 'right' form and a 'wrong' or 'perverted' form. There are thus three 'right' constitutions and three 'deviant' ones (III. 6–7).

Among the 'right' forms of constitution kingship is the rule of one man for the common interest. Aristotle recognizes that it is likely to be rare but argues that it is the appropriate form of constitution for a people in which there is one man or one family of outstanding merit (1288^{a}15–29). The 'wrong' or 'perverted' form of constitution corresponding to kingship is tyranny, the rule of one man in his own interest. The 'right' form of government by a few is aristocracy (literally 'rule by the best people'). But Aristotle's conception of aristocracy is not quite the traditional one. Genuine aristocrats, in his eyes, owe their position not to the deeds of their ancestors, but to their own virtues (1279^{a}34–9). This form of constitution would be appropriate for a population which contained a small number of families of outstanding merit (1286^{b}3–7). The 'wrong' form of government by a few is oligarchy—a constitution in which a small number of people govern in their own interest. The right form of government by the many is not, as we might expect, government by the whole population in the general interest. Aristotle believes that it is impossible for the whole population to have the virtuous character needed to govern well. So the right form of government by the many is one in which political participation is restricted to those who can afford the armour of a hoplite soldier (1239^{a}37–^{b}4). To

describe this form of government Aristotle uses the word
politeia—the very word which he and other authors normally
use with the meaning 'constitution'. (Translators often distinguish between these two uses by coining the word 'polity' to
use as a translation of *politeia* when it is used in this special
sense, but that, of course, blurs a significant point. Aristotle
clearly thinks of this form of constitution as being the genuine
constitution or constitutional government *par excellence*.) The
wrong or perverted form of government by the many is
democracy, which Aristotle sees as government by the masses
in their own interest.

This sixfold schema has considerable limitations and Aristotle himself quickly moves beyond it. In fact he modifies it
almost immediately by arguing that the distinction between
oligarchy and democracy is not primarily one of numbers but
of wealth. Oligarchy is the rule of the wealthy, while democracy is the rule of the poor. It is true that the wealthy are
generally few in number while the poor are more numerous,
but this need not necessarily be the case (III. 8). The economic
division is thus fundamental. One might expect Aristotle,
having made this point, to argue that political problems can
be solved only by economic means, but this is not in fact the
line he takes. Indeed he is critical of the proposal in Plato's
Republic for the abolition of private property and of schemes
put forward by other would-be reformers for the equalization
of property (II. 5 and 7). Instead he offers a diagnosis of
political conflict in terms of competing conceptions of justice.
All are agreed that justice consists in some kind of equality.
The democrats argue that those who are equal in being free-
born citizens should have equal access to offices and honours.
The oligarchs, on the other hand, argue that political privileges
should be distributed in proportion to wealth, so that those
whose wealth is greater receive greater privileges. Others might
argue that these privileges should be proportioned to excellence of character or to nobility of birth (1280^{a}7–25). Different
kinds of constitution thus rest on different conceptions of
justice. The upshot might appear to be that justice is relative—that what is just in a democratic state is different from
what is just in an oligarchic state and that that is all there is

to be said about the matter. This, however, is not Aristotle's own position. He argues that in distributing offices and honours we should consider the end or purpose of the city. Those who make the largest contribution to that end should be assigned the greatest privileges. Thus if wealth was the end for which the city existed then those with the greatest wealth should receive the greatest privileges. But Aristotle holds that the purpose of the city is the good life which consists in noble actions—the kind of activity that is worth while in itself. Wealth and free birth are necessary conditions of the existence of the city and thus deserve some consideration but the excellence of character which makes possible the kinds of activity that are truly worth while must have pre-eminence (1280^a25–1281^b10).

Although Aristotle's account of justice may at first sight seem to be purely formal it provides the basis for a distinctive and cogently argued approach to the problems of politics. Although political divisions rest on economic ones they are primarily, as we might say, disputes about values. Different values lead to different views as to what constitutional forms should be adopted as well as to disputes about particular policies. Aristotle argues that we should seek to solve such disputes by asking what the end of the city is, or in other words by asking what the city is for. Of course this too can be a subject of disagreement. Some think the city exists simply to protect its citizens, or as Aristotle puts it, that it exists simply for the sake of life; others think that it exists to create wealth. Aristotle is scathing about both these views, which are, of course, at least as prevalent today as they were in ancient Greece. Those who hold them fail to see the difference between a mere alliance and a city. The former at most prevents people from injuring one another. The latter is concerned to ensure that its citizens are good men. The argument here depends in part on that in the *Ethics* where Aristotle demonstrates that the good life consists in more than mere survival and cannot even be identified with the accumulation of riches, but must consist in a life of virtuous activity. The city must, so far as possible, be constituted so as to promote this kind of life.

As Aristotle himself is the first to acknowledge, recognizing that the city exists for the good life does not solve all political problems. Even if one concedes the pre-eminent claims of virtue there could still be disputes about which constitutional arrangements are appropriate. Some may argue that a single individual of outstanding excellence should be supreme. Others may claim that the excellence of the people as a whole, taken collectively, outweighs that of any individual. Still others hold that law should be supreme. The situation is even more complicated if one concedes that some account should also be taken of other claims such as those of wealth and free birth and of the varying circumstances of particular cities. In Books VII and VIII Aristotle describes a constitution for a city in which circumstances are as favourable as they are ever likely to be. In this city the citizens will receive an appropriate upbringing and training, while demeaning manual work and trade will be left to slaves and aliens. Thus all the citizens can be assumed to be men of virtue and to have time for political activity and for a cultivated leisure. But of course most legislators are less fortunate; they have to grapple with circumstances which are anything but propitious. Since politics, as Aristotle conceives it, is a practical as well as a theoretical science, the Aristotelian political scientist cannot confine himself to describing ideals. He must be able to give advice about the affairs of cities as they actually are.

The practical focus of the *Politics* is most apparent in Books IV–VI. In these books he concentrates much of his attention on democracy and oligarchy, describing their different varieties and the means by which they may be preserved. In doing so he demonstrates an extensive and detailed knowledge of the political affairs of the Greek cities and makes plenty of shrewd observations. Aristotle is acutely aware that situations vary from city to city and from time to time and that a policy which is appropriate for one kind of population may not work for another. He offers plenty of advice but does not pretend that there are universal remedies for political problems. His general approach may, however, be summed up rather crudely in three words: 'law', 'moderation' and 'mixture'.

Law plays an important part in Aristotle's discussion of these problems because he believes that there is a crucial distinction between those constitutions, on the one hand, where government is in accordance with law and those, on the other, where decisions depend purely on the ruling body. This distinction applies whatever the size of the ruling body. Aristotle has an evident horror of what he sees as extreme democracy in which the popular assembly has the power to do whatever it likes, untrammelled by law, but he has an equal horror of lawless monarchy (tyranny) or lawless oligarchy (what he calls 'dynasty'). This does not mean that the sovereignty of law is a panacea. Laws themselves may be biased. But Aristotle believes, no doubt rightly, that a ruling body which has to conform to law will be less likely to exercise its power in an arbitrary way or to exploit other sections of the population and will be more likely to consider the general good.

The theme of moderation takes several different forms. Aristotle believes that any ruling body, be it a tyrant, an oligarchy, or a democracy, will do well to adopt conciliatory policies and not to push its own interests too far. But Aristotle also argues for moderation in the constitution itself. The best kind of democracy is one which does not allow everyone indiscriminately to take part in political affairs, while the best kind of oligarchy is one which has only a moderate property qualification. There is, it appears, very little difference between the best kind of oligarchy and the best kind of democracy. Not surprisingly therefore, when Aristotle comes to discuss the type of constitution which is most generally practicable it is one with a moderate property qualification in which those whom Aristotle sees as 'the men in the middle' are dominant. The best source of stability and security is a large middle class, for the men in the middle will avoid the excesses of both the rich and the poor. Thus the constitution which Aristotle recommends as the best which could be achieved by most states in normal conditions differs little, if at all, from what he elsewhere calls 'constitutional government' or polity, the constitution where political participation is confined to those who can afford a hoplite's armour.

The idea of mixture is closely linked to that of moderation. Aristotle thinks of the constitution with a moderate property qualification as a mixture of democracy and oligarchy, but he also makes use of the distinct, and in some respects incompatible, idea that the constitution should include distinct democratic, oligarchic, and perhaps also aristocratic elements. He has some ingenious suggestions about how such mixtures might be achieved.

Problems in Aristotle's Theory

Like any great political thinker, Aristotle has attracted criticism as well as admiration, and, characteristically, the features of his thought which have been found most disturbing are closely connected to some of those which have proved most attractive. His advocacy of moderation is a case in point. There is clearly much good sense in what he has to say. If the main problem is to ensure political stability then it makes sense to seek solutions which everyone, or at least the largest possible section of the population, can live with, to make everyone feel that the considerations they hold to be most important have been taken into account, and to ensure that no single party can use the mechanisms of state to pursue its own sectional interests. Some of the measures Aristotle suggests have proved of permanent importance. He was, for example, the main source in the medieval and early modern periods for the idea that law should be sovereign—a doctrine whose lasting importance it would be difficult to deny. Nevertheless, one suspects that behind Aristotle's judicious moderation there are assumptions and values which are highly questionable. Consider for example the suggestion that the best practicable constitution is one with a moderate property qualification. A constitution of that kind would give the opportunity to participate in political affairs to the rich, even though they would have to share this privilege with the men in the middle. The really poor, on the other hand, would be excluded altogether. So from the point of view of the poor there has been no compromise at all—they have lost everything. The only reason why Aristotle could regard this kind of constitution as the best one generally practicable is that he is deeply suspicious of the political capacities of the poor. If it is not possible to ensure that political privileges are confined to those whom Aristotle considers to be of good character and education, then a moderate property qualification can at least exclude the least suitable characters. It is significant here that Aristotle recommends, not that the constitution should be acceptable to the largest number of people, but that it should be constructed in such a way that those who favour its continuance just outweigh those who do not ($1296^{b}15$–16, $1309^{b}16$–18). In other words, participation is to be kept to the minimum consistent with stability. This makes good sense in the light of Aristotle's belief that the purpose of the city is the good life but that this can be achieved only by a few. It means, however, that the large numbers who have no possibility of achieving the good life as Aristotle conceives it are excluded from any real form of participation.

No doubt Aristotle's belief that the labouring poor should not be full members of the city reflects a deep anti-democratic prejudice. But it is not simply an expression of prejudice. It is, rather, connected with some of the leading themes in Aristotle's political and ethical philosophy. Part of the trouble is that Aristotle assumes an exalted view of what constitutes the good life. It is a life of leisure requiring freedom from the toils of manufacture, agriculture, and trade. Aristotle believes, moreover, that these latter kinds of occupation not only take up too much time but by their nature render us unfit for the good life ($1337^{b}4$–22). Given such a view, in any society which has existed or is likely to exist in the foreseeable future those able fully to participate in the good life must inevitably be a minority. But one might object here that Aristotle simply has too restricted a view of what might constitute human flourishing. We might for example argue that the life of, shall we say, a potter who exercises his skill and shares a social life with his workmates, family, and friends provides as much scope for the exercise of a distinctively human excellence as that of the leisured aristocrat who spends his time in political activity and in cultural pursuits. A less restricted conception of what constitutes human good could thus render the idea of the city as a partnership for the good life less exclusive.

Another consequence of Aristotle's view which is not particularly obvious in his text but has been emphasized by some modern critics is that it apparently leaves the citizens of an Aristotelian state with very little freedom to choose their own ways of life. Aristotle believes that any form of constitution if it is to survive must ensure that its citizens receive the appropriate education and have an appropriate style of life. A constitution is not just an organization of offices but embodies a view about the way in which the citizens ought to live. That Aristotle takes this seriously is clear from the account of his own ideal city. As this stands it is much more concerned with the ways in which citizens will be educated and the ways in which they will live their lives than it is with political organization in the narrow sense. The purpose of the city is to make possible the living of the good life as Aristotle understands it, but this necessarily precludes the living of other forms of life and the pursuit of other values. Barker, in his Introduction, laid some stress on this aspect of the *Politics* which he connected with what he saw as the dominant nature of the Greek *polis*. Other critics have pointed to Aristotle's view that the individual is part of the city in much the same way that a hand is part of the body. Taken at its face value this might seem to suggest that the individual has no value apart from his contribution to the larger whole which is the city.

This extreme criticism would clearly be a mistake. For Aristotle the city is not an entity over and above the citizens who are its members. It exists for the sake of the good life but it is the citizens themselves who live that life. To live well is to exercise rational choice, so the good life must leave scope for choice. This is one reason why Aristotle evidently values personal relationships and private property. But, although Aristotle values freedom, he does not see it as a matter of doing what one likes or of the right to follow one's own conception of the good life (1310ª28–38, 1317ª40–ᵇ17). What counts as a good life is not a matter of individual taste but can be objectively determined by an investigation of human nature. It is the task of the statesman to know what constitutes

human excellence and to ensure that citizens are brought up
to live accordingly. So although Aristotle can be acquitted of
any charge of authoritarianism or of subordinating the individual to the state, it is clear that his conception of the city as
existing for the sake of the good life commits him to rejecting
the liberal conception of freedom which most of us now take
for granted.

Aristotle Today

Barker included in his introduction to the *Politics* an account
of the later history of Aristotle's political theory in which he
noted that while Aristotle himself was still active, his one-time
pupil Alexander was bringing to an end the kind of world
which is presupposed by the *Politics*—a world in which the
basic political unit was the independent self-sufficient *polis*, a
world in which the distinction between Greek and barbarian
was fundamental. In consequence, no doubt, of this change,
the *Politics* underwent a long period of oblivion from which it
was rescued by St Thomas Aquinas, through whom some of
its essential doctrines passed into the general thought of the
later Middle Ages. These included 'the doctrine that the law is
sovereign, and that governments are the servants of the law;
the doctrine that there is a fundamental difference between
the lawful monarch and the tyrant who governs by his arbitrary will; the doctrine that there is a right inherent in the
people, by virtue of their collective capacity for judgement, to
elect their rulers and call them to account'. These ideas were
absorbed by later writers such as Hooker, Locke, and Burke.
Thus, Barker claimed, the legacy of the *Politics* could be
summarized in one word: 'constitutionalism'.

We may baulk here at the use of the term 'legacy', as
though Aristotle's will (which, as it happens, is preserved by
Diogenes Laertius) included, alongside the provisions for his
dependants, a neatly labelled bequest for twentieth-century
political thinkers. Philosophers do not, of course, leave lega-
cies of this kind. Rather their successors choose consciously
or unconsciously to take over and adapt some of their doctrines while discarding others. But even with this qualification,

Barker's account would now seem insular. What he does not mention is that Aristotle exercised a powerful influence on both Hegel and Marx. Much of Hegel's political philosophy is inspired by a vision, largely derived from Aristotle, of the Greek *polis* as an integrated ethical community which had made it possible for men to find their own identity in the collective life of their city. Marx, who had been a student of Greek philosophy, derived from the same source the idea that society is a substance, a whole, which is prior to the individual. Of course the totalitarian states erected by Marx's twentieth-century followers were about as far removed from Aristotle's ideal as anything could be, which is one reason why some of those who seek a different understanding of Marx now emphasize his Aristotelian roots.

If one was to ask what was the most important lesson which can be derived today from a reading of the *Politics*, most scholars and political theorists would probably point to the doctrine of man as a social being. This doctrine sharply distinguishes Aristotle's political philosophy from the individualism which has dominated western political thought since the Renaissance. Whereas Aristotle sees society as prior to the individual, the prevailing view sees the individual as prior to society—in Aristotelian terms society is seen as an alliance or an aggregation rather than as a whole. This individualist attitude is most starkly presented by Hobbes, who describes men in a state of nature covenanting together to set up a sovereign and thus establish civil society in order to save their skins. Central to the individualist view is the picture of human beings as having needs and desires which are independent of the society in which they live. The function of society is to make it possible for individuals to satisfy their desires. Individualist theories may take different forms depending on how these desires and needs are conceived. Hobbes, assuming that the need for security is all-important, argued for an authoritarian state. Others, like Locke, see the function of the state as the protection of property, a view which is easily transformed into the idea that the main function of the state is to provide the conditions for increasing wealth. Still others, like Mill, have stressed the variability of human needs and desires and the variety of ways in which the personality may develop. They have, therefore, seen it as the role of the state to maximize individual freedom.

Such individualist views may be opposed to what is often called communitarianism, the idea that human beings are necessarily social so that society in a sense precedes the individual. The identity of any individual depends on his place in society. On this view an individual existing wholly outside society, if that were physically possible, would barely be human. On such a view society is not simply a means which enables individuals to achieve independently specifiable needs and desires. Being part of a society is a necessary part of being human and it is society which shapes the individuals and determines what sort of people they are. Society must therefore be based implicitly or explicitly on a conception of the good life. It is in Aristotle's terms an association or partnership for the sake of the good.

In western societies, at least, individualist views have been overwhelmingly predominant for the last three hundred years. In the twentieth century they have gained strength because the only alternative to individualism seemed to be a totalitarian state of the kind erected in eastern Europe by Marx's followers. It may be no accident that as the communist regimes have crumbled there has been in the West a resurgence of interest in communitarian ideas. In this resurgence Aristotle plays a key role, for he is of all philosophers the one who affirms most clearly the social nature of man. Aristotelian ideas are thus central to the communitarian critique of individualism. To acknowledge in this way the contemporary importance of Aristotle is not, of course, to say that he is necessarily right. As we have seen, his picture of society is both attractive and disturbing. The same can be said for contemporary communitarianism. It is attractive because it offers a picture of the citizen as a member of a community seeking the common good. It thus offers an alternative to a society in which the only values seem to be those of the market and in which relations founded on competition are increasingly taken to be the norm. But it also faces precisely the same kinds of problem which we encountered in Aristotle's theory. We may ask whether a strong sense of community can be developed without drawing a sharp distinction between those who are and those who are not members, that is without inciting discrimination and prejudice against those who do not seem to belong. We may also question whether a society based on a common conception of what constitutes the good life for a human being can grant its members the freedom, which most of us would cherish, to develop their own lifestyles and personalities. The power of Aristotle's *Politics* is that it still raises such issues more clearly and forcefully than any other text.

Reading the *Politics*

In the ancient world Aristotle was praised for his elegant literary style, but sadly none of the works which he produced for general publication has survived intact. We have instead a very large amount of writing which was apparently intended, not for the general public, but for the private use of Aristotle himself, his colleagues, and pupils. So the writings of Aristotle, as we have them, are more like lecture notes than finished literary works. There are passages which are brief, allusive, and note-like alongside others in which Aristotle's thought is explained in a fuller and clearer way. Aristotle's method is often aporetic, that is he is concerned to raise and explore problems rather than to produce clearly defined answers. Sometimes he approaches the same issue from different directions in successive passages. To make matters more complicated, it is evident that Aristotle was in the habit of reworking what he had written, so that a single work may contain passages written at different times and there are even places where what seem to be different versions of the same material appear alongside each other. There are also passages where marginal notes or additions, whether by Aristotle or by his successors, appear to have been incorporated into the text. For these reasons Aristotle's works are less easy to read than, for example, the writings of Plato's early and middle periods, but they can be especially rewarding. Those who take the time and trouble to read them with care gain an unparalleled sense of contact with a great philosopher as he puzzles his way through problems which he himself finds genuinely difficult.

Some of Aristotle's longer works are more like sets of loosely connected essays than unified treatises. This is particularly so in the case of the *Politics*. Books VII and VIII are clearly part of a single, incomplete, treatise on the ideal *polis*. Books V and VI are less tightly bound together but may still be thought of as constituting a single treatise on the ways in which constitutions change and the methods of ensuring their stability. But each of the others seems to constitute a course or *methodos*, to use Aristotle's term. One might thus think of the *Politics* as containing at least six different courses, but these courses are not entirely separate. They are bound together by cross-references which indicate that Aristotle did in some sense see them as constituting a single whole.

A problem which vexed scholars of the late nineteenth and early twentieth centuries was that of determining the correct order of the different parts of the *Politics*. The starting-point of discussions on this point is that Books VII and VIII which describe the ideal polis do not seem to follow very naturally on Books IV, V, and VI, which have a strong empirical basis and deal with the problems of existing states in the real world. In their general approach Books VII and VIII seem to belong more naturally with Book II, which deals with the ideal states proposed by other thinkers and with some actual constitutions that were widely admired in Aristotle's day, and perhaps also with Book III, which deals with citizenship and constitutions in a largely theoretical way. Moreover, the closing sentence of Book III is more or less identical with the opening sentence of Book VII, which strongly suggests that there must at some time have been a version of the *Politics* in which Books VII and VIII followed immediately after Book III. The fact that there are no cross-references from Books VII and VIII to Books IV–VI seems to support this view. Thus some scholars rearranged the books. For example, the order followed in Newman's great edition is I, II, III, VII, VIII, IV, V, VI. Against this it can be pointed out that Books IV to VI do not follow at all naturally on Books VII and VIII, and IV, at least, is closely tied by cross-references to III. Thus the revised order has as many difficulties as the traditional one. For this reason most scholars have now given up the attempt to establish a right order. The most obvious interpretation of the situation as we find it is that the various books of the *Politics* originated as notes which Aristotle prepared in connection with his own teaching and that he handled the material in different ways on different occasions.

The question of the order of the Books in the *Politics* was closely bound up with questions about their dating. The great German scholar Werner Jaeger proposed an interpretation of Aristotle based on the assumption that he began as a committed Platonist who followed an idealistic method in philosophy and moved very gradually towards a more realistic, empirically based philosophy of his own. As applied to the *Politics* this meant that Books VII and VIII, which Jaeger saw as idealistic, were written very early in Aristotle's career, whereas the more empirical Books IV to VI must have been very late. The late dating of these books receives some confirmation from the fact that they contain references to events as late as the 330s and also from the sheer amount of empirical data they include. We know from Diogenes Laertius that Aristotle wrote or caused to have written accounts of the constitutions of 158 different states. Of these only the *Constitution of Athens* survives. It is reasonable to assume that he drew on this material in composing the more empirical books of the *Politics*. But the constitutions are unlikely to have been completed before Aristotle's final period in the Lyceum. So if he did draw on them in writing Books IV–VI these books must be relatively late. In an article published in 1931 Barker accepted a view broadly in line with Jaeger's but by the time he had completed his translation he had changed his mind. In his introduction he criticized what he saw as the 'subjectivity' of Jaeger's approach and argued that the evidence of the text, particularly its cross-references, favours a view of the *Politics* as a single work composed in the period 335–322. Exercising his own subjectivity he wrote: 'Any translator of the *Politics*, who has lived with the book day on day, and month after month, is bound to become familiar with his author; and such familiarity breeds in the mind a deep sense of the unity of the author, which is perhaps the strongest argument for the unity of the structure and composition of his book' (xliv). More recently Jaeger's account of Aristotle's general philosophical development has been subject to searching criticism, particularly by G.E.L. Owen. Barker's judgement on the unity and date of the *Politics* would therefore be widely accepted. This is, of course, quite compatible with the belief that in composing the *Politics* as we now have it Aristotle drew on earlier material. The point is simply that the work as it stands is almost certainly a product of his final years and not simply a collection of pieces composed at different periods. We may still think of the work as combining idealistic and empirical elements, but the reason for that must be that Aristotle continued to see both methods as having validity.

It may finally be helpful to add something here about the relation of the *Politics* to Aristotle's ethical works. It will be obvious from the account of Aristotle's theory given above that there is a close connection between his political and ethical theories. The basis of this connection is that he sees the *polis* as existing for the sake of the good life. The basis of the *Politics* is thus fundamentally ethical. Not surprisingly therefore there are many references in it to the *Ethics*. Two versions of the *Ethics* have come down to us under the titles the *Eudemian Ethics* and the *Nicomachean Ethics*. These versions have three books in common. Otherwise they cover similar ground but in different ways. Traditionally the Nicomachean version has been regarded as the later and more authoritative work, though this view has been challenged. Most references in the *Politics* are to the common books though there are a few passages where Aristotle seems to be thinking of doctrines in their Eudemian rather than their Nicomachean forms. On the other hand, the *Nicomachean Ethics* is more explicit than the Eudemian version on the connections between ethics and politics. At the beginning Aristotle argues that it is incumbent on the statesman to know about ethics because he is above all concerned with the good life for the individual and for the city as a whole. The last chapter of the *Nicomachean Ethics* is clearly intended to make a transition to the *Politics*. Aristotle argues that legislation is needed to ensure that the citizens receive the kind of training without which virtue is impossible. The chapter ends with a (slightly inaccurate) description of the *Politics'* programme. While this final passage may be an interpolation the general picture is clear enough. For Aristotle the good life is possible only within a properly ordered state. It is therefore the task of the statesman to make virtue possible. This ethical purpose is the most characteristic feature of Aristotle's approach to politics.

The Vocabulary of the *Politics*

Anyone who attempts to translate a text in a foreign language has to face the fact that the words of one language seldom have exact equivalents in another. The problems are serious enough when we are handling a modern text that originated in a society not very different from our own. They are obviously far more severe when the text in question originated in a culture as remote as that of fourth-century BC Greece. In this Introduction and in the notes I have indicated some ways in which Aristotle's vocabulary diverges from our own. The index is intended to serve as a glossary of Greek words and of the English terms which are used to translate them, as well as to draw attention to passages where these problems of vocabulary are discussed. But there are barriers to understanding which no glossary can overcome. The words of a language are part of a form of life. They take their meaning from the practices in which they are embedded and from their associations with one another. As this Introduction has sought to make clear, the institutions and patterns of thought which Aristotle took for granted were very different from those which constitute our world. To understand the *Politics* we have to enter imaginatively into the world of the Greek *polis* while at the same time seeking to relate it to the world of the modern state in which we live. But it is precisely because it enables us to see the problems of our own day from a very different perspective that reading the *Politics* can be so valuable.

One feature of the *Politics* which is particularly liable to be lost in translation is the way in which its thought is structured by the etymological associations of some of its key terms. I shall mention here three word families which are introduced in the first chapter of Book I and continue to play an important part throughout the work.

The first of these is the *polis* family. As we have seen, *polis* is the Greek term for a city-state and has no real equivalent in English. Barker sometimes simply used 'polis' as though it was an English word and sometimes translated it as 'state'. I have standardized the translation by rendering it throughout as 'city'. Etymologically connected with it are: *politēs*, a citizen or member of the *polis*; *politeia*, the constitution or organizational structure of the *polis*; *politeuma*, the citizen body; *politikē*, the art or science concerned with the affairs of the *polis*; and *politikos*, the statesman, the one who conducts the affairs of the *polis*. The translator is forced to render these terms with words from a variety of sources: Latin, Greek, and Germanic. There is a danger that in doing so we will lose track of the way in which the *Politics* focuses on the *polis* and on the relationships which constitute it.

The second family is the *archē* family. The noun *archē* can be used generally to describe any kind of beginning, origin, or cause but in politics it has the meaning of 'rule'. The verb *archein* means to rule, to govern, or to occupy public office. Its passive form, *archesthai*, means to be ruled or be subject to someone or something else. The noun form *archōn* can mean a ruler or anyone who occupies an office of authority. Thus one of the major concerns of *Politics* I is to distinguish different kinds of rule, to distinguish the rule of the master of slaves, for example, from the kind of rule exercised by a statesman over free citizens. Aristotle believes that the role of the free citizen of a *polis* is characteristically one of ruling and being ruled (*archein kai archesthai*).

The third family is the *koinōnia* family. Here there is the verb *koinōnein*, which means 'to share' or 'to participate' in something. The noun *koinōnia* means literally a 'sharing' or 'participation' and is generally rendered in English as 'association', 'partnership', or 'community'. It is connected with the adjective *koinos* which describes something which is shared or held in common and often refers to the public property of the city (which is held in common by all the citizens). Aristotle sees the city as a *koinōnia* and in this context the translation 'community' may seem most attractive, but there are other contexts where it is misleading (it would be strange for example to talk of the *koinōnia* partnership of husband and wife as a 'community'). I have therefore followed Barker in using the translation 'association' though this does not convey the full sense of the Greek word. In particular it may obscure one of the central and most attractive features of Aristotle's thought, his view of the *polis* as a shared undertaking or partnership among the citizens.

NOTE ON THE TEXT

IN preparing his translation of the *Politics* Sir Ernest Barker sought to produce a version in a modern idiom which could be used by students in a wide range of disciplines. It is a mark of his success in achieving this aim that the translation is still widely recommended almost fifty years after it was first published. However, in preparing an edition for the World's Classics series I have taken the opportunity for some fairly drastic revision. The most notable change is the elimination of a very large number of passages where Barker expanded his translation by adding words in square brackets which did not represent anything in the Greek text but which helped to clarify what he took to be Aristotle's meaning. While Barker's expansions were often very helpful they made it very difficult for the reader to distinguish what was being attributed to Aristotle from what were, in effect, Barker's own comments. I have therefore deleted Barker's additions except in a small number of passages where it was impossible to produce an intelligible version without some addition. In many cases this has involved a substantial rewriting of the relevant passages. I have also revised many other passages to bring them closer to the Greek or to remove expressions which are no longer in current English use or which might mislead the modern reader. I have not, however, attempted any wholesale modernization of Barker's style, which is in general elegant and intelligible. Where possible, I have tried to achieve a greater consistency in the translation of key terms.

Barker's translation was based primarily on Newman's edition of the Greek text, although he also made use of the edition by Immisch. Two more recent editions are those by Ross and Dreizehnter. Ross's edition, though in many ways admirable, was not based on a full review of all the manuscripts and is marred by some unlikely emendations. In revising the translation I have in general therefore followed Dreizehnter's text, which is based on a more thorough examination of the available manuscripts and is usually more cautious in

adopting emendations. I have, however, departed from
Dreizehnter's version in a very small number of passages
mentioned in the notes and I have on occasion adopted a
different punctuation.

Barker's version included a long introduction, extensive
notes, and several appendices. Although these contained some
very helpful material, advances in scholarship together with
changes in philosophical fashion and in political realities have
made them seem dated in some respects. I have therefore
provided a new introduction and explanatory notes of my
own in a format appropriate for this series. In doing so I have
drawn heavily on Barker. Passages taken verbatim from his
notes are acknowledged but there are many other places
where I have drawn on the substance of his comments without
acknowledgement. The same goes for the titles which Barker
added to each of the books and in some cases to parts of
books and for the italicized summaries with which he headed
each chapter. I have retained these with very few modifications
(mostly to keep the summaries in line with the revised
translation).

Each Book of the *Politics* has traditionally been divided
into chapters. These divisions do not have Aristotle's own
authority and sometimes interrupt the flow of the argument,
but since they provide the customary way of referring to
substantial sections of the text I have used them throughout.
Book and chapter numbers are given at the head of each
page. In making more detailed references it is customary to
use the page, column, and line numbers of the Berlin edition
of Aristotle's works published under the editorship of
I. Bekker in 1831. The reference for the opening of *Politics* I
under this system is 'page 1252, column a, line 1', or, more
briefly '1252^{a}1'. References are given in this form at the
beginning of each paragraph. The same system is used for the
cross-references in the notes.

SELECT BIBLIOGRAPHY

Texts, Translations, and Commentaries

DREIZEHNTER, A., *Aristotles' Politik*, text (Munich, 1970).

EVERSON, S., *Aristotle, The Politics*, Jowett's translation as revised by J. Barnes (Cambridge, 1988).

LORD, C., *Aristotle, The Politics,* translation with introduction, notes, and glossary (Chicago, 1984).

NEWMAN, W. L., *The Politics of Aristotle*, text, introduction, notes critical and explanatory, 4 vols. (Oxford, 1887–1902; repr. 1973).

RACKHAM, H., *Aristotle, Politics*, text and translation, Loeb Classical Library (Cambridge, Mass., 1932).

ROBINSON, R., *Aristotle's Politics Books III and IV*, translation, introduction, and comments, Oxford Clarendon Series (Oxford, 1962).

ROSS, W. D., *Aristotelis Politica*, Oxford Classical Texts (Oxford, 1957).

SINCLAIR, T. A., *Aristotle, The Politics,* translation; 2nd rev. edn. by T. J. Saunders (Harmondsworth, 1983).

SUSEMIHL, F., and HICKS, R. D., *The Politics of Aristotle*, text, introduction, analysis, and commentary to Books I–V [i.e. Books I–III, VII–VIII in the standard order] (London, 1894; repr. 1976).

General Accounts of Aristotle's Thought

ACKRILL, J., *Aristotle the Philosopher* (Oxford, 1981).

BARNES, J., *Aristotle* (Oxford, 1982).

GUTHRIE, W. K. C., *History of Greek Philosophy*, vi. *Aristotle: an Encounter* (Cambridge, 1981).

IRWIN, T. H., *Aristotle's First Principles* (Oxford, 1988).

Aristotle's Life and Background

CHROUST, A.-H., *Aristotle*, vol. i (London, 1973).

The Greek World

AUSTIN, M. M., and VIDAL-NAQUET, P., *Economic and Social History of Greece: An Introduction* (London, 1977).

CARTLEDGE, P., *The Greeks* (Oxford, 1993).

Aristotle's Political Theory

Collections

BARNES, J., SCHOFIELD, M., and SORABJI, R. (eds.), *Articles on Aristotle*, 2: *Ethics and Politics* (London, 1977).

KEYT, D., and MILLER, F., *A Companion to Aristotle's Politics* (Oxford, 1991).

PATZIG, G., *Aristotles' Politik* (Göttingen, 1990) (contains many articles in English).

Books and Articles

ADKINS, A. W. H., 'The Connection Between Aristotle's *Ethics* and *Politics*', *Political Theory*, 12 (1984), 29–49.

ALLAN, D. J., 'Individual and State in the *Ethics* and *Politics*', in Fondation Hardt, *Entretiens sur l'Antiquité Classique*, IX. La *'Politique' d'Aristote* (Geneva, 1964), 53–95.

BARKER, E., 'The Life of Aristotle and the Composition and Structure of the *Politics*', *Classical Review*, 45 (1931), 162–72.

——*The Political Thought of Plato and Aristotle* (London,1906; repr. 1959).

BARNES, J., 'Aristotle and Political Liberty' with commentary by R. Sorabji in Patzig (1990), 250–64.

BRADLEY, A. C., 'Aristotle's Conception of the State', in Keyt and Miller (1991), 13–56.

COOPER, J. M., 'Political Animals and Civic Friendship' with commentary by J. Annas in Patzig (1990), 221–42.

DEFOURNY, M., 'The Aim of the State: Peace', in Barnes *et al.* (1977), 195–201.

DEPEW, D. J., 'Politics, Music and Contemplation in Aristotle's Ideal State', in Keyt and Miller (1991), 346–80.

EVERSON, S., 'Aristotle on the Foundations of the State', *Political Studies*, 36 (1988), 89–101.

FORTENBAUGH, W. W., 'Aristotle on Prior and Posterior Correct and Mistaken Constitutions', in Keyt and Miller (1991), 226–37.

——'Aristotle on Slaves and Women', in Barnes *et al.* (1977), 135–9.

IRWIN, T. H., 'Aristotle's Defense of Private Property', in Keyt and Miller (1991), 200–25.

——'The Good of Political Activity' with commentary by G. Striker in Patzig (1990), 73–99.

——'Moral Science and Political Theory in Aristotle', in P. A. Cartledge and F. D. Harvey (eds.), *Crux* (London, 1985), 150–68.

KAHN, C. H., 'The Normative Structure of Aristotle's *Politics*', in Patzig (1990), 369–84.

KELSEN, H., 'The Philosophy of Aristotle and the Hellenic-Macedonian Policy', *International Journal of Ethics*, 48 (1937), 1–64; partially repr. in Barnes *et al.* (1977), 170–94.

KEYT, D., 'Aristotle's Theory of Distributive Justice', in Keyt and Miller (1991), 238–78.

——'Three Basic Theorems in Aristotle's Politics', in Keyt and Miller (1991), 118–41.

KULLMANN, W., 'Man as a Political Animal in Aristotle', in Keyt and Miller (1991), 94–117.

LEYDEN, W. VON, *Aristotle on Equality and Justice: His Political Argument* (London, 1985).

LINTOTT, A., *Violence, Civil Strife and Revolution in the Classical City* (London, 1985), 239–51.

MEIKLE, S., 'Aristotle and Exchange Value', in Keyt and Miller (1991), 156–81.

MILLER, F. D. Jr., 'Aristotle on Natural Law and Justice', in Keyt and Miller (1991), 279–306.

MORROW, G. R., 'Aristotle's Comments on Plato's *Laws*', in I. During and G. E. L. Owen (eds.), *Aristotle and Plato in the Mid-Fourth Century* (Göteborg, 1960), 145–62.

MULGAN, R. G., 'Aristotle and the Democratic Conception of Freedom', in B. F. Harris (ed.), *Auckland Classical Studies Presented to E. M. Blaiklock* (Auckland, 1970), 95–111.

——'Aristotle's Analysis of Oligarchy and Democracy', in Keyt and Miller (1991), 307–22.

——*Aristotle's Political Theory* (Oxford, 1977).

NUSSBAUM, M. C., 'Nature, Function and Capability: Aristotle on Political Distribution', with commentary by D. Charles and reply by Nussbaum in Patzig (1990), 153–87.

——'Shame, Separateness and Political Unity: Aristotle's Criticism of Plato', in A. R. Rorty (ed.), *Essays on Aristotle's Ethics* (Berkeley, Calif., 1980), 395–435.

OKIN, S. M., *Women in Western Political Thought* (Princeton, NJ, 1979), ch. 4.

POLANSKY, R., 'Aristotle on Political Change', in Keyt and Miller (1991), 323–45.

POPPER, K. R., *The Open Society and its Enemies*, 5th edn. (London, 1966), vol. ii, ch. 11.

ROWE, C. J., 'Aims and Methods in Aristotle's *Politics*', in Keyt and Miller (1991), 57–74.

SCHOFIELD, M., 'Ideology and Philosophy in Aristotle's Theory of Slavery', with commentary by C. H. Kahn in Patzig (1990), 1–27.

SMITH, N. D., 'Aristotle's Theory of Natural Slavery', in Keyt and Miller (1991), 142–55.

STALLEY, R. F., 'Aristotle's Criticism of Plato's *Republic*', in Keyt and Miller (1991), 182–99.

STOCKS, J. L., 'The Composition of Aristotle's *Politics*', *Classical Quarterly*, 21 (1927), 177–87.

VANDER WAERDT, P. A., 'Kingship and Philosophy in Aristotle's Best Regime', *Phronesis*, 30 (1985), 249–73.

WHEELER, M., 'Aristotle's Analysis of the Nature of the Political Struggle', in Barnes *et al.* (1977), 159–69.

CHRONOLOGICAL TABLE

ARISTOTLE AND GREEK POLITICS
510–322

510   The tyranny of Peisistratus and his sons who have ruled Athens off and on for around fifty years is overthrown.

508–507   Under the leadership of Cleisthenes a democratic constitution is established at Athens.

490   Persian invasion defeated by the Athenians at the battle of Marathon.

480–479   A second much larger Persian invasion defeated by the co-operative efforts of many Greek cities at the battles of Salamis and Plataea. The Athenian fleet is mainly responsible for the victory at sea and the Spartan army for the victory on land.

477   Many of the city-states around the Aegean sea join in establishing a military alliance (called the Delian League). The Athenians gradually convert this league into an empire. Other Greek states (mostly with oligarchic governments) look to Sparta for leadership. So there is a situation of what we would call 'cold war' between the democratic states led by Athens and more conservative oligarchic states led by Sparta.

431   Outbreak of Peloponnesian War between Athens and her empire on the one side and Sparta and her allies on the other. Initially the Athenians fare quite well but Sparta eventually gets the upper hand. Many ascribe Athens' failures to bad decisions taken by the democratic assembly.

404   Athens defeated.

404–403   The Spartans establish an oligarchy in Athens but the democracy is soon restored.

395–386   The Corinthian War: Athens, Corinth, and Thebes challenge Spartan supremacy. The war is ended by the Persian-sponsored King's Peace.

384   Aristotle born at Stagira, the son of Nicomachus, a doctor who has served as personal physician to King Amyntas III of Macedon.

371   The Thebans under Epaminondas defeat Sparta at the battle
      of Leuctra. This effectively ends Sparta's career as an impor-
      tant power.

367   Aristotle goes to Athens. (The traditional view is that the
      purpose of his going there was to study in Plato's Academy.
      But Plato himself was away in Sicily at this time and it is
      possible that Aristotle's reason for going to Athens was as
      much for safety as for study. Amyntas had been assassinated
      in 369 and Nicomachus had also died. There have been
      suggestions, based on slender evidence, that Aristotle
      studied for a short period with the rhetorician Isocrates
      before joining the Academy.)

362   The death of Epaminondas at the battle of Mantinea brings
      Theban supremacy to an end.

359   Philip assumes power in Macedonia.

353   The Sacred War gives Philip the chance to begin military
      interference in Greece. Demosthenes rouses the Athenians
      to oppose him.

348/7 Aristotle leaves Athens for Atarneus. (The traditional view
      is that he left in anger at not being appointed to succeed
      Plato as head of the Academy. It is more likely that he was
      forced to leave by anti-Macedonian sentiment following the
      capture of Olynthus, a city allied to Athens.)

347–345 Aristotle joins Erastus and Coriscus, fellow members of the
      Academy, at Atarneus, where they enjoy the patronage of
      the ruler Hermias. Hermias establishes them at Assos. Aristo-
      tle's marriage to Hermias' niece, Pythias, may date from
      this period.

345/4 Aristotle moves to Mytilene on Lesbos.

343/2 Aristotle moves to Macedon. He is traditionally supposed
      to have acted as tutor to Alexander, the son of King Philip,
      but there is little contemporary evidence for this.

341/40 Hermias is betrayed to the Persians and dies under torture.

338   Battle of Chaeronea. Philip defeats the Athenians and The-
      bans and acquires effective control over Greece. At the
      congress in Corinth he announces his intention to invade
      Persia.

336   Philip is assassinated; his son Alexander succeeds to the
      throne of Macedon and to the leadership of Greece.

335/4 Aristotle returns to Athens, where he establishes his own
      school in the Lyceum. During this period he evidently

enjoys close relations with Antipater, the Macedonian general who is left in charge of Greece by Alexander.

334   Alexander invades Persia.

323   Alexander dies. Athens and some other Greek cities stage an unsuccessful attempt to throw off Macedonian control.

323   Aristotle leaves Athens for Chalcis in Euboea. His departure is almost certainly connected with the Athenian revolt against Macedon following the death of Alexander.

322   Aristotle dies at Chalcis.

THE POLITICS

CONTENTS

BOOK I
THE HOUSEHOLD AND THE CITY

A: The Political Association and its Relation to other Associations (Chapters 1–2)

CHAPTER 1

All associations have ends: the political association has the highest; but the principle of association expresses itself in different forms, and through different modes of government.

1252ᵃ1 Observation shows us, first, that every city [*polis*] is a species of association,* and, secondly, that all associations come into being for the sake of some good—for all men do all their acts with a view to achieving something which is, in their view, a good.* It is clear therefore that all associations aim at some good, and that the particular association which is the most sovereign of all, and includes all the rest, will pursue this aim most, and will thus be directed to the most sovereign of all goods. This most sovereign and inclusive association is the city [or *polis*], as it is called, or the political association.

1252ᵃ7 It is a mistake to believe that the statesman is the same as the monarch of a kingdom, or the manager of a household, or the master of a number of slaves.* Those who hold this view consider that each one of these differs from the others not with a difference of kind, but according to the number, large or small, of those with whom he deals. On this view someone who is concerned with few people is a master, someone who is concerned with more is the manager of a household, and someone who is concerned with still more is a statesman,* or a monarch. This view abolishes any real difference between a large household and a small city; and it also reduces the difference between the 'statesman' and the monarch to the one fact that the latter has an uncontrolled and sole authority, while the former exercises his authority in conformity with the rules imposed by the art of statesmanship and as one who rules and is ruled in turn. But this is a view which cannot be accepted as correct.*

1252ª18 Our point will be made clear if we proceed to consider the matter according to our normal method of analysis. Just as, in all other fields, a compound* should be analysed until we reach its simple elements (or, in other words, the smallest parts of the whole which it constitutes), so we must also consider analytically the elements of which a city is composed. We shall then gain a better insight into the way in which these differ from one another; and we shall also be in a position to discover whether there is any kind of expertise to be acquired in connection with the matters under discussion.

CHAPTER 2

To distinguish the different forms of association we must trace the development successively of the association of the household, that of the village, and that of the city or polis. *The* polis, *or political association, is the crown: it completes and fulfils the nature of man: it is thus natural to him, and he is himself 'naturally a* polis-*animal'; it is also prior to him, in the sense that it is the presupposition of his true and full life.*

1252ª24 In this, as in other fields, we shall be able to study our subject best if we begin at the beginning and consider things in the process of their growth.* First of all, there must necessarily be a union or pairing of those who cannot exist without one another. Male and female must unite for the reproduction of the species—not from deliberate intention, but from the natural impulse, which exists in animals generally as it also exists in plants, to leave behind them something of the same nature as themselves. Next, there must necessarily be a union of the naturally ruling element with the element which is naturally ruled, for the preservation of both. The element which is able, by virtue of its intelligence, to exercise forethought, is naturally a ruling and master element; the element which is able, by virtue of its bodily power, to do the physical work, is a ruled element, which is naturally in a state of slavery; and master and slave have accordingly a common interest.

1252ᵇ2 The female and the slave are naturally distinguished from one another. Nature makes nothing in a miserly spirit, as smiths do when they make the Delphic knife* to serve a number of purposes: she makes each separate thing for a separate end; and she does so because the instrument is most perfectly made when it serves a single purpose and not a variety of purposes. Among barbarians, however, the female and the slave occupy the same position*—the reason being that no naturally ruling element exists among them, and conjugal union thus comes to be a union of a female who is a slave with a male who is also a slave. This is why our poets have said,

Meet it is that barbarous peoples should be governed by the Greeks*

the assumption being that barbarian and slave are by nature one and the same.

The first result of these two elementary associations is the household or family. Hesiod spoke truly in the verse,

First house, and wife, and ox to draw the plough,*

for oxen serve the poor in lieu of household slaves. The first form of association naturally instituted for the satisfaction of daily recurrent needs is thus the family; and the members of the family are accordingly termed by Charondas 'associates of the breadchest', as they are also termed by Epimenides* the Cretan 'associates of the manger'.

1252ᵇ17 The next form of association—which is also the first to be formed from more households than one, and for the satisfaction of something more than daily recurrent needs —is the village. The most natural form of the village appears to be that of a colony [or offshoot] from a family;* and some have thus called the members of the village by the name of 'sucklings of the same milk', or, again, of 'sons and the sons of sons'. This, it may be noted, is the reason why cities were originally ruled, as the peoples of the barbarian world still are, by kings. They were formed of people who were already monarchically governed, for every household is monarchically governed by the eldest of the kin, just as villages, when they are offshoots from the household, are similarly governed in virtue of the kinship between their members. This is what Homer describes:

> Each of them ruleth
> Over his children and wives,*

a passage which shows that they lived in scattered groups, as indeed men generally did in ancient times. The fact that men generally were governed by kings in ancient times, and that some still continue to be governed in that way, is the reason that leads everyone to say that the gods are also governed by a king. People make the lives of the gods in the likeness of their own—as they also make their shapes.

1252b27 When we come to the final and perfect association,* formed from a number of villages, we have already reached the city [or *polis*]. This may be said to have reached the height of full self-sufficiency;* or rather we may say that while it comes into existence for the sake of mere life, it exists for the sake of a good life.* For this reason every city exists by nature,* just as did the earlier associations [from which it grew]. It is the end or consummation to which those associations move, and the 'nature' of things consists in their end or consummation; for what each thing is when its growth is completed we call the nature of that thing, whether it be a man or a horse or a family. Again the end, or final cause, is the best and self-sufficiency is both the end, and the best.

1253a2 From these considerations it is evident that the city belongs to the class of things that exist by nature, and that man is by nature a political animal.* He who is without a city, by reason of his own nature and not of some accident, is either a poor sort of being, or a being higher than man: he is like the man of whom Homer wrote in denunciation:

> Clanless and lawless and heartless is he.*

The man who is such by nature at once plunges into a passion of war; he is in the position of a solitary advanced piece in a game of draughts.

1253a7 It is thus clear that man is a political animal, in a higher degree than bees or other gregarious animals. Nature, according to our theory, makes nothing in vain; and man alone of the animals is furnished with the faculty of language. The mere making of sounds serves to indicate pleasure and pain, and is thus a faculty that belongs to animals in general: their nature enables them to attain the point at which they have perceptions of pleasure and pain, and can signify those perceptions to one another. But language serves to declare what is advantageous and what is the reverse, and it is the peculiarity of man, in comparison with other animals, that he alone possesses a perception of good and evil, of the just and the unjust, and other similar qualities; and it is association in these things which makes a family and a city.

1253ª18 We may now proceed to add that the city is prior in the order of nature to the family and the individual. The reason for this is that the whole is necessarily prior to the part.* If the whole body is destroyed, there will not be a foot or a hand, except in that ambiguous sense in which one uses the same word to indicate a different thing, as when one speaks of a 'hand' made of stone; for a hand, when destroyed [by the destruction of the whole body], will be no better than a stone 'hand'.* All things derive their essential character from their function and their capacity; and it follows that if they are no longer fit to discharge their function, we ought not to say that they are still the same things, but only that, by an ambiguity, they still have the same names.

1253ª25 We thus see that the city exists by nature and that it is prior to the individual.* For if the individual is not self-sufficient when he is isolated he will stand in the same relation to the whole as other parts do to their wholes. The man who is isolated, who is unable to share in the benefits of political association, or has no need to share because he is already self-sufficient, is no part of the city, and must therefore be either a beast or a god. There is therefore a natural impulse in all men towards an association of this sort. But the man who first constructed such an association* was none the less the greatest of benefactors. Man, when perfected, is the best of animals; but if he be isolated from law and justice he is the worst of all. Injustice is all the graver when it is armed injustice; and man is furnished from birth with weapons which are intended to serve the purposes of wisdom and goodness,* but which may be used in preference for opposite ends. That is why, if he be without goodness [of mind and character], he is a most unholy and savage being, and worse than all others in the indulgence of lust and gluttony. The virtue of justice belongs to the city; for justice is an ordering of the political association, and the virtue of justice consists in the determination of what is just.

B: The Association of the Household and its Different Factors (Chapters 3–13)

CHAPTER 3

1. The constituent elements of the household. The three relations of master and slave, husband and wife, parent and child. The fourth element of 'acquisition'.

1253ᵇ1 Having ascertained, from the previous analysis, what are the elements of which the city is constituted, we must first consider the management of the household; for every city is composed of households. The parts of household management will correspond to the parts of which the household itself is constituted. A complete household consists of slaves and freemen. But every subject of inquiry should first be examined in its simplest elements; and the primary and simplest elements of the household are the connection of master and slave, that of the husband and wife, and that of parents and children. We must accordingly consider each of these connections, examining the nature of each and the qualities it ought to possess. The factors to be examined are therefore three: first, the relationship of master and slave; next, what may be called the marital relationship (for there is no word in our language which exactly describes the union of husband and wife); and lastly, what may be called the parental relationship, which again has no single word in our language peculiar to itself. But besides the three factors which thus present themselves for examination there is also a fourth, which some regard as identical with the whole of household management, and others as its principal part. This is the element called 'the art of acquisition';* and we shall have to consider its nature.

1253^b14 We may first speak of master and slave, partly in order to gather lessons bearing on the necessities of practical life, and partly in order to discover whether we can attain any view, superior to those now generally held, which is likely to promote an understanding of the subject. There are some who hold that the exercise of authority over slaves is a kind of knowledge. They believe (as we said in the beginning)* that household management, slave ownership, statesmanship, and kingship are all the same. There are others, however, who regard the control of slaves by a master as contrary to nature. In their view the distinction of master and slave is due to law or convention; there is no natural difference between them:* the relation of master and slave is based on force, and so has no warrant in justice.

CHAPTER 4

2. Slavery. The instruments of the household form its stock of property: they are animate and inanimate: the slave is an animate instrument, intended (like all the instruments of the household) for action, and not for production.

1253^b23 Property is part of the household and the art of acquiring property is part of household management, for it is impossible to live well, or indeed at all, unless the necessary conditions are present. Thus the same holds true in the sphere of household management as in the specialized arts: each must be furnished with its appropriate instruments if its function is to be fulfilled. Instruments are partly inanimate and partly animate:* the steersman of a ship, for instance, has an inanimate instrument in the rudder, and an animate instrument in the look-out man (for in the arts a subordinate is of the nature of an instrument). Each article of property is thus an instrument for the purpose of life, property in general is a quantity of such instruments, the slave is an animate article of property, and subordinates, or servants, in general may be described as instruments which are prior to other instruments.

We can imagine a situation in which each instrument could do its own work, at the word of command or by intelligent anticipation, like the statues of Daedalus or the tripods made by Hephaestus, of which the poet relates that

> Of their own motion they entered the conclave of Gods on
> Olympus.*

A shuttle would then weave of itself, and a plectrum would do its own harp-playing. In this situation managers would not need subordinates and masters would not need slaves.

1254^{a}1 The instruments of which we have just been speaking are instruments of production; but property is an instrument of action.* From the shuttle there issues something which is different, and exists apart, from the immediate act of its use; but from garments or beds there comes only the one fact of their use. We may add that, since production and action are different in kind, and both of them need instruments, those instruments must also show a corresponding difference. Life is action and not production; and therefore the slave is a servant in the sphere of action.

1254^{a}8 The term 'article of property' is used in the same way in which the term 'part' is also used. A part is not only a part of something other than itself: it also belongs entirely to that other thing. It is the same with an article of property. Accordingly, while the master is merely the master of the slave, and does not belong to him, the slave is not only the slave of his master; he also belongs entirely to him.

1254^{a}13 From these considerations we can see clearly what is the nature of the slave and what is his capacity: anybody who by his nature is not his own man, but another's, is by his nature a slave; anybody who, being a man, is an article of property is another's man; an article of property is an instrument intended for the purpose of action and separable from its possessor.

CHAPTER 5

There is a principle of rule and subordination in nature at large: it appears especially in the realm of animate creation. By virtue

of that principle, the soul rules the body; and by virtue of it the
master, who possesses the rational faculty of the soul, rules the
slave, who possesses only bodily powers and the faculty of
understanding the directions given by another's reason. But
nature, though she intends, does not always succeed in achieving
a clear distinction between men born to be masters and men
born to be slaves.

1254ᵃ17 We have next to consider whether there are, or are
not, some people who are by nature such as are here defined;
whether, in other words, there are some people for whom
slavery is the better and just condition, or whether the reverse
is the case and all slavery is contrary to nature.* The issue is
not difficult, whether we study it philosophically in the light
of reason, or consider it empirically on the basis of the actual
facts. The relation of ruler and ruled is one of those things
which are not only necessary, but also beneficial; and there
are species in which a distinction is already marked, immediately at birth, between those of its members who are intended
for being ruled and those who are intended to rule. There are
also many kinds both of ruling and ruled elements. (Moreover
the rule which is exercised over the better sort of subjects is a
better sort of rule—as, for example, rule exercised over a man
is better than rule over an animal. The reason is that the value
of something which is produced increases with the value of
those contributing to it; and where one element rules and the
other is ruled, there is something which they jointly produce.)
In all cases where there is a compound, constituted of more
than one part but forming one common entity, whether the
parts be continuous or discrete, a ruling element and a ruled
can always be traced. This characteristic is present in animate
beings by virtue of the whole constitution of nature; for even
in things which are inanimate there is a sort of ruling principle,
such as is to be found, for example, in a musical harmony.*
But such considerations perhaps belong to a more popular
method of inquiry; and we may content ourselves here with
saying that animate beings are composed, in the first place, of
soul and body, with the former naturally ruling and the latter
naturally ruled. When investigating the natural state of things,

we must fix our attention, not on those which are in a
corrupt, but on those which are in a natural condition.* It
follows that we must consider the man who is in the best state
both of body and soul, and in whom the rule of soul over
body is accordingly evident; for with vicious people or those
in a vicious condition, the reverse would often appear to be
true—the body ruling the soul as the result of their evil and
unnatural condition.

1254ᵇ2 It is possible, as we have said, to observe first in
animate beings the presence of a ruling authority, both of the
sort exercised by a master over slaves and of the sort exercised
by a statesman over fellow citizens. The soul rules the body
with the authority of a master: reason rules the appetite with
the authority of a statesman or a monarch.* In this sphere it
is clearly natural and beneficial to the body that it should be
ruled by the soul, and again it is natural and beneficial to the
affective part of the soul that it should be ruled by the reason
and the rational part; whereas the equality of the two elements, or their reverse relation, is always detrimental. The
same principle is true of the relation of man to other animals.
Tame animals have a better nature than wild, and it is better
for all such animals that they should be ruled by man because
they then get the benefit of preservation. Again, the relation
of male to female is naturally that of the superior to the
inferior, of the ruling to the ruled. This general principle must
similarly hold good of all human beings generally.

1254ᵇ16 We may thus conclude that all men who differ from
others as much as the body differs from the soul, or an
animal from a man (and this is the case with all whose
function is bodily service, and who produce their best when
they supply such service)—all such are by nature slaves. In
their case, as in the other cases just mentioned, it is better to
be ruled by a master. Someone is thus a slave by nature if he
is capable of becoming the property of another (and for this
reason does actually become another's property) and if he
participates in reason to the extent of apprehending it in
another, though destitute of it himself. Other animals do not
apprehend reason* but obey their instincts. Even so there is
little divergence in the way they are used; both of them (slaves

and tame animals) provide bodily assistance in satisfying essential needs.

1254ᵇ27 It is nature's intention also to erect a physical difference between the bodies of freemen and those of the slaves, giving the latter strength for the menial duties of life, but making the former upright in carriage and (though useless for physical labour) useful for the various purposes of civic life—a life which tends, as it develops, to be divided into military service and the occupations of peace. The contrary of nature's intention, however, often happens: there are some slaves who have the bodies of freemen, as there are others who have a freeman's soul. But, if there were men who were as distinguished in their bodies alone as are the statues of the gods, all would agree that the others should be their slaves.* And if this is true when the difference is one of the body, it may be affirmed with still greater justice when the difference is one of the soul; though it is not as easy to see the beauty of the soul as it is to see that of the body.

1254ᵇ39 It is thus clear that, just as some are by nature free, so others are by nature slaves, and for these latter the condition of slavery is both beneficial and just.

CHAPTER 6

Legal or conventional slavery: the divergence of views about its justice, and the reason for this divergence. In spite of the divergence, there is a general consensus—though it is not clearly formulated—that superiority in goodness justifies the owning and controlling of slaves. Granted such superiority in the master, slavery is a beneficial and just system.

1255ᵃ3 But it is easy to see that those who hold an opposite view are also in a way correct. 'Slavery' and 'slave' are terms which are used in two different senses; for there is also a kind of slave, and of slavery, which owes its existence to law. (The law in question is a kind of understanding that those vanquished in war are held to belong to the victors.) That slavery can be justified by such a convention is a principle against which a number of jurists bring an 'indictment of illegality',* as

one might against an orator. They regard it as a detestable notion that someone who is subjugated by force should become
the slave and subject of one who has the capacity to subjugate
him, and is his superior in power. Even among men of judgement there are some who accept this and some who do not.
The cause of this divergence of view, and the reason why the
opposing contentions overlap one another, is to be found in
the following consideration. There is a sense in which good
qualities, when they are furnished with the right resources,
have the greatest power to subjugate; and a victor is always
pre-eminent in respect of some sort of good. It thus appears
that 'power never goes without good qualities'; and the dispute
between the two sides thus comes to turn exclusively on the
point of justice.* (In this matter some think that being just consists in goodwill* while others hold that the rule of the stronger
is in itself justice.) If these different positions are distinguished
from one another, no other argument has any cogency, or even
plausibility, against the view that one who is superior in
goodness ought to rule over, and be the master of, his inferiors.

1255ª21 There are some who, clinging, as they think, to a
sort of justice (for law is a sort of justice), assume that slavery
in war is just. Simultaneously, however, they contradict that
assumption; for in the first place it is possible that the original
cause of a war may not be just, and in the second place no
one would ever say that someone who does not deserve to be
in a condition of slavery is really a slave. If such a view were
accepted, the result would be that men reputed to be of the
highest rank would be turned into slaves or the children of
slaves, if they [or their parents] happened to be captured and
sold into slavery. This is the reason why they do not like to
call such people slaves, but prefer to confine the term to
barbarians. But by this use of terms they are, in reality, only
seeking to express that same idea of the natural slave which
we began by mentioning. They are driven, in effect, to admit
that there are some who are everywhere slaves, and others
who are everywhere free. The same line of thought is followed
in regard to good birth. Greeks regard themselves as well
born not only in their own country, but absolutely and in all
places; but they regard barbarians as well born only in their

own country—thus assuming that there is one sort of good birth and freedom which is absolute, and another which is only relative. We are reminded of what Helen says in the play of Theodectes:*

> Scion of Gods, by both descent alike,
> Who would presume to call me serving-maid?

When they use such terms as these, men are using the one criterion of the presence, or absence, of goodness for the purpose of distinguishing between slave and freeman, or again, between the well-born and the low-born. They are claiming that just as man is born of man, and animal of animal, so a good man is born of good men. It is often the case, however, that nature wishes but fails to achieve this result.*

1255^{b}4 It is thus clear that there is some reason for the divergence of view which has been discussed—it is not true that the one group are natural slaves and the other natural freemen. It is also clear that there are cases where such a distinction exists, and that here it is beneficial and just that the former should actually be a slave and the latter a master —the one being ruled, and the other exercising the kind of rule for which he is naturally intended and therefore acting as master. But a wrong exercise of his rule by a master is a thing which is disadvantageous for both master and slave. The part and the whole, like the body and the soul, have an identical interest; and the slave is a part of the master, in the sense of being a living but separate part of his body. There is thus a community of interest, and a relation of friendship, between master and slave, when both of them naturally merit the position in which they stand. But the reverse is true, when matters are otherwise and slavery rests merely on legal sanction and superior power.

CHAPTER 7

The training of slaves, and the art of using them properly. How they may be justly acquired.

1255^{b}16 The argument makes it clear that the rule of the master and that of the statesman are different from one another, and that it is not the case that all kinds of rule are, as some thinkers hold, identical.* One kind of rule is exercised over those who are naturally free; the other over slaves; and again the rule exercised over a household by its head is that of a monarch (for all households are monarchically governed), while the rule of the statesman is rule over freemen and equals. Now masters are not so termed in virtue of any knowledge which they have acquired, but in virtue of their own endowment; and the same is true of slaves and freemen generally. But there may be a kind of knowledge which belongs to masters, and another which belongs to slaves; and the latter would be of the nature of the knowledge taught by the man of Syracuse, who instructed servants for pay in the discharge of their ordinary duties. Instruction in such subjects might be extended further: it might include, for example, the art of cookery and other similar forms of skilled domestic service. The reason why this might be done is that the duties differ; some are of a higher standing, even if others are needed more. As the proverb says:

Slave may go before slave, and master may go before master.*

All such forms of knowledge are necessarily of a servile character. But there is also a form of knowledge belonging to the master, which consists in the use of slaves: a master is such in virtue not of acquiring, but of using slaves. This knowledge belonging to the master is something which has no great or majestic character: the master must simply know how to command what the slave must know how to do. This is why those who are in a position to escape from being troubled by it delegate the management of slaves to a steward, and spend on politics or philosophy the time they are thus able to save. The art of acquiring slaves for ownership differs both from the art of being a master and from that of being a slave—that is to say, when it is justly practised; for in that case it is a particular form of the art of war, or of the art of hunting.

1255ᵇ39 This should be an adequate account of the distinction between master and slave.

CHAPTER 8

3. Property and the art of acquisition. *The art of household management is distinct from that of acquisition. It has to provide a stock of requisites for the household; and the different methods by which this is done produce different ways of life—the hunting, the pastoral, the agricultural, and so forth. Nature intends and provides the requisites for household use; and the acquisition of such requisites is a natural mode of acquisition. Property in them is limited to the amount required by household needs; and it is the nature of all true wealth to be so limited.*

1256ᵃ1 We may now study generally all forms of property and the art of acquiring it,* following our normal method; for we have already seen that the slave is an article of property. The first problem which may be raised is whether the art of acquiring property is identical with that of household management, or is a part of it, or is ancillary to it; and whether, if it is ancillary, it is so in the sense in which the art of making shuttles is ancillary to the art of weaving, or in the sense in which the art of casting bronze is ancillary to the art of sculpture. These are ancillary in a different way; the one provides instruments, and the other the material. (By 'material' we mean the substance from which a product is made; as wool, for instance, serves the weaver; and bronze the sculptor.) That the art of household management is not identical with the art of acquiring property is obvious. It is the function of the latter simply to provide, but it is the function of the former to use what has been provided; for what art can there be, other than that of household management, which will use the resources of the household? But the question whether the art of acquisition is a part of it, or a separate art altogether, is one which admits of a divergence of views. If someone who is engaged in acquisition has to consider from what different sources he can get goods and property, and if property and wealth include many different parts, we shall first have to consider whether farming is a part of the art of acquisition, or a separate art: indeed we shall have to ask that question generally, in regard to all modes of occupation and gain which are concerned with the provision of subsistence. There are a number of different modes of subsistence; and the result is a number of different ways of life, among both animals and human beings. It is impossible to live without means of subsistence; and among the animals we may notice that differences in the means of subsistence have produced consequent differences in ways of life. Some wild animals live in herds, and others are scattered in isolation, according as they find it convenient for the purpose of getting subsistence—some of them being carnivorous, some herbivorous, and some, again, omnivorous. Nature has thus distinguished their ways of life, with a view to their greater comfort and their better attainment of these things: indeed, as the same sort of food is not naturally agreeable to all the members of a class, and as different sorts suit different species, there are also different ways of life even within the class of carnivorous animals—and equally in that of the herbivorous. The same is also true of men. Their ways of life also differ considerably. The most indolent are the pastoral nomads. They acquire a subsistence from domestic animals, at their leisure, and without any trouble; and as it is necessary for their flocks to move for the sake of pasturage, they also are forced to follow and to cultivate what may be called a living farm. There are others who live by hunting; and of these, again, there are different kinds, according to their different modes of hunting. Some live by being freebooters;* some, who live near lakes and marshes and rivers, or by a sea which is suitable for the purpose, gain a livelihood by fishing; others live by hunting birds or wild animals. Most of mankind, however, derive their livelihood from the soil, and from cultivated plants.

1256ª40 The different ways of life (at any rate if we take into account only those who follow an occupation dependent on their own labours, and do not provide themselves with subsistence by exchange and petty trade) may be roughly classified as pastoral, freebooting, fishing, hunting, and farming. But there are some who live comfortably by means of a combination of different methods, and who supplement the shortcomings of one way of life, when it tends to fall short of being sufficient in itself, by adding some other way. For example, some combine the pastoral way of life with the freebooting; others combine farming with hunting; and similar combinations may be made of other ways of life; as need impels people so they shape their lives.

1256^b7 This kind of capacity for acquisition is evidently given by nature to all living beings, from the moment when they are first born to the days when their growth is finished. There are animals which, when their offspring is born, bring forth along with it food enough to support it until it can provide for itself: this is the case with those which reproduce themselves by grubs, and with animals which do so by eggs. Animals which are viviparous have food for their offspring in themselves, for a certain time, of the nature of what is called milk.

1256^b15 Likewise we must evidently believe that similar provision is made for adults. Plants exist for the benefit of animals, and some animals exist for the benefit of others.* Those which are domesticated, serve human beings for use as well as for food; wild animals, too, in most cases if not in all, serve to furnish us not only with food, but also with other kinds of assistance, such as the provision of clothing and similar aids to life. Accordingly, if nature makes nothing purposeless or in vain, all animals must have been made by nature for the sake of men. It also follows that the art of war is in some sense a natural mode of acquisition. Hunting is a part of that art; and hunting ought to be practised, not only against wild animals, but also against human beings who are intended by nature to be ruled by others and refuse to obey that intention, because this sort of war is naturally just.

1256^b26 It follows that one form of acquisition is naturally a part of the art of household management, in the sense that the manager of a household must either have available or ensure the availability of a supply of objects which are capable of being stored and are either necessary for life or useful to the association of the city [polis] or the household. These are the objects which may be regarded as constituting true wealth, for the amount of household property which suffices for a good life is not unlimited, nor of the nature described by Solon* in the verse,

There is no bound to wealth stands fixed for men.

There is a bound fixed, as is also the case in the means required by the other arts. All the instruments needed by all the arts are limited, both in number and size, and wealth may be defined as a number of instruments used in a household or city.

1256ᵇ37 It is thus clear that there is a natural art of acquisition* which has to be practised by managers of households and statesmen; and the reason for its existence is also clear.

CHAPTER 9

The 'art of acquisition', as a way of acquiring property distinct from the natural way of the household. It originates in exchange, when exchange is conducted through the medium of currency and for profit. The view thus arises that the art of acquisition is specially concerned with accumulating a fund of currency. But there is a contrary view that currency is a mere convention, and not the true object of the art of acquisition. This contrary view has its truth. There is a natural form of the art of acquisition, which is not distinct from, but a part of, the art of household management. This natural form of acquisition aims at the accumulation not of currency, but of true wealth—and therefore not at the infinite, but at the finite.

1256ᵇ40 But there is a second form of the art of getting property, which is particularly called, and which it is just to call, 'the art of acquisition'.* It is this second form which gives rise to the opinion that there is no limit to wealth and property. There are many who hold it to be identical with the other form previously mentioned, because it has affinities with it. In fact it is not identical, and yet it is not far removed. The other form previously mentioned is natural: this second form is not natural, but is rather the product of a certain sort of experience and skill.

1257ª5 We may start our discussion of this [second] form from the following point of view. All articles of property have two possible uses.* Both of these uses belong to the article as such, but they do not belong to it in the same manner, or to the same extent. The one use is proper and peculiar to the article concerned; the other is not. A shoe, for example, can be used both for wearing and for exchange. Both of these uses are uses of the shoe as such. Even the man who exchanges a shoe, in return for money or food, with someone who needs the article, is using the shoe as a shoe; but since the shoe has not been made for the purpose of being exchanged, the use which he is making of it is not its proper and peculiar use. The same is true of all other articles of property. Exchange is possible in regard to them all: it arises from the natural facts of the case, and is due to some men having more, and others less, than suffices for their needs. We can thus see that retail trade is not naturally a part of the art of acquisition. If that were the case, it would only be necessary to practise exchange to the extent that sufficed for the needs of both parties.

1257ª19 In the first form of association, which is the household, it is obvious that there is no purpose to be served by the art of exchange. Such a purpose only emerged when the scope of association had already been extended. The members of the household had shared all things in common: those who lived separately from one another, had at their disposal a number of different things, which they had to exchange as need arose, by way of barter—much as many barbarian tribes still do to this day. On this basis things which are useful are exchanged themselves, and directly, for similar useful things, but the transaction does not go any further; wine, for instance, is given, or taken, in return for wheat, and other similar commodities are similarly bartered for one another. When used in this way, the art of exchange is not contrary to nature, nor in any way a form of the art of acquisition. Exchange simply serves to satisfy the natural requirements of sufficiency. None the less it was from exchange, as thus practised, that the art of acquisition developed,* in the sort of way we might reasonably expect. The supply of men's needs came to depend on more foreign sources, as men began to import for themselves what they lacked, and to export what they had in superabundance: and in this way the use of a money currency was inevitably instituted.* The reason for this was that all the naturally necessary commodities were not easily portable; and people therefore agreed, for the purpose of their exchanges, to give and receive some commodity which itself belonged to the category of useful things and possessed the advantage of being easily handled for the purpose of getting the necessities of life. Such commodities were iron, silver, and other similar metals. At first their value was simply determined by their size and weight; but finally a stamp was imposed on the metal which, serving as a definite indication of the quantity, would save people the trouble of determining the value on each occasion.

1257^{a}41 When in this way a currency had once been instituted, there next arose, from the necessary process of exchange, the second form of the art of acquisition, the one which consists in retail trade. At first, we may allow, it was perhaps practised in a simple way: but in process of time, and as the result of experience, it was practised with a more studied technique, which sought to discover the sources from which, and the methods by which, the greatest profit could be made. The result has been the emergence of the view that the art of acquisition is specially concerned with currency, and that its function consists in an ability to discover the sources from which a fund of money can be derived. In support of this view it is urged that the art is one which produces wealth and money; indeed those who hold the view often assume that wealth is simply a fund of currency, on the ground that the arts of acquisition and of retail trade are concerned with currency. In opposition to this view it is sometimes held that currency is a sham, and entirely a convention. Naturally and inherently [the supporters of the view argue] a currency is a nonentity; for if those who use a currency give it up in favour of another, that currency is worthless, and useless for any of the necessary purposes of life. A man rich in currency [they proceed to urge] will often be at a loss to procure the necessities of subsistence; and surely it is absurd that a thing should be counted as wealth which a man may possess in abundance, and yet none the less die of starvation—like Midas* in the fable, when everything set before him was turned at once into gold through the granting of his own avaricious prayer.

1257^{b}17 For this reason some people seek a different conception of wealth and of the art of acquisition. They are right to do so. The natural form of the art of acquisition, like the natural form of wealth, is something different.* It is part of the management of the household while retail trade serves to make money, and that only by the exchange of commodities. The latter may be seen as concerned with currency; for currency is both a basic unit and a limiting factor in exchange.

1257^{b}23 A further point of difference is that the wealth produced by this [second] form of the art of acquisition is unlimited.* The art of medicine recognizes no limit in respect of the production of health, and the arts generally admit no limit in respect of the production of their ends (each seeking to produce its end to the greatest possible extent)—though medicine, and the arts generally, recognize and practise a limit to the means they use to attain their ends, since the end itself constitutes a limit.* The same is true of the retail form of the art of acquisition. There is no limit to the end it seeks; and the end it seeks is wealth of the sort we have mentioned and the mere acquisition of money. But the art of household management, as distinct from the art of acquisition, has a limit; and the object of that art is not an unlimited amount of wealth. It would thus appear, if we look at the matter in this light, that all wealth must have a limit. In actual experience, however, we see the opposite happening, and all who are engaged in acquisition increase their fund of currency without any limit or pause.

1257^{b}35 The cause [of this contradiction] lies in the close connection between the two different modes of acquisition. They overlap in the sense that they both use the same object, that is, they use the same property but not in the same way. The object of the one is simply accumulation, and that of the other something quite different.* This explains why some men believe that mere accumulation is the object of household management; and why they stick to the idea that they must keep intact their wealth in currency, or increase it indefinitely.

But the fundamental cause of this state of mind is concern about living, rather than about living well; and since their desire for that is unlimited, their desire for the things that produce it is equally unlimited. Even those who do aim at well-being seek the means of obtaining physical enjoyments; and, as what they seek appears to depend on the activity of of acquisition, they are thus led to occupy themselves wholly in the making of money. This is why the second form of the art of acquisition has come into vogue. Because enjoyment depends on superfluity, men address themselves to the art which produces the superfluity necessary to enjoyment; and if they cannot get what they want by the art of acquisition, they attempt to do so by other means, using each and every capacity in a way not consonant with its nature. The proper function of courage, for example, is not to produce money but to give confidence. The same is true of military and medical ability: neither has the function of producing money: the one has the function of producing victory, and the other that of producing health. But those of whom we are speaking turn all such capacities into forms of the art of acquisition, as though to make money were the one aim and everything else must contribute to that aim.

$1258^{a}14$ We have thus discussed the unnecessary form of the art of acquisition: we have described its nature, and we have explained why men need its services. We have also discussed the necessary form: we have shown that it is different from the other, and is naturally a branch of the art of household management, concerned with the provision of subsistence, and not therefore unlimited in its scope, as the other form is, but subject to definite bounds.

CHAPTER 10

Household management is concerned with the use, and not (except in the way of general supervision) with the acquisition, of property; generally the householder should be able to count on nature supplying the means he needs. Acquisition for acquisition's sake shows its worst side in usury, which makes barren metal breed.

1258ª19 The argument of the last chapter provides a clear solution to the problem which we originally raised. 'Does the art of acquisition belong to the province of the manager of the household and the statesman? Or is it outside that province, and should property be regarded as something which they can simply take as given?' It may be urged, in favour of the second alternative, that just as the art of the statesman does not produce human stock, but counts on its being supplied by nature and proceeds to use her supply, so nature must also provide the physical means of subsistence—the land, or sea, or whatever it be. Then, and upon that basis, it is the province of the householder to manage properly these means. It is not the business of the art of weaving to produce wool, but to use it, and to distinguish the sorts of wool which are good and suitable from those which are poor and unsuitable. If the art of acquisition were held to be a part of the art of household management, the question might be raised why the art of medicine should not equally be held to be a part; and it might be argued that the members of a household must needs have health, in the same way as they must needs have life or any of the other necessaries. There is a sense in which it is the business of the manager of a household or of a ruler to see to the health of the members of his household or city; but there is another sense in which it is not their business but that of the doctor. Similarly, in the matter of property, there is a sense in which it is the business of the manager of a household to see to its acquisition and another sense in which that is not his business, but part of an ancillary art. But in general, as we have already noticed, a supply of property should be ready to hand.

1258ª35 It is the business of nature to furnish subsistence for each being brought into the world; and this is shown by the fact that the offspring of animals always gets nourishment from the residuum of the matter that gives it its birth. The natural form, therefore, of the art of acquisition is always, and in all cases, acquisition from fruits and animals. That art, as we have said, has two forms: one which is connected with retail trade, and another which is connected with the management of the household. Of these two forms, the latter is

necessary and laudable; the former is a method of exchange
which is justly censured, because the gain in which it results is
not naturally made, but is made at the expense of other men.
The trade of the petty usurer is hated with most reason: it
makes a profit from currency itself, instead of making it from
the process which currency was meant to serve. Currency
came into existence merely as a means of exchange; usury
tries to make it increase. This is the reason why it got its
name; for as the offspring resembles its parent, so the interest
bred by money is like the principal which breeds it, and it
may be called 'currency the son of currency.'* Hence we can
understand why, of all modes of acquisition, usury is the most
unnatural.

CHAPTER 11

*A practical consideration of the art of acquisition. The divisions
of that art which may be made on practical grounds. Instances
of the successful practice of the art, especially by the creation
of monopolies.*

1258^{b}9 We have now discussed sufficiently that part of our
subject which is related to pure knowledge: it remains to
consider the part which is related to actual use. All subjects of
this nature may be treated liberally in theory, but have to be
handled in practice as circumstances demand. The parts of
the art of acquisition which are of actual use are the following.
The first is an experience of farm-stock. This involves knowing
which are the most profitable breeds, and on what soil, and
with what treatment, they will give us the greatest profit—
knowing, for example, the right way of stocking horses, or
cattle, or sheep, or any other kind of farm-stock. We need
experience to tell how different breeds compare with one
another in point of profit, or what breeds are most profitable
on what sorts of soil: for some breeds thrive on one sort of
soil, and some on another sort. Other useful parts of the art
of acquisition are experience in cultivation, not only of cornland but also of land planted with vines and olives; experience
in bee-keeping; and experience in the rearing of such fish and

fowl as may help to provide subsistence. These are the parts and the original elements of the art of acquisition in its most proper form. We now come to exchange. This includes, first and foremost, commerce (which is divided into the three operations of the provision of a ship, the carriage of freight, and offering for sale—operations which differ from one another in the sense that some have a greater margin of safety, and others a greater margin of profit); it includes, in the second place, investment at interest; and it also includes, in the third place, service for hire. This last part of exchange is partly a matter of skilled craftsmen in the mechanical arts, and partly of unskilled workers who can render only the service of bodily labour. A third form of the art of acquisition is a form intermediate between the first and second; for it possesses elements both of the first, or natural, form, and of the form which consists in exchange. It is concerned with things extracted from the earth or with products of the earth which bear no fruit but are still of use; and we may thus cite, as examples, lumbering and all [forms of] mining.* Mining, in its turn, has many forms, because there are many species of metals extracted from the earth.

1258ᵇ33 A general account has now been given of the various forms of acquisition: to consider them minutely, and in detail, might be useful for practical purposes; but to dwell long upon them would be in poor taste. Suffice it to say that the occupations which require most skill are those in which there is least room for chance: the meanest are those in which most damage is done to physique: the most servile are those in which most use is made of physical strength: the least noble are those in which there is least need for the exercise of goodness.

1258ᵇ39 There are books on these subjects by several writers: Charetides of Paros and Apollodoros of Lemnos have written on the cultivation of cornland and land planted with vines and olives: others have written on other themes; anyone who is interested should study these subjects with the aid of these writings. A collection ought also to be made of the scattered stories about the ways in which different people have succeeded in making a fortune. They are all useful to those who value the art of acquisition. There is, for example, the story which is told of Thales of Miletus.* It is a story about a scheme for making money, which is fathered on Thales owing to his reputation for wisdom; but it involves a principle of general application. He was reproached for his poverty, which was supposed to show the uselessness of philosophy; but observing from his knowledge of meteorology (so the story goes) that there was likely to be a heavy crop of olives, and having a small sum at his command, he paid deposits, early in the year, for the hire of all the olive-presses in Miletus and Chios; and he managed, in the absence of any higher offer, to secure them at a low rate. When the season came, and there was a sudden and simultaneous demand for a number of presses, he let out the stock he had collected at any rate he chose to fix; and making a considerable fortune he succeeded in proving that it is easy for philosophers to become rich if they so desire, though it is not the business which they are really about. The story is told as showing that Thales proved his own wisdom; but as we have said, the plan he adopted, which was, in effect, the creation of a monopoly, involves a principle which can be generally applied in the art of acquisition. Some cities, therefore, as well as individuals, adopt this resource when in need of money: they establish, for instance, a monopoly in provisions. In Sicily a man with whom a sum of money had been deposited bought up all the iron from the ironworks; and afterwards, when retailers came from their shops to get a supply, he was the only seller from whom they could buy. He did not raise the price to any extent; but he gained, none the less, a profit of a 100 talents on an outlay of 50. This speculation came to the notice of Dionysius [the ruler of Syracuse] and he ordered the man to leave the city, though he allowed him to take his gains: the reason was his discovery of a way of making profit which was injurious to the interests of Dionysius himself. Yet his idea was simply the same as that of Thales; and what both of them did was merely to establish a private monopoly. But a knowledge of these methods is useful to statesmen—cities, like households, but to an even greater extent, are often in want of financial resources and in need of more ways of gaining them. This is the reason why

some of those who adopt a political career confine their
political activity to matters of finance.

CHAPTER 12

*4. Marriage, parenthood, and the general management of the
household. The nature of marital authority, which is like that
exercised by a statesman over his fellow citizens. The nature of
parental authority, which is like that of a king over his subjects.*

1259^{a}37 We said, in a previous passage, that there were
three parts of the art of household management—the first,
of which we have already spoken, being the art of controlling
slaves: the second, the art of exercising paternal authority;
and the third, that of exercising marital authority. While the
head of the household rules over both wife and children,
and rules over both as free members of the household, he
exercises a different sort of rule in each case. His rule over
his wife is like that of a statesman over fellow citizens; his
rule over his children is like that of a monarch over
subjects.* The male is naturally fitter to command than the
female, except where there is some departure from nature;
and age and maturity are similarly fitter to command than
youth and immaturity. In most cases where rule of the statesman's sort is exercised there is an interchange of ruling and
being ruled: the members of a political association aim by
their very nature at being equal and differing in nothing. It is
none the less true that when one rules and the other is ruled, [the
former] desires to establish a difference, in outward forms, in
modes of address, and in titles of respect. This may remind us of
the saying of Amasis about his foot-pan.* The relation of the
male to the female is permanently that in which the statesman
stands to his fellow citizens. Paternal rule over children, on the
other hand, is like that of a king over his subjects. The male
parent is in a position of authority both in virtue of the affection
to which he is entitled and by right of his seniority; and his
position is thus in the nature of royal authority. Homer was
right, therefore, to use the invocation

Father of Gods and of men

to address Zeus, who is king of them all. A king ought to be
naturally superior to his subjects, and yet of the same stock as
they are; and this is the case with the relation of age to youth,
and of parent to child.

CHAPTER 13

The art of household management is a moral art, aiming at the
moral goodness of the members of the household; and this is
true in regard to slaves as well as to other members. The
goodness of the head of the household has a quality of its own:
the different classes of members have also different qualities of
goodness. This is part of a general law that goodness is relative
to function, and that it is the function of some to guide, and of
others to be guided—and guided, too, in different ways. The
master's duty of guiding the slaves of the household. The
subjects of marriage and parenthood (only briefly mentioned in
the previous chapter) are to be reserved for future treatment, in
connection with the city and the proper mode of its government
(Book VII, Chapters 17–18).

1259^{b}18 It is clear from the previous argument that the
business of household management is concerned more with
human beings than it is with inanimate property; that it is
concerned more with the good condition of human beings
than with a good condition of property (which is what we call
wealth); and, finally, that it is concerned more with the
goodness of the free members of the household than with that
of slaves. Here a preliminary question may be raised in regard
to the slave. Has he any 'goodness' beyond that of discharging
his function as an instrument and performing his menial
service—any goodness of a higher value, such as temperance,
fortitude, justice, and the rest of such moral qualities?* Or
has he no 'goodness' outside the area of the bodily services he
renders? Either alternative presents difficulties. If slaves have
a 'goodness' of the higher sort, in what respect will they differ
from freemen? If they have not it would be surprising since
they are human beings, with a share in reason.* Practically
the same question may be asked in regard to a woman and a

child. Do they have their own forms of goodness? Must a woman be temperate, brave, and just? Is it, or is it not, possible for a child to be licentious or temperate?

1259ᵇ32 In general we must raise the following question about those who are naturally ruled and about those who rule: 'Is their goodness the same or does it differ?' If we say that both of them ought to share in the nobility of goodness, why should one of them permanently rule, and the other be permanently ruled? The difference between them cannot be simply a difference of degree: the difference between ruler and ruled is one of kind, and degree has nothing to do with the matter. On the other hand, it would be strange if one of them ought to share and the other ought not. How can the ruler rule properly, or the subject be properly ruled, unless they are both temperate and just? Anyone who is licentious or cowardly will utterly fail to do his duty. The conclusion which clearly emerges is that both classes must share in goodness, but that there must be different kinds of goodness, just as [there are also different kinds of goodness] among those who are naturally ruled.

1260ᵃ4 The view here suggested takes us straight to the nature of the soul. The soul has naturally two elements, a ruling and a ruled; and each has its different goodness, one belonging to the rational and ruling element, and the other to the irrational and ruled. What is true of the soul is evidently also true of the other cases; and we may thus conclude that it is natural in most cases for there to be both a ruling element and one that is ruled.* The rule of the freeman over the slave is one kind of rule; that of the male over the female another; that of the grown man over the child another still. It is true that all these people possess in common the different parts of the soul; but they possess them in different ways. The slave is entirely without the faculty of deliberation; the female indeed possesses it, but in a form which lacks authority; and children also possess it, but only in an immature form. We must assume that the same holds with regard to moral goodness: they must all share in it, but not in the same way—each sharing only to the extent required for the discharge of his or her function. The ruler, accordingly, must possess moral goodness in its full and perfect form, because his function is essentially that of a master-craftsman,* and reason is such a master-craftsman; but other people need only to possess moral goodness to the extent required of them. It is thus clear that while moral goodness is a quality of all those mentioned, the fact still remains that temperance—and similarly courage and justice—are not, as Socrates held,* the same in a woman as they are in a man. One kind of courage is concerned with ruling, the other with serving; and the same is true of the other forms of goodness.

1260ª24 This conclusion also emerges clearly when we examine the subject in more detail. To speak in general terms, and to maintain that goodness consists in 'a good condition of the soul', or in 'right action', or in anything of the kind, is to be guilty of self-deception. Far better than such general definitions is the method of simple enumeration of the different forms of goodness, as followed by Gorgias.* We must therefore hold that what the poet said of women

A modest silence is a woman's crown*

contains a general truth—but a truth which does not apply to men. And since a child is immature its goodness is obviously not a matter of its relation to itself, but of its relation to its end and to the authority that guides it. Similarly, too, the goodness of the slave is a matter of his relation to his master.

1260ª33 We laid it down, in treating of slaves, that they were useful for the necessary purposes of life. It is clear, on that basis, that they need but little goodness; only so much, in fact, as will prevent them from falling short of their duties through intemperance or cowardice. If this be true, the question may be raised whether artisans too ought not to have goodness, seeing that they often fall short of their duties through intemperance. But does not the case of the artisan differ greatly from that of the slave? The slave is a partner in his master's life: the artisan is less closely attached to a master. The extent of the goodness incumbent on him is proportionate to the extent of the servitude to which he is subject; since the mechanical type of artisan is subject only to what may be called a limited servitude.* Again the slave belongs to the class of those who are naturally what they are; but no shoe-maker, or any other artisan, belongs to that class. It is therefore clear that the task of producing in the slave the sort of goodness we have been discussing belongs to the master of the household, not to whoever instructs him in his work. This is why those who withhold reason from slaves, and argue that only command should be employed,* are making a mistake: admonition ought to be applied to slaves even more than it is to children.

1260ᵇ8 This may be sufficient as a discussion of these topics. There remain for discussion a number of questions: the relation of husband and wife, and that of parent and child; the nature of the goodness proper to each partner in these relations; the character of the mutual association of the partners, with its qualities and defects and the methods of attaining those qualities and escaping those defects. All these are questions which must be treated later in the discourses which deal with constitutions.* Every household is a part of a city and the relationships we have mentioned are parts of the household. Moreover, the goodness of every part must be considered with reference to the goodness of the whole. We must therefore consider the constitution before we proceed to deal with the training of children and women—at any rate if we hold that the goodness of children and of women makes any difference to the goodness of the city. And it must make a difference. Women are a half of the free population: children grow up to be partners in the constitution.

1260ᵇ20 As we have already discussed some aspects [of the household], and as we are to discuss the rest at a later stage, we may dismiss our present inquiry as finished, and make a new start. Let us first examine the theories of those who have expressed opinions about the best form of constitution.*

BOOK II
REVIEW OF CONSTITUTIONS

A: Constitutions in Theory (Chapters 1–8)

CHAPTER 1

1. Plato's Republic. Before describing our own conception of the best constitution we must consider both those constitutions that are in force in cities considered to be well governed and those constitutions that have been proposed by our predecessors. In doing so we should note that political association is a sharing: so we may ask 'How much should be shared?' In Plato's Republic it is proposed that women, children, and property should be held in common.

1260ᵇ27 Our purpose is to consider what form of political association is best for people able so far as possible to live as they would wish.* We must therefore consider not only constitutions actually in force in cities that are said to be well governed, but also other forms of constitution which people have proposed if these are thought to have merit.* In this way we will be able to see in what respects these constitutions are properly designed and useful. What is more, when we proceed to look for something different from them, we shall not seem to be the sort of people who desire at all costs to show their own ingenuity, but rather to have adopted our method in consequence of the defects we have found in existing forms.

1260ᵇ36 Our starting-point must be the one that is natural for such a discussion. It is necessary either that the citizens have all things in common, or that they have nothing in common, or that they have some things in common, and others not.* It is clearly impossible that they should have nothing in common: the constitution of a city involves in itself some sort of association, and its members must in the first place share a common locality. Just as a single city [*polis*] must have a single locality, so citizens are those who share in a single city. But is it better that a city which is to be well conducted should share in all the things in which it is possible for it to share, or that it should share in some things and not in others? It is certainly possible that the citizens should share children and women and property with one another. This is the plan proposed in the *Republic* of Plato, where 'Socrates'* argues that children and women and property should be held in common. We are thus faced by the question whether it is better to remain in our present condition or to follow the rule of life laid down in the *Republic*.*

CHAPTER 2

*Community of women and children. Criticisms of the end or object (unity) which Plato proposes to attain by it: (*a*) carried to its logical extreme, that object would produce a one-man city; (*b*) it neglects the social differentiation necessary in a city (a differentiation which, even in a city of 'equals and likes', produces the distinction of rulers and ruled); (*c*) it thus makes self-sufficiency impossible, because self-sufficiency involves different elements making different contributions.*

1261ᵃ10 A system in which women are common to all involves, among many others, the following difficulties. The *object* for which Socrates states that it ought to be instituted is evidently not established by the arguments which he uses.* Moreover, the end which he states as necessary for the city [*polis*] is impracticable;* and yet he gives no account of the lines on which it ought to be interpreted. I have in mind here the idea, which Socrates takes as his premiss, that the greatest possible unity of the whole city is the supreme good. Yet it is obvious that a city which goes on becoming more and more of a unit, will eventually cease to be a city at all. A city, by its nature, is some sort of plurality. If it becomes more of a unit, it will first become a household instead of a city, and then an individual instead of a household; for we should all call the household more of a unit than the city, and the individual more of a unit than the household. It follows that, even if we could, we ought not to achieve this object: it would be the destruction of the city.*

1261ª22 Not only is the city composed of a *number* of people: it is also composed of different *kinds* of people, for a city cannot be composed of those who are like one another.* There is a difference between a city and a military alliance. An alliance, formed by its very nature for the sake of the mutual help which its members can render to one another, possesses utility purely in virtue of its quantity, even if there is no difference of kind among its members. It is like a weight which depresses the scales more heavily in the balance. In this respect a *city* will also differ from a tribe, assuming that the members of the tribe are not scattered in separate villages, but [are united in a confederacy] like the Arcadians.* A real unity must be made up of elements which differ in kind. It follows that the stability of every city depends on each of its elements rendering to the others an amount equivalent to what it receives from them—a principle already laid down in the *Ethics.** This has to be the case even among free and equal citizens. They cannot all rule simultaneously;* they must therefore each hold office for a year, unless they adopt some other arrangement or some other period of time. In this way it comes about that all are rulers, just as it would if shoemakers and carpenters changed their occupations so that the same people were not always following these professions. Since the arrangement [followed in the arts and crafts] is also better when applied to the affairs of the political association, it would clearly be better for the same people always to be rulers wherever possible. But where this is impossible, through the natural equality of all the citizens—and also because justice requires the participation of all in office (whether office be a good thing or a bad)—there is an imitation of it, if equals retire from office in turn and are all, apart from their period of office, in the same position. This means that some rule, and others are ruled, in turn, as if they had become, for the time being, different people. We may add that even those who are rulers differ from one another, some holding one kind of office and some another.

1261ᵇ6 These considerations are sufficient to show, first, that it is not the nature of the city to be a unit in the sense in which some thinkers say that it is, and secondly, that what is said to be the supreme good of a city is really its ruin. But surely the 'good' of each thing is what preserves it in being.

1261ᵇ10 There is still another consideration which may be used to prove that the policy of attempting an extreme unification of the city is not a good policy. A household is something which attains a greater degree of self-sufficiency than an individual; and a city, in turn, is something which attains self-sufficiency to a greater degree than a household. But it becomes fully a city, only when the association which forms it is large enough to be self-sufficing. On the assumption, therefore, that the higher degree of self-sufficiency is the more desirable thing, the lesser degree of unity is more desirable than the greater.*

CHAPTER 3

Community of women and children (continued). Criticisms of such community considered as a means for producing the end of unity: (a) as all collectively, and not each individually, are parents, there will be no real feeling, but rather a general apathy; (b) kinship will be fractional kinship (when 1,000 are father to the same child, each father is only 1/1,000 father); (c) nature will 'recur', and spoil the scheme.

1261ᵇ16 Even if it were the supreme good of a political association that it should have the greatest possible unity, this unity does not appear to follow from the formula of 'All men saying "Mine" and "Not mine" at the same time', which, in the view of 'Socrates',* is the index of the perfect unity of a city. The word 'all' has a double sense:* if it means 'each separately', the object which 'Socrates' desires to realize may perhaps be realized in a greater degree: each and all separately will then say 'My wife' (or 'My son') of one and the same person; and each and all separately will speak in the same way of property, and of every other concern. But it is not in the sense of 'each separately' that all who have children and women in common will actually speak of them. They will all call them 'Mine'; but they will do so collectively, and not individually.* The same is true of property also; [all will call it

'Mine'] but they will do so in the sense of 'all collectively', and not in the sense of 'each separately'. It is therefore clear that there is a certain fallacy in the use of the term 'all'. 'All' and 'both' and 'odd' and 'even' are liable by their ambiguity to produce captious arguments* even in reasoned discussions. We may therefore conclude that the formula of 'all men saying "Mine" of the same object' is in one sense something fine but impracticable, and in another sense does nothing to promote harmony.

1261ᵇ32 In addition to these problems the formula also involves another disadvantage. What is common to the greatest number gets the least amount of care. People pay most attention to what is their own: they care less for what is common; or, at any rate, they care for it only to the extent to which each is individually concerned. Even where there is no other cause for inattention, people are more prone to neglect their duty when they think that another is attending to it: this is what happens in domestic service, where many attendants are sometimes of less assistance than a few. [The scheme proposed in the *Republic* means that] each citizen will have a thousand sons: they will not be the sons of each citizen individually: any son whatever will be equally the son of any father whatever. The result will be that all will equally neglect them.

1262ᵃ1 Furthermore each person, when he says 'Mine' of any citizen who is prosperous or the reverse, is speaking fractionally. He means only that he is 'Mine' to the extent of a fraction determined by the total number of citizens. When he says 'He is mine' or 'He is so-and-so's', the term 'Mine' or 'So-and-so's' is used with reference to the whole body concerned—the whole thousand, or whatever may be the total number of citizens. Even so he cannot be sure; for there is no evidence who had a child born to him, or whether, if one was born, it managed to survive. Which is the better system—that each of two thousand, or ten thousand, people should say 'Mine' of a child in this fractional sense, or that each should say 'Mine' in the sense in which the word is now used in ordinary cities? As things are, one man calls by the name of '*My* son' the same person whom a second man calls by the name of '*My* brother': a third calls him '*My* cousin' or '*My* relative', because he is somehow related to him, either by blood or by connection through marriage; while besides these different modes of address someone else may use still another, and call him '*My* clansman' or '*My* tribesman'. It is better to be someone's own cousin than to be his son after this fashion.* Even on Plato's system it is impossible to avoid the chance that some of the citizens might guess who are their brothers, or children, or fathers, or mothers.* The resemblances between children and parents must inevitably lead to their drawing conclusions about one another. That this actually happens in real life is stated as fact by some of the writers on descriptive geography. They tell us that some of the inhabitants of upper Libya have their women in common; but the children born of such unions can still be distinguished by their resemblance to their fathers. Indeed there are some women, and some females in the animal world (mares, for instance, and cows), that show a strong natural tendency to produce offspring resembling the male parent: the Pharsalian mare which was called the 'Just Return'* is a good example.

CHAPTER 4

Community of women and children (continued). Problems arise when parents do not know their children, or children their parents. At best such a community produces a watery sort of friendship. The addition to it of a scheme of transposition of ranks raises further difficulties.

1262ª25 There are also other difficulties which those who construct such a community will not find it easy to avoid. We may take as examples cases of assault, homicide, whether unintentional or intentional, fighting, and slander. All these offences, when they are committed against father or mother or a near relative, differ from offences against people who are not so related, in being breaches of natural piety.* Such offences must happen more frequently when men are ignorant of their relatives than when they know who they are; and when they do happen, the customary penance can be made if people know their relatives, but none can be made if they are ignorant of them. It is also surprising that, after having made sons common to all, he should simply forbid lovers from engaging in carnal intercourse.* Nor does he forbid other familiarities which, if practised between son and father, or brother and brother, are the very height of indecency, all the more as this form of love [even if it is not expressed] is in itself indecent. It is surprising, too, that he should debar male lovers from carnal intercourse on the one ground of the excessive violence of the pleasure, and that he should think it a matter of indifference that the lovers may be father and son, or again that they may be brothers.

1262ª40 Community of women and children would seem to be more useful if it were practised among the farmers rather than among the guardians. The spirit of friendship* is likely to exist to a lesser degree where women and children are common; and the governed class ought to have little of that spirit if it is to obey and not to attempt revolution. Generally, such a system must produce results directly opposed to those which a system of properly constituted laws should produce, and equally opposed to the very object for which, in the view of 'Socrates', this community of women and children ought to be instituted. Friendship, we believe, is the chief good of cities, because it is the best safeguard against the danger of factional disputes. 'Socrates' himself particularly commends the ideal of the unity of the city; and that unity is commonly held, and expressly stated by him, to be the result of friendship. We may cite the argument of the discourses on love,* where 'Aristophanes', as we know, speaks of lovers desiring out of friendship to grow together into a unity, and to be one instead of two. Now in that case it would be inevitable that both or at least one of them should cease to exist. But in the case of the political association there would be merely a watery sort of friendship: a father would be very little disposed to say 'Mine' of a son, and a son would be as little disposed to say 'Mine' of a father. Just as a little sweet wine, mixed with a great deal of water, produces a tasteless mixture, so family feeling is diluted and tasteless when family names have as little meaning as they have in a constitution of this sort, and when there is so little reason for a father treating his sons as sons, or a son treating his father as a father, or brothers one another as brothers. There are two things which particularly move people to care for and love an object. One of these is that the object should belong to yourself: the other is that you should like it. Neither of these motives can exist among those who live under a constitution such as this.

1262^{b}24 There is still a further difficulty. It concerns the way in which children born among the farmers and craftsmen are to be transferred to the guardian class,* and vice versa. How such transposition is actually to be effected is a matter of great perplexity; and in any case those who transfer such children, and assign them their new place, will be bound to know who are the children so placed and with whom they are being placed. In addition, those problems of assault, unnatural affection, and homicide, which have already been mentioned, will occur even more in the case of these people. Those transferred from the guardian class to that of the other citizens will cease for the future to address the guardians as brothers, or children, or fathers, or mothers, as the case may be; and it will have the same effect for those who have been transferred from among the other citizens to the guardians. Such people will no longer avoid committing these offences on account of their kinship.

1262^{b}35 This may serve as a determination of the issues raised by the idea of community of women and children.

CHAPTER 5

Community of property. Three possible systems of property. The difficulties of a system under which ownership and use are both common: the merits of a system under which ownership is private and use is common—it gives more pleasure, and it encourages goodness more. Communism cannot remedy evils which really spring from the defects of human nature: it is also based on a false conception of unity, and neglects the true unity which comes from education; finally, it is contradicted by experience. Plato's particular scheme of community of property leaves the position of the farming class obscure. The system of govern-

*ment which he connects with his scheme is too absolute, and is
likely to cause discontent: it also deprives the ruling class of any
happiness.*

1262ᵇ39 The next subject for consideration is property.*
What is the proper system of property for citizens who are to
live under the best form of constitution? Should property be
held in common or not? This is an issue which may be
considered in itself, and apart from any proposals for community of women and children. Even if women and children are
held separately, as is now universally the case, questions
relating to property still remain for discussion. Should use
and ownership both be common?* For example, there may be
a system under which plots of land are owned separately, but
the crops (as actually happens among some tribal peoples) are
brought into a common stock for the purpose of consumption.
Secondly, and conversely, the land may be held in common
ownership, and may also be cultivated in common, but the
crops may be divided among individuals for their private use:
some of the barbarian peoples are also said to practise this
second method of sharing. Thirdly, the plots and the crops
may both be common.

1263ᵃ8 When the cultivators of the soil are a different body
from the citizens who own it, the position will be different
and easier to handle; but when the citizens who own the soil
do the work themselves, the problems of property will cause a
good deal of trouble. If they do not share equally in the work
and in the enjoyment of the produce, those who do more
work and get less of the produce will be bound to raise
complaints against those who get a large reward and do little
work. In general it is a difficult business to live together and
to share in any form of human activity, but it is specially
difficult in such matters. Fellow-travellers who merely share
in a journey furnish an illustration: they generally quarrel
about ordinary matters and take offence on petty occasions.
So, again, the servants with whom we are most prone to take
offence are those who are particularly employed in ordinary
everyday services.

1263ᵃ21 Difficulties such as these, and many others, are involved in a system of community of property. The present system would be far preferable, if it were embellished with social customs and the enactment of proper laws. It would possess the advantages of both systems, and would combine the merits of a system of community of property with those of the system of private property. For, although there is a sense in which property *ought* to be common, it should in general be private. When everyone has his own separate sphere of interest, there will not be the same ground for quarrels; and they will make more effort, because each man will feel that he is applying himself to what is his own.

1263ª30 On such a scheme, too, moral goodness will ensure that the property of each is made to serve the use of all, in the spirit of the proverb which says 'Friends' goods are goods in common'.* Even now there are some cities in which the outlines of such a scheme are so far apparent, as to suggest that it is not impossible; in well-ordered cities, more particularly, there are some elements of it already existing, and others which might be added. [In these cities] each citizen has his own property; part of which he makes available to his friends, and part of which he uses as though it was common property. In Sparta, for example, men use one another's slaves, and one another's horses and dogs, as if they were their own; and they take provisions on a journey, if they happen to be in need, from the farms in the countryside. It is clear from what has been said that the better system is that under which property is privately owned but is put to common use; and the function proper to the legislator is to make men so disposed that they will treat property in this way.

1263ª40 In addition, to think of a thing as your own makes an inexpressible difference, so far as pleasure is concerned. It may well be that regard for oneself is a feeling implanted by nature, and not a mere random impulse. Self-love is rightly censured, but that is not so much loving oneself as loving oneself in excess.* It is the same with one who loves money; after all, virtually everyone loves things of this kind. We may add that a very great pleasure is to be found in doing a kindness and giving some help to friends, or guests, or comrades; and such kindness and help become possible only when property is privately owned. But not only are these pleasures impossible under a system in which the city is excessively unified; the activities of two forms of goodness are also obviously destroyed. The first of these is temperance in the matter of sexual relations* (it is an act of moral value to keep away from the wife of another through temperance): the second is generosity in the use of property.* In a city which is excessively unified no man can show himself generous, or indeed do a generous act; for the function of generosity consists in the proper use which is made of property.

1263ᵇ15 This kind of legislation may appear to wear an attractive face and to demonstrate benevolence. The hearer receives it gladly, thinking that everybody will feel towards everybody else some marvellous sense of friendship—all the more as the evils now existing under ordinary forms of government (lawsuits about contracts, convictions for perjury, and obsequious flatteries of the rich) are denounced as due to the absence of a system of common property.* None of these, however, is due to property not being held in common. They all arise from wickedness. Indeed it is a fact of observation that those who own common property, and share in its management, are far more often at variance with one another than those who have property separately—though those who are at variance in consequence of sharing in property look to us few in number when we compare them with the mass of those who own their property privately.*

1263ᵇ27 What is more, justice demands that we should take into account not only the evils which people will be spared when they have begun to hold their property in common, but also the benefits of which they will be deprived. Their life can be seen to be utterly impossible.

1263ᵇ29 The cause of the fallacy into which 'Socrates' falls must be held to be his incorrect premiss.* It is true that unity in some respects is necessary both for the household and for the city, but unity in all respects is not. There is a point at which a city, by advancing in unity, will cease to be a city: there is another point at which it will still be a city, but a worse one because it has come close to ceasing altogether to be a city. It is as if you were to turn harmony into mere unison, or to reduce a theme to a single beat. The truth is that the city, as has already been said, is a plurality; and education is therefore *the* means of making it a community and giving it unity. It is therefore surprising that one who intends to introduce a system of education, and who believes that the city can achieve goodness by means of this system, should none the less think that he is setting it on the right track by such methods as he actually proposes, rather than by the method of social customs, of mental culture, and of legislation.* An example of such legislation may be found in Sparta and Crete, where the legislator has made the institution of property serve a common use by the system of common meals.

1264ª1 There is another matter which must not be ignored: we are bound to pay some regard to the long past and the passage of the years, in which these things would not have gone unnoticed if they had been really good. Almost everything has been discovered already;* though some things have not been combined with one another, and others are not put into practice. It would shed a great deal of light on these matters, if we could watch the actual construction of such a constitution. The foundation of any city will always involve the division and distribution of its members into classes, partly in the form of associations for common meals, and partly in that of clans and tribes. It follows that the only peculiar feature of the legislation* is the rule that the guardians are not to farm the land; and even that is a rule which the Spartans are already attempting to follow.

1264ª11 'Socrates' does not explain the character of the whole constitution so far as concerns those who share in it, nor indeed is it easy to explain. The mass of the citizens who are not guardians will be, in effect, nearly the whole of the citizen body. But their position is left undefined.* We are not told whether the farmers are also to have property in common, or to own it individually; nor do we learn whether their women and children are to be common to them all, or to belong to each separately.

1264ª17 The first alternative is that all things should belong to them all in common. In that case, what will be the difference between them and the guardians? What advantage will they gain by accepting the government of the guardians? What convinces them actually to accept it?—unless it be some device such as is used in Crete, where the serfs are allowed to enjoy the same general privileges as their masters, and are excluded only from athletic exercises and the possession of arms.

1264ª22 The second alternative is that these institutions should be the same for the farmers as they are in most cities today. In that case, we may inquire, what the character of their association* will be? There will inevitably be two cities in one, and those cities will be opposed to one another—the guardians being made into something of the nature of an army of occupation, and the farmers, artisans, and others being given the position of ordinary civilians. Again, legal complaints, and actions at law, and all the other evils which he describes as existing in cities as they are, will equally exist among them. Certainly 'Socrates' says that, in virtue of their education, they will not need a number of regulations* (such as city ordinances, market by-laws, and the like); but it is also true that he provides education only for the guardians. A further difficulty is that he has the farmers control their holdings on condition that they pay a quota of their produce to the guardians. This is likely to make them far more difficult to handle, and much more filled with high ideas of their own importance, than other people's helots, penestae,* or serfs.

1264ª36 In any case there is no indication whether it is necessary for these arrangements to be the same [for the farmers as for the guardians] or not, nor are other matters connected with this made clear—matters such as the position of the farmers in the political system, the nature of their education, and the character of the law they are to observe. We thus find it difficult to discover what the farming class will be like, and yet this is a matter of the highest importance if the common life of the guardians is to be preserved. The third and last alternative is that the farmers should have a system of community of women, combined with a system of private property. In that case, who will see to the house while the men are seeing to the business of the fields? And, for that matter, who will see to the house, when the farmers have property as well as women in common? It is strange, too, that Plato should draw an analogy from the animal world in order to prove that women should follow the same pursuits as men. Animals do not have households to manage.*

1264^b6 There is also an element of danger in the method of government which 'Socrates' proposes to institute. He makes the same people be rulers all the time. This is a system which must cause factional conflict even among the elements which have no particular standing, and all the more, therefore, among the high-spirited and martial elements. It is obviously necessary for him to make the same people rulers all the time. The 'divine gold'* cannot be sometimes mixed in the souls of one group and sometimes in those of another, but must always be in the same people. This is why he says that when they were first created 'the god mixed gold in the composition' of some, silver in that of others, and brass and iron in that of the rest, who were to be craftsmen and farmers. It is a further objection that he deprives his guardians even of happiness,* maintaining that the object of the legislator should be for the whole city to be happy. It is impossible for the whole city to be happy unless all, or most, or at least some of its parts are happy. The quality of being happy is not of the same order as the quality of being even. That may exist in a whole without existing in either of its parts: the quality of being happy cannot. Furthermore, if the guardians are not happy, who else is? Certainly not the craftsmen, or the mass of the common people.

1264^b24 We may thus conclude that the constitution which 'Socrates' describes raises all the difficulties we have mentioned, and others which are no less serious.

CHAPTER 6

2. Plato's Laws. *The scheme of the* Laws *is not greatly different from that of the* Republic. *It postulates too large a territory, but fails to pay proper attention to the problem of foreign relations. It does not sufficiently define the amount of property required, or the object for which it is required; nor does it make*

*proper provision for a balance between property and population.
The system of government is a sort of 'constitutional government', but it is not properly balanced: the method of electing
officials and councillors is too oligarchical.*

1264ᵇ26 The same, or nearly the same, is true of the *Laws*;*
which is a later work. This makes it advisable for us to
examine briefly the constitution there described. A further
reason for doing so is that in the *Republic* 'Socrates' attempted
to resolve only a very small number of issues—mainly the
proper method for ensuring community of women and children and community of property, and the structure of the
constitution. He divides the population into two parts: one
consists of the farmers, the other of the military class; and
from this last is selected a third part, the deliberative and
sovereign class. But so far as the farmers and artisans are
concerned, 'Socrates' leaves it unsettled whether they are to
share in some offices or in none, and whether or not they are
to bear arms and join in military service. He thinks that the
women should join in the military service and enjoy the same
education as the male guardians; but otherwise he has filled
up the dialogue with digressions extraneous to the main
theme, and with a discussion of the proper manner of educating the guardians.

1265ᵃ1 The great bulk of the *Laws* is concerned with legislation. He says little about the constitution;* and in what he
does say, though he speaks of desiring to institute a form of
government which will be more in the reach of existing cities,
he gradually brings the form he proposes round again to the
other type* [i.e. to that described in the *Republic*]. In all
matters other than community of women and property, he
provides identical institutions for both of his constitutions.
Education is the same in both: the members of both are to
live a life free from menial duties: there is the same arrangement for common meals in both. The only differences are that
in the *Laws* there are to be common meals for women and the
number of citizens who bear arms,* which in the *Republic* is
only 1,000, is to be fixed at a total of 5,000.

1265ᵃ10 All the Socratic dialogues are original:* they show ingenuity, novelty of view, and a spirit of inquiry. To handle everything well is perhaps a difficult thing. Take, for example, the number of citizens which has just been mentioned. We cannot overlook the fact that such a number will require a territory of the size of Babylon or some space which is similarly unlimited in extent. It will need all that to support 5,000 people in idleness, especially when we reflect that they will be augmented by a crowd of women and attendants many times as great as themselves. It is right to assume the most desirable conditions but not to assume anything which is plainly impossible.

1265ᵃ18 It is stated [in the *Laws*] that there are two factors to which the legislator should pay regard in enacting laws: the territory of the city, and the inhabitants of that territory.* But there is also a third factor. If a city is to live a political life, and not a life of isolation, it is a good thing that its legislator should also pay regard to neighbouring countries. For example, a city should employ not only such instruments of war as are serviceable in its own territory but also such as are serviceable for use abroad. Even if one does not accept this way of life* as desirable for the individual or for the city as a whole it is none the less essential to be formidable to enemies both when they are invading one's territory and when they are in retreat.

1265ᵃ28 The amount of property should also be considered; and we have to ask whether it is not better to determine it in a different, or rather a more definite, way. He states that the amount should be 'sufficient for a life of temperance', as though this was equivalent to 'sufficient for a good life'; the latter is, of course, a more general expression and it is, moreover, possible for a life to be both temperate and miserable. A better definition would be, 'sufficient for a life of temperance *and* generosity',* for if these qualities are separated, generosity will be accompanied by luxury, and temperance by hardship. They are the only qualities to be desired in the use of wealth: one cannot, for example, [be said to] use wealth in a meek or in a manly spirit; but one can use it both in a temperate and in a generous spirit. These must therefore be the qualities involved in the use of wealth.

1265ᵃ38 It is strange that he should distribute landed property in equal lots, without making any corresponding arrangements to fix the number of citizens.* He imposes no restriction on the production of children, on the assumption that however many children may be born [in some families], infertility [in others] will keep the number level. The reason [why he makes this assumption] is that it appears to be what actually happens in existing cities. But a constant population will need to be maintained with far more accuracy than it is in existing cities. As things are now, properties can be freely divided to cover the whole population, however large it may be, and nobody need be destitute, but under these proposals the properties are indivisible, and any surplus population which may arise, whether it be large or small, will have no property at all. One would have thought that it was even more necessary to limit the rate of reproduction so that no more than a certain number of children should be produced, than to limit property. The rate of reproduction should be fixed to allow for the chances both of mortality among children and of infertility among married couples. If no restriction is imposed on the rate of reproduction (and this is the case in most of our existing cities), poverty is the inevitable result; and poverty produces, in its turn, factional disputes and wrongdoing. Pheidon of Corinth, one of the earliest legislators, held that the number of family plots and the number of citizens should be kept equal to one another, even if the citizens had all started originally with plots of unequal size; but what we find in the *Laws* is the opposite.

1265ᵇ16 We must leave to a later occasion* any discussion of the improvements which might be suggested in this scheme. Another omission in the *Laws* is the failure to explain how the rulers are to differ from the ruled. He simply uses a simile: the relation of ruler and ruled, he suggests, should be like that of warp and woof,* which are made out of different wools. It is a further omission that while he allows someone's whole property to be increased fivefold,* he does not explain why his plot of land should not also be allowed to increase up to some given point. The distribution of the farmhouses is another subject which needs further consideration: it hardly seems to conduce to efficiency of household management. He assigns two quite separate plots of land* to each of its citizens but it is difficult to live in two houses.

1265^{b}26 The whole system tends to be one neither of democracy nor of oligarchy, but rather an intermediate form, of the sort which is usually called 'constitutional government' [or polity]:* the citizens, for example, are drawn only from those who bear arms. If his view in constructing this constitution is that it represents the form which is most readily attainable by most cities, he may very well be right; but if he regards it as the form which comes next in merit to his first form of constitution [i.e. that in the *Republic*], he is mistaken: one might commend more highly the constitution of Sparta, or some other form of a more aristocratic character.* There are, indeed, some thinkers who hold that the best constitution should be a mixture of all constitutions; and they commend, for this reason, the constitution of Sparta. Some say that the Spartan constitution is composed of all the three elements, monarchy, oligarchy, and democracy: monarchy is represented by the two kings; oligarchy by the Council of Elders; and democracy by the Ephors, who are drawn from the ranks of the people. Others, however, regard the Ephoralty as representing tyranny; and these consider that the element of democracy appears in the system of common meals, and in the general habit of daily life. But in the *Laws* it is claimed that the best constitution should be composed of democracy and tyranny, forms which one would classify either as not constitutions at all or as the worst of all constitutions.* Those who combine more forms put forward a better view; for a constitution is better when it is composed of more numerous elements.

1266^{a}5 It is a further objection that this constitution has really no element of monarchy, but only the elements of oligarchy and democracy, with a particular inclination towards oligarchy.* This appears clearly in the method proposed for appointing officials.* The use of the lot for the purpose of finally choosing officials from those who have been previously elected combines democracy with oligarchy. But compelling the richer citizens to attend the assembly, to vote in elections of officials, and to discharge other forms of political duty, while the other citizens are allowed to abstain is oligarchical. So is the attempt to secure a greater number of office-holders from the wealthier class, and to fill the highest offices from the ranks of those whose assessments are highest. He also makes the method of electing councillors oligarchical. All the citizens, it is true, are compelled to take part in the election of candidates from the first assessment class, and of an equal number from the second. They then elect candidates from the third class, but it is not compulsory for everyone to take part in election of candidates from the third and fourth classes, indeed in the election from the fourth class only the members of the first and second classes are compelled to vote. [All this relates to the process of pre-election.] Then, from those [chosen in this way], there must next, he says, be elected, an equal number for each assessment class. The result will be that the electors who have the largest assessments and are of better character will form the majority, because many of the common people, not being compelled to vote, will not do so.

1266ª22 These considerations, and others which will be mentioned when the time comes for us to examine this sort of constitution, are sufficient to prove that it should not be formed by combining democracy and monarchy. We may add that there is also a danger in the method of electing the officials by the double process of pre-election and a final election. If a knot of people, even of moderate size, decide to act in combination the elections will always be decided according to their preference.

1266ª28 These are the considerations which are raised by the constitution described in the *Laws*.

CHAPTER 7

3. Phaleas of Chalcedon. His proposal for the equalization of property in land. It would involve regulation of the population: it would also involve determination of the exact standard on which equality was to be achieved. Generally, equality matters more in the moral, or educational, sphere than in the material: disorder and crime are due to moral defects as well as to

*economic causes. The amount and distribution of property in a
city are affected by considerations of foreign as well as domestic
policy; but the essential criticism of Phaleas is that he lays too
much emphasis on material factors.*

1266ᵃ31 There are also a number of other schemes for new
constitutions, some of them proposed by laymen, and others
by men who were versed in philosophy or statesmanship.
They all come nearer to the existing constitutions, under
which people are now actually living, than does either of the
schemes proposed by Plato. No other thinker has proposed
such novelties as community of wives and children or common
meals for women: on the contrary, thinkers have rather started
from the immediate necessities of life. Thus there are some
who hold that the proper regulation of property is more
important than any other object, because, so they say, it is
about this issue that factional conflicts always arise. Phaleas
of Chalcedon* was the first to suggest this and he proposed
accordingly that all the citizens should have equal amounts of
property. He thought that in new colonies this could be
achieved, without any difficulty, at the moment of their foundation. Cities which were already established would present a
greater problem; but even here equality could be introduced—and that in the shortest possible time—if the rich
gave dowries but did not receive them, and the poor, conversely, received but did not give them. Plato, when he was
writing the *Laws,* was of the opinion that the amount of
property should be left unrestricted up to a given point;
beyond that point, he was in favour of restriction, proposing,
as has already been said, that no citizen should be allowed to
accumulate to an extent which would make his property more
than five times as large as the smallest property owned by any
other citizen.

1266ᵇ8 Those who propose such legislation ought not to
forget, as they continually do, that regulation of the amount
of property ought to be accompanied by regulation of the
number of children in the family. If the number of children
gets out of proportion to the amount of the property, the
abrogation of the law must necessarily follow; and, apart

from this abrogation, it is a sorry thing that a large number of people should be reduced from comfort to penury. It is difficult for men who have suffered that fate not to be revolutionaries. Even in times past, there were some who clearly recognized that such equality had an influence on the character of a political association. We may cite the example of Solon's legislation;* and in other cities too there is a law which prevents men from acquiring land to any extent they desire. Similarly there are laws to be found which prevent the *sale* of property: among the Locrians, for instance, there is a law to the effect that men cannot sell their property unless they can prove that an evident misfortune has befallen them. There are also laws which provide that the original lots must be maintained intact: it was the abrogation of such a law at Leucas, to mention one instance, which made the constitution excessively democratic; as a result, those who possessed the necessary legal qualification no longer came into office. But it is possible that equality of property may exist, and yet the amount possessed by each individual may be either unduly large, which leads to luxury, or unduly small, which results in penury. It is therefore clear that it is not enough for the legislator to establish the equality of property: it is [also] necessary to aim at a moderate amount. But even if one were to fix the same moderate amount for each, there would still be no gain. It is more necessary to equalize people's desires than their properties; and that is a result which cannot be achieved unless they are adequately trained by the influence of laws. Phaleas, however, might possibly retort that this is just the view which he himself propounds; for it is his opinion that cities should practise equality in two things: property and education. But in that case we ought to be told what is to be the character of the education. There would be no real gain if it were merely one and the same for all; for it is possible for education to be one and the same for all, and yet to be of a character which will produce a disposition to covet wealth, or to covet office, or to covet both. This raises a further point: factional conflict arises not only from inequality of property, but also from inequality of offices. But these two kinds of inequality work in opposite ways. The masses become revolutionary when the distribution of property is *unequal*. Men of education become revolutionary when the distribution of office is *equal*.* This is the point of the saying:

> Office and honour are one and the same for the good and the bad man.*

1267ª2 But people do not commit crimes solely because of a lack of necessities, a condition for which Phaleas thinks equality of property will be a remedy since it will serve to prevent men from stealing simply through cold or hunger. They also commit crimes to get the pleasure it gives and to rid themselves of desire. If they have a desire which goes beyond the simple necessities of life, they will turn criminals to cure it. This is not the only reason: even when they do not have any desire they do wrong just in order to enjoy those kinds of pleasure which are unaccompanied by pain.

1267ª9 What is the remedy for these three kinds of crime? For the first kind, we may answer, some modicum of property and some sort of work; for the second, a temperate disposition; as for the third kind, we can only say that if there are men who want to get unmixed pleasure purely by their own effort, they will find no cure except in the aid of philosophy; for all pleasures other than that of philosophy need the assistance of others. The greatest crimes are committed not for the sake of necessities, but for the sake of superfluities. Men do not become tyrants in order to avoid exposure to cold. This is the reason why great honours are paid to someone who kills not a mere thief, but a tyrant. We thus see that the general scheme of the constitution proposed by Phaleas avails only against the lesser crimes.

1267ª17 Furthermore, while Phaleas seeks to arrange most of the details of his scheme with a view to the proper working of the constitution internally, he ought also to make arrangements to meet the problem of defence against all neighbouring and foreign cities. It is therefore necessary that the constitution should be constructed with a view to military strength; and of this Phaleas has nothing to say. The same applies to property. It should be adequate not only as a basis for the political activities of the citizens internally, but also as a resource for meeting external dangers. This latter consideration suggests the proper amount. On the one hand, it should not be so large that neighbouring and more powerful cities will covet it, while its owners are unable to repel an attack: on the other hand, it should not be so small that those who own it are unable to sustain the burden of a war even with cities equal and similar to their own. Phaleas has given us no indication; but we must not forget that *some* amount of property is an advantage. Perhaps, therefore, the best criterion of that amount is that stronger cities shall find no advantage in going to war with a city because its wealth is excessive, but will go to war with it only in circumstances in which they would do so even if its wealth were less than it is. There is an historical incident which illustrates our argument. When the Persian Autophradates was planning to besiege Atarneus, Eubulus* asked him to consider the length of time which it would take to capture it, and to calculate the expense which a siege of that duration would mean. He was willing, he said, to surrender the town immediately for less than that amount. By saying this he caused Autophradates, after a little reflection, to abandon the siege.

1267ᵃ37 A system which gives equal properties to all the citizens has a certain advantage, in that it helps to prevent mutual discord; but the advantage, on the whole, is inconsiderable. The educated would be aggrieved by the system, feeling that they deserved something more than mere equality; indeed, as a matter of actual observation, they often rise in revolt and cause civic discord for this very reason. The wickedness of human beings is insatiable: at first two obols were a sufficient allowance,* but now that this has become the tradition men are always wanting something more, and are never contented until they get to infinity. It is the nature of desire to be infinite, and most people live for the satisfaction of desire. The source from which a remedy for such evils may be expected is not the equalization of property, but rather a method of training which ensures that the better sort of people have no desire to make themselves richer while the poorer sort have no opportunity to do so. The latter object

will be attained if those concerned are put in an inferior
position without being subjected to injustice.

1267**b**9 Even in regard to his proposal for equality of property Phaleas has expressed himself imperfectly. He would
equalize property only in land; but wealth may also consist in
slaves, cattle, and money, and in addition there will be a
considerable stock of what are called movables. The proper
course is either to deal with all these forms of wealth by an
equal distribution or by fixing a moderate maximum, or to
leave all alike unregulated. It is also evident, from the legislation proposed by Phaleas, that he proposes to institute only a
small body of citizens: the artisans are all to be public slaves,
and are not to furnish any addition to the citizen body. It
may be the case that one class of artisans—those who are
employed on public property—should be made public slaves.
If so, it ought to be done on the lines which are followed at
Epidamnus, or on the scheme which Diophantus once sought
to introduce at Athens.*

1267**b**19 These observations on the constitution proposed by
Phaleas will enable one to judge whether his suggestions are
good or bad.

CHAPTER 8

*4. Hippodamus of Miletus. A planner of towns, who also sought
to plan cities on new lines. His advocacy of 'triads'—three
social classes; three divisions of the territory; three sorts of
laws. Criticism of his three classes and three divisions of territory. Criticism of his legal novelties, and especially of his
proposal to reward the inventors of reforms. Tradition has its
claims; and the value of a law-abiding habit may be greater
than that of legal reforms.*

1267**b**22 Hippodamus* the son of Euryphon, a citizen of
Miletus, was the first man without practical experience of
politics who attempted to handle the theme of the best form
of constitution. He was a man who invented the planning of
towns in separate quarters, and laid out the Piraeus with
regular roads. In his general life, too, he was led into some

eccentricity by a desire to attract attention; and this made some people feel that his way of life was too studied and artificial. He wore his hair long and expensively adorned: he had flowing robes, made from a cheap but warm material, which he wore in summer-time as well as in winter; and he aspired to be learned about nature generally.

1267^b30 The city which he planned to construct was one of 10,000 citizens, divided into three classes: the first of artisans, the second of farmers, and the third a defence force equipped with arms. The territory was to be similarly divided into three parts. One was intended for religious purposes; the second for public use; and the third was to be private property. The first part was to meet the expenses of the regular worship of the civic deities; the second part, that devoted to public use, was to support the defence force; and the third was to be the private property of the farming class. Hippodamus also believed that there are only three classes of laws,* for he held that there are three main issues, wanton assault, damage, and homicide, from which lawsuits arise. He proposed, too, that there should be a single supreme court, to which all cases that appeared to have been improperly decided should be referred; and this court, on his plan, was to be constituted of elders selected for the purpose. He also held that judgements should not be given in the courts by the method of dropping a pebble into the voting urn: each juryman should deposit a tablet. If he gave an absolute verdict of condemnation against the defendant, he would write that verdict on the tablet: if he gave an absolute verdict of acquittal, he would leave the tablet blank; if he wished to record a [qualified] verdict, partly of condemnation, and partly of acquittal, he would specify the nature of this verdict. He considered that the present arrangement results from poor legislation: it compels a juryman to violate his judicial oath by deciding the case in favour of one side or the other.

1268^a6 He also proposed a law that honours should be conferred on those responsible for any invention of benefit to the city; and he further suggested, as a novelty not hitherto included in the legislation of any city, that the children of those who had been killed in action should be supported at the public expense. (Actually, such a law is already in existence at Athens, and also in other cities.) Finally, the public officials, on his scheme, were all to be elected by the people: the people was to be constituted of the three classes already mentioned; and the officials whom they elected would take charge of public matters, matters relating to aliens, and matters relating to orphans.

1268ª14 These are the main and most notable features in the political arrangements proposed by Hippodamus. The first criticism which we may raise concerns the division of the citizen body. The artisans, the farmers, and those who bear arms all share in the constitution; but the farmers do so without possessing arms, and the artisans without possessing either land or arms. This makes them both, in effect, the slaves of the class in possession of arms. It is thus impossible that they should share in all the [offices and] honours; for necessarily members of the class which possesses arms must be appointed as generals and protectors of the citizens, and must thus hold, in the main, the highest offices. But how can those who do not share in the constitution be disposed in a friendly way towards the constitution? It may be rejoined that the class which possesses arms ought to be superior to both of the other classes. [We may answer that] it will be difficult for them to be superior unless they are also numerous. But, in that case, is there any need for the other two classes to share in the constitution, or to control the appointment of officials? And are the farmers really of any service to the city? Artisans are necessary (for every city needs artisans), and they can earn a living from their crafts in the city proposed by Hippodamus as they do in other cities. If the farmers had provided the means of subsistence for those who bear arms, they might reasonably have been counted as an integral part of the city; but on the scheme of Hippodamus they own their own land as private property, and they will farm it for their private benefit.

1268ª35 A further difficulty arises with regard to the third part of the territory which is to be common property, and from which the members of the defence force are to draw their subsistence. If the members of the defence force farm this common land themselves, there will be no distinction, such as Hippodamus wishes to establish, between the military and the farming class. If, on the other hand, those who farm this common land are to be distinct both from the class of those who farm their own land and from the military class, we shall have a fourth class in the city; and this class will have no share in anything whatsoever and will be extraneous to the constitution. Again, if one makes the same persons who farm their own land farm the common land as well, the crops produced by each farmer will not be sufficient in quantity for two households; and the question may also be fairly asked, 'Why not start at once with a system by which the farmers, using all the same land, and the same estates, will at one and the same time get subsistence for themselves and provide it for the military class?' There is great confusion on all these matters.

1268ᵇ4 The law he proposes in regard to judicial decisions is also unsatisfactory. He prescribes that a juryman should give a qualified verdict, even though the case on which he gives his decision is stated without qualification. This is, in effect, to prescribe that the juryman should become an arbitrator. A qualified verdict is possible in a court of arbitration, even when there are several arbitrators (for they can confer with one another in order to determine their verdict); but in courts of law this is impossible, since most legislators, far from permitting this, lay down measures to ensure that the jurymen shall *not* communicate.* How could a decision not produce confusion when a juryman is of the opinion that damages should be given, but not to the amount for which the plaintiff sues? A plaintiff, for example, may sue for 20 minae but a juryman will give a verdict for 10 (or a plaintiff may sue for a still larger sum and a juryman will give a verdict for something still less); another juryman will give a verdict for 5, and still another a verdict for 4. In this way, it is obvious, the various jurymen who give a qualified verdict will each award a different proportion of the amount claimed. Some will award the whole sum claimed, while some will award nothing at all. What is the method of estimating [the total effect of] the decisions thus given?

1268ᵇ17 Furthermore, we must notice that a plain verdict of pure acquittal or pure condemnation never compels a juryman to violate his oath,* provided that the case itself has been duly laid in a plain and unqualified form. The juryman who gives a verdict for acquittal does not decide that the defendant owes nothing; he only decides [for example] that he does not owe 20 minae. The only juryman who really violates his oath is one who gives a verdict *against* the defendant although he does not believe that he owes the 20 minae claimed by the plaintiff.

1268ᵇ22 As for the idea that some honour ought to be conferred on those who suggest an improvement which is of benefit to the city, legislation in such a sense cannot be safely enacted, and has only a specious sound. It might encourage malicious accusations and changes in the constitution. But the proposal also involves another problem, and suggests a further argument. Some people raise a doubt whether cities lose or gain by changing their traditional laws even if some other law is better. If [on this issue we take the line that] change is *not* a gain, it is difficult to agree readily with the proposal made by Hippodamus; it is possible that people might propose the overthrow of the laws, or of the constitution, as being for the common good. However, as the issue has now been mentioned, it will be as well to define our views about it a little further. It is, as we have said, an issue which is open to debate; and a case may be made for the view that change is the better policy. Certainly in other branches of knowledge change has proved beneficial. We may cite in evidence the changes from traditional practice which have been made in medicine, in physical training, and generally in all kinds of craft and skill; and since politics must be seen as one of these, it seems that the same must also be true of it. It can also be argued that the actual facts provide an indication. In ancient times customs were exceedingly simple and barbaric: Greeks went about armed, and bought their brides from each other. Indeed the relics of ancient customs which are still in existence, here and there, are absurd. There is, for instance, a law at Cyme, relating to homicide, that if an accuser can produce a certain number of witnesses from his own kinsmen, the person accused shall be liable to the charge of murder. All men, as a rule, seek, not what is sanctioned by tradition, but what is good; and the earliest known human beings, whether they were 'earth-born', or the survivors of some cataclysm, were in all probability similar to ordinary or even foolish people [today]. (Indeed that is actually the tale that is told of the 'earth-born' men.) It would therefore be an absurdity to remain constant to their notions. But besides these considerations, it may also be urged that to leave *written* laws unchanged is not a good policy. The reason is that in matters of political organization, as in the arts generally, it is impossible for everything to be written down precisely: what is written down must be in general terms, but actions are concerned with particulars.*

1269^{a}12 But while these arguments go to show that in *some* cases, and at *some* times, law ought to be changed, there is another point of view from which it would appear that change is a matter which needs great caution. When we reflect that the improvement likely to be effected may be small, and that it is a bad thing to accustom men to abrogate laws lightheartedly, it becomes clear that there are some errors made by legislators and by rulers which had better be left untouched. The benefit of change will be less than the loss which is likely to result if men fall into the habit of disobeying the government. We must also notice that the analogy drawn from the arts is false. To change the practice of an art is not the same as to change a law. The law has no other source of strength through which to secure obedience apart from habit. But habit can be created only by the passage of time; and a readiness to change from existing to new and different laws will accordingly tend to weaken the general power of law. Further questions may also be raised. Even if it is allowable to make a change, does that hold true or not of all laws and in all constitutions? And again, should change be attempted by anyone whatsoever, or only by certain people? These points make a great difference. We may therefore dismiss this question for the present. It belongs to a different occasion.

B: Actual Constitutions which Approach the Ideal
(Chapters 9–12)

CHAPTER 9

1. The Spartan constitution. The problem of finding a leisured class for the purposes of government: serfdom as a solution: the Spartan Helots. The undue influence of women at Sparta: the bad distribution of property, and its bad effects on the army. The defects of the Ephorate, the Council of Elders, and the dual kingship: defects of the Spartan system of common meals. The bad results of Spartan militarism, and the bad state of the public finances at Sparta.

1269ª29 When we consider the constitutions of Sparta and Crete—or indeed, for that matter, of any other city*—two questions emerge. The first is whether any of their provisions is good or bad when judged by the standard of the best system: the second is whether any provision runs contrary to the principles and character of their constitutions as established.* It is generally agreed that leisure, or in other words freedom from the necessity of labour, should be available in a well-ordered city; but it is difficult to see by what mode of organization this leisure is to be secured.* The Penestae [or serfs] of Thessaly have often revolted against the Thessalians; and the Helots have similarly revolted against the Spartans, for whose misfortunes they are always on the watch, just as if they lay in an ambush. Nothing similar, it is true, has hitherto happened in Crete. Perhaps the reason is that the neighbouring cities, although engaged in mutual hostilities, never enter into any alliance with revolting serfs: it is not to the interest of any, as each has serfs of its own. The neighbours of Sparta, on the other hand, Argos, Messenia, and Arcadia, have been her enemies. Likewise the early revolts of their serfs against the Thessalians were due to the fact that they were still engaged in hostilities with the peoples on their borders, the Achaeans, the Perrhaebians, and the Magnesians. Even if there were no added trouble, in the handling of serfs there is the irksome business of deciding on what footing one should associate with them: if they are kept on a loose rein, they become insolent, and proceed to claim equality with their masters: if they have a hard life, they fall into conspiracy and hatred. The moral is plain. Those who suffer in this way from having a system of serfdom have not discovered the best mode of organization.

1269ᵇ12 The indulgence permitted to women is damaging both to the purpose of the constitution and to the happiness of the city. Just as husband and wife are parts of the family, so it is clear that a city should also be considered as divided almost equally into the male and female populations. In all constitutions, therefore, where the position of women is poorly regulated, one half of the citizen body must be considered as left untouched by the laws. This is what has actually happened at Sparta. The legislator who made the Spartan code intended to make the whole citizen body hardy; but if he fulfilled that intention, as he obviously did, in regard to the men, he has wholly neglected to achieve it in regard to the women, whose lives are full of every kind of licence and luxury. The inevitable result, in such a constitution, is the worship of wealth, especially if, as happens with most military and martial races, the citizens are dominated by the women. (But the Celts are an exception to this general rule: so, too, are such peoples as openly approve of homosexual attachments.) There was wisdom in the earliest author of myths when he paired Ares and Aphrodite: the facts show that such peoples are prone to passionate attachments either to men or to women. It was attachments of the latter sort which were common in Sparta; and the result was that, in the days of her hegemony, affairs largely fell into the hands of women. But what is the difference between rulers being ruled by women and women being actually rulers? The result is the same. Even in the matter of courage, which is useless in all life's ordinary affairs and only of use, if it has a use, in time of war, the women of Sparta have had a most mischievous influence. They showed this during the Theban invasion;* unlike the women of other cities, they were of no use whatever, and caused more confusion than the enemy.

1269ᵇ39 The licence enjoyed by women seems to have come about originally at Sparta in a way which it is easy to understand. The men were absent from their own country for long periods on military expeditions: they were at war with the Argives, and then with the Messenians and Arcadians. When the men returned to a life of leisure and submitted themselves to the legislator they were well prepared by their experience of military life (a life which requires many kinds of human excellence). But, as the story goes, when Lycurgus* attempted to bring the women within the range of his laws, they opposed him, and he had to abandon the attempt. These are the causes of what happened, and are thus the source of [the Spartans'] error; but we have to remember that we are not concerned with what can, or cannot, be excused, but with what is right or wrong.

1270ᵃ11 The defects in the position of women in Sparta, as we have already suggested, seem not only calculated to produce some lack of harmony in the constitution, if we take that by itself, but also to foster the growth of avarice. One might, indeed, pass from the observations just made to a criticism of the unequal distribution of property. While some of the Spartans have come to possess far too much property, others have been reduced to the tiniest amount; and in this way the land has mostly passed into the hands of a very few people. This matter has been badly handled in their laws. The legislator, very rightly, made it improper to buy or sell property in land; but he also allowed any person who so desired to give or bequeath his property—though the same results must necessarily follow in the one case as in the other. About two-fifths of the whole country actually belongs to women; this is due to the number of heiresses and the practice of giving dowries. It would have been better to have had no dowries at all, or to have fixed them at a small, or at any rate a moderate, amount. As it is, a citizen may give the daughter who inherits his property to any man whom he likes (rich or poor); and if he dies intestate before he has done so, the man who is left in the position of guardian gives her to whoever he chooses. The result has been that while the territory could have supported 1,500 horse and 30,000 foot, the actual

number was less than 1,000. The history of the Spartans has
shown that the effects of this arrangement have been bad for
them. The city was unable to withstand a single blow* and
was ruined for want of men. It is said that, under the early
kings, the Spartans were in the habit of sharing [citizenship
with foreigners], and that, as a result, there was no want of
men, in spite of the long wars they were fighting: indeed they
are said to have numbered, at one time, as many as 10,000
citizens. Whether this statement is true or false, Sparta would
have done better to keep her ranks filled by maintaining an
equal distribution of property. Such a reform is, however,
impeded by the law concerning the birth-rate. Anxious for the
Spartans to be as numerous as possible, the legislator encouraged citizens to have as many children as possible; they have
a law that the father of three sons should be exempt from
military service, and the father of four entirely free from all
taxes. Yet it is obvious that, if many children are born, and
the land is divided accordingly, a large number of the citizens
must necessarily be reduced to poverty.

1270^{b}6 Moreover there are deficiencies in the way the
Ephorate is organized. The Ephors at Sparta have a sovereign
authority in matters of the highest importance; but they are
all drawn from the people at large, and it often happens that
very poor men, whose lack of means renders them open to
bribery, attain this office. They have often shown this tendency in the past; and there is a recent instance in the affair at
Andros,* when some of the Ephors, by taking bribes, did
everything in their power to ruin the whole city. Furthermore,
this institution is so important, and so much in the nature of
a dictatorship, that even the kings have been compelled to
court the favour of the Ephors. As a result, damage has also
been done to the whole constitution, which, from being an
aristocracy has tended to turn into a democracy. But the
Ephorate does hold the constitution together. The people at
large are contented because they have a share in the most
important office; and this result, whether it be due to the
legislator or to chance, has a beneficial effect on their affairs.
If the constitution is to survive, every part of the city must
have a common desire for its existence and for the continuance

of its arrangements.* The kings have this because of the honour that is paid to them; the upper classes have it because there is the Council of Elders (this office is a reward for excellence); and the general population have it because of the Ephorate (which is open to all citizens).

1270ᵇ26 It is right and proper that all should be eligible for the office, but not that the election should be conducted on the present method, which is far too childish.* Again, the Ephors are just ordinary men, but they have power to decide important cases; and it would be better, therefore, that they should not decide at their discretion, but on the basis of written rules set down in legal form. Finally, their mode of life is not in agreement with the aim of the city. It permits too much indulgence, whereas for the other citizens, the arrangements incline so much to the opposite extreme of severity that men cannot endure their rigour, and escape from the law into the secret enjoyment of sensual pleasures.

1270ᵇ35 The institution of the Council of Elders has also its defects. If the members of the council were men of probity, and adequately trained in manly virtues, it might be argued that the institution was of benefit to the city. Even so, it would be dubious whether councillors should be life-judges in important cases: the mind, as well as the body, is subject to old age. But when, as a matter of fact, the training of the councillors is such that even the legislator has no confidence in their character as good men, the arrangement is unsafe. It is evident from experience that those who have held the office of councillor have often been influenced by bribery and favouritism in dealing with public affairs. This is a reason why they should not be free from scrutiny of their conduct. It is true that the Ephors can apparently scrutinize the conduct of every official; but this is too sweeping a prerogative for them to possess, nor is it the way in which, in our view, the councillors should be subjected to scrutiny.

1271ᵃ9 The system by which they appoint councillors involves a childish method of selection;* and there is an impropriety in requiring that, to be eligible, a man should openly seek election. The man who deserves the office should have it whether he wants it or not. Here the legislator is plainly doing what he did with the rest of the constitution. He has imposed this requirement [that candidates *seek* election] on the election of councillors because he wants to make his citizens generally ambitious of honours; for no one would seek to hold office unless he was ambitious. Yet ambition and avarice are exactly the motives which lead men to commit nearly all intentional crimes.

1271ª18 The general theme of kingship, and the question whether it is good or bad for cities to have kings, may be left to another occasion. But it would be better if they did not come to the throne on the principle now followed [in Sparta]; instead the choice of a king should in every case be based on his manner of life. On the present system it is clear that even the legislator himself must be of the opinion that he cannot produce good and honourable kings. At any rate he shows no confidence that they will be sufficiently good men; this is why it was the practice to send opponents of the kings with them on embassies, and why it was considered that factional disputes between the kings served as a political safeguard.

1271ª26 The legal arrangements made by its founder for regulating the system of common meals (or, as the Spartans call them, *phiditia*), may also be criticized. The cost of such gatherings ought to be defrayed from public funds, as it is in Crete; but the rule at Sparta is for each man to bring his own contribution, in spite of the fact that some of the citizens are extremely poor and unable to bear the expense. The natural result is the very opposite of the legislator's intention. The system of common meals is meant to be democratic, but with these regulations it is the reverse of democratic. Citizens who are extremely poor find it difficult to share in the common meals; and yet it is the traditional rule of the constitution that those who cannot contribute their quota are debarred from participating in it.

1271ª37 Other writers have also censured, not without justice, the law relating to the office of admiral. They are right to do so since it is a cause of factional conflict. The office of admiral is a sort of second kingship, rivalling the kings, who are supreme commanders for life.

1271ª41 There is another criticism one might make of the

principle that underlies the Spartan legislation, a criticism also made by Plato in his *Laws*.* The whole system of legislation is directed to fostering only one part [or element] of goodness, goodness in war, because that sort of goodness is useful for gaining power. As a result the Spartans remained secure as long as they were at war; but they collapsed as soon as they acquired an empire. They did not know how to use their leisure and they had never accustomed themselves to any discipline other than and superior to that of war. There is another defect at Sparta which is equally grave. The Spartans hold that the 'goods' for which men strive are to be attained through goodness rather than badness of character. They are right in thinking this; but they are wrong in supposing that these 'goods' are greater than goodness of character.*

1271ᵇ10 Another defect at Sparta is the state of the public finances. The public treasury is empty, at a time when they are compelled to wage major wars; and the taxes are not properly paid. Because most of the land is in the hands of citizens, they do not look closely at each other's payments. The effect of the legislator's work is here the reverse of beneficial: he has reduced the city to penury while encouraging private avarice. This may serve as an account of the Spartan constitution, and these are the defects which are particularly open to censure.

CHAPTER 10

2. The Cretan constitution. Crete possibly the model of Sparta: similarities between the two. The Cretan system of common meals is superior to the Spartan; but the Cretan Cosmoi, who correspond to the Spartan Ephors, are inferior to them. Cretan 'feudalism': confederations of nobles: feuds and factions: Crete hitherto saved from their evil effects by its geographical isolation.

1271ᵇ20 The Cretan constitution* is close to that of the Spartans; in some ways it is no worse but in most respects it is less polished. It is said that most features of the Spartan constitution were copied from the Cretan. This may well be the case, for institutions of an older origin are generally less elaborate than the more modern. Tradition records* that Lycurgus, when he relinquished the office of guardian to King Charillus and went abroad, spent most of his time in Crete, to which he was drawn by ties of connection, the people of Lyctus being a colony from Sparta. Those who came to the colony adopted the system of law which they found existing among the inhabitants at the time of their settlement. This is why these laws are still in use among the subject peoples [of Crete], who regard them as a system of law created by Minos.*

1271ᵇ32 The island seems to be naturally designed,* and admirably situated, for ruling in the Greek world. It commands the whole of the sea on whose shores nearly all of the Greeks are settled: it is not far from the Peloponnese on the one side, and close to the corner of Asia round Triopium and Rhodes on the other. This explains why Minos could establish a maritime empire. He subdued some of the neighbouring islands, and sent colonies to others. Finally he carried his attacks as far as Sicily, where he died near Camicus.

1271ᵇ40 The Cretan system parallels the Spartan. The Helots cultivate the land for the Spartans while the subject peoples [Perioikoi], do so for the Cretans; and in both places there is a system of common meals, which the Spartans, in former times, used to call *andria* (and not, as they now do, *phiditia*), a term still used by the Cretans, and a proof that the institution came from Crete. The same goes for the constitutional system. The Spartan Ephors have the same power as the Cretan *Cosmoi*: the only difference is that the Ephors are five in number, and the *Cosmoi* ten. Similarly the Spartan elders are equivalent to the Cretan; but the latter are called the Council. The Cretans formerly had a monarchy; but afterwards abolished it, and the *Cosmoi* are now in command of the army. All citizens can take part in the assembly; but its only power is that of ratifying the decisions of the elders and the *Cosmoi*.

1272ᵃ12 The arrangements for common meals in Crete are better than they are at Sparta. At Sparta each citizen contributes individually the quota allotted to him, and if he fails to do so he is legally debarred, as has already been noted, from a share in the constitution. In Crete things are placed on a more communal footing. The whole of the agricultural produce and livestock raised on the public land, and all the rents paid by the subject peoples, are divided, with one part going to the cult of the gods and the discharge of public services, and the other to the provision of common meals. This makes it possible for all alike, men, women, and children, to be fed at the public cost.* The legislator devised a number of ingenious measures both to encourage an abstemious form of diet (something he saw as beneficial) and to ensure the segregation of women, to prevent them from having too many children. For the same reason he encouraged homosexual connections. (Whether he was right or wrong is a question which may be left for a later occasion.)*

1272ª26 It is clear that the arrangements for common meals in Crete are superior to those at Sparta. On the other hand, those for the *Cosmoi* are inferior even to the Ephoralty. They share the defect of the board of Ephors—that of being appointed without any proper qualification—but do not present the same constitutional advantage as the Ephors. In the Spartan system, under which every citizen is eligible for the Ephoralty, the people at large share in this highest of offices, and therefore wish the constitution to survive. In Crete, however, the *Cosmoi* are drawn from a limited number of families, and not from the citizens as a whole; while the members of the Council of Elders are drawn, in their turn, from those who have served as *Cosmoi*. This Cretan Council of Elders may be criticized on the same grounds as the Spartan. Their lack of accountability, and their life-tenure, are both prerogatives beyond their desert; and their power of acting at their own discretion—and not on the basis of written rules—is dangerous. It is not proof of the institutions being properly organized that the people should remain contented in spite of their exclusion from it. The *Cosmoi,* unlike the Ephors, have no opportunity of using their powers for their own profit: they live on an island, remote from those who might corrupt them.

1272ᵇ1 The remedy which the Cretans provide for the defects of this institution is curious, and more fitted to government by clique* than to a constitutional state. Again and again a faction is formed—either by some of their own colleagues, or by a group of private citizens—which proceeds to eject the *Cosmoi* from office; and they are also allowed to resign their office before their term has expired. Surely it is better that all such matters should be regulated by law, and not settled by the mere will of men, which is a dangerous standard for action. Worst of all, however, is the practice of suspending the office of the *Cosmoi,* to which powerful people often resort when they are unwilling to submit to justice. This proves that the Cretan system, if it has some of the elements of a constitution, is not really a constitution at all, but a government by a clique. It has become customary for powerful men to cause dissension among the people and among their own friends to set up monarchies of their own, to form factions, and to fight among themselves. In effect such a state of things simply means that for a time the city goes out of existence and the political association is dissolved. A city which is brought to this pass is in danger: those who wish to attack it will now have also the power to do so. But Crete itself, as has already been noted, is saved from this danger by its geographical position; and distance has here the same effect as laws for the expulsion of aliens.* This also explains why the subject peoples there stay quiet, while the Helots of Sparta are often in revolt. The Cretans have no share in dominions overseas; and it is only lately that foreign forces have penetrated into the island*—with results which have gone to show the frailty of their laws.

So much for the Cretan type of constitution.

CHAPTER 11

3. The Carthaginian constitution. Similarities of Carthage and Sparta, with the balance, in some respects, in favour of Carthage. The constitution of Carthage is generally based on the principle of aristocracy; but it deviates from that principle, partly towards democracy and partly towards oligarchy. Its main defect is that it attaches too much importance to wealth, and is thus, in effect, a moneyed oligarchy. Another defect is

*the habit of pluralism. Carthage has sought to correct her
defects by a policy of encouraging the emigration of the poor;
but while this policy has been fortunate in its results, it is not an
adequate remedy.*

1272^{b}24 The constitution of Carthage* is generally accounted a good constitution, and one which is in many
respects different from others; but the chief thing about it is
its likeness, at a number of points, to the Spartan. Indeed the
three constitutions with which we are here concerned—the
Cretan, the Spartan, and the Carthaginian—are all closely
related to one another, and they all differ greatly from other
constitutions. Many of the institutions at Carthage are certainly good. It is a proof of a well-ordered constitution that
the people has stood firm by the political system: there have
been no factional conflicts worth mentioning, nor any attempt
at a tyranny. There are the following similarities with the
Spartan constitution: the common meals shared by the
'messes' at Carthage are similar to the Spartan *phiditia*. The
office of the 'Hundred and Four' is similar to the Ephoralty,
but better in so far as the elections to the office are made on
the basis of merit, while the Ephoralty is recruited haphaz-
ardly. Finally, the kings and the Council of Elders at Carthage
are analogous to the Spartan kings and Council of Elders.
But here again it is to the credit of Carthage that her kings
are drawn neither from a single family nor [indiscriminately]
from any family. Rather they are drawn from any family
which is outstanding at the time, and they are drawn from it
by election, and not by seniority. Kings, after all, have considerable powers: and if they are worthless characters, they can
do a great deal of harm—as, indeed, they have actually done
at Sparta.

1273^{a}2 Most of the features which may be criticized as
deviations,* are features common to all of the constitutions
with which we are here concerned. But [in the case of the
Carthaginian constitution] some of the deviations from its
underlying principle of aristocracy or 'constitutional government' are in the direction of democracy, while others are in that
of oligarchy. It is a deviation in the former direction that while

the kings and the Elders, if they are both agreed, can freely decide whether or not they will submit any issue to the assembly, the assembly is equally free to deal with an issue if they are *not* agreed about its submission. Again, when the kings and the Elders submit a proposal, the assembly is not confined to hearing and approving the decision of the rulers: it has the power of decision, and any of its members who so desire may oppose the proposal. This does not happen under the other constitutions [i.e. those of Sparta and Crete]. On the other hand, the following features are oligarchic: the boards of five, which are in control of many important matters, select their own members; these boards choose the 'Hundred and Four', who are the highest authority; what is more, the members of these boards hold office longer than other officials (they are virtually in office both before and after the period of regular tenure). Aristocratic features are the fact that the officials are not paid or appointed by lot, and other similar practices; and the rule that *all* lawsuits may be decided by the boards, and not some by one body and some by another, as is the case at Sparta.

1273^{a}21 The Carthaginian system deviates most markedly from aristocracy in the direction of oligarchy by following the widely held view that office-holders should be chosen on grounds of means as well as on grounds of merit, because poor men are unable to rule well and have no leisure.

1273^{a}25 If selection on grounds of means is characteristic of oligarchy and selection by merit of aristocracy, the way in which the constitutional affairs of the Carthaginians are organized would seem to be something different from either. Both grounds are taken into consideration in the elections, especially in those for the highest offices, the kings and the generals. This deviation from the pure principle of aristocracy must be regarded as an error on the part of the lawgiver. From the outset one of his most pressing duties is to see that the most meritorious have the opportunity to be at leisure and to refrain from unworthy occupations, not only when they are in office, but even when they are not. Even if it is right to take means too into consideration, in order to secure men of leisure, it is disgraceful to make the highest of offices (those of the kings and the generals) open to purchase. This custom puts riches in a more honourable position than merit, and imbues the whole city with a spirit of avarice. When the sovereign body in a city attaches value to something, the opinion of the other citizens will necessarily follow its lead, and where merit does not receive the highest place of honour an aristocratic constitution cannot have a secure existence. Besides, when money has been spent to get office, the purchasers may naturally be expected to fall into the habit of trying to make a profit on the transaction. If people who are poor but honest want to make profit, we can hardly expect worse characters who are already out of pocket to refrain from doing so. So those who would make the best rulers should rule; and even if the legislator abandons any attempt to make honest citizens wealthy, he ought at any rate to provide for their having leisure during the period for which they hold office.

1273^{b}8 It would also appear to be a defect that one person should hold a number of offices, which is a practice in vogue at Carthage. Each job is done best when it is done by one man; and the lawgiver should see that this rule is followed, and not set the same man to be both flute-player and cobbler. Accordingly, except in a small city, it is at once more statesmanlike and more democratic that a larger number of citizens should share in office. Then, as we have already argued,* the work is shared more widely and each particular job is done better and more quickly. This is clearly evident in military and naval matters. In both, the practice of ruling and being ruled extends to everyone concerned.

1273^{b}18 The Carthaginians have a constitution which is in practice oligarchical; but they get away with this by an excellent means—from time to time a section of the populace is planted out among the dependent cities and thus grows wealthy. In this way they remedy defects of the constitution and give it stability. But this may be said to be the effect of chance; they ought to be kept free of factional conflict by the work of the legislator. In the present position of affairs the law provides no remedy to ensure internal peace if some misfortune occurs and the masses revolt against their rulers.

1273^b24 Such is the character of the three constitutions—the
Spartan, the Cretan, and the Carthaginian—which are justly
held in high regard.

CHAPTER 12

4. Postscript on other legislators. Solon and the constitution of
Athens. The earliest legislators. Various notes (e.g. on the
severity of Draco's laws, and on the legislation of Pittacus
about the offences committed under the influence of drink).

1273^b27 Some of those who have put forward a view about
constitutional matters* have taken no part in political affairs
of any kind or description, but have lived for the whole of
their lives in a private capacity; we have already mentioned
practically everything worthy of note concerning these.
Others, again, were experienced statesmen who served as
lawgivers, some for their own and others for foreign cities.
Some of these simply drew up laws: others were authors of
constitutions as well as of laws. Lycurgus and Solon* are
both in the latter category: they established both laws and
constitutions.

1273^b35 The constitution of Sparta has already been described. Solon is held by some to have been an excellent
lawgiver. They say that he swept away an oligarchy which
was far too absolute, that he emancipated the people from
serfdom, and that he instituted the 'ancestral democracy',
thereby establishing an admirably 'mixed' constitution: the
Council of the Areopagus is oligarchic; the method of electing
office-holders is aristocratic; and the lawcourts are democratic. In actual fact, however, it would appear that two of
these elements (the council and the election of office-holders)
existed before his time; he simply refrained from abolishing
them. But he certainly put the people into power by making
membership of the lawcourts open to every citizen; and that is
the reason why he is blamed by some of his critics, who argue
that he really destroyed the other elements by making these
popular lawcourts, with their members appointed by lot,
supreme in every case. Later, as these courts grew in strength,

they sought to flatter the people in the way that men flatter a tyrant, and transformed the constitution into its present form of democracy. Ephialtes and Pericles curtailed the Council of the Areopagus; Pericles introduced the system of paying the members of the lawcourts; and thus each demagogue, in his turn, increased the democratic element until the constitution reached its present form.* This, however, appears to be due to accident rather than to any deliberate design on the part of Solon. The people, who had been the cause of the acquisition of a maritime empire during the course of the Persian wars, acquired a conceit of themselves; and in spite of the opposition of the respectable citizens they found worthless demagogues to support their cause. Solon himself would seem to have given the people only the necessary minimum of power, allowing them simply to elect office-holders and to call them to account. (A people which does not have this power is a people of slaves, and an enemy [to the city].) He arranged that office-holders should be drawn exclusively from those who were notable and well-to-do, from the Pentacosiomedimni, from the Zeugitae, and from the third class, the Hippeis—while the lowest class, that of the Thetes, was ineligible for any office.*

1274ᵃ22 Other legislators* were Zaleucus, for the Epizephyrian Locrians, and Charondas of Catana, for his own city and for others in Italy and Sicily which had been settled from Chalcis. There are some writers, however, who would go farther back, and argue that Onomacritus was the earliest expert in legislation. They make him a Locrian, who was trained in Crete during a visit paid there in the course of his vocation as a soothsayer: they make Thales his colleague: finally, they make Lycurgus and Zaleucus the disciples of this Thales, and Charondas the disciple of Zaleucus. In saying this they speak with too little regard to chronology; but Philolaus of Corinth certainly framed laws for Thebes. He belonged by birth to the Bacchiad family in his native city; but he was the friend and lover of Diocles, an Olympic victor who left Corinth in disgust at his mother Halcyone's incestuous passion for himself, and he accompanied Diocles to Thebes, where they lived and died together. Their tombs are still shown today: they stand in full view of one another, but one of them can be seen from the soil of Corinth, and the other cannot; and the story goes that the two friends deliberately arranged to be buried in this way—Diocles remembering his past with horror, and anxious that Corinth should not be visible from the mound under which he lay, but Philolaus desiring that it should be from his. This was the reason of their settling at Thebes; and this was how Philolaus came to make laws for that city. Among his laws there are some which deal with the production of children. They are called the 'laws of adoption'; and they are a peculiar feature of the legislation of Philolaus, intended to keep the number of family plots constant and undisturbed.

1274^b5 The only peculiar feature of the legislation of Charondas is that relating to suits brought against those guilty of perjury (he was the first to institute the practice of denunciation for false witness); but in the general precision of his laws he showed himself a still better draftsman than our modern legislators. The peculiar feature of the legislation proposed by Phaleas is the equalization of property; the peculiar features of Plato's legislation* are: the community of property and of wives and children; a system of common meals for women; the rule about drinking, which provides that the sober must be in the chair at a drinking-party; and the rule about military training, which provides that soldiers must practise ambidexterity, since it is wrong for one hand to be useful and the other not.

1274^b15 There are laws of Draco but he drew up these laws for an existing constitution and they have no peculiar feature worth mentioning, except the severity which they show in fixing the amount of punishments. Pittacus, like Draco, was the author only of laws, and not of a constitution. One of the laws peculiar to him is the law that a drunken man should be punished more heavily for an offence than a sober one. He noted that drunken men commit offences of violence more frequently than sober ones; but instead of holding that this entitled them to greater consideration, he preferred to take his stand on the ground of expediency. Androdamas of Rhegium was another legislator, who made laws for the Chalcidian settlements in Thrace. Some of them are concerned with homicide, and with the succession of women to property; but his legislation has no peculiar feature that need be mentioned.

1274^b26 This may conclude our inquiry into matters connected with both types of constitutions, those which are actually in force, and those planned by political theorists.

BOOK III
THE THEORY OF CITIZENSHIP AND CONSTITUTIONS

A: Citizenship (Chapters 1–5)

CHAPTER 1

*To understand what a constitution (*politeia*) is, we must inquire into the nature of the city (*polis*); and to understand that— since the city is a body of citizens (*politai*)—we must examine the nature of citizenship. Citizenship is not determined by residence, or by merely having access to the courts of law. Rather 'a citizen is one who permanently shares in the adminis- tration of justice and the holding of office'. This definition is more especially true in a democracy: to make it generally applicable, we must modify it to run, 'a citizen is one who shares for any period of time in judicial and deliberative office'.*

1274ᵇ32 When we are dealing with constitutions, and seeking to discover the essence and the attributes of each form, our first investigation may well be directed to the city [the *polis*] itself; and we may begin by asking, 'What is the city?'* This is at present a disputed question—while some say, 'It was the city that did such and such an act', others say, 'It was not the city, but the oligarchy or the tyrant.'* All the activity of the statesman and the lawgiver is obviously concerned with the city, and a constitution is a way of organizing the inhabitants of a city.

1274ᵇ38 A city belongs to the order of 'compounds',* just like any other thing which forms a single 'whole', while being composed, none the less, of a number of different parts. This being the case, it clearly follows that we must inquire first about the citizen.* In other words, a city is a certain number of citizens; and so we must consider who should properly be called a citizen and what a citizen really is.* The definition of a citizen is a question which is often disputed: there is no general agreement on who is a citizen. It may be that someone who is a citizen in a democracy is not one in an oligarchy. We may leave out of consideration those who enjoy the title of 'citizen' in some special sense, for example, naturalized citizens. A citizen proper is not one by virtue of residence in a given place: for even aliens and slaves may share the common place of residence. Nor [can the title of 'citizen' be given to] those who share in legal processes only to the extent of being entitled to sue and be sued in the courts. This is something which belongs also to aliens who share it by virtue of a treaty; though it is to be noted that there are many places where resident aliens are obliged to choose a legal protector, so that they only share to a limited extent in this form of association. They are like children who are still too young to be entered on the roll of citizens, or men who are old enough to have been excused from civic duties. There is a sense in which these may be called citizens, but it is not altogether an unqualified sense: we must add the reservation that the young are undeveloped, and the old superannuated citizens, or we must use some other qualification; the exact term we apply does not matter, for the meaning is clear.

1275ª19 We are seeking to discover the citizen in the strict sense, who has no such defect to be made good. Similar questions may also be raised and answered about those who are exiled or disenfranchised. The citizen in this strict sense is best defined by the one criterion that he shares in the administration of justice and in the holding of office. Offices may be divided into two kinds. Some are discontinuous in point of time: in other words, they are of the sort that either cannot be held at all for more than a single term or can only be held for a second term after some definite interval. Others, however, have no limit of time, for example, the office of jurymen, or the office of a member of the popular assembly. It may possibly be contended that such people are not holders of 'office', and do not share in 'office' by virtue of their position. But it would be ridiculous to exclude from the category of holders of office those who actually hold the most sovereign position in the city; and, since the argument turns on a word, we should not let it make a difference. The point is that we have no word to denote what is common to the juryman and the member of the assembly, or to describe the position held by both. Let us, in the interest of a clear analysis, call it 'indeterminate office'. On that basis we may lay it down that citizens are those who share in the holding of office as so defined.*

1275ᵃ33 The definition of citizen which will most satisfactorily cover the position of all who bear the name is of this general kind. We must also notice that there are certain kinds of thing which may be based on different kinds of principle, one of them standing first, another second, and so on down the series.* Things belonging to this class, when considered purely as such, have no common denominator whatever, or, if they have one, they have it only to a meagre extent. Constitutions obviously differ from one another in kind, with some of them coming later in the order and others earlier; for constitutions which are defective and perverted (we shall explain later in what sense we are using the term 'perverted') are necessarily secondary to those which are free from defects. It follows that the citizen under each different kind of constitution must also necessarily be different. We may thus conclude that the citizen of our definition is particularly and especially the citizen of a democracy. Citizens living under other kinds of constitution may possibly, but do not necessarily, correspond to the definition. There are some cities, for example, in which there is no popular element: such cities have no regular meetings of the assembly, but only meetings specially summoned; and they decide different kinds of legal case by different means. In Sparta, for example, the Ephors take cases of contracts (not as a body, but each sitting separately); the Council of Elders take cases of homicide; and some other authority may take other cases. Much the same is also true of Carthage, where a number of official bodies are entitled to decide cases of all kinds.

1275ᵇ13 But our definition of citizenship can be amended. In other kinds of constitution members of the assembly and the courts do not hold that office for an indeterminate period. They hold it for a limited term; and it is to some or all of these that the citizen's function of deliberating and judging (whether on all issues or only a few) is assigned. From these considerations it emerges clearly who a citizen is. We say that one who is entitled to share in deliberative or judicial office is thereby a citizen of that city, and a city, in its simplest terms, is a body of such people adequate in number for achieving a self-sufficient existence.*

CHAPTER 2

A popular and pragmatic view of citizenship makes it depend on birth, i.e. descent from a citizen parent or two citizen parents. This does not carry us far, and in any case it only relates to old established citizens. A more serious question is raised when we consider new citizens, who have been allowed to participate in the constitution as the result of a revolution. Are they actually citizens? On the criterion of sharing in judicial and deliberative office (which is a functional criterion), they are actually citizens when once they possess that function.

1275^{b}22 For practical purposes, it is usual to define a citizen as 'one born of citizen parents on both sides', and not on the father's or mother's side only; but sometimes this requirement is carried still farther back, to the length of two, three, or more stages of ancestry. This popular and facile definition has induced some thinkers to raise the question, 'How did the citizen of the third or fourth stage of ancestry himself come to be a citizen?' Gorgias of Leontini—perhaps partly from a sense of this difficulty and partly in irony—said, 'As mortars are things which are made by the craftsmen who are mortar-makers, so Larissaeans are made by the craftsmen who are Larissaean-makers'.* But the matter is really simple. If, in their day, they had a share in the constitution in the sense of our own definition, they were certainly citizens. It is obviously impossible to apply the requirement of descent from a citizen father or a citizen mother to those who were the first inhabit-ants or original founders of a city.

1275^{b}34 A more serious difficulty is perhaps raised by the case of those who have acquired a share as the result of a change in the constitution. We may take as an example the action of Cleisthenes* at Athens, when after the expulsion of the tyrants he enrolled in the tribes a number of resident aliens both foreigners and slaves. The question raised by such an addition to the civic body is not 'Who is actually a citizen?' but, 'Are they rightly or wrongly such?'* It must be admitted, however, that someone might also raise the further question whether a man who is not justly a citizen is really a citizen, on the grounds that the unjust comes to the same as the false. Obviously there are office-holders who have no just title to their office; but we still say that they hold office, though we do not say it is just for them to do so. The citizen also is defined by the fact of holding a sort of office (for the definition we have given to the citizen involves his sharing in office of the deliberative and judicial kind); and it follows, therefore, that these people must be called citizens.

CHAPTER 3

The question, 'Are they justly citizens?' leads to the further question 'When can a given act be considered an act of the city or polis?' *This in turn raises the general question of the identity of the city. Is the city identical with the government for the time being? Generally, what are the factors which constitute its identity? The identity of a city does not depend on its being surrounded by one set of walls, or on its consisting of one stock of inhabitants. The city is a compound; and its identity, like that of all compounds, is determined by the scheme of its composition, i.e. by its constitution.*

1276^{a}6 The question whether these people are, in justice, citizens or not is a different matter, which is closely connected with a larger question already mentioned.* Some people have wondered when a given act can, and when it cannot, be considered to be the act of the city. We may take as an example the case of an oligarchy or tyranny which changes into a democracy. In such a case some people are reluctant to fulfil public contracts, on the grounds that these were made, not by the city, but by the governing tyrant, and they are unwilling to meet other obligations of a similar nature because they hold that some constitutions exist by virtue of force, and not for the sake of the common good. It would follow that if a democracy exists in this fashion [i.e. by force] we have to admit that acts done under the government of such a democracy are no more acts of the city concerned than were acts done under the oligarchy or tyranny.

1276ᵃ17 Our discussion would seem to be closely connected with the following problem: 'On what principles ought we to say that a city has retained its identity, or conversely, that it has lost its identity and become a different city?' The most obvious mode of dealing with this question is to consider simply territory and population. On this basis we may note that the territory and population of a city may be divided into sections, with some of the population residing in one block of territory, and some of it in another. This question need not be regarded as particularly difficult: the issue which it raises can easily be met if we remember that the word 'city' is used in different senses.*

1276ᵃ24 In the case of a population which inhabits a single territory, we may likewise ask 'When should we consider that there is a single city?' For, of course, the identity of a city is not constituted by its walls—it would be possible to surround the whole of the Peloponnese by a single wall. Babylon (which, it is said, had been captured for three whole days before some of its inhabitants knew of the fact) may perhaps be counted a city of this dubious nature: so, too, might any city which had the dimensions of a people [ethnos] rather than those of a city [or polis]. But it will be better to reserve the consideration of this question for some other occasion.* (To determine the size of a city—to settle how large it can properly be, and whether it ought to consist of the members of several races—is a duty incumbent on the statesman.)

1276ᵃ34 Assuming a single population inhabiting a single territory, shall we say that the city retains its identity as long as the stock of its inhabitants continues to be the same (although the old members are always dying and new members are always being born), and shall we thus apply to the city the analogy of rivers and fountains, to which we ascribe a constant identity in spite of the fact that part of their water is always flowing in and part always flowing out? Or must we take a different view, and say that even though the population remains the same, the city, for the reason already mentioned, may none the less change?

1276^b1 If a city is a form of association, and if this form of association is an association of citizens in a constitution, it would seem to follow inevitably that when the constitution undergoes a change in form, and becomes a different constitution, the city will likewise cease to be the same city. We say that a chorus which appears at one time as a comic and at another as a tragic chorus is not the same—and this in spite of the fact that the members often remain the same. What is true of the chorus is also true of every other kind of association, and of all other compounds generally. If the form of its composition is different, the compound becomes a different compound. A scale composed of the same notes will be a different scale depending on whether it is in the Dorian or the Phrygian mode. If this is the case, it is obvious that in determining the identity of the city we must look to the constitution. Whether the same group of people inhabits a city, or a totally different group, we are free to call it the same city, or a different city. It is a different question* whether it is right to pay debts or to repudiate them when a city changes its constitution into another form.

CHAPTER 4

Aristotle now raises the question, 'What is the relation of the excellence of the good citizen to the excellence of the good man?' If we look at constitutions generally, we must note that different constitutions require different types of good citizen, while the good man is always the same. If we look at the best constitution, we may argue that even here there must be different types of good citizen, because there are different sorts of civic function; and thus here too the good citizen cannot be identified with the good man. On the whole, therefore, the good citizen and the good man cannot be identified. But there is one case in which they can be. This is the case of the good ruler who

possesses the quality of moral wisdom required for being a good
subject. The quality of moral wisdom which he possesses is the
essential quality of the good man; and in his case the excellence
of the good citizen is identical with that of the good man.

1276^b16 A question connected with those which have just
been discussed is the question whether the excellence of a
good man and that of a good citizen are identical or
different.* If this question is to be investigated, we must first
describe the excellence of the citizen in some sort of outline.
Just as a sailor is a member of an association,* so too is a
citizen. Sailors differ from one another in virtue of the different capacities in which they act: one is a rower, another a
steersman, another a look-out man; and others will have still
other such titles. It is, nevertheless, clear that, while the most
accurate definition of the excellence of each sailor will be
special to the man concerned, a common definition of excellence will apply to all, inasmuch as safety in navigation is the
common task of all and the object at which each of the sailors
aims. The same is also true of citizens. Though they differ, the
end which they all serve is the safety of their association; and
this association consists in the constitution. The conclusion to
which we are thus led is that the excellence of the citizen must
be an excellence relative to the constitution. It follows that if
there are several different kinds of constitution there cannot
be a single absolute excellence of the good citizen.* But the
good man is a man so called in virtue of a single absolute
excellence.

1276^b34 It is thus clear that it is possible to be a good
citizen without possessing the excellence by which one is a
good man. But we may reach the same conclusion in another
way,* by discussing the question with particular reference to
the best constitution. Although it is impossible for a city to be
composed entirely of good men, each citizen must, none the
less, perform well his particular function and this requires [the
appropriate kind of] excellence. But, since it is impossible for
all the citizens to be alike, the excellence of a citizen cannot be
identical with that of a good man. The excellence of a good
citizen must belong to all citizens, because that is the condition

necessary for the city being the best city; but the excellence of a good man cannot possibly belong to all—unless, indeed, we hold that every citizen of a good city must also be a good man. Furthermore, the city is composed of unlike elements. Just as a living being is composed of soul and body, or the soul of the different elements of reason and appetite, or the household of man and wife, or property of master and slave, so the city too is composed of different and unlike elements, among them not only the various elements already mentioned, but also others in addition. It follows that there cannot be a single excellence common to all the citizens, any more than there can be a single excellence common to the leader of a dramatic chorus and his assistants.

1277ᵃ12 Although it is clear from these considerations why they are not in all cases identical, the question may still be raised whether there are not some cases in which the excellence of the good man and that of the good citizen are the same. We say that a good ruler is a good man and possesses practical wisdom, while the citizen does not need to have practical wisdom. Indeed there are some who hold that the very training of the ruler should be, from the first, of a different kind; and it is a matter of observation that the sons of kings are specially trained in riding and the art of war. Thus Euripides says

> No subtleties for me,
> But what the city most needs,*

which implies a special training for the ruler. We may thus assume that the excellence of the good ruler is identical with that of the good man. But subjects too are citizens. It follows that the excellence of the good citizen cannot be identical with that of the good man in all cases, though it may be so in a particular case.* The excellence of the ordinary citizen is different from that of the ruler; and this may well be the reason why Jason [the tyrant of Pherae] said that he was 'a hungry man except when he was tyrant', meaning that he did not know how to live as an ordinary person.

1277ᵃ25 On the other hand, people hold in esteem the capacity both to rule and to obey, and they regard the excellence of a good citizen as being a matter of ruling and obeying well. Now if the excellence of the good man is in ruling, while that of the good citizen is in both ruling and obeying, these two excellences cannot be held in the same esteem.

1277ᵃ29 Since it thus seems that ruler and ruled should acquire different kinds of knowledge, rather than the same kind, while the citizen should have both sorts of knowledge, and share in both, we can now see the next step which our argument has to take.* There is rule of the sort which is exercised by a master; and by this we mean the sort of rule connected with the necessary functions of life. Here it is not necessary for the ruler to know how to do the task himself, but only to know how to use those who do: indeed the former kind of knowledge (by which we mean an ability to do menial services personally) has a servile character. There are a number of kinds of servant, because there are a number of kinds of menial service which have to be rendered. One of these forms of service is that which is rendered by manual labourers. These, as their very name signifies, are those who live by the work of their hands; and the menial craftsman [or mechanic] belongs to this class. This is the reason why in some cities the manual workers were once upon a time excluded from office, in the days before the institution of the extreme form of democracy. The occupations pursued by those who are subject to rule of the sort just mentioned need never be studied by the good man, or by the statesman, or by the good citizen—except occasionally and in order to satisfy some personal need, in which case there ceases to be any question of the relation of master and slave.

1277ᵇ7 But there is also rule of the sort which is exercised over those who are similar in birth to the ruler, and are similarly free. Rule of this sort is what we call political rule; and this is the sort of rule which the ruler must begin to learn by being ruled—just as one learns to be a commander of cavalry by serving under another commander, or to be a general of infantry by serving under another general and by acting first as colonel and, even before that, as captain. This is why it is a good saying that 'you cannot be ruler unless you have first been ruled'. Ruler and ruled have indeed different excellences; but the fact remains that the good citizen must possess the knowledge and the capacity requisite for ruling as well as for being ruled, and the excellence of a citizen may be defined as consisting in 'a knowledge of rule over free men from both points of view'.

1277ᵇ16 A good man, also, will need both, even though the temperance and justice required for ruling have a different character. Equally, the excellence (justice, for example) of a good man who is a subject in a free city will not be of a single kind. It will include different sorts: one sort which fits him to act as a ruler, and one which fits him to act as a subject. The temperance and the courage of a man differ from those of a woman in much the same sort of way. A man would be thought cowardly if his courage were only the same as that of a courageous woman; and conversely a woman would be thought a gossip if she showed no more decorum than that which befits a good man. The function of the man in the household is different from that of the woman: it is the function of the one to acquire, and of the other to keep.

1277ᵇ25 Practical wisdom is the only form of excellence which is peculiar to the ruler. The other forms must, it would seem, belong equally to rulers and subjects. The excellence of subjects cannot be practical wisdom, and may be defined as 'right opinion'. The ruled may be compared to a flute-maker: the ruler is like a flute-player who uses what the flute-maker makes.

1277ᵇ30 These considerations will show whether the excellence of the good man and that of the good citizen are identical or different—or in what sense they are identical and in what sense they are different.

CHAPTER 5

There is a further question relating to citizenship, 'Can mechanics and labourers be citizens, and if they cannot be citizens, how are they to be described?' They should not be citizens, because they cannot achieve the excellence of the good citizen, though they are necessary to the existence of the city. But the answer

*varies from one kind of constitution to another: in an aristocratic
constitution, mechanics and labourers cannot be citizens; in an
oligarchy, a rich mechanic may.*

1277^{b}33 There is still a question which remains to be considered in regard to the citizen. Is the citizen in the true sense
one who is entitled to share in office, or must mechanics* be
also included in the ranks of citizens? If we hold that those,
who have no share in public offices, are also to be included,
we shall have some citizens who can never achieve the excellence of the good citizen (for this man will also be a citizen).
If, on the other hand, someone of this sort is not a citizen, in
what class is he to be placed? He is not a resident alien,
neither is he a foreigner. Or shall we say that this point does
not involve us in any absurdity? For the same is true of slaves
and freedmen. The truth is that we cannot include as citizens
all who are necessary to the city's existence.* Similarly, too,
children are not citizens in the same sense as adult males.
Adults are citizens absolutely; children are citizens only in a
qualified sense—they are citizens but undeveloped ones. There
were some places, in ancient times, where the class of mechanics was actually composed of slaves or foreigners only, and
this explains why a great number of mechanics are slaves or
foreigners even today.

1278^{a}8 The best form of city will not make the mechanic a
citizen. Where mechanics are admitted to citizenship we shall
have to say that the citizen excellence of which we have
spoken cannot be attained by every citizen, by all who are
simply free men, but can only be achieved by those who are
free from the necessary tasks of life. Those who do the
necessary tasks may be divided into two classes, slaves, who
do them for individuals, and mechanics and labourers, who
do them for the community.

1278^{a}13 If we start from this basis, and carry our inquiry a
little further, the position of these mechanics and labourers
will soon become evident; in fact, enough has already been
said* to make it clear, once the bearing of the argument is
grasped. Constitutions are various: there must thus be various
kinds of citizens; more especially, there must be various kinds

of citizens who are subjects. In one variety of constitution it will be necessary that mechanics and labourers should be citizens: in other varieties it will be impossible. It will be impossible, for example, where there is a constitution of the type termed 'aristocratic', with offices distributed on the basis of worth and excellence; for one who lives the life of a mechanic or labourer cannot pursue the things which belong to excellence. The case is different in oligarchies. Even there, it is true, a labourer cannot be a citizen (participation in office depending on a high property qualification); but a mechanic may, for the simple reason that craftsmen often become rich. Yet in Thebes there was a law that no one could share in office who had not abstained from selling in the market for a period of ten years. On the other hand, there are many constitutions where the law goes to the length of admitting aliens to citizenship. There are, for example, some democracies where someone who has only a citizen mother is admitted; and there are many cities where the same privilege is given to those of illegitimate birth. But the policy of extending citizenship so widely is [generally] due to a dearth of genuine citizens; and it is only shortage of population which produces such legislation. When they have sufficient numbers they gradually disqualify such people: first sons of a slave father or slave mother are disqualified; then those who are born of a citizen mother but an alien father; and finally citizenship is confined to those who are of citizen parentage on both sides.*

1278ᵃ34 These considerations prove two things: that there are several different kinds of citizens, and that the name of citizen is particularly applicable to those who share in the offices and honours of the city. Homer accordingly speaks in the *Iliad* of a man being treated

like an alien man, without honour;*

and it is true that those who do not share in positions of honour in the city are just like resident aliens. When restrictions are imposed by subterfuge their only object is to hoodwink those inhabitants who are not citizens.

1278ᵃ40 Two conclusions also emerge from our discussion* of the question, 'Is the excellence of the good man identical

with that of the good citizen, or different from it?' The first is
that there are some cities in which the good man and the
good citizen are identical, and some in which they are different. The second is that, in cities of the former type, it is not all
good citizens who are also good men, but only those among
them who hold the position of statesmen—in other words,
those who direct or are capable of directing, either alone or in
conjunction with others, the conduct of public affairs.

B: Constitutions and their Classification
(Chapters 6–8)

CHAPTER 6

The definition of a constitution. The classification of constitu-
tions depends on (1) the ends pursued by cities, and (2) the kind
of rule exercised by their governments. The true end of a city is
a good life, and it is the common interest to achieve this: the
right kind of rule is authority exercised in the common interest.
We may thus distinguish 'right' constitutions, which are directed
to the common interest, and 'wrong' or 'perverted' constitutions
directed to the selfish interest of the ruling body.

1278^{b}6 Having determined these matters we have next to
consider whether there is a single type of constitution, or
whether there are a number of types. If there are a number of
types, what are these types; how many of them are there; and
how do they differ? A constitution [or *politeia*] may be defined
as 'the organization of a city [or *polis*], in respect of its offices
generally, but especially in respect of that particular office
which is sovereign in all issues'.* The civic body is everywhere
the sovereign of the city; in fact the civic body is the constitution itself. In democratic cities, for example, the people
[*dēmos*] is sovereign:* in oligarchies, on the other hand, the
few [or *oligoi*] have that position; and this difference in the
sovereign bodies is the reason why we say that the two types
of constitution differ—as we may equally apply the same
reasoning to other types besides these.

1278^{b}15 We must first ascertain two things: the nature of

the end for which a city exists, and the various kinds of rule
to which mankind and its associations are subject. It has
already been stated, in our first book (where we were concerned with the management of the household and the control
of slaves), that 'man is a political animal'.* For this reason
people desire to live a social life even when they stand in no
need of mutual succour; but they are also drawn together by
a common interest, in proportion as each attains a share in
the good life. The good life is the chief end, both for the
community as a whole and for each of us individually. But
people also come together, and form and maintain political
associations, merely for the sake of life; for perhaps there is
some element of the good even in the simple fact of living, so
long as the evils of existence do not preponderate too heavily.
It is an evident fact that most people cling hard enough to life
to be willing to endure a good deal of suffering, which implies
that life has in it a sort of healthy happiness and a natural
quality of pleasure.

1278ᵇ30 It is easy enough to distinguish the various kinds of
rule of which people commonly speak; and indeed we have
often had occasion to define them ourselves in works intended
for the general public.* The rule of a master is one kind;* and
here, though there is really a common interest which unites
the natural master and the natural slave, the fact remains that
the rule is primarily exercised with a view to the master's
interest, and only incidentally with a view to that of the slave,
who must be preserved in existence if the rule is to remain.
Rule over wife and children, and over the household generally,
is a second kind of rule, which we have called by the name of
household management.* Here the rule is either exercised in
the interest of the ruled or for the attainment of some advantage common to both ruler and ruled. Essentially it is exercised
in the interest of the ruled, as is also plainly the case with
other arts besides that of ruling, such as medicine and gymnastics—though an art may incidentally be exercised for the
benefit of its practitioner, and there is nothing to prevent
(say) a trainer from becoming occasionally a member of the
class he instructs, in the same sort of way as a steersman is
always one of the crew. Thus a trainer or steersman primarily

considers the good of those who are subject to his authority; but when he becomes one of them personally, he incidentally shares in the benefit of that good—the steersman thus being also a member of the crew, and the trainer (though still a trainer) becoming also a member of the class which he instructs.

1279ª8 For this reason, when the constitution of a city is constructed on the principle that its members are equals and peers, the citizens think it proper that they should hold office by turns. At any rate this is the natural system, and the system which used to be followed in the days when people believed that they ought to serve by turns, and each assumed that others would take over the duty of considering his benefit, just as he himself, during his term of office, had considered their interest.* Today because of the profits to be derived from office and the handling of public property, people want to hold office continuously. It is as if they were invalids, who got the benefit of being healthy by being permanently in office: at any rate their ardour for office is just what it would be if that were the case.* The conclusion which follows is clear: those constitutions which consider the common interest are right constitutions, judged by the standard of absolute justice. Those constitutions which consider only the personal interest of the rulers are all wrong constitutions, or perversions of the right forms.* Such perverted forms are despotic;* whereas the city is an association of freemen.

CHAPTER 7

These two types of constitution each fall into three subdivisions on the basis of number, i.e. according as the One, or the Few, or the Many are the ruling authority in each type. We have thus, as the three subdivisions of the 'right' type, Kingship, Aristocracy, and 'Constitutional Government' or 'Polity': as the three subdivisions of the 'wrong' type, Tyranny, Oligarchy, and Democracy.

1279ª22 Now that these matters have been determined, the next subject for consideration is the number and nature of the different constitutions. We may first examine those constitutions that are rightly formed, since, when these have been determined, the different perversions will at once be apparent.

1279ª25 The term 'constitution' [*politeia*] signifies the same thing as the term 'civic body' [*politeuma*]. The civic body in every city [*polis*] is the sovereign [*to kurion*]; and the sovereign must necessarily be either One, or Few, or Many. On this basis we may say that when the One, or the Few, or the Many rule with a view to the common interest, the constitutions under which they do so must necessarily be right constitutions.* On the other hand, the constitutions directed to the personal interest of the One, or the Few, or the Masses, must necessarily be perversions. Either we should say that those who do not share in the constitution are not citizens, or they ought to have their share of the benefits. According to customary usage, among monarchical forms of government the type which looks to the common interest is called Kingship; among forms of government by a few people (but more than one) it is called Aristocracy—that name being given to this species either because the best [*aristoi*] are the rulers, or because its object is what is best [*ariston*] for the city and its members. Finally, when the masses govern the city with a view to the common interest, the form of government is called by the generic name common to all constitutions (or polities)—the name of 'Constitutional Government'.* There is a good reason for this usage: it is possible for one man, or a few, to be of outstanding excellence; but when it comes to a large number, we can hardly expect precision in all the varieties of excellence. What we can expect particularly is the military kind of excellence,* which is the kind that shows itself in a mass. This is the reason why the defence forces are the most sovereign body under this constitution, and those who possess arms are the ones who participate in it.

1279ᵇ4 The perversions that correspond to the constitutions just mentioned are: Tyranny, [the perversion of] Kingship; Oligarchy [the perversion of] Aristocracy; and Democracy [the perversion of] 'Constitutional Government' [or polity]. Tyranny is a government by a single person directed to the interest of that person; Oligarchy is directed to the interest of the well-to-do; Democracy is directed to the interest of the poor. None of these benefits the common interest.

CHAPTER 8

The basis of number is not, however, adequate. The real basis, at any rate so far as oligarchy and democracy are concerned, is social class: what makes an oligarchy is the rule of the rich (rather than the few), and what makes a democracy is the rule of the poor (rather than the many). Number is an accidental, and not an essential, attribute; but the accidental generally accompanies the essential.

1279^{b}11 We must consider at somewhat greater length what each of these constitutions is. There are certain difficulties involved; and when one is pursuing a philosophical method of inquiry in any branch of study, and not merely looking to practical considerations, the proper course is to set out the truth about every particular with no neglect or omission.

1279^{b}16 Tyranny, as has just been said, is single-person government of the political association on the lines of despotism; oligarchy exists where those who have property are the sovereign authority of the constitution; and, conversely, democracy exists where the sovereign authority is composed of the poorer classes, who are without much property.*

1279^{b}20 The first difficulty which arises is a matter of definition. It could be that the majority are well-to-do and that these hold the sovereignty in a city; but when the majority is sovereign there is [said to be] democracy. Similarly it could happen that the poorer classes were fewer in number than the well-to-do, and yet were stronger and had sovereign authority in the constitution; but where a small number has sovereignty there is said to be oligarchy. Thus it may seem that the definitions we have given of these constitutions cannot be correct.

1279^{b}26 We might attempt to overcome the difficulty by combining both of the factors: wealth with paucity of numbers, and poverty with mass. On this basis oligarchy might be defined as the constitution under which the rich, being also few in number, hold the public offices; and similarly democracy might be defined as the constitution under which the poor, being also many in number, are in control. But this involves us in another difficulty. If there are no forms of oligarchy and democracy other than those enumerated, what names are we to give to the constitutions just suggested as conceivable—those where the wealthy form a majority and the poor a minority, and where the wealthy majority in the one case, and the poor minority in the other, are the sovereign authority of the constitution? The course of the argument thus appears to show that whether the sovereign body is small or large in number (as it is respectively in oligarchies or in democracies) is an accidental attribute, due to the simple fact that the wealthy are generally few and the poor are generally numerous. Therefore the causes originally mentioned are not in fact the real causes of the difference between oligarchies and democracies. The real ground of the difference between oligarchy and democracy is poverty and riches. It is inevitable that there should be an oligarchy where the rulers, whether they are few or many, owe their position to riches; and it is equally inevitable that there should be democracy where the poor rule.

1280ª2 It happens, however, as we have just remarked, that the former [i.e. the wealthy] are few and the latter [i.e. the poor] are numerous. It is only a few who have riches, but all alike share in free status; and it is on these grounds that the two parties dispute the control of the constitution.

C: The Principles of Oligarchy and Democracy and the Nature of Distributive Justice (Chapters 9–13)

CHAPTER 9

The principle of a constitution is its conception of justice; and this is the fundamental ground of difference between oligarchy and democracy. Democrats hold that if men are equal by birth, they should in justice have an equal share in office and honours: oligarchs hold that if they are unequal in wealth, they should in justice have unequal shares in these things. True justice means that those who have contributed to the end of the city should have privileges in proportion to their contribution to that end. The end of the city is not mere life, nor an alliance for mutual defence; it is the common promotion of a good quality of life. Thus although the citizens of a city must always inhabit a single territory, engage in intermarriage, and co-operate with each other in economic matters, the operative aim is always the promotion of a good quality of life. Those who contribute most to the realization of that aim should in justice have the largest share of office and honour.

1280ª7 We must next ascertain what are said to be the distinctive principles of oligarchy and democracy, and what are the oligarchical and the democratic conceptions of justice.* All parties have a hold on a sort of conception of justice; but they both fail to carry it far enough, and do not express the true conception of justice in the whole of its range. For example, justice is considered to mean equality. It does mean equality—but equality for those who are equal, and not for all.* Again, inequality is considered to be just; and indeed it is—but only for those who are unequal, and not for all. These people fail to consider for whom there should be equality or inequality and thus make erroneous judgements. The reason is that they are judging in their own case; and most people, as a rule, are bad judges where their own interests are involved. Justice is concerned with people; and a just distribution is one in which there is proportion between the things distributed and those to whom they are distributed, a point which has already been made in the *Ethics.** There is general agreement about what constitutes equality in the thing, but disagreement about what constitutes it in people.* The main reason for this is the reason just stated, they are judging, and judging erroneously, in their own case; but there is also another reason, they are misled by the fact that they are professing a sort of conception of justice, and professing it up to a point, into thinking that they profess one which is absolute and complete. Some think that if they are superior in one point, for example in wealth, they are superior in all:

others believe that if they are equal in one respect, for instance in free birth, they are equal all round.

1280ᵃ25 Both sides, however, fail to mention the really cardinal factor.* If property is the end for which people come together and form an association, one's share of the city would be proportionate to one's share of the property; and in that case the argument of the oligarchical side would appear to be strong: they say that is not just for someone who has contributed one mina to share in a sum of a hundred minae on equal terms with one who has contributed all the rest and that this applies both to the original sum and to the interest accruing upon it. But the end of the city is not mere life; it is, rather, a good quality of life. Otherwise, there might be a city of slaves, or even a city of animals; but in the world as we know it any such city is impossible, because slaves and animals do not share in happiness* nor in living according to their own choice. Similarly, it is not the end of the city to provide an alliance for mutual defence against all injury, nor does it exist for the purpose of exchange or [commercial] dealing.* If that had been the end, the Etruscans and the Carthaginians would be in the position of belonging to a single city; and the same would be true to all peoples who have commercial treaties with one another. It is true that such peoples have agreements about imports; treaties to ensure just conduct; and written terms of alliance for mutual defence. On the other hand, they have no common offices to deal with these matters: each, on the contrary, has its own offices, confined to itself. Neither party concerns itself to ensure a proper quality of character among the members of the other; neither of them seeks to ensure that all who are included in the scope of the treaties are just and free from any form of vice; and they do not go beyond the aim of preventing their own members from committing injustice against one another. But it is the goodness or badness in the life of the city which engages the attention of those who are concerned to secure good government.

1280ᵇ6 The conclusion which clearly follows is that any city which is truly so called, and is not merely one in name, must devote itself to the end of encouraging goodness. Otherwise, a political association sinks into a mere alliance, which only differs in space [i.e. in the contiguity of its members] from other forms of alliance where the members live at a distance from one another. Otherwise, too, law becomes a mere covenant—or (in the phrase of the sophist Lycophron)* 'a guarantor of just claims'—but lacks the capacity to make the citizens good and just.

1280^b12 That this is the case may be readily proved. If two different sites could be united in one, so that the city [i.e. the *polis*] of Megara and that of Corinth were embraced by a single wall, that would not make a single city. If the citizens of two cities intermarried with one another, that would not make a single city, even though intermarriage is one of the forms of social life which are characteristic of a city. Nor would it make a city if a number of people, living at a distance from one another, but not at so great a distance but they could still associate, had a common system of laws to prevent their injuring one another in the course of exchange. We can imagine, for instance, one being a carpenter, another a farmer, a third a shoemaker, and others producing other goods; and we can imagine a total number of as many as 10,000. But if these people were associated in nothing further than matters such as exchange and alliance, they would still have failed to reach the stage of a city. Why should this be the case? It cannot be ascribed to any lack of contiguity in such an association. The members of a group so constituted might come together on a single site; but if that were all—if each still treated his private house as if it were a city, and all of them still confined their mutual assistance to action against aggressors (as if it were only a question of a defensive alliance)—if, in a word, they associated with each other in the same fashion after coming together as they did when they were living apart—their association, even on its new basis, could not be deemed by any accurate thinker to be a city.

1280^b29 It is clear, therefore, that a city is not an association for residence on a common site, or for the sake of preventing mutual injustice and easing exchange. These are indeed conditions which must be present before a city can exist; but the presence of all these conditions is not enough, in itself, to constitute a city. What constitutes a city is an association of households and clans in a good life, for the sake of attaining a perfect and self-sufficing existence. This, however, will not come about unless the members inhabit one and the self-same place and practise intermarriage. It was for this reason that the various institutions of a common social life—marriage-connections, kin-groups, religious gatherings, and social pastimes generally—arose in cities. This sort of thing is the business of friendship, for the pursuit of a common social life is friendship. Thus the purpose of a city is the good life, and these institutions are means to that end. A city is constituted by the association of families and villages in a perfect and self-sufficing existence; and such an existence, on our definition, consists in living a happy and truly valuable life.

1281ᵃ2 It is therefore for the sake of actions valuable in themselves,* and not for the sake of social life, that political associations must be considered to exist. Those who contribute most to this association have a greater share in the city than those who are equal to them (or even greater) in free birth and descent, but unequal in civic excellence, or than those who surpass them in wealth but are surpassed by them in excellence. From what has been said it is plain that all sides in the dispute about constitutions profess only a partial conception of justice.*

CHAPTER 10

What person or body of people should be sovereign in a city: the people, the rich, the better sort of citizens, the one best, or the tyrant? All these alternatives present difficulties; and there is a difficulty even in a further alternative, that no person or body of people, but law, should be sovereign.

1281ᵃ11 A difficulty arises when we turn to consider what body should be sovereign in the city. The people at large, the wealthy, the better sort, the one who is best of all, the tyrant. But all these alternatives appear to involve unpleasant results:* indeed, how can it be otherwise? What if the poor, on the ground of their being a majority, proceed to divide among themselves the possessions of the wealthy—will not this be unjust? 'No, by heaven' (someone may reply); 'it has been justly decreed so by the sovereign body.' But if this is not the extreme of injustice, what is? Whenever a majority takes everything and divides among its members the possessions of a minority, that majority is obviously ruining the city. But goodness does not ruin whatever possesses it, nor can justice be such as to ruin a city. It is therefore clear that a law of this kind cannot possibly be just. The tyrant's acts too would necessarily be just; for he too uses coercion by virtue of superior power in just the same sort of way as the people coerce the wealthy. Is it just that a minority composed of the wealthy should rule? Then if they too behave like the others —if they plunder and confiscate the property of the people— their action is just. If it is, then this behaviour would also be just in the former case. It is clear that all these acts of oppression are mean and unjust. But should the better sort have authority and be sovereign in all matters? In that case, the rest of the citizens will necessarily be deprived of honour, since they will not enjoy the honour of holding civic office. We speak of offices as honours; and when the same people hold office all the time, the rest of the community must necessarily be deprived of honour. Is it better that the one best man should rule? This is still more oligarchical because the number of those deprived of honour is even greater. It may perhaps be urged that it is a poor sort of policy to vest sovereignty in a human being, rather than in law; for human beings are subject to the passions that beset their souls. But the law itself may incline either towards oligarchy or towards democracy; and what difference will the sovereignty of law then make in the problems which have just been raised?* The consequences already stated will follow just the same.

CHAPTER 11

It is possible, however, to defend the alternative, that the people should be sovereign. The people, when they are assembled, have a combination of qualities which enables them to deliberate wisely and to judge soundly. This suggests that they have a claim to be the sovereign body; it also suggests the scope of affairs in which they should be sovereign, or the powers which they should exercise. They should exercise deliberative and judicial functions; in particular, they should elect the magistrates and examine their conduct at the end of their tenure. Two objections may be raised. (1) It may be argued that experts are better judges than the non-expert; but this objection may be met by reference to (a) the combination of qualities in the assembled people (which makes them collectively better judges than the expert), and (b) the fact that in some cases laymen are in as good a position to judge as experts (which enables them to pass judgement on the behaviour of magistrates). (2) It may be urged that the people, if they have such powers, have more authority than the better sort of citizens who hold office as magistrates, though they are not of so good a quality; but we may answer to this that the people as a whole may well be of a high quality. We have always, however, to remember that rightly constituted laws should be the final sovereign, and that personal authority of any sort should only act in the particular cases which cannot be covered by a general law.

1281ª39 The other alternatives may be reserved for later inquiry;* but the suggestion that the people at large should be sovereign* rather than the few best men would [seem to present problems which]* need resolution, and while it presents some difficulty it perhaps also contains some truth. There is this to be said for the many: each of them by himself may not be of a good quality; but when they all come together it is possible that they may surpass—collectively and as a body, although not individually—the quality of the few best, in much the same way that feasts to which many contribute may excel those provided at one person's expense. For when there are many, each has his share of goodness and practical wisdom; and, when all meet together, the people may thus become something like a single person, who, as he has many feet, many hands, and many senses, may also have many qualities of character and intelligence. This is the reason why the many are also better judges of music and the writings of poets: some appreciate one part, some another, and all together appreciate all. The thing which makes a good man differ from a unit in the crowd—as it is also the thing which is generally said to make a beautiful person differ from one who is not beautiful, or an artistic representation differ from ordinary reality—is that elements which are elsewhere scattered and separate are here combined in a unity. If the elements are taken separately, one may say of an artistic representation that it is surpassed by the eye of this person and by some other feature of that.

1281ᵇ15 It is not clear, however, that this contrast between the many, on the one hand, and the few good men, on the other, can apply to every people and to every large group. Perhaps, by heaven, there are some of which it clearly cannot be true; for otherwise the same argument would apply to the beasts. Yet what difference, one may ask, is there between some men and the beasts?* All the same, there is nothing to prevent the view we have stated from being true of a particular group.

1281ᵇ21 It would thus seem possible to solve, by the considerations we have advanced, both the problem raised in the previous chapter ['Which people should be sovereign?'] and the further problem which follows upon it, 'What are the matters over which freemen, or the general body of citizens —the sort of people who neither have wealth nor can make any claim on the ground of goodness—should properly exercise sovereignty?'* Of course there is a danger in people of this sort sharing in the highest offices, as injustice may lead them into wrongdoing, and thoughtlessness into error. But there is also a serious risk in not letting them have some share of power; for a city with a body of disfranchised citizens who are numerous and poor must necessarily be a city which is full of enemies. The alternative left is to let them share in the deliberative and judicial functions. This is why Solon, and some of the other legislators, allow the people to elect officials and to call them to account at the end of their tenure of office, but not to hold office themselves in their individual capacity. When they all meet together, the people display a good enough gift of perception, and combined with the better class they are of service to the city (just as impure food, when it is mixed with pure, makes the whole concoction more nutritious than a small amount of the pure would be); but each of them is imperfect in the judgements he forms by himself.

1281^b38 But this arrangement of the constitution presents some difficulties. The first difficulty is that it may well be held that the function of judging when medical attendance has been properly given should belong to those whose profession it is to attend patients and cure the complaints from which they suffer—in a word, to members of the medical profession.* The same may be held to be true of all other professions and arts; and just as medical men should have their conduct examined before a body of medics, so, too, should those who follow other professions have theirs examined before a body of members of their own profession. But the term 'medic' is applied to the ordinary practitioner, to the specialist who directs the course of treatment, and to someone who has some general knowledge of the art of medicine. (There are people of this last type to be found in connection with nearly all the arts.) We credit those who have a general knowledge with the power of judging as much as we do the experts. When we turn to consider the matter of election, the same principles would appear to apply. To make a proper election is equally the work of experts. It is the work of those who are versed in geometry to choose a geometrician, or again, of those who are acquainted with steering to choose a steersman; and even if, in some occupations and arts, there are some non-experts who also share in the ability to choose, they do not share in a higher degree than the experts. It would thus appear, on this line of argument, that the people should not be made sovereign, either in the matter of election of magistrates or in that of their examination.

1282^a14 It may be, however, that these arguments are not altogether well founded for the reason given above—provided, that is to say, that the people is not too debased in character. Each individual may indeed be a worse judge than the experts; but all, when they meet together, are either better than experts or at any rate no worse. In the second place, there are a number of arts in which the craftsman is not the only, or even the best, judge. These are the arts whose products can be understood even by those who do not possess any skill in the art. A house, for instance, is something which can be understood by others besides the builder: indeed the user of a house, or in other words the householder, will judge it even better than he does. In the same way a steersman will judge a rudder better than a shipwright does; and the diner, not the cook, will be the best judge of a feast.

1282ᵃ23 The first difficulty would appear to be answered sufficiently by these considerations. But there is a second difficulty still to be faced, which is connected with the first. It would seem to be absurd that people of poor character should be sovereign on issues which are more important than those assigned to the better sort of citizens. The election of officials, and their examination at the end of their tenure, are the most important of issues; and yet there are constitutions, as we have seen, under which these issues are assigned to the people, since the assembly is sovereign in all such matters. To add to the difficulty, membership of the assembly, which carries deliberative and judicial functions, is vested in people of little property and of any age; but a high property qualification is demanded from those who serve as treasurers or generals, or hold any of the highest offices.

1282ᵃ32 This difficulty too may, however, be met in the same way as the first; and the practice followed in these constitutions is perhaps, after all, correct. It is not the individual juryman, councillor, or assemblyman, who is vested with office, but the court, the council, or the popular assembly; and in these bodies each member, whether he be a councillor, an assemblyman, or a juryman, is simply a part of the whole. It is therefore just that the people should be sovereign on the more important issues, since the assembly, the council, and the court consist of many people. Moreover, the property owned by all these people is greater than that of those who either as individuals or as members of small bodies hold the highest offices.

1282ᵃ41 This may serve as a settlement of the difficulties which have been discussed. But the discussion of the first of these difficulties leads to one conclusion above all others.

Rightly constituted laws should be [the final] sovereign;* but rulers, whether one or many, should be sovereign in those matters on which law is unable, owing to the difficulty of framing general rules for all contingencies, to make an exact pronouncement. But what rightly constituted laws ought to be is a matter that is not yet clear; and here we are still confronted by the difficulty stated at the end of the previous chapter. Laws must be good or bad, just or unjust in the same way as the constitutions to which they belong. The one clear fact is that laws must be laid down in accordance with constitutions; and if this is the case, it follows that laws which are in accordance with right constitutions must necessarily be just, and laws which are in accordance with perverted constitutions must be unjust.

CHAPTER 12

Justice is the political good. It involves equality, or the distribution of equal amounts to those who are equal. But who are equals, and by what criterion are they to be reckoned as equals? Many criteria can be applied; but the only proper criterion, in a political society, is that of contribution to the function of that society. Those who are equal in that respect should receive equal amounts: those who are superior or inferior should receive superior or inferior amounts, in proportion to the degree of their superiority or inferiority. If all are thus treated proportionately to the contribution they make, all are really receiving equal treatment; for the proportion between contribution and reward is the same in every case. The sort of equality which justice involves is thus proportionate equality; and this is the essence of distributive justice.

1282^{b}14 In all branches of knowledge and in every kind of craft the end in view is some good. In the most sovereign of these, the capacity for [leadership in] political matters, the end in view is the greatest good and the good which is most to be pursued. The good in the sphere of politics is justice;* and justice consists in what tends to promote the common interest. General opinion makes it consist in some sort of equality. Up to a point this agrees with the philosophical inquiries which contain our conclusions on ethics.* In other words, it holds that justice involves two factors—things, and those to whom things are assigned—and it considers that those who are equal should have assigned to them equal things. But here there arises a question which must not be overlooked. Equals and unequals—yes; but equals and unequals in what? This is a question which raises difficulties, and involves us in philosophical speculation on politics. It is possible to argue that offices and honours ought to be distributed unequally on the basis of superiority in any kind of goodness whatsoever—even if those concerned are similar, and do not differ, in any other respect. The reason is that where people differ from one another there must be a difference in what is just and proportionate to their merits. If this argument were right, the mere fact of a better complexion, or greater height, or any other such advantage, would establish a claim for a greater share of political rights to be given to its possessor. But is not the argument obviously wrong? To be clear that it is, we have only to consider other kinds of knowledge and ability. In dealing with a number of equally skilled flute-players, you should not assign a better supply of flutes to those who are better born. Rather those who are better at the job should be given the better supply of tools. If our point is not yet plain, it can be made so if we push it still further. Let us suppose someone who is superior to others in flute-playing, but far inferior in birth and beauty. Even if birth and beauty are greater goods than ability to play the flute, and even if those who possess them may surpass the flute-player proportionately more in these qualities than he surpasses them in his flute-playing, the fact remains that he is the one who ought to get the superior flutes. Superiority, whether in birth or in wealth, ought to contribute something to the performance of that function; and here these qualities contribute nothing to such performance.

1283ᵃ3 There is a further objection. If we accept this argument, every quality will have to be commensurable with every other. You will begin by reckoning a given degree of (say) height as superior to a given degree of some other quality,

and you will thus be driven to pit height in general against
(say) wealth and birth in general. But on this basis—i.e. that,
in a given case, A is counted as excelling in height to a greater
degree than B does in goodness, and that, *in general*, height is
counted as excelling to a greater degree than goodness does—
qualities are made commensurable. [We are involved in mere
arithmetic]; for if amount X of some quality is 'better' than
amount Y of some other, some amount which is other than X
must clearly be equal to it [i.e. must be *equally* good].* This is
impossible. It is therefore clear that in matters political there
is no good reason for basing a claim to the exercise of
authority on any and every kind of superiority. (Some may be
swift and others slow; but this is no reason why the one
should have more, and the other less—it is in athletic contests
that the superiority of the swift receives its reward.) Claims
must be based on the elements which constitute the being of
the city. There are thus good grounds for the claims to
honour which are made by people of good descent, free birth,
or wealth, since those who hold office must necessarily be free
men and pay the property assessment. (A city could not be
composed entirely of those without means, any more than it
could be composed entirely of slaves.) But we must add that if
wealth and free birth are necessary elements, the qualities of
being just and being a good soldier are also necessary. These
too are elements which must be present if people are to live
together in a city. The one difference is that the first two
elements are necessary for the simple existence of a city, and
the last two for its good life.

CHAPTER 13

*This raises the question, What constitutes a contribution to the
purpose of a political society? Wealth, birth, goodness, and the
aggregate quality of numbers, may all claim to be contributors.
How are these rival claims to be reconciled when they all
coexist in the same society? A case may be made in favour of
the aggregate quality of numbers; but a case may also be made
in favour of the single man of exceptional and outstanding
goodness. Such a man must either be made a king or sent into*

exile. The democratic policy of ostracism means a choice of the latter alternative; and the proportion, or balance, needed in a constitution is certainly disturbed if any one element is outstandingly eminent. On the other hand it cannot be just, in a good constitution, to refuse the recognition which is due to a man of outstanding goodness; and such a man should not be banished, but should rather be made a king. We are thus brought to the subject of kingship.

1283ᵃ23 If we are thinking in terms of contribution to the state's existence, all of the elements mentioned, or at any rate several of them, may properly claim to be recognized [in the award of honours and office]; but if we are thinking in terms of contribution to its good life, then culture and goodness,* as we have noted already, may be regarded as having the justest claim. On the other hand—since it is not right for those who are equal in one respect, and only in one, to have an equal share of all things, or for those who are unequal in one respect to have unequal shares of everything—all such constitutions must be perversions. We have noted already that there is a certain sense in which all are justified in the claims they advance, though none of them is absolutely justified. (a) The rich are justified to the extent that they have a larger share of the land, which is a matter of common concern: they are also, as a rule, more reliable in matters of contract. (b) The free and the nobly born may claim recognition together as being closely connected. The better-born are citizens to a greater extent than the low-born; and good birth has always honour in its own country. In addition the descendants of better men are likely to be better; good birth means goodness of stock. (c) Similarly we may also allow that goodness [of mind and character] has a just claim; for in our view the virtue of justice is goodness in matters of common concern and is necessarily accompanied by all other forms of goodness.* (d) Lastly, the many have a justified claim against the few: taken together and compared with the few they are stronger, richer, and better.

1283ᵃ42 Suppose these—I mean the good, the wealthy, and well-born, and some general body of citizens—all living together in a single city. Will there or will there not be a dispute about which of them is to rule? The decision about who should rule is not a matter of dispute in any of the constitutions we have mentioned. These constitutions differ in virtue of different groups being sovereign: one of them is distinguished by sovereignty being vested in the wealthy; another by its being vested in the good; and so with each of the rest. But we should consider how the matter is to be decided when these claims are present at the same time. Suppose, for example, that the good are exceedingly few in number: how are we to settle their claim? Should we consider the fact that they are few in the light of the function they have to discharge and ask therefore whether they will be able to manage a city? Or should we ask whether they are numerous enough to compose one?

1283ᵇ13 Here there arises a difficulty which applies to all the different claimants for political honours. It may be held that those who base their claim to rule on the ground of wealth have no case, and neither do those who base it on birth. The reason for thinking this is that if there is any one man who in turn is richer than all the rest, this one man must rule over all on the very same ground of justice; and similarly any one man who is pre-eminent in point of good birth must carry the day over those who base their claim on the ground of free birth. The same thing could perhaps happen even in aristocracies based on the claim of goodness. If someone is a better man than all the other good men who belong to the civic body, this one man should be sovereign on the very same ground of justice. Similarly if the reason why the Many should be sovereign is their being stronger than the Few, then if one man is stronger than all the rest—or if a group of more than one, but fewer than the Many, is stronger—these should be sovereign instead of the Many.

1283ᵇ27 All these considerations would seem to prove that none of the principles, in virtue of which people claim to rule and to have all others subject to their rule, is right. Take, for example, those who claim to be sovereign over the citizen body on the ground of goodness; or, equally, those who base their claim on the ground of wealth. The claims of both may be justly challenged by the masses; for there is nothing to prevent the Many—collectively if not individually—from being better, or richer, than the Few. This last reflection enables us to meet a difficulty which is sometimes raised and discussed. The difficulty is this. Suppose that the situation just mentioned does occur [i.e. that the Many are actually better, taken as a whole, than the Few]: what, in that case, is the proper policy for a lawgiver who wishes to enact right laws to the best of his power? Should he direct his legislation to the benefit of the better sort or should he direct it to that of the majority? [We may reply that] what is 'right' should be understood as what is 'equally right'; and what is 'equally right' is what is for the benefit of the whole city and for the common good of its citizens. The citizen is, in general, one who shares in the civic life of ruling and being ruled in turn. But this varies from constitution to constitution; and under the best constitution he must be one who is able and willing to rule and be ruled with a view to attaining a way of life in keeping with goodness.

1284ᵃ3 If there is one person (or several people, but yet not enough to form the full complement of a city) so pre-eminently superior in goodness that there can be no comparison between the goodness and political capacity which he shows (or several show, when there is more than one) and what is shown by the rest, such a person, or such people, can no longer be treated as part of a city. An injustice will be done to them if they are treated as worthy only of an equal share, when they are so greatly superior to others in goodness and political capacity; for someone of this sort may very well be like a god among men. This being the case, it is clear that legislation is necessarily limited to those who are equal in birth and capacity. There can be no law governing people of this kind. They are a law in themselves. It would be a folly to attempt to legislate for them: they might reply to such an attempt with the words used by the lions,* in the fable of Antisthenes, when the hares were making orations and claiming that all the animals should have equal status.

1284ᵃ17 Reasons of this nature will serve to explain why democratic cities institute the rule of ostracism.* Such cities are held to aim at equality above anything else; and with that aim in view they used to pass a sentence of ostracism on those whom they regarded as having too much influence owing to their wealth or the number of their connections or any other form of political strength. There is a story that the Argonauts left Heracles behind for this sort of reason; and the Argo itself refused to have him among the crew because he was so greatly superior to all the others. From this point of view we cannot altogether regard as just the strictures passed by the critics of tyranny on the advice once given by Periander to Thrasybulus.* According to the story, Periander said nothing to the messenger who had been sent [by Thrasybulus] for his advice; he simply chopped off the outstanding ears and thus levelled the corn [in the field where he was standing]. The messenger did not understand the meaning of his action, and merely reported the incident; but Thrasybulus guessed that he should cut off the outstanding men in the city. It is not only tyrants who may derive some benefit from this policy; nor is it only tyrants who put it into practice. Oligarchies and democracies are both in the same position; and ostracism has, in its way, the same effect of pulling down and banishing men of outstanding influence. Those who have gained an ascendancy apply the same sort of policy to other cities and peoples. The Athenians, for instance, acted in this way to Samos, Chios, and Lesbos:* once they had gained a firm grip of their empire, they humbled these cities, in violation of their former treaties. The King of the Persians did the same to the Medes, the Babylonians, and any of the others who were made presumptuous by memories of having once had an empire themselves.

1284^{b}3 The difficulty which we are discussing is one which is common to all forms of government, the right as well as the wrong; perverted forms adopt this policy of levelling with a view to their own particular interest, but the same is also true even of forms which look to the common good. This rule of proportion may also be observed in the arts and sciences generally. A painter would not permit a figure to have a foot which exceeded the bounds of symmetry, however beautiful it might be. A shipwright would not tolerate a stern, or any other part of a ship, which was out of proportion. A choir-master would not admit to a choir a singer with a stronger and a finer voice than any of the other members. For this reason nothing prevents monarchs who behave in this way from being in harmony with the cities [over which they rule]—provided that their own rule is beneficial to these cities; and thus the argument in favour of ostracism possesses a kind of political justice in relation to any recognized forms of pre-eminence. It is better if the legislator so frames a constitution initially that it never needs any such remedy; but the next best course, should the need arise, is to correct it by this sort of device. Actually, this is not what has happened in cities; instead of looking to the interest of their own particular constitution, they have resorted to acts of ostracism in a spirit of faction.

1284ᵇ22 So far as perverted forms are concerned, it is clear that the ostracism is expedient and just from their own point of view—though perhaps it is also clear that it is not absolutely just. But in the best constitution a serious difficulty arises. It does not arise in regard to pre-eminence in other qualities such as political strength, or wealth, or an abundance of connections but where there is someone of outstanding excellence. 'What is to be done in that case?' Nobody would say that such a man ought to be banished and sent into exile. But neither would any one say that he ought to be subject to others. That would be like claiming to rule over Zeus, according to some division of offices.* The only alternative left—and this would also appear to be the natural course—is for all others to pay a willing obedience to the man of outstanding goodness. Such men will accordingly be the permanent kings in their cities.

D: Kingship and its Forms (Chapters 14–18)

CHAPTER 14

*There are five forms of kingship: (1) the Spartan form; (2)
kingship among barbarian peoples; (3) the dictatorship or elective form of tyranny; (4) the kingship of the Heroic Age; (5)
absolute kingship, with the king exercising a plenary power like
that which a father exercises over his household.*

1284ᵇ35 It will perhaps be well, after the previous discussion,
to make a transition, and to proceed to consider kingship,
since this is, in our view, one of the right constitutions. The
question we have to consider is whether this form of government is to the advantage of cities or territories which are to be
properly governed; or whether this is not so and some other
form is more advantageous—or, at any rate, more advantageous in some cases, even if it is not in others. We must
begin by determining whether there is only one kind of
kingship, or whether it has several varieties. It is easy to see
that it includes a number of different kinds, and that the style
of government is not the same in all these kinds.

1285ᵃ3 The kind of kingship to be found in the constitution
of Sparta is regarded as the best example of kingship under
law. But it involves no general sovereignty: a Spartan king
simply has charge of military matters when he goes outside
the country; matters of religious observance are also vested in
the kings. This form of kingship is like a generalship with
absolute command and permanent tenure. A king of this sort
does not have the power to put anyone to death, except on
grounds of cowardice, as happened on military expeditions in
ancient times, by right of superior force. Homer may be cited
as evidence: for Agamemnon was patient under abuse in the
presence of the assembly, but exercised the power of life and
death on the field of battle. At any rate he says:

> Whomso I find apart from the fight . . . he shall have no hope of
> escaping:

Dogs and vultures shall rend him; for mine is the power to command
death.*

One type of kingship is thus a military command held for life;
some of these are hereditary and others elective.

1285ª16 Another type of kingship is the sort which is to be
found among some barbarian peoples. Kingships of this sort
all possess an authority similar to that of tyrannies; but they
are, none the less, governed by law, and they descend from
father to son. The reason is that these barbarian peoples are
more servile in character than Greeks (as the peoples of Asia
are more servile than those of Europe); and they therefore
tolerate despotic rule without any complaint. So these kingships have the nature of tyrannies; but, being in accordance
with law, they are at the same time stable. For the same
reason the bodyguards used in such cities are such as suit
kings, and not tyrants. Kings are guarded by the arms of their
subjects; tyrants by a foreign force. Ruling according to law,
and with the consent of their subjects, kings have bodyguards
drawn from their subjects: the tyrant has a [foreign] bodyguard to protect himself against them.

1285ª29 These are two types of monarchy; but there is
also a third, which used to exist among the ancient
Greeks, and which goes by the name of *aisumnēteia*. This
may be roughly described as an elective form of tyranny.
It differs from kingship among the barbarians, not in
being outside the law, but only in being non-hereditary.
Some of these held office for life: others for a fixed
period, or for the discharge of a definite task. Pittacus,*
for instance, was elected at Mytilene to deal with the attacks of the exiles commanded by Antimenides and the
poet Alcaeus. The fact of the election of Pittacus is attested by Alcaeus, in one of his drinking songs, where he
bitterly says:

Meanly born Pittacus over their gall-less and heaven-doomed city
Was enthroned by them for their tyrant, with clamour of praise, in
    the throng of the hustings.

1285ᵇ2 These forms of government were, and still are,

tyrannies in their despotic power, but kingships in being elective and in resting on the assent of their subjects. But there is a fourth type of kingship—those of the Heroic Age rested on consent, and descended from father to son, in accordance with law. The founders of royal lines had been benefactors of their people in the arts or in war: they had drawn them together in a city, or provided them with territory; and they had thus become kings by general consent, and had established kingships which descended to their successors. Such kings had the sovereign functions of being commanders in war, and of offering such sacrifices as did not require a priest; they were also judges in legal actions. Sometimes they judged upon oath, and sometimes without oath: the form of the oath, when they took one, was the lifting up of their sceptre. In ancient times they enjoyed a permanent authority, which included urban, rural, and foreign affairs: at a later date they relinquished some of their prerogatives: others were taken away by the masses; in some cities only the [conduct of] sacrifices was left to the kings. Even where it could be said that a real kingship still existed, they kept only the power of military command in foreign expeditions.

1285ᵇ20 There are thus these four types of kingship: (1) the kingship of the Heroic Age, based on general consent but limited to a number of definite functions, with the king acting as general and judge and the head of religious observances; (2) the type of kingship among barbarian peoples, with the king exercising, by right of descent, a despotic authority, albeit in accordance with law; (3) kingship of the type which is termed *aisumnēteia*, and which is an elective form of tyranny; and (4) the Spartan type of kingship, which may be roughly defined as a permanent command of the army exercised by right of descent. These four types differ from one another in the ways just mentioned; but there is still a fifth type of kingship. This is the absolute type, where a single person is sovereign on every issue, with the same sort of power that a tribe or a city exercises over its public concerns. It is a type which corresponds to paternal rule over a household. Just as household government is kingship over a family, so conversely this type of kingship may be regarded as household government exercised over a city, or a tribe, or a collection of tribes.

CHAPTER 15

Only the last of the five forms of kingship mentioned in the last chapter needs special examination. It raises the problem of personal rule versus the rule of law. There are arguments on either side: personal rule has the quality of initiative; the rule of law has that of impartiality. The rule of law is of major importance, and should be the main factor in all constitutions, including kingship, which should therefore be a constitutional kingship limited by law. There are, however, matters of detail which cannot be settled by law. Even so, the question arises whether such matters are best settled by one person, or by a number of people. The balance is in favour of a number of people. Where government by a single person exists, in the form of kingship, it raises two special problems: should it be hereditary, and should it be backed by a guard or standing army?

1285^{b}33 For practical purposes there are only two types of kingship which we need consider—the type just mentioned, and the Spartan type. Most of the others are intermediate between these two: their kings are sovereign to a lesser extent than they are in the absolute type but to a greater extent than in the Spartan type. Thus our inquiry is practically reduced to two issues. The first is the issue whether it is expedient for cities to have a permanent general (either on a hereditary basis, or on some scheme of rotation). The second is the issue whether it is expedient or not that one man should be sovereign in all matters.

1286^{a}2 Examining generalship of the kind just mentioned is more a matter of laws than of constitutions, since it may exist under any form of constitution; and we may therefore dismiss the first question for the present. The other type of kingship [absolute kingship] is a form of constitution; and we are therefore bound to study it philosophically, and to examine briefly the difficulties which it involves. Our inquiry starts from the general problem, 'Is it more advantageous to be ruled by the one best man, or by the best laws?'*

1286ᵃ9 Those who hold that kingship is advantageous argue that law can only lay down general rules; it cannot issue commands to deal with events as they happen; and following written rules is therefore foolish in any art whatever.* In Egypt doctors are rightly permitted to alter the rules of treatment after the first four days, though a doctor who alters them earlier does so at his own risk. It is clear, for the same reason, that a constitution based on the letter and rules of law is not the best constitution. But, of course, that general principle must also be present in the rulers. That from which the element of passion is wholly absent is better than that to which passion naturally clings. This element [of passion] is not to be found in law but must always be present in the human mind. The rejoinder may, however, be made that the individual mind, for its part, can deliberate better, and decide better, on particular issues.

1286ᵃ21 It is surely clear that [the one best man] must be a lawgiver, and there must be a body of laws, but these laws must not be sovereign where they fail to hit the mark—though they must be so in all other cases. But in cases which cannot be decided at all, or cannot be decided properly, by law, should rule be exercised by the one best man or by the whole of the people?

1286ᵃ26 In the actual practice of our own day the people gather together to judge, to deliberate, and to make decisions. These decisions are all concerned with particular matters. Any individual, so far as his own contribution is concerned, may be inferior. But the city is composed of many individuals; and just as a feast to which many contribute is better than one provided by a single person, so, and for the same reason, a crowd can come to a better decision, in many matters, than any one individual.

1286ᵃ31 Again, a numerous body is less likely to be corrupted. In the same way that a larger volume of water [is not so liable to pollution], the people is not so liable to corruption as the few. The judgement of a single man is bound to be corrupted when he is overpowered by anger, or by any other similar emotion; but it is no easy task to make everyone get angry and go wrong simultaneously. Suppose that the people are all freemen, do nothing contrary to law, and act outside it only in matters which law is obliged to omit. This may not be easy when many people are involved but if the majority are both good men and good citizens, which will be the more likely to be free from corruption—the one man, or the greater number who are all good men? Is not the balance clearly in favour of the greater number?

1286ᵇ1 May the many not be subject to faction, from which the one man will be free? It is perhaps an answer to this objection that they will be of good mental character just as the one man is. If we call by the name of aristocracy the rule of a number of people who are all good men, and by the name of kingship the rule of a single person, we may say that aristocracy is better for cities than kingship (whether rule is exercised by force or without force)—provided only that a number of people of similar character can be found.

1286ᵇ8 Perhaps the reason why kingship was formerly common was because it was rare to find a number of men of outstanding goodness—all the more as the cities they inhabited were small. A further reason why kings were appointed was that they were benefactors—as is the function of good men. Later when it came about that there were a number of people of equal goodness, they no longer held back but sought to have something they could share in common, and so established a constitution. Later still, they deteriorated in character and enriched themselves from the public property. It is to some such origin that we may reasonably ascribe the rise of oligarchy, since they began to hold wealth in honour. From oligarchies there was first a change to tyrannies, and then from tyrannies to democracy. The reason was that, greedy for the gains which office conferred, they limited it to a narrower and narrower circle; and by this policy they strengthened the masses until they rose in rebellion and established democracies. Since cities have become still larger, we may perhaps say that it is now difficult for any form of constitution apart from democracy to exist.*

1286ᵇ22 If kingship be accepted as the best form of government for cities, what is to be the position of the king's children? Are we to say that his descendants should also be kings? If they turn out as some of them have done, the result will be mischievous. It may be argued that a king, even if he has the power to do so, will not hand over the crown to his children [if they are unsuitable]. But that is hardly to be believed: it is a difficult thing to do, and it needs a degree of goodness greater than is consonant with human nature.

1286ᵇ27 Another question, which raises difficulties, is that of the force which the one who is to be king should have; should he have his own bodyguard which will enable him to coerce those who are unwilling to obey? If not, how can he possibly manage to govern? Even if he were a sovereign who ruled according to law and who never acted according to his own wishes outside the law, he must necessarily have a force in order to guard the law. In the case of a king of this sort [who rules according to law] it is perhaps easy to settle the question. He ought to have some force, which should be enough to make his power greater than that commanded by any one individual or any group of individuals but less than that of the people. This was the nature of the bodyguard assigned in ancient times, when someone was made head of the city under the title of *aisumnētēs* or tyrant. It was also the size of the force which someone at Syracuse advised the people to give to Dionysius when he asked for a bodyguard.

CHAPTER 16

The general considerations of the previous chapter, so far as they favour kingship at all, are in favour of a constitutional and limited kingship. But the question still remains whether a case can be made in favour of an absolute kingship. It may be objected to such a form of kingship that it is contrary to the idea of a free society of equals, and adverse to the rule of law. True, the rule of an absolute king may be defended on the ground of his expert knowledge; and the analogy of science and the arts may be invoked in his favour. But the analogy does not really hold; and in any case expert knowledge is more likely to reside in a number of people than in one. So far, therefore, the conclusion would seem to be adverse to absolute monarchy—at any rate on general grounds.

1287ª1 The argument which now confronts us, and the inquiry we have still to attempt, is concerned with the king who does everything at his own discretion. What is called 'kingship under the law', as has already been noted,* is not in itself a form of constitution. A permanent military command may exist in any form of constitution—for example, in a democracy or an aristocracy; and in the sphere of civil administration too there are a number of cities with different forms of constitution which make a single person sovereign: there is an office of this kind at Epidamnus, for instance, and another, though with somewhat more limited powers, at Opus. But what is called a *pambasileia* is a form of constitution in which a king governs at his own discretion over the whole population. Now there are some who take the view that the sovereignty of one man over all the other members of a city is not even natural in any case where a city is composed of equals. On this view those who are alike by nature are naturally entitled to receive the same justice and enjoy the same status. It is harmful for our bodies if those who are unequal have equal amounts of food and clothing; the same goes for [offices and] honours. Similarly it is harmful for those who are equal to have unequal shares. For this reason justice means being ruled as well as ruling, and therefore involves rotation of office. But when we come to that, we already come to law; for such an arrangement is law. The rule of law is therefore preferable, according to the view we are stating, to that of a single citizen. In pursuance of the same view it is argued that, even if it be the better course to have individuals ruling, they should be made 'law-guardians'* or 'servants' of the law. There must, it is admitted, be public offices; but these, it is urged, cannot be vested in one man, consistently with justice, when all are alike.

1287ª23 Furthermore, if there are a number of cases which law seems unable to determine, it is also true that a human being would be equally unable to find an answer to these cases. Law trains the holders of office expressly in its own spirit, and then sets them to decide and settle those residuary issues which it cannot regulate, 'as justly as in them lies'.* It also allows them to introduce any improvements which may seem to them, as the result of experience, to be better than the existing laws. He who commands that law should rule may thus be regarded as commanding that God and reason alone should rule; he who commands that a man should rule adds the character of the beast.* Appetite has that character; and high spirit, too, perverts the holders of office, even when they are the best of men. Law is thus 'reason without desire'.

1287ª32 The parallel of the arts is false since medical treatment according to the rules of a textbook is a poor sort of thing, and it is very much better to use the services of those who possess professional skill. Physicians never act in defiance of reason from motives of partiality: they cure their patients and earn their fee. Politicians in office have a habit of doing a number of things in order to spite [their enemies] or favour [their friends]. If patients suspected physicians of conspiring with their enemies to destroy them for their own profit, they would be more inclined to seek for treatment by the rules of a textbook. Again, physicians, when they are ill, call in other physicians to attend them; and trainers, when they are in training, use the services of other trainers, on the grounds that they cannot judge truly themselves because they are judging in their own case under the influence of their own feelings. This shows that to seek for justice is to seek for a neutral standard; and law is a neutral* standard. But laws resting on unwritten custom are even more sovereign, and concerned with issues of still more sovereign importance, than written laws; and this suggests that, even if the rule of a man be safer than the rule of written law, it need not therefore be safer than the rule of unwritten law.

1287ᵇ8 A further objection [to the rule of a single man] is that it is difficult for one person to exercise oversight over many things. He will thus find it necessary to appoint a number of officers to give him assistance. But is there any real difference between having these officers at the start and having them appointed by the choice of a single man? We may add a point which has already been made. If the good man has a just title to rule because he is better than others, then two good men are better than one. This is what is meant by

Two men going together*

and the prayer of Agamemnon

Would that I had ten men for my counsellors like unto Nestor.*

In our own day, too, we find a number of offices, such as jurymen, for example, who are vested with a power of decision on certain issues on which the law is not competent to pronounce; for no one disputes the fact that law will be the best ruler and judge on the issues on which it is competent.

1287^{b}19 It is because there are some matters which law can include within its scope and others which it cannot, that difficulties arise and the question comes to be debated, 'Is the rule of the best law preferable to that of the best man?' Matters which belong to the sphere of deliberation, are obviously ones on which it is not possible to lay down a law. Those who advocate the rule of law do not deny that such matters ought to be judged by men; they claim only that they ought to be judged by many men rather than one.

1287^{b}25 Anyone in office, if he has been trained by the law, will have a good judgement; and it may well be regarded as an absurdity that a single man should do better in seeing with two eyes, judging with two ears, or acting with two hands and feet, than many could do with many. Indeed, it is actually the practice of monarchs to take to themselves, as it were, many eyes and ears and hands and feet, and to use as colleagues those who are friendly towards their government and to them personally. If they are not friends they will not act in accordance with the monarch's policy. But if they are friends both to him personally and to his government, they will also be, as a man's friends always are, his equal and peers; and in believing that his friends should have office he is also committed to the belief that his equals and peers should have office.

These are the main arguments pressed by those who argue against the cause of kingship.

CHAPTER 17

*There may, however, be a particular sort of society in which
absolute kingship ought to be instituted. This is the sort of
society in which one family, or one person, is of merit so
outstanding as to surpass all the other members. Here justice
and propriety may be argued to require that there should be
absolute kingship, with plenary power and no limit to tenure.*

1287ᵇ36 These arguments, however, may be true when applied to some peoples, but not when applied to others. There
is one sort of people which is meant by its nature for rule of
the despotic type, another for rule by a king, and another still
for rule of a constitutional type;* what is just and expedient
varies accordingly. (But there is no society which is meant by
its nature for rule of the tyrannical type, or for rule of the
other types found in wrong or perverted constitutions: the
societies that are under such types of rule have fallen into an
unnatural condition.) What has just been said is sufficient to
show that in a group whose members are equal and peers it is
neither expedient nor just that one man should be sovereign
over all others. This is equally true whether laws are absent,
with the one man ruling as a law in himself, or are present; it
is true whether the one man is a good man ruling over the
good, or a bad man ruling over the bad; it is even true when
the one man is superior in goodness unless his superiority be
of a special character. We have now to say what that character
is—though it has already been in some sense explained in an
earlier passage.*

1288ᵃ6 We must first determine what sorts of group are
suitable for kingship, for aristocracy, and for government of
the constitutional type. A people suitable for kingship is one
of the sort which naturally tends to produce some particular
stock [or family] pre-eminent in its capacity for political
leadership. A people suitable for aristocracy is one which
naturally tends to produce a stock capable of being ruled, in a
manner suitable to free men, by those with the quality of
leadership in their capacity for political rule. A people suitable

for government of the constitutional type is one in which there naturally exists a stock possessing military capacity who can rule and be ruled under a system of law which distributes offices among the wealthy in proportion to merit.*

1288ª15 When it happens that the whole of a family, or a single individual among the ordinary people, is of merit so outstanding as to surpass that of all the rest, it is only just that this family should be vested with kingship and absolute sovereignty, or that this single person should become king. As we said earlier,* this is in accordance with the kind of justice which is usually pleaded in establishing any form of constitution—be it aristocratic or oligarchic, or be it, again, democratic. All forms alike recognize the claim of some sort of superiority, though the kind of superiority in question varies. Here, however, there is a special ground which we have already had reason to mention, namely that it would be improper, of course, to execute a man of outstanding superiority, to banish him permanently, to ostracize him, or to require him to take his turn at being a subject under a system of rotation. A whole is never intended by nature to be inferior to a part; and a man so greatly superior to others stands to them in the relation of a whole to its parts. The only course which remains is that he should receive obedience, and should have sovereign power without any limit of tenure, not turn by turn* with others.

1288ª30 These may serve as our conclusions in regard to kingship, and as our answers to the questions: what are its different forms? is it, or is it not, advantageous to cities? and, if it be so, to what cities, and under what conditions, is it advantageous?

CHAPTER 18

We may now turn to inquire by what means a good constitution, be it an aristocracy or a kingship, should be brought into existence. The same means must be used to make a good constitution as are used to make a good man. We are thus led to inquire into the nature of the good life, which is the aim of both the good man and the good constitution.

1288ᵃ32 We have laid it down that there are three types of right constitution, and that the best of these must be the one which is administered by the best. This is the type in which there is a single man, or a whole family, or a number of people, surpassing all others in goodness and where ruled as well as rulers are fitted to play their part in the attainment of the most desirable mode of life. We have also shown, at the beginning of our inquiry, that the goodness of the good man, and that of the good citizen of the best city, must be one and the same. It clearly follows that just the same method, and just the same means, by which a man becomes good, should also be used to achieve the creation of a city on the pattern of aristocracy or kingship; and thus the training and habits of action which make a good man are the same as those which make a good statesman or a good king.

1288ᵇ2 These issues determined, we must next attempt to treat of the best form of constitution, asking ourselves, 'Under what conditions does it tend to arise, and how can it be established?' In order to make a proper inquiry into this subject it is necessary . . .*

BOOK IV
ACTUAL CONSTITUTIONS AND
THEIR VARIETIES

A: Introductory (Chapters 1–2)

CHAPTER 1

Politics, like other branches of knowledge, must consider not only the ideal, but also the various problems of the actual—e.g. which is the best constitution practicable in the given circumstances; what are the best means of preserving actual constitutions; which is the best average constitution for the majority of cities; what are the different varieties of the main types of constitution, and especially of democracy and oligarchy. Politics, too, must consider not only constitutions, but also laws, and the proper relation of laws to constitutions.

1288ᵇ10 It is true of all those practical arts and those branches of knowledge which are complete in the sense that they cover the whole of a subject rather than dealing with it in a piecemeal fashion, that each of them has to consider the different methods appropriate to the different categories of its subject. For instance, the art of physical training has to consider (1) which type of training is appropriate to which type of physique; (2) which is the best type of training (for the best type of training must be one which is suitable for the best endowed and best equipped physique); and (3) which is the type of training that can be generally applied to the majority of physiques—for that too is one of the problems to be solved by the art of physical training. Nor is this all. (4) If someone wants to have physical training, but does not want to attain the standard of skill and condition which is needed for competitions, it is the task of the trainer and the gymnastic master to impart the level of ability he requires. The same is obviously true of medicine, of shipbuilding, tailoring, and of all the other arts.

1288ᵇ21 It follows that it is the task of the same branch of knowledge [i.e. politics] to consider first which is the best constitution, and what qualities a constitution must have to come closest to the ideal when there are no external factors to hinder its doing so, and secondly which sort of constitution suits which sort of civic body.* The attainment of the best constitution is likely to be impossible for many cities; and the good lawgiver and the true statesman must therefore have their eyes open not only to what is the absolute best, but also to what is the best in relation to actual conditions. A third task is to consider the sort of constitution which depends upon an assumption*—in other words, to study a given constitution with a view to explaining how it may have arisen and how it may be made to enjoy the longest possible life. The sort of case which we have in mind is one where a city has neither the [ideally] best constitution (nor even the elementary conditions needed for it) nor the best constitution possible under the actual conditions, but has only a constitution of an inferior type. In addition to all these tasks, it is important also to know the type of constitution which is best suited to cities in general. For this reason most of the writers who treat of politics, even if they deal well with other matters, fail when they come to matters of practical utility.* We have to study not only the best constitution, but also the one which is practicable, and likewise the one which is easiest to work and most suitable to cities generally.

1288ᵇ39 As things are, some confine their investigations to the extreme of perfection, which requires large resources. Others, addressing themselves to what is more generally attainable, still do away with the constitutions that now exist, and simply extol the Spartan constitution or some other type. The sort of constitutional system which ought to be proposed is one such that people will have little difficulty in accepting it or taking part in it, given the system they already have. It is as difficult a matter to reform an old constitution as it is to construct a new one; as hard to unlearn a lesson as it was to learn it initially. The statesman [*politikos*], therefore, must not confine himself to the matters we have just mentioned: he must also be able, as we said previously,* to help any existing constitution. He cannot do so unless he knows how many different kinds of constitutions there are. As things are, people believe that there is only one sort of democracy and one sort of oligarchy. This is an error. To avoid that error, we must keep in mind the different varieties of each constitution; we must be aware of their number, and of the number of different ways in which they are constituted.

1289ᵃ11 The same kind of understanding is needed to see which laws are [absolutely] best and which are appropriate to each constitution. Laws ought to be made to suit constitutions (as indeed in practice they always are), and not constitutions made to suit laws. The reason is this. A constitution is an organization of offices in a city, by which the method of their distribution is fixed, the sovereign authority is determined, and the nature of the end to be pursued by the association and all its members is prescribed.* Laws, apart from those that frame the constitution, are the rules by which the magistrates should exercise their powers, and should watch and check transgressors. It follows that one must always bear in mind both the varieties and the definition of each constitution, with a view to enacting appropriate laws. If there are several forms of democracy, and several forms of oligarchy, rather than a single form of each, the same laws cannot possibly be beneficial to all oligarchies or to all democracies.

CHAPTER 2

On this basis, after the general considerations of the previous book and the account of kingship and aristocracy there given, it remains to discuss the 'right' form of constitution called 'constitutional government' (polity) and the three 'perverted' forms called democracy, oligarchy, and tyranny. These three perversions may be graded in an ascending order—tyranny the worst; oligarchy the next worst; and democracy the least bad. The general programme of future inquiry is outlined.

1289ᵃ26 In our first discussion of constitutions* we distinguished three varieties of right constitution (kingship, aristocracy, and 'constitutional government' [polity]), and three corresponding perversions of those varieties (tyranny being the perversion of kingship, oligarchy of aristocracy, and democracy of 'constitutional government'). Aristocracy and kingship have already been treated. To consider the best constitution is, in effect, to consider the two constitutions so named;* for, like the best constitution, they both aim to produce goodness of character duly equipped with the necessary means for its exercise. We have also defined, in a previous passage, the nature of the difference between aristocracy and kingship,* and we have explained when kingship should be established. It only remains, therefore, to discuss (1) 'constitutional government', which is called by the generic name common to all constitutions, and (2) the remaining constitutions: oligarchy, democracy, and tyranny.*

1289ª38 It is also obvious which of these perversions is the worst, and which of them is the next worst. The perversion of the first and the most nearly divine of the right constitutions must necessarily be the worst. Kingship must either be merely a name, without any substance, or be based on the fact of a king's great personal superiority. Tyranny, therefore, is the worst, and at the farthest remove of all the perversions from a true constitution: oligarchy, being as it is far removed from aristocracy, is the next worst: democracy is the most moderate [and so the least bad]. One of our predecessors* has already advanced the same view, but he used a different principle. On his principle all constitutions could have a good as well as a bad form; oligarchy, for example, could be good as well as bad; and going on this principle he ranked the good form of democracy as the worst of all the good forms of constitution, and the bad form of it as the best of all the bad. In our opinion these two constitutions, in any of their forms, are wholly on the side of error. It cannot properly be said that one form of oligarchy is better than another; it can only be said that one is not so bad as another.

1289ᵇ11 But for the present we may leave aside discussion of this sort of judgement. We have, first, to enumerate the varieties of each type of constitution, on the assumption that democracy and oligarchy have each several different forms. Secondly, we have to examine what type of constitution, short of the best, is the most generally acceptable, and the most to be preferred; and if there is any other constitution of an aristocratic and well-constructed character but suitable, none the less, for adoption in most cities, we have to ask what that constitution is. Thirdly, and in regard to constitutions generally, we have to inquire which constitution is desirable for which sort of civic body. It is possible, for instance, that democracy rather than oligarchy may be necessary for one sort of civic body, and oligarchy rather than democracy for another. Fourthly, we have to consider how someone who wishes to do so should set to work to establish these various constitutions—i.e. the different varieties both of democracy and oligarchy. Fifthly, when we have given a concise account of all these subjects, to the best of our power, we must attempt to handle a final theme. How are constitutions generally, and each constitution severally, liable to be destroyed; how can they be preserved; and what are the causes which particularly tend to produce these results?*

B: The Varieties of the Main Types of Constitution especially Democracy, Oligarchy, and 'Constitutional Government' or Polity (Chapters 3–10)

CHAPTER 3

The reason for the variety of constitutions is the varieties to be found in the 'parts' or social elements of the city—especially among the populace and the notables. A constitution is an arrangement of offices; and there will be as many constitutions as there are methods of distributing offices among the different parts of the city. There is a general opinion that there are only two sorts of constitutions, just as there are only two sorts of winds and two sorts of musical modes; but this is a simplification which cannot be accepted.

1289ᵇ27 The reason why there are many different constitutions is to be found in the fact that every city has many different parts.* In the first place, every city is obviously composed of households. Secondly, in this number there are bound to be some rich, some poor, and some in the middle, with the rich possessing and the poor being without the equipment of the heavy-armed soldier. Thirdly, the common people [or *dēmos*] are engaged partly in agriculture, partly in trade, and partly in menial jobs. Fourthly, there are also differences among the notables—differences based on their wealth and the amount of their property; and these differences appear, for example, in the matter of keeping horses. This can only be done by the very wealthy, which is the reason why cities whose strength lay in cavalry were in former times the homes of oligarchies. These oligarchies used their cavalry in wars with adjoining cities: we may cite the examples of Eretria and Chalcis [in the island of Euboea] and of Magnesia on the Maeander and many other cities in Asia Minor. Besides differences of wealth, there is also difference of birth, and difference of merit; and there are differences based on other factors of the same order—factors already described as being parts of a city in our discussion of aristocracy,* where we distinguished and enumerated the essential parts from which every city is composed.

1290ᵃ3 Sometimes all these parts share in the control of the constitution; sometimes only a few of them share; sometimes a number of them share. It thus follows clearly that there must be a number of constitutions, which differ from one another in kind. This is because the parts differ in kind from one another. A constitution is an arrangement in regard to the offices of the city. By this arrangement the citizen body distributes office, either on the basis of the power of those who participate in it, or on the basis of some sort of general equality (i.e. the equality of the poor, or of the rich, or an equality existing among both rich and poor). There must therefore be as many constitutions as there are modes of arranging the distribution of office according to the superiorities and the differences of the parts of the city.

1290ᵃ13 There is indeed a prevalent opinion that there are only two constitutions. Just as winds, in ordinary speech, are simply described as north or south, and all other winds are treated as deviations from these, so constitutions are also described as democratic or oligarchical. On this basis aristoc-

racy is classified as being a sort of oligarchy, under the
heading of oligarchical, and similarly the so-called 'constitutional government' [polity] is classified under the heading of
democracy—just as westerly winds are classified under the
head of northerly, and easterly winds under that of southerly.
The situation is much the same, so some people think, with
the modes in music. In their case also two modes (the Dorian
and the Phrygian)* are treated as basic and other arrangements are called by one or other of these two names. But
though this is the prevalent view about constitutions in current
opinion, we shall do better, and we shall come nearer the
truth, if we classify them on a different basis, as has already
been suggested.* On that basis we shall have one or two
constitutions which are properly formed; all the others will be
perversions of the best constitution (just as in music we may
have perversions of the properly tempered modes); and these
perversions will be oligarchical when they are too severe and
dominant, and democratic when they are soft and relaxed.

CHAPTER 4

*Democracy does not mean only the rule of number: it also
means the rule of a social class. Both criteria must be used to
define democracy, as both number and social class must also be
used to define oligarchy. On this basis we may now study the
different varieties of democracy and oligarchy, which (as stated
in the previous chapter) will depend on the varieties to be found
in the 'parts' of different cities—i.e. on the different natures of
their social composition. We shall accordingly classify the varieties of constitutions as we should classify the various species of
animals—by the varieties of their parts and of the composition
of those parts. We therefore proceed to enumerate the ten or so
parts which go to the composition of a city, contrasting our
enumeration with the different enumeration of Plato. We must
also take note of the different forms assumed by the* dēmos, *or
populace, and also by the upper class, according as one or
another part predominates in its make-up. This enables us to
distinguish five varieties of democracy, in a descending scale
which ends in 'extreme democracy'—a variety of democracy,*

analogous to tyranny, where law has ceased to be sovereign
and the notion of a constitution has practically disappeared.

1290ª30 It ought not to be assumed, as some people are
nowadays in the habit of doing, that democracy can be
defined, without any qualification, as a form of constitution
in which the greater number are sovereign.* Even in oligarchies, and indeed in all constitutions, the majority is
sovereign.* Similarly, oligarchy cannot be simply defined as a
form [of government] in which a few people have sovereignty
over the constitution. Suppose that the total population is
1,300, that 1,000 of the 1,300 are wealthy, and that these
1,000 assign no share in office to the remaining 300 poor,
although they are men of free birth and like them in other
respects. Nobody will say that these people are democratically
governed. Or suppose, again, that there are only a few poor
men, but that they are stronger than the rich men who form
the majority. Nobody would term such a constitution an
oligarchy, if no share in official honours is given to the group
that is rich. It is better, therefore, to say that democracy exists
wherever the free-born are sovereign, and that oligarchy exists
wherever the rich are sovereign, though it so happens that the
former are many and the latter few—there are many who are
free-born, but few who are rich. Otherwise* we should have
an oligarchy if offices were distributed on the basis of height
(as they are said to be in Ethiopia), or on the basis of looks;
for the number of tall or good-looking men must always be
small.

1290ᵇ7 Yet even this criterion [of poverty and wealth] is not
sufficient to distinguish the constitutions in question. We
have to remember that the democratic and the oligarchical
city both contain a number of parts. We cannot, therefore,
apply the term 'democracy' to a constitution under which
those who are free-born rule a majority who are not free-
born. (A system of this sort once existed at Apollonia, on the
Ionian Gulf, and at Thera. In both of these cities honours and
offices were reserved for those who were of the best birth—in
the sense of being the descendants of the original settlers
—though they were only a handful of the whole population.)

Nor can we apply the term democracy to a constitution under which the rich are sovereign simply because they are more numerous than the poor. An example of such a constitution formerly existed at Colophon, where before the war with Lydia a majority of the citizens were the owners of large properties. There is a democracy when the free-born and poor control the government, being at the same time a majority; and similarly there is an oligarchy when the rich and better-born control the government, being at the same time a minority.

1290^b21 The fact that there are a number of constitutions, and the cause of that fact, have been established. We must now explain why there are more constitutions than the two just mentioned [i.e. democracy and oligarchy], indicate what they are, and suggest the reasons for their existence. In doing so we may start from the principle which was previously stated, and which we can now take as agreed, that every city consists, not of one, but of many parts.

1290^b25 If we aimed at a classification of the different kinds of animals, we should begin by enumerating what is necessary to every animal. These will include, for example, some of the sensory organs, organs for getting and digesting food, such as the mouth and the stomach, and, in addition, the organs of locomotion which are used by the different animals. Assuming that there are only so many of these organs and that they come in different forms—I mean that there are different forms of mouth, of stomach, of sensory organs, and of organs of locomotion, the number of possible combinations of these varieties will inevitably produce several different kinds of animals (for the same kind of animal cannot exhibit several varieties of mouth, or of ears). Thus when all the possible combinations have been taken into account they will produce different kinds of animals—as many kinds of animals as there are combinations of the necessary organs.

1290^b37 It is just the same with the constitutions which have been mentioned. Cities too, as we have repeatedly noticed, are composed not of one but of many parts. One of these parts consists of all those people concerned with the production of food, or, as it is called, the farming class. A second, which is called the mechanical class, consists of those who are occupied in the various arts and crafts without which a city cannot be inhabited—some of them being necessities, and other contributing to luxury or to the living of a good life. A third part is what may be termed the marketing class; it includes all those who are occupied in buying and selling, either as merchants or as retailers. A fourth part is the class of hired labourers; and a fifth element is the defence force, which is no less necessary than the other four, if the population is not to be enslaved by invaders. For it is surely not possible to call a city by that name if it is naturally servile. Self-sufficiency is the mark of a city whereas the slave is not self-sufficient.

1291ª10 For this reason the account of this matter in the *Republic* [369d – 371e] is inadequate, though ingenious. 'Socrates' begins by stating that four elements are most necessary for the constitution of a city. He says that these are weavers, farmers, shoemakers, and builders. He then proceeds, on the ground that these four are not self-sufficient, to add other parts—smiths, herdsmen to tend the necessary cattle, merchants, and retail dealers. These are the parts which form the whole complement of the 'first city' which he sketches—as though every city merely existed for the supply of necessities, and not rather to achieve the Good, and as though it needed the shoemaker as much as it needs the farmer.

1291ª19 'Socrates' gives no part to the defence force until the growth of the city's territory, and contact with that of its neighbours, gets them involved in war. Moreover, even among the four original parts—or whatever may be the number of the elements forming the association—there needs to be someone to dispense justice, and to determine what is just. If the mind is to be reckoned as more essentially a part of a living being than the body, parts of a similar order must equally be reckoned as more essentially parts of the city than those which serve its basic needs. By this we mean the military part, the part concerned in the legal organization of justice, and (we may also add) the part engaged in deliberation, which is a function that needs the gift of political understanding. Whether the people these functions belong to are separate groups or the same, makes no difference to the argument. It often falls to the same people both to serve in the army and to till the fields. It is clear therefore that if these people are to be considered parts of the city alongside those first mentioned, then the element, at any rate, which bears arms is an essential part of the city.

1291ª33 The seventh part* consists of those who serve the city with their property. We call these the 'wealthy'. The eighth part serves the public and undertakes duties connected with public office. No city can exist without rulers; and there must therefore be people capable of discharging the duties of office and rendering the city that service, permanently or in rotation. There remain the parts we mentioned above: the deliberative part and the part which determines what is just when there is a dispute. If these parts ought not only to exist in all cities, but to exist in a way that is fine and just, it is essential that some of the citizens possess excellence [of mind and character].

1291ᵇ2 The different capacities belonging to the other parts may, it is generally held, be shown by one and the same set of people. The same people, for example, may serve as soldiers, farmers, and craftsmen; the same people, again, may act both as a deliberative council and a judicial court. Goodness [of mind and character], too, is a quality to which all men pretend; and everybody thinks himself capable of filling most offices. But the same people cannot be both rich and poor. This explains why these two classes, the rich and the poor, are regarded as parts of the city in a special sense. Nor is this all. Since one of these classes is generally small, and the other large, they appear to have the status of opposed elements among the parts of the city. This is why the constitutions which are established are based on the predominance of one or other of these elements. It is also the reason why it is thought that there are only two constitutions, democracy and oligarchy.

1291ᵇ14 The fact that there are a number of constitutions, and the causes of that fact, have already been established. We may now go on to say that there are also a number of varieties of both democracy and oligarchy. This is already clear from what has been previously said.* The reason for this is that both the populace [the *dēmos*] and the notables vary in kind. So far as the populace is concerned, one sort is engaged in farming; a second is engaged in the arts and crafts; a third is the marketing sort, which is engaged in buying and selling; a fourth is the maritime sort, which in turn is partly naval, partly mercantile, partly employed on ferries, and partly engaged in fisheries. (We may note that there are many places where one of these subdivisions forms a considerable body; as the fishermen do at Tarentum and Byzantium, the naval crews at Athens, the merchant seamen in Aegina and Chios, and the ferrymen at Tenedos.) In addition to these there is the sort of populace that is composed of unskilled labourers and those whose means are too small to enable them to enjoy any leisure; finally there are those who are not of free birth on both sides; and there may also be other sorts of populace of similar character. The notables fall into different sorts according to wealth, birth, merit, culture, and other qualities of the same order.

1291^b30 The first variety of democracy is the one which is said to follow the principle of equality closest. In this variety the law declares equality to mean that the poor are to count no more than the rich: neither is to be sovereign and both are to be on a level. For if we hold, as some thinkers do, that liberty is chiefly to be found in democracy and that the same goes for equality, this condition is most fully realized when all share, as far as possible, on the same terms in the constitution. A constitution of this order is bound to be a democracy; for the people are the majority, and the decision of the majority is sovereign.

1291^b38 This is one variety of democracy; another is that in which offices are assigned on the basis of a property qualification, but the qualification is low; those who attain it have to be admitted to a share in office, and those who lose it are excluded. A third variety is one in which every citizen of unimpeachable descent can share in office, but the law is the final sovereign. A fourth variety is one in which everyone, provided only that he is a citizen, can share in office, but the law is still the final sovereign. A fifth variety of democracy is the same in other respects but the people, and not the law, is the final sovereign. This is what happens when popular decrees are sovereign instead of the law;* and that is a result which is brought about by leaders of the demagogue type.

1292ᵃ7 In cities which have a democracy under the law there are no demagogues; it is the best of the citizens who preside over affairs. Demagogues arise in cities where the laws are not sovereign. The people then becomes a monarchy—a single composite monarch made up of many members, with the many playing the sovereign, not as individuals, but collectively. It is not clear what Homer means when he says [*Iliad* II. 204] that 'it is not good to have the rule of many masters': whether he has in mind a situation of this kind, or one where there are many rulers who act as individuals. However, a democracy of this sort, since it has the character of a monarch and is not governed by law, sets about ruling in a monarchical way and grows despotic; flatterers are held in honour and it becomes analogous to the tyrannical form of monarchy. For this reason both show a similar temper; both behave like despots to the better citizens; the decrees of the one are like the edicts of the other; the popular leader in the one is the same as, or at any rate like, the flatterer in the other; and in either case the influence of favourites predominates—that of the flatterer in tyrannies, and that of the popular leader in democracies of this variety.

1292ᵃ24 It is popular leaders who, by referring all issues to the decision of the people, are responsible for substituting the sovereignty of decrees for that of the laws. The source of their great position is that the people are sovereign in all matters while they themselves, since the multitude follows their guidance, are sovereign over the people's decision. In addition opponents of those who occupy official positions argue 'The people ought to decide': the people accept that invitation readily; and thus all offices lose authority.

1292ᵃ28 Those who attack this kind of democracy saying that it is not a [true] constitution would appear to be right. Where the laws are not sovereign, there is no constitution. Law should be sovereign on every issue, and the officials and the constitution* should decide about details. It is thus clear that, even if democracy is a form of constitution, this particular system, under which everything is managed by decrees, is not really a democracy, in the proper sense of the word, for decrees can never be general in character.

The different forms of democracy may thus be defined in this way.

CHAPTER 5

We may similarly classify four varieties of oligarchy. But constitutions which are formally and legally democratic, or formally and legally oligarchical, may in their actual working be of a different character. Legal form and actual working are two different things, and this is particularly liable to be the case after a revolution.

1292ᵃ39 Among oligarchies one variety is that in which the holding of office depends on property qualifications, high enough to exclude the poor, even though they form the majority, but where it is possible for anyone who can acquire the appropriate amount of property to have a share in the constitution. A second variety is that in which the property qualification is high, and in which they themselves choose replacements for any vacancies.* (Where they choose replacements from the whole body of qualified people, the constitution may be held to incline in the direction of aristocracy: where they are made only from a limited section, it may be held to be oligarchical.) A third variety is when sons succeed to their fathers. The fourth variety has the same arrangement but, instead of the rule of law, the officials are the rulers. This variety is the equivalent, among oligarchies, of tyranny among monarchies or the variety of democracy last mentioned among democracies. An oligarchy of this sort is called a 'dynasty'.*

1292ᵇ11 These are the several varieties of oligarchy and democracy. It should be noted, however, that in actual life it often happens that constitutions which are not legally democratic are made to work democratically by the habits and training of the people. Conversely, there are other cases where the legal constitution inclines towards democracy, but is made by training and habits to work in a way which inclines more towards oligarchy. This happens particularly after a revolution. The citizens do not change their temper immediately; and in the first stages the triumphant party is content to leave things largely alone, without seeking to take any great advantage of its opponents. The result is that the old laws remain in force, even though those who are changing the constitution are actually in power.

CHAPTER 6

Classifying once more the varieties of democracy, we may distinguish an agricultural or 'peasant' form from three other forms—the main criterion being the degree of leisure which its social conditions enable a people to devote to politics. In the same way, and on the same general social–economic basis, we may also distinguish four varieties of oligarchy, according to the distribution of property and the relative degree of importance attached to its ownership.

1292^{b}21 What we have already said is sufficient of itself to prove that there must be all these varieties of democracy and oligarchy.* For it is necessary either that all the groups of the people previously mentioned share in the constitution, or that some share and others do not. When the farming class and the class with moderate means are the sovereign power in the constitution, they conduct the government under the rule of law. Because they are able to live by their work, but cannot enjoy any leisure, they make the law supreme, and confine the meetings of the assembly to a minimum; while the remaining citizens are allowed to participate in the constitution as soon as they attain the property qualification determined by the law. Thus all who have acquired this amount of property have a share.* In general it is characteristic of oligarchies that the opportunity to participate is not open to everyone. Of course, there cannot be opportunity for leisure where there is no income.

1292^{b}33 This is one form of democracy; and these are its causes. A second form is based on the criterion which comes logically next, the criterion of birth. Here all who possess irreproachable descent are legally allowed to participate, but do so in practice only when they are able to find the necessary leisure. In a democracy of this sort the laws are accordingly sovereign, simply because there are not the revenues. A third form is that in which all those of free birth are allowed to participate, but they do not actually do so for the reason already given; and here, once more, the rule of law is the necessary consequence. A fourth form of democracy is the one which comes chronologically last in the actual development of cities. Here, under the influence of two causes—the large increase in the population of cities, compared with their original size, and the accumulation of a considerable revenue—all alike participate, owing to the numerical superiority of the masses, and all alike join in political activity, owing to the facilities for leisure which are provided even for the poor by the system of state-payment [for attendance in the assembly and the courts]. A populace of this kind has more leisure than anyone else, for the need to attend to their private affairs does not constitute any hindrance, while it does for the well-to-do, with the result that the latter often absent themselves from the assembly and the courts. Under these conditions the mass of the poor become the sovereign power in the constitution, in place of the laws.

1293ª10 These then are the forms of democracy; we have discussed how many of them there are, their [various] characters, and the causes that necessitate them. Turning to the forms of oligarchy, we may rank first the form in which a majority of the citizens have property, but the amount they possess is moderate and not excessively large, while all who acquire this moderate amount are allowed to participate in the constitution. Since the mass of the people are thus included among those who have a share in the business of government, it follows that sovereignty, under this form, will be vested in the law, rather than in mere human beings. A moderate oligarchy of this type is totally different from the personal rule of a monarch; and as its members have neither so much property that they are able to enjoy a leisure free from all business cares, nor so little that they depend on the city for support, they will be bound to ask that the law should rule for them, and they will not claim to rule themselves.

1293ª21 The second form of oligarchy arises when the owners of property are fewer than they were in the first form, and the property they own is larger. Under these conditions they have greater power; and they expect to get more advantage. They themselves therefore select the members of the other classes who are to be admitted to the civic body; and not being powerful enough, as yet, to rule without law, they enact a law to this effect. A further advance is made, and a third form of oligarchy arises, when matters are strained still further and still fewer people become the owners of still larger properties. The members of the governing oligarchy now keep the offices entirely in their own hands; but they still act in terms of law—the law which provides that sons shall succeed to their fathers. The fourth and last form of oligarchy arises when matters are strained to the last degree, alike in the size of properties and the influence of connections. A 'dynasty' of the type which now emerges is closely akin to the personal rule of a monarch; and it is human beings, and not the law, who are now the sovereign. This fourth form of oligarchy corresponds to the last form of democracy.

CHAPTER 7

Having classified the varieties of democracy and oligarchy, we may now classify the varieties of the other forms. Aristocracy —apart from the true aristocracy which is really the government of the Best—has three varieties, which are all, more or less, of the nature of mixed constitutions, and thus approximate to 'constitutional government'.

1293ª35 There are still two forms of constitution left, besides democracy and oligarchy.* One of these is usually reckoned, and has indeed already been mentioned, as one of the four main forms of constitution, which are counted as being kingship, oligarchy, democracy, and the form called aristocracy.* There is, however, a fifth form, which is called by the generic name common to all the forms—for people call it a 'constitu-

tional government' [or polity]—but being of rare occurrence
it has not been noticed by the writers who attempt to classify
the different forms of constitution—in their [accounts of]
constitutions they usually limit themselves, like Plato, to an
enumeration of only four forms.* The name 'aristocracy'
should properly be applied to the form of constitution which
has already been treated in our first part. The only constitution which can with strict justice be called an aristocracy is
one where the members are not merely 'good' in relation to
some standard or other, but are absolutely the 'best' [aristoi]
so far as excellence [of mind and character] is concerned.
Only in such a constitution can the good man and the good
citizen be absolutely identified; in all others the 'good' are
only so relatively to the particular constitution. Nevertheless
there are some further forms of constitution, which differ
both from oligarchies and from the so-called 'constitutional
government' and are also called aristocracies. This is the case
when elections to office are based not only on wealth but also
on excellence. This type of constitution differs from both of
the forms [just mentioned]; and is called aristocracy. [This
usage is just, because] even in cities which do not make the
encouragement of excellence a matter of public policy, there
may still be found individuals who have a good reputation
and are seen as respectable people. Accordingly, a constitution
which pays regard to wealth, goodness, and [the will of] the
people, as the Carthaginian does, may be called an aristocratic
constitution; and the same may also be said of constitutions
such as the Spartan, which pay regard to excellence and to
[the will of] the people, and where there is thus a mixture of
the two factors, democracy and excellence. There are thus
these two forms of aristocracy in addition to the first or best
form of that constitution; and there is also a third form
presented by those varieties of the so-called 'constitutional
government' which incline particularly to oligarchy.*

CHAPTER 8

*We now come to the 'constitutional government' or polity and
its varieties. Generally, a 'constitutional government' is a mix-*

ture of democracy and oligarchy; but in common usage the term 'constitutional government' is reserved for mixtures which incline more towards democracy, and the mixtures which incline more towards oligarchy are called aristocracies. This leads us into a digression on the uses of the term 'aristocracy' and the reasons why that term—through being associated in men's minds partly with the rule of gentlefolk, and partly with the rule of law—is somewhat vaguely and widely applied. The proper use of terms depends on a recognition of the fact that there are three elements to be considered in a city, the free-born poor, the wealthy, and the men of merit, and not only the two elements of the poor and the wealthy. On this basis we shall confine the term 'aristocracy' to constitutions which recognize merit in some way or other; and we shall use the term 'constitutional government', and only that term, for constitutions which recognize only the two elements of free birth and wealth.

1293^b22 It remains for us to speak of the so-called 'constitutional government' [polity] and of tyranny.* Here we are associating 'constitutional government' with a perverted constitution, although it is not in itself a perversion, any more than are the forms of aristocracy which we have just mentioned. But, to tell the truth, all these constitutions really fall short of the best form of right constitution, and are therefore to be reckoned among perversions; and we may add that, as has already been mentioned in our first part, the perversions among which they are reckoned are those to which they themselves give rise.* It is reasonable to mention tyranny last, because we are engaged in an inquiry into constitutions; and tyranny, of all others, has least the character of a constitution. We have thus explained the reason for the order we propose to follow; and we must now proceed to treat of 'constitutional government'. Its character will emerge the more clearly now that we have already defined the nature of oligarchy and democracy.

1293^b33 'Constitutional government' may be described, in general terms, as a mixture of oligarchy and democracy; but in common usage the name is confined to those mixtures which incline to democracy, while those which incline more to oligarchy are called aristocracies, the reason being that culture and breeding are more associated with the wealthier classes. Furthermore, the wealthy are generally supposed to possess already the advantages for want of which wrongdoers fall into crime; and this is the reason why they are called 'gentlemen' or 'notables'.* Now as aristocracy aims at giving preeminence to the best, people tend to describe oligarchies too as cities governed by gentlemen.

1294ª1 It seems impossible that there should be good government* in a city which is ruled by the poorer sort, and not by the best of its citizens; and, conversely, it is equally impossible for a city which is not well governed to be an aristocracy. But good government does not consist in having a good set of laws which are not actually obeyed. We have to distinguish two senses of good government—one which means obedience to such laws as have been enacted and another which means that the laws obeyed have also been well enacted. (Obedience can also be paid to laws which have been enacted badly.) The latter sense admits, in its turn, of two subdivisions: people may render obedience to laws which are the best that are possible for them, or to ones which are absolutely the best.

1294ª9 Aristocracy is thought to consist primarily in the distribution of office according to merit: merit is the criterion of aristocracy, as wealth is the criterion of oligarchy, and free birth of democracy. The principle of the rule of majority-decision is present in all constitutions. Alike in oligarchies, in aristocracies, and in democracies, the decision of the majority of those who share in the constitution is final and sovereign. In most cities the form of government is called 'constitutional government', since the mixture attempted in it seeks only to blend the rich and the poor, or wealth and free birth, and the rich are regarded by common opinion as holding the position of gentlemen. But in reality there are three elements which may claim an equal share in the mixed form of constitution: free birth, wealth, and merit. (So-called 'nobility' of birth, which is sometimes reckoned a fourth, is only a corollary of the two latter, and simply consists in inherited wealth and merit.) Obviously, therefore, we ought always to use the term

'constitutional government' for a mixture of only two elements, where these elements are the rich and the poor; and we
ought to confine the name 'aristocracy' to a mixture of three,
which is really more of an aristocracy than any other form so
called, except the first and true form. We have now shown
that there are other forms of constitution besides monarchy,
democracy, and oligarchy; what the nature of these other
forms is; how aristocracies differ from one another, and
'constitutional governments' differ from aristocracy; and,
finally, that these are not far removed from one another.

CHAPTER 9

*We may now consider finally the various forms which 'constitu-
tional government' proper may take. There are three possible
ways of combining democracy and oligarchy. The first is to mix
democracy as a whole with oligarchy as a whole. The second is
to take the mean between the two. The third is to take some
elements from democracy and some from oligarchy. It is a good
criterion of a proper mixture of democracy and oligarchy that
you should be able to describe a mixed constitution indifferently
as either. Sparta may be cited as an example of such a mixture.*

1294ª30 We may now discuss, in continuation of our argument, how what is called 'constitutional government' [polity]
comes into existence by the side of democracy and oligarchy
and in what way it ought to be organized. In the course of
that discussion it will also be evident what are the distinguishing marks of democracy and oligarchy; for we have first to
ascertain the difference between these two forms, and then to
form a combination between them by taking, as it were, a
token* from each. There are three different principles on
which such a combination or mixture may be based. The first
is to take and use simultaneously both democratic and oligarchical laws. We may take as an example those about jury
service.* In oligarchies the rich are fined if they do not serve
on juries, and the poor receive no pay for serving. In democracies, on the other hand, the poor are given pay [for jury
service] while the rich are not fined [if they fail to serve on

juries]. To follow both of these practices is to adopt a common or middle term between them; and for that reason such a method is characteristic of a 'constitutional government', which is a mixture of the two constitutions. This is, accordingly, one of the possible ways of combination. A second is to take the mean, between the two different systems. Some cities, for example, require no property qualification at all, or only a very low qualification, for membership of the assembly: others require a high qualification. Here we cannot use both practices to provide a common term; we have, rather, to take the mean between the two. The third way is to combine elements from both, and to mix elements of the oligarchical rule with elements of the democratic. In the appointment of magistrates, for example, the use of the lot is regarded as democratic, and the use of the vote as oligarchical. Again, it is considered to be democratic that a property qualification should not be required, and oligarchical that it should be. Here, accordingly, the method appropriate to an aristocracy or a 'constitutional government' [polity] is to take one element from one form of constitution and another from the other—that is to say, to take from oligarchy the practice of choosing office-holders by voting, and from democracy the practice of requiring no property qualification.

1294^{b}13 This is the general method of mixture. The sign that a good mixture of democracy and oligarchy has been achieved is that the same constitution is described both as a democracy and as an oligarchy. Obviously the feelings of those who speak in this way are due to the excellence of the mixture. This happens in the case of the mean because each of the two extremes can be traced within it. The constitution of Sparta is an example. There are many who wish to describe it as a democracy, on the ground that its organization has a number of democratic features. The first such feature concerns the way in which the young are brought up: the children of the rich have the same upbringing as those of the poor, and the type of education they receive is one which the children of the poor could afford. The same policy is followed in the next stage of their lives and when they become adults. No difference is made between the rich and the poor: the provision of food at the common mess is the same for all, and the dress of the rich is such as any of the poor could also provide for themselves. Another such feature is the fact that, of the two most important offices, one is elected by the people and the other is open to them (that is, they elect the Council of Elders and are eligible for the Ephorate). On the other hand, some people describe the Spartan constitution as an oligarchy, on the ground that it has many oligarchical features. For example, office-holders are all appointed by vote, and none by lot, the power of inflicting the penalty of death or banishment rests in the hands of a few people, and there are many other similar features. A properly mixed constitution should look as if it contained both democratic and oligarchical elements—and as if it contained neither. It should owe its stability to its own intrinsic strength, and not to external support; and its intrinsic strength should be derived from the fact, not that a majority are in favour of its continuance* (that might well be the case even with a poor constitution), but rather that no section at all in the city would favour a change to a different constitution.

We have now described the way in which a 'constitutional government', and what are called aristocracies, ought to be organized.

CHAPTER 10

It now remains to consider, in conclusion, the varieties of tyranny. Two of its varieties, as we have already incidentally noticed (in Book III, ch. 14), are kingships rather than tyrannies: i.e. the kingships found among 'barbarians', and the dictatorships, or 'elective' tyrannies, of the early Greeks. The third variety is tyranny proper—the irresponsible rule of an autocrat acting for his own advantage.

1295ª1 It remains to speak of tyranny, not because there is much to be said about it; but because it, too, has been included in our classification of constitutions and must therefore have a place in our inquiry. Kingship has already been discussed in our first part,* where we dealt with kingship in the most usual sense of the term and inquired whether it was beneficial or prejudicial to cities, what sort of person should be king, from what source he should be drawn, and how he should be established in office. Two forms of tyranny were distinguished in the course of our discussion,* because, as both of them are forms of government conducted in obedience to law, the nature of their power in some sense overlaps with that of kingship. There are some among the barbarian peoples who have monarchs elected with absolute power and monarchs of the same type, termed *aisumnētai* [or dictators], once existed among the early Greeks. There are some differences between the two forms; but they may both be called royal, because they rule in accordance with law and over consenting subjects, and also tyrannical, because they rule as masters [over slaves], and follow their own judgement. But there is also a third form of tyranny, which seems to be a tyranny in the strictest sense of the term and is the converse of absolute kingship.* This form of tyranny is bound to exist where a single person rules over people who are all his peers or superiors, without any form of accountability, and with a view to his own advantage rather than that of his subjects. It is thus a form of rule exercised over unwilling subjects, for no free man will voluntarily endure such a system.

These, for the reasons that have just been given, are the forms of tyranny; and this is their number.

C: The Type of Constitution which is most Generally Practicable (Chapter 11)

CHAPTER 11

We are here concerned with the best constitution and way of life for the majority of people and cities. Goodness itself consists in a mean; and in any city the middle class is a mean between the rich and the poor. The middle class is free from the ambition of the rich and the pettiness of the poor: it is a natural link which helps to ensure political cohesion. We may thus conclude that a constitution based on this class, i.e. a 'constitutional government' or polity, is most likely to be generally beneficial. It will be free from faction, and will be likely to be stable. But 'constitutional governments' have been historically rare, partly for internal reasons, and partly because the policy of the Athenian and the Spartan empires has encouraged extremes in preference to a middle way. Still, the 'constitutional government' may serve as a standard in judging the merits of actual constitutions.

1295ª25 We have now to consider what is the best constitution and the best way of life for the majority of cities and the majority of mankind.* In doing so, we shall not employ a standard of excellence above the reach of ordinary people, or a standard of education requiring exceptional natural endowments and equipment, or the standard of a constitution which attains an ideal level. We shall be concerned only with the sort of life which most people are able to share and the sort of constitution which it is possible for most cities to enjoy. The 'aristocracies', so called, of which we have just been treating, either lie at one extreme, beyond the reach of most cities, or they approach so closely to what is called 'constitutional government' [polity] that the two can be considered as a single form.

1295ª34 The issues we have just raised can all be decided in the light of one body of fundamental principles. If we were right when, in the *Ethics*, we stated that the truly happy life is one of goodness lived in freedom from impediments and that goodness consists in a mean, it follows that the best way of life is one which consists in a mean, and a mean of the kind attainable by each individual.* Further, the same criteria should determine the goodness or badness of the city and that of the constitution;* for a constitution is the way in which a city lives. In all cities there are three parts: the very rich, the very poor, and the third class which forms the mean between these two.* Now, since it is admitted that moderation and the mean are always best it is clear that in the ownership of all gifts of fortune a middle condition will be the best. Those who are in this condition are the most ready to listen to reason. Those who are over-handsome, over-strong, over-noble, or over-wealthy, and, at the opposite extreme, those who are over-poor, over-weak, or utterly ignoble, find it hard

to follow the lead of reason. Those in the first class tend more
to arrogance and serious offences: those in the second tend
too much to criminality and petty offences; and most wrongdoing arises either from arrogance or criminality. [It is a
further characteristic of those in the middle that] they are
least prone either to refuse office or to seek it,* both of which
tendencies are dangerous to cities.

1295^b13 It must also be added that those who enjoy too
many advantages—strength, wealth, friends, and so forth—
are both unwilling to obey and ignorant how to obey. This
[defect] appears in them from the first, during childhood
and in home-life: nurtured in luxury, they never acquire a
habit of obedience, even in school. But those who suffer from
a lack of such things are far too mean and poor-spirited.
Thus there are those who are ignorant how to rule and only
know how to obey, as if they were slaves, and, on the other
hand, there are those who are ignorant how to obey any sort
of authority and only know how to rule as if they were
masters [of slaves]. The result is a city, not of freemen, but
only of slaves and masters: a state of envy on the one side and
of contempt on the other. Nothing could be further removed
from the spirit of friendship or of a political association. An
association depends on friendship—after all, people will not
even take a journey in common with their enemies. A city
aims at being, as far as possible, composed of equals and
peers, which is the condition of those in the middle, more
than any group. It follows that this kind of city is bound to
have the best constitution since it is composed of the elements
which, on our view, naturally go to make up a city. The
middle classes enjoy a greater security themselves than any
other class. They do not, like the poor, desire the goods of
others; nor do others desire their possessions, as the poor
desire those of the rich, and since they neither plot against
others, nor are plotted against themselves, they live free from
danger. Phocylides* was therefore right when he prayed:

> Many things are best for those in the middle;
> I want to be at the middle of the city.

1295^b34 It is clear from our argument, first, that the best

form of political association is one where power is vested in
the middle class, and, secondly, that good government is
attainable in those cities where there is a large middle
class—large enough, if possible, to be stronger than both of
the other classes, but at any rate large enough to be stronger
than either of them singly; for in that case its addition to
either will suffice to turn the scale, and will prevent either of
the opposing extremes from becoming dominant. It is therefore the greatest of blessings for a city that its members
should possess a moderate and adequate property. Where
some have great possessions, and others have nothing at all,
the result is either an extreme democracy or an unmixed
oligarchy; or it may even be, as a result of the excesses of
both sides, a tyranny. Tyranny grows out of the most immature type of democracy, or out of oligarchy, but much less
frequently out of constitutions of the middle order, or those
which approximate to them.* We shall explain the reason for
this later, when we come to treat of the ways in which
constitutions change.*

1296a7 Meanwhile, it is clear that the middle type of constitution is best. It is the one type free from faction; where the
middle class is large, there is less likelihood of faction and
dissension than in any other constitution. Large cities are
generally more free from faction just because they have a
large middle class. In small cities, on the other hand, it is easy
for the whole population to be divided into only two classes;
nothing is left in the middle, and all, or almost all, are either
poor or rich. Democracies are generally more secure and
more permanent than oligarchies because of their middle
class. This is more numerous, and has a larger share of
[offices and] honours, than it does in oligarchies. Where
democracies have no middle class, and the poor are greatly
superior in number, trouble ensues, and they are speedily
ruined. It must also be considered a proof of its value that the
best legislators have come from the middle class. Solon was
one, as he makes clear in his poems: Lycurgus was another
(after all he was not a king); and the same is true of Charondas
and most of the other legislators.*

1296a22 What has just been said also serves to explain why

most constitutions are either democratic or oligarchical. The middle class in these cities is often small; and the result is that as happens whenever one class—be it the owners of property or the masses—gains the advantage, it oversteps the mean, and draws the constitution in its own direction so that either a democracy or an oligarchy comes into being. In addition, factious disputes and struggles readily arise between the masses and the rich; and the side, whichever it is, that wins the day, instead of establishing a constitution based on the common interest and the principle of equality, exacts as the prize of victory a greater share in the constitution. It then institutes either a democracy or an oligarchy. Furthermore, those who have gained ascendancy in Greece* have paid an exclusive regard to their own types of constitution; one has instituted democracies in the cities [under its control], while the other has set up oligarchies: each has looked to its own advantage, and neither to that of the cities it controlled. These reasons explain why a middle or mixed type of constitution has never been established—or, at the most, has only been established on a few occasions and in a few cities. One man, and one only,* of all who have hitherto been in a position of ascendancy, has allowed himself to be persuaded to allow this sort of system to be established. And now it has also become the habit for cities not even to want a system of equality. Instead they seek to dominate or, if beaten, to submit.

1296^{b}2 It is clear, from these arguments, which is the best constitution, and what are the reasons why it is so and it is easy to see which of the others (given that we distinguish several varieties of democracy and several varieties of oligarchy) should be placed first, which second, and so on in turn, according as their quality is better or worse. The nearest to the best must always be better, and the one farthest removed from the mean must always be worse, unless we are judging on the basis of a particular assumption. I use the words 'on the basis of a particular assumption' because it often turns out that, although one sort of constitution may be preferable, there is nothing to prevent another sort from being better suited to certain peoples.

D: What Sort of Constitution is Desirable for What Sort of Civic Body? (Chapters 12–13)

CHAPTER 12

In constitutions quantity and quality have to be balanced against one another. When the weight of numbers among the poor more than balances the quality of the other elements, a democracy is desirable. When the quality of the other elements more than balances the weight of numbers among the poor, an oligarchy is desirable. When the middle class more than balances both the others—or even one of the others—a 'constitutional government' (polity) is desirable. Considerations on the value of such constitutional governments and on the folly of devices intended to trick men into believing that they have rights when they have none.

1296^{b}13 The next topic to consider, after what we have said, is: 'What particular constitution is suited to what particular people and what sort of constitution is suited to what sort of population?'* Now, we must first grasp a general principle which holds for all constitutions—that the part of a city which wishes a constitution to continue must be stronger than the part which does not.*

1296^{b}17 Quality and quantity both go to the making of every city.* By 'quality' we mean free birth, wealth, culture, and nobility of descent; by 'quantity' we mean superiority in numbers. Now quality may belong to one of the parts which compose a city, and quantity to another. For example, those who are low-born may be more numerous than the high-born, or the poor than the rich; but the superiority of one side in quantity may not be as great as their inferiority in quality. Quantity and quality must thus be placed in the balance against one another. Where the number of the poor exceeds the proportion just described,* there will naturally be a democracy; and the particular variety of democracy will depend on the form of superiority which is shown, in each particular case, by the mass of the people. If, for example, the farmers exceed the others in number, we shall have the first form of democracy: if the mechanics and day-labourers are most numerous, we shall have the 'extreme' form, and the same will be true of the intermediate forms between these.* Where the superiority of the rich and the notables in point of quality is greater than their inferiority in point of quantity, there will be an oligarchy; and the particular variety of oligarchy will similarly depend on the particular form of superiority which is shown by the oligarchical body.

1296^{b}34 A legislator should always make the members of the middle class partners in the constitution. If the laws he makes are oligarchical, he should direct his attention to the middle class, and, if they are democratic, he should seek to attach that same class to those laws. Where the middle class outweighs in numbers both the other classes, or even one of them, it is possible for a constitution to be permanent. There is no risk, in such a case, of the rich uniting with the poor to oppose the middle class: neither will ever be willing to be subject to the other; and if they try to find a constitution which is more in their common interest than this, they will fail to find one. Neither class would tolerate a system of ruling in turns: they have too little confidence in one another. A [neutral] arbitrator always gives the best ground for confidence; and the 'man in the middle' is such an arbitrator. The better, and the more equitable, the mixture in a constitution, the more durable it will be. An error often made by those who desire to establish aristocratic constitutions is that they not only give more power to the well-to-do, but they also deceive the people. Illusory benefits must always produce real evils in the long run; and the encroachments made by the rich are more destructive to a constitution than those of the people.

CHAPTER 13

A number of devices are used to deceive the masses and there are counter-devices used by democracies. But a better policy is to pursue a middle way, and to aim at an honest compromise rather than to use such devices. This policy may be illustrated from a study of the proper nature of a civic army and the methods by which it can be honestly recruited. This leads us to consider the effects of the nature and composition of the army on Greek constitutional development.

1297ᵃ14 The devices adopted in constitutions* for appearance's sake in order to fob off the masses are five in number. They relate to the assembly; to public offices; to the lawcourts; to the possession of arms; and to the practice of athletics. As regards the assembly, all alike are allowed to attend; but fines for non-attendance are imposed on the rich alone, or are imposed on them at a far higher rate. As regards public offices, those who possess a property qualification are not allowed to decline office on oath,* but the poor are allowed to do so. As regards the lawcourts, the rich are fined for non-attendance, but the poor may absent themselves with impunity; or, alternatively, the rich are heavily fined and the poor are only fined lightly—as happens under the laws of Charondas. In some cities a different device is adopted in regard to attendance at the assembly and the lawcourts. All who have registered themselves may attend but those who fail to attend the courts and the assembly after registration are heavily fined. Here the intention is to stop people registering, through fear of the fines they may thus incur, and ultimately to stop them from attending the courts and assembly as a result of their failure to register. Similar measures are also employed in regard to the possession of arms and the practice of athletics. The poor are allowed not to have any arms, and the rich are fined for not having them. The poor are not fined if they absent themselves from physical training while the rich are; and so while the latter are induced to attend by the sanction of a fine, the former are left free to abstain in the absence of any deterrent.

1297ᵃ34 The legal devices just mentioned are of an oligarchical character. Democracies have their counter-devices: they give the poor payment for attendance at the assembly and the lawcourts; but they do not fine the rich if they fail to attend. It is thus clear that if anyone wants to achieve a mixture that is just, he must combine elements drawn from both sides: in other words, he must provide pay for the one class and impose fines on the other. On this scheme all would share in a common constitution: otherwise, the constitution belongs to one side only. The constitution should draw only on those who have arms. But it is not possible to define the qualification [required for this purpose] absolutely, or to say that it must consist of a fixed amount in all cases. One must seek to discover the highest amount which ensures that those who have a part in the constitution are in a majority over those who do not and fix that as the qualification. Even when they have no part in the constitution, the poor are ready enough to keep quiet, provided that no one handles them violently or deprives them of any of their property. But this is not easy, since it is not always the case that the members of the citizen body are obliging. For example, in time of war, the poor are usually reluctant to serve, if they are given no subsistence allowance, and are thus left without any means. But if they are provided with subsistence they are willing enough to fight.

1297^{b}12 There are some places where the constitution includes not only those who are actually serving as soldiers, but also those who have previously served.* The Malian constitution, for example, included both, but only those who were actually serving could be elected to office. The first form of constitution which succeeded to monarchy in Greece was one composed of those who were soldiers. At first it consisted only of cavalry. (Military strength and superiority were then the prerogative of that arm; infantry is useless without a systematic organization; and as the experience and organization in such matters did not exist in early times, the strength of armies lay in their cavalry.) When, however, cities began to increase in size, and infantry forces acquired a greater degree of strength, more people were given a part in the constitution. For this reason, what we now call 'constitutional governments' [polities] were in the past called 'democracies'. It is not surprising that the old constitutions should have been oligarchical and, earlier still, monarchical. With their populations still small, cities had no large middle class; and the body of the people, still few in number, and poor in organization, were more ready to tolerate being ruled by others.

1297ᵇ28 We have now explained* why there is a variety of constitutions, and why there are forms other than those commonly enumerated. (Democracy is not one form; and the same is true of other constitutions.) We have also explained the differences between the various forms, and the causes of the character of each. In addition we have explained which generally speaking is the best constitution, and also, so far as other constitutions are concerned, which sort of constitution suits which sort of civic body.

E: The Methods of Establishing Constitutions, in Relation to the Three Powers—Deliberative, Executive, and Judicial (Chapters 14–16)

CHAPTER 14

There are three elements or powers in the government of a city. The first is the deliberative; and that may be arranged on three different systems. The first system assigns all matters of deliberation to all the citizens: it is the system of democracy, and it may be carried into effect in four different ways. The second system assigns all matters to some of the citizens: it is the system of oligarchy, and it may be carried into effect in three ways. A third system assigns some matters to all the citizens, and others to some of them: this system is characteristic of an aristocracy and of 'constitutional governments' (polities). How the deliberative element may best be arranged, as a matter of policy, in democracies and in oligarchies.

1297ᵇ35 Now, in treating of the topics that come next, we have to find a proper basis on which to treat them and then to speak both in general terms and separately for each constitution. There are three elements in every constitution* and a good legislator must bear these in mind when he considers what is suitable in each case. If all these elements are in good order, then the whole constitution will also be in good order and, to the extent that these elements differ, so constitutions will also differ. The first of the three is the deliberative element concerned with common affairs: the second is the element concerned with public offices (and here it has to be settled what these offices are to be, what matters they are to control, and how their occupants are to be appointed): the third is the judicial element.

1298ª3 The deliberative element is sovereign (1) on the issues of war and peace, and the making and breaking of alliances; (2) in the enacting of laws; (3) in cases where the penalty of death, exile, and confiscation is involved; and (4) in the appointment of officials and in calling them to account* [on the expiration of their office]. It is necessary either to give the decision on all these issues to all the citizens, or, to give the decision on all the issues to some of the citizens (by referring them all to one official body or to a combination of such bodies, or by referring different issues to different bodies), or, to give the decision on some issues to all the citizens, and on other issues to some of them.

1298ª9 The arrangement which assigns all issues to all the citizens, is characteristic of democracies, for this sort of equality is what the people desire. But there are a number of different ways in which all decisions might be given to them.* First, all the citizens may meet to deliberate in turn, and not in a single body. (This was the scheme in the constitution of Telecles of Miletus;* and there are other constitutions in which the different boards of officials meet together for deliberation in a single body, but the citizens join the boards in turns—drawn from the tribes and the smallest units [within the tribes]—until they have all been included in the cycle.) Under this scheme the citizens assemble only for the purpose of enacting laws, for dealing with constitutional matters, and for hearing the announcements of the magistrates. A second scheme is that all the citizens should meet to deliberate in a single body, but only for the purposes of appointing officials, enacting laws, dealing with issues of war and peace, and examining officials. The other matters will then be left for the deliberation of the officials assigned to deal with each branch; but appointment to such offices, whether this is done by election or by lot, will be open to all the citizens. A third scheme is that the citizens should meet for the purposes of appointing and examining the magistrates, and deliberating on issues of war and foreign policy, but other matters should be left to the control of boards of officials which, as far as possible, are kept elective—boards, that is, of the kind to which knowledgeable people must be appointed. A fourth scheme is that all should meet to deliberate on all issues, and boards of officials should have no power of giving a decision on any issue, but only that of making preliminary investigations. This is the way in which extreme democracy*—a form of democracy analogous, as we have suggested, to the form of oligarchy called 'dynasty' and to the tyrannical form of monarchy—is nowadays conducted.

1298ᵃ33 All these schemes are democratic, whereas the system under which some citizens deliberate about all matters is oligarchic. This system also has a number of different varieties. One of these is when the members of the deliberative body are eligible on the basis of a moderate property qualification, and are therefore fairly numerous. They do not make changes in matters where the law prohibits change, but obey its rules, and all who acquire property to the amount of the qualification required are allowed to share in deliberation. This is an oligarchy, but one of a constitutional kind by virtue of its moderation. When membership of the deliberative body belongs only to selected people—and not to all [those who acquire property to the amount of the qualification required] —but these people act in obedience to the rules of law, the system, like the previous one, is oligarchic in character.* When those who possess the power of deliberation recruit themselves by co-optation, or simply succeed by heredity, and have the power of overruling the laws, the arrangement is one which inevitably means oligarchy.

1298ᵇ5 A third system of arrangement is that some of the citizens should deliberate on some matters, but not on all. When, for example, all the citizens exercise the deliberative power in regard to war and peace and the examination of officials but the officials (who may be elected or chosen by lot) exercise that power alone on issues other than these, then the constitution is an aristocracy or a constitutional government [polity]. If some issues of deliberation are assigned to people appointed by election, and others to people chosen by lot (whether that is open to all or only to candidates selected in advance), or if all issues go to a mixed body with some elected and some chosen by lot, then the arrangement is in one way an aristocratic constitution and in another a constitutional government [polity].

1298ᵇ11 These are the different forms of the deliberative body which correspond to the different constitutions. Each constitution is organized on the basis of one or other of the systems we have distinguished.

1298ᵇ13 A democracy of the type which is nowadays held to be most fully democratic (by which I mean one where the people has sovereignty even over the laws) will find it advantageous, so far as improving the quality of the deliberative body is concerned, to apply to it the scheme which oligarchies apply to the lawcourts. Oligarchies impose a fine to ensure that those whom they want to have serving as jurymen do actually do so, whereas democrats provide pay for the poor. It is in the interest of a democracy to apply the same scheme to the assembly, since they will deliberate better when all deliberate together, the populace along with the notables and the notables along with the populace. It is also in the interest of a democracy that the members of the deliberative body should be either elected or chosen by lot with equal numbers from each section.* It is also in its interest, when the members of the populace greatly exceed in number those [notables] who have political experience, that payment for attendance at the assembly shouldn't be given to all the citizens, but only to so many as will balance the number of the notables or, alternatively, that the lot should be used to eliminate the excess of ordinary citizens over the notables.

1298ᵇ26 In oligarchies it is advantageous either to co-opt [to the deliberative body] some members drawn from the populace, or, alternatively, to erect an institution of the type which exists in some cities, under the name of 'preliminary councillors' or 'guardians of the laws', and then to allow the citizen body to deal only with such issues as have already been considered, in advance, by these people. On this plan the people at large will share in deliberation, but they will not be able to abrogate any rule of the constitution. Another line of

policy which is in the interest of oligarchies is that the people
should only be free to vote for measures which are identical,
or at any rate in agreement, with those submitted to them; or,
alternatively, that the people as a whole should be allowed to
give advice but that decisions should be taken by those who
hold office. In fact they should do the opposite of what
happens in [so-called] 'constitutional governments' [polities].
The people should be sovereign for the purpose of rejecting
proposals, but not for the purpose of passing them; and any
proposals which they pass should be referred back to those in
office. In constitutional governments [polities] they do the
reverse of this.* The few [i.e. the officials] are sovereign for
the purpose of rejecting proposals, but not for the purpose of
passing them; and any proposal which they pass is referred
back to the many.

This is our analysis of the deliberative or sovereign element
in the constitution.

CHAPTER 15

*The second element is the executive, or the system of offices.
Differences in the system of offices turn on four points—number; functions; tenure; and methods of appointment. Definition
of the term 'office'; and a general consideration of the number,
functions, and tenure of offices, with a discussion of the relation
of different offices [e.g. the* Boule *and the* Probouloi] *to different constitutions. The methods of appointment: the three main
factors to be considered, the choice of alternatives presented by
each, and the various modes of handling the choice of alternatives. The arrangements for the appointment of public officials
best suited to different constitutions: democracy, constitutional
government [polity], oligarchy, and aristocracy.*

1299ª3 The next subject, after those we have just considered,
is the classification of offices.* This element of the constitution
also admits of a number of different arrangements. These
concern: (1) the number of the offices; (2) the subjects with
which they deal; and (3) the length of the tenure of each. (In
some cities they are held for six months; in some for a shorter

period; in others for a year; and in others, again, for an even longer time. We have also to inquire whether offices should be held for life, or for a long term of years, or neither for life nor for a long term but only for shorter periods, and whether, in that case, the same person should hold office more than once, or each should be eligible only for a single term.) A further point to be considered (4) is the method of appointment. This raises three questions—who should be eligible; who should elect them; and how should the election be conducted?

1299ª12 We have first to distinguish the various methods which it is possible to apply to each of these questions, and then, on that basis, we have to determine the particular forms of office which suit a particular form of constitution. We are confronted, however, with an initial difficulty of definition. What is to be included under the term 'office'? A political association needs many positions of responsibility. We cannot, therefore, reckon as office-holders all those appointed to a position by election or lot. We can hardly include, for example, the priests of the public cults, whose position must be reckoned as something different from the political offices. The same is true of those responsible for producing plays, and of heralds. People are also elected to go on embassies. Political functions are those which involve the task of directing either the whole body of the citizens in some particular sphere of action (as, for example, a general directs them on a military expedition), or some section of the citizens (as happens, for example, with the inspectors of women and children). Others functions are economic; and here the officers elected to measure the corn for distribution (they are to be found in many cities) may be cited as an example. Still other functions are subordinate in character, involving duties which, in wealthy cities, the public slaves are set to discharge. The title of 'office' should, on the whole, be reserved for those which are charged with the duty, in some given field, of deliberating, deciding, and giving instructions, particularly the last since giving instructions is the special mark of one who holds office. But these matters make no difference in practice. No decision has been reached about what is merely a dispute over terminology, though it offers an opportunity for speculative inquiry.

1299ᵃ31 In dealing with all constitutions, but especially in dealing with those of small cities, it is a matter of more importance to distinguish what sort and number of offices are necessary to the city's existence, and what sort are of value—even if they are not actually necessary—in ensuring a good constitution. In large cities it is both possible and proper that a separate office should be allotted to each separate function. Because there are a great many citizens it is possible for a large number of people to enter office: it permits some of the offices to be held only once in a lifetime, and others (though held more than once) to be held again only after a long interval; and each function gets better attention when it is the only one undertaken, and not one among a number of others.

1299ᵇ1 In small cities, on the other hand, a large number of functions have to be accumulated in the hands of but a few people. The small numbers of the citizens makes it difficult for many people to be in office together; and if there were, who would be their successors? It is true that small cities sometimes need the same offices, and the same laws, as large ones. But it is also true that large cities have frequent need of their offices, while small cities need theirs only at long intervals. There is thus no reason why small cities should not impose a number of duties simultaneously, since they will not interfere with one another; and anyhow it is necessary, where the population is small, to make official positions like spithooks* [with many functions].

1299ᵇ10 If we can say how many offices must necessarily exist in every city and how many are valuable, though not necessary—someone who knows this will easily be able to combine together those offices which ought to be combined into one office. In addition, we must not omit to consider which matters need the attention of different offices in different places,* and which ought to be controlled by one office with overall responsibility. The maintenance of order is an example: should there be one person to keep order in the market-place and another somewhere else, or should there be a single person to keep order everywhere. We must consider, too, whether functions should be allocated according to the subject to be handled, or according to the sorts of people concerned: for example, should there be one officer for the whole subject of the maintenance of order, or a separate officer for children and another for women?

1299^b20 We have also to take into account the difference of constitutions. Does the scheme of offices vary from one constitution to another, or is it the same for all? Do the same offices form the government in democracy, oligarchy, aristocracy, and monarchy—with the one difference that those who hold office do not come from the same, or a similar, social class, but are drawn from a different class in each different constitution (in aristocracies, for example, from the cultured class; in oligarchies from the wealthy; and in democracies from the free-born)? Or do some kinds of office exist as a result of these very differences, so that in some cases the same offices are suitable, but in other cases they are bound to differ? It may be appropriate, for example, that in some constitutions offices should be powerful while in others the same offices should be weak.

1299^b30 Some offices, it is true, are altogether peculiar to one type of constitution. A preliminary council [the *probouloi*] is an example. Such a body is not democratic, whereas the ordinary council, or *boulē*, is democratic.* There ought, indeed, to be some sort of body charged with the duty of preliminary deliberation on behalf of the people; otherwise the people will not be able to attend to their ordinary business. But if such a body is small in size, it becomes an oligarchical institution; the preliminary councillors must be few in number, and must therefore be oligarchical. Where both kinds of office are to be found, the preliminary councillors are a check on the councillors; they are an oligarchical element, and the council is democratic. Yet even the authority of the council itself is subverted in democracies of the extreme type, where the people assembles in person to transact the whole business of the city. This usually happens when there is a high rate of pay to those who attend the assembly. People then have the leisure to hold frequent meetings and decide all issues themselves.

1300ª4 Officers for the maintenance of order among women and children, and other officials charged with similar duties of supervision, are aristocratic in character, not democratic (how could one prevent the wives of the poor from going out?); nor are they oligarchic, since the wives of a ruling oligarchy live a life of luxury.

1300ª8 Enough has been said, for the present, about these matters: and we must now attempt to give a full account of the appointment of public officials.* The differences here are connected with three factors, which produce, in combination, all the possible modes. The three factors are:

(1) those appointing;

(2) those eligible for appointment;

(3) the method of appointment.

Each of these three factors involves two alternatives. Thus:

(1) those appointing may be all the citizens, or only a section;

(2) those eligible for appointment may be all the citizens, or only a section—a section determined by a property qualification, or birth or merit or some similar characteristic (in Megara, for example, only those who had returned from exile together and fought together against the populace were eligible for appointment);

(3) The method of appointment may be election, or it may be lot.

In addition we may also have a conjunction of both alternatives, with the result that:

(1) for some offices those appointing may be all the citizens, and for others only a section;

(2) for some offices those eligible may be all the citizens, and for others only a section;

(3) for some offices the method of appointment may be election, and for others it may be lot.

1300ª22 Four modes are possible in handling each of the choices of alternatives [given the alternative which consists in all the citizens appointing];

(1) all may appoint from all by election;

(2) all may appoint from all by lot; or
(3) all may appoint from a section by election;
(4) all may appoint from a section by lot.

Similarly if a section of the citizens appoints:

(1) they may appoint from all by election;
(2) they may appoint from all by lot;
(3) they may appoint from a section by election;
(4) they may appoint from a section by lot.

1300ª26 If they appoint from all, they may do so either successively from sections—such as tribes and wards and clans—until all have eventually been included, or continuously from all, appointing to some offices in one of these ways and to others in another. By this I mean that they may appoint to some offices 'from all by election' and to others 'from all by lot'. There are thus twelve modes in all, if we omit the other two conjunctions.

1300ª31 Of these methods of making appointments, two are democratic:*

(a) all appoint from all either by election or lot;
(b) all appoint from all both by election and lot, using the one method for some offices and the other for others.

A method characteristic of constitutional government [polity] is:

all should appoint but not at the same time. They may either make these appointments from all using election or lot or both these methods, or they may appoint from all to some of the offices, but appoint from a section to others. By 'using both these methods' I mean appointing to some offices by lot and to some by election.*

1300ᵇ1 An arrangement which suits an oligarchy is:

a section appoints from a section—by election, or lot (it does not matter that this does not actually occur), or a mixture of both.

An arrangement which suits an aristocracy is:

a section appoints from all, or all appoint from a section, by the method of election.*

1300ᵇ5 Such is the number of the methods which may be used in connection with [the appointment of officials], and such is their distribution among different types of constitution. As we consider the different kinds of offices and their functions, it will become clear which method is suitable to each office and how the appointments ought to be made. By the function of an office I mean functions such as control of the revenue or control of the defence force. The functions of offices differ in kind, for example, between that of a general and that of an officer charged with the superintendence of contracts made in the market.

CHAPTER 16

The third element is the judicial element, or the system of lawcourts (dikastēria). An enumeration of eight different types of lawcourts, and a consideration of the three main ways in which courts may be constituted. The types of constitution to which these different ways are best suited.

1300ᵇ13 Of the three elements in the constitution, the judicial alone remains to be considered. We must follow the same plan in determining the different forms which this may take. The ways in which lawcourts differ are: (1) in their membership; (2) in the subjects with which they deal; and (3) the manner of appointing the members. By 'their membership' I mean whether the courts are to be constituted from all the citizens or from a section; by 'the subjects with which they deal' I mean how many kinds of courts there should be; by 'the manner of appointment' I mean whether appointment should be by vote or by lot.

1300ᵇ17 We must first determine how many kinds of courts there are. These may be said to be eight. There is one for the review of the conduct of public officials; a second for dealing with any offence against any point of public interest; a third for cases which bear on the constitution; a fourth (which includes in its scope both officials and private persons) for cases of disputes about the amount of fines; a fifth for contracts between private persons, where a considerable amount is involved; in addition there are those which deal with homicide and with cases concerning aliens. [It should be noted that] the court which deals with homicide has a number of divisions, which may either be combined under one set of judges or come before different sets. One of these divisions is concerned with deliberate homicide; a second with involuntary homicide; a third with homicides where the act is admitted, but its justification is disputed; and a fourth for actions brought, upon their return, against those who have previously been exiled for involuntary homicide. An example of the last division is the court at Athens which is known as the 'Court at Phreatto', but cases of this sort are always infrequent, even in large cities. The court for cases of aliens has two divisions: one for cases between alien and alien, and one for cases between alien and citizen. Finally, there is an eighth court for contracts which only involve a small sum—a matter of a drachma, or five drachmas, or some sum a little larger. Here a decision has to be given, but there is no need for a large court to give it.

1300ᵇ35 We need not go further into these courts and those dealing with homicide and aliens. We must speak of those which have a political character, as they deal with issues which, unless properly handled, create factional divisions and constitutional disturbance. Here we must have one or other of the following systems. (1) All the citizens [are eligible to] judge on all the matters we have distinguished, and are chosen for the purpose either (a) by vote or (b) by lot. (2) All the citizens [are eligible to] judge on all these matters; but for some of them the courts are appointed by election, and for others by lot. (3) [All citizens are eligible to judge, but] only on part of these matters; and the courts concerned with that part should all be similarly recruited, partly by vote and partly by lot. This means four different systems [if we count the two alternatives under (1) as separate systems]. There will be an equal number of systems if a sectional method be followed [i.e. if it is only a section of the citizens, and not all,

who are eligible to sit in the courts]. In that case we may have
(1) judges drawn from a section by vote to judge on all
matters; or (2) judges drawn from a section by lot to judge on
all matters; or (3) judges drawn from a section by vote for
some matters and by lot for others; or (4) some courts,
dealing with the same matters, recruited partly by vote and
partly by lot. It will be seen that these last four systems, as
has just been said, correspond exactly to the previous four. In
addition, we may have a conjunction of both sorts of systems;
for example, we may have some courts with members drawn
from the whole civic body, others, again, with a mixed membership (the same court being, in that case, composed of members
drawn from the whole and of members drawn from a section);
and again we may have the members appointed either by
vote, or by lot, or by a mixture of both.

1301ª10 This gives us a complete list of all the possible
systems on which courts can be constituted. The first sort of
system, in which the membership of the courts is drawn from
all, and the courts decide on all matters, is democratic. The
second sort, in which the membership is drawn from a section,
and the courts decide on all matters, is oligarchical. The third
sort, [which is a conjunction of the first two, and] in which
the membership of some courts is drawn from all, and that of
others from a section, is characteristic of aristocracies and
'constitutional governments' [polities].

BOOK V
CAUSES OF FACTIONAL CONFLICT
AND CONSTITUTIONAL CHANGE

A: The General Causes of Factional Conflict and Change in all Types of Constitution (Chapters 1–4)

CHAPTER 1

Different interpretations of justice and equality lead to the making of different claims by different parties; and the conflict of these claims causes political struggles and changes. The different forms which programmes of political change may take either imply the overthrow of the existing constitution, or involve some sort of modification. Whatever the difference of form may be, the general motive is always a passion for some conception of equality, which is held to be involved in the very idea of justice. There are two main conceptions of equality, the numerical and the proportionate: democracy is based on the one, and oligarchy on the other. Neither conception should be exclusively followed; but, of the two, the democratic is the safer, and the less likely to provoke factional conflict.

1301ª19 We have now discussed practically all the topics stated in our programme apart from the following.* What are the general causes which produce changes in constitutions, and what is the number and nature of these causes? In what particular ways is each constitution liable to degenerate—i.e. what forms of constitution are most likely to change to what? In addition we must ask which policies are likely to ensure the stability of constitutions, collectively and individually, and what means may best be employed to secure each particular constitution. We must now consider these questions.

1301ª25 We must first assume, as a basis of our argument, that the reason why there is a variety of different constitutions is the fact, already mentioned,* that while everybody is agreed about justice, and the principle of proportionate equality, people fail to achieve it in practice. Democracy arose out of an opinion that those who were equal in any one respect were equal absolutely, and in all respects. (People are prone to think that the fact of their all being equally free-born means that they are all absolutely equal.) Oligarchy similarly arose from an opinion that those who were unequal in some one respect were altogether unequal. (Those who are superior in point of wealth readily regard themselves as absolutely superior.) Thus those on one side claim an equal share in everything, on the ground of their equality, while those on the other press for a greater share, on the ground that they are unequal, since to be greater is to be unequal. Both sides are based on a sort of justice; but they both fall short of absolute justice. For this reason each side engages in factional conflict* if it does not enjoy a share in the constitution in keeping with the conception of justice it happens to entertain. Those who are pre-eminent in merit would be the most justified in forming factions (though they are the last to make the attempt); for they, and they only, can reasonably be regarded as enjoying an absolute superiority. There are also those who possess an advantage of birth and regard themselves as entitled to more than an equal share on the ground of this advantage, for those whose ancestors had merit and wealth are commonly regarded as 'well-born'.

1301ᵇ4 These, in a general sense, are the sources and springs of faction, and the reasons why people engage in faction-fighting. These considerations will also explain the two different ways in which constitutional changes may happen. (1) Sometimes factions are directed against the existing constitution, and are intended to change it from its established form—to turn democracy into oligarchy, or oligarchy into democracy; or, again, to turn democracy and oligarchy into 'constitutional government' [polity] and aristocracy, or, conversely, these latter [constitutions] into the former. (2) Sometimes, however, they are not directed against the existing constitution. Those forming a faction may choose to maintain the system of government—an oligarchy, for example, or a monarchy—as it stands; but they desire to get the administration into their own hands. Or they may wish to make the constitution more pronounced or more moderate. They may wish, for example, to make an oligarchy more, or less, oligarchical. They may wish to make a democracy more, or less, democratic. They may similarly seek to tighten, or loosen, any of the other forms of constitution. They may also direct their efforts towards changing only one part of the constitution. They may wish, for example, to erect, or to abolish, some particular office. Some writers state that Lysander attempted to abolish the kingship at Sparta, and King Pausanias* the 'ephoralty'. At Epidamnus, again, there was a partial change of the constitution; and a council was substituted for the tribal leaders. But even at the present time those holding office are the only members of the civic body who are obliged to attend the public assembly, when the appointment to an office is being put to the vote; and the existence of a supreme official [called an *archōn*] was another oligarchical feature.

1301ᵇ26 Factional conflict is always the result of inequality except, that is, where unequals are treated in proportion to the inequality existing between them. An hereditary monarchy only involves inequality when it exists among equals. It is the passion for equality which is thus at the root of faction. But equality is of two sorts. One sort is numerical equality: the other sort is equality proportionate to desert.* 'Numerical equality' means being treated equally, or identically, in the number and volume of things which you get; 'equality proportionate to desert' means being treated on the basis of equality of ratios. To give an example—numerically, the excess of 3 over 2 is equal to the excess of 2 over 1; but proportionally the excess of 4 over 2 is equal to the excess of 2 over 1, 2 being the same fraction of 4 as 1 is of 2. Now people are ready to agree to the principle that absolute justice consists in proportion to desert; but, as we noted above, they differ [in practice]. Some consider that if they are equal in one respect, they are equal in all: others consider that if they are superior in one respect, they may claim superiority in everything.

1301ᵇ39 For this reason two types of constitution—democ-

racy and oligarchy—are particularly prevalent. Good birth
and merit are found in few people; but the qualities on which
democracy and oligarchy are based are found in a much
larger number. In no city would you find as many as a
hundred people of good birth and merit: there are many in
which you would find that number of wealthy people. But a
system based absolutely, and at all points, on either kind of
equality is a poor sort of thing. The facts are evidence enough:
no constitution of this sort ever endures. The reason is simple.
When one begins with an initial error, it is inevitable that one
should end badly. The right course is to use the principle of
numerical equality in some cases, and that of equality proportionate to desert in others. Yet it must be admitted that
democracy is a form of government which is safer, and less
vexed by faction, than oligarchy. Oligarchies are prone to two
sorts of faction-fighting—among themselves, and between
themselves and the populace. In democracies there is only
faction-fighting against the oligarchs; and there are no internal
dissensions—at any rate none worth mentioning—which
divide the populace against itself. Furthermore, the form of
constitution based on the middle [group of citizens],* which is
the most stable of all the forms with which we are here
concerned, is nearer to democracy than to oligarchy.

CHAPTER 2

*In dealing with the general origins and causes of factional
conflict, we may do so under three heads: (1) psychological
motives; (2) the objects in view; and (3) the initial occasions,
which in turn are of two main kinds.*

1302ª16 Since we have to consider the various reasons
which lead to the rise of factions and changes in constitutions,
we had better begin with a general view of their origins and
causes. They may be said to be three in number; and we must
begin by giving a brief outline of each of them separately. We
have to investigate (1) the state of mind which leads to
faction; (2) the objects which are at stake; and (3) the causes
which give rise to political disturbance and factional disputes.

1302^{a}22 The principle and general cause of an attitude of mind which disposes people towards change is the cause of which we have just spoken. There are some who engage in factional disputes because their minds are filled by a passion for equality, which arises from their thinking that they have less in spite of being the equals of those who have more. There are others who do it because their minds are filled with a passion for inequality (i.e. superiority), which arises from their conceiving that they get no advantage over others (but only an equal amount, or even a smaller amount) although they are really more than equal to others. (Either of these passions may have some justification; and either may be without any.) Thus inferiors form factions in order to be equals, and equals in order to be superiors.

1302^{a}31 This is the state of mind which creates faction. The objects which are at stake are profit and honour and their opposites, for people start factional disputes in cities with the object of avoiding some disgrace, or a fine, on themselves or on their friends.

1302^{a}34 The causes and origins of disturbances—i.e. the factors which encourage the attitude of mind and lead to the pursuit of the objects which have just been mentioned—may be counted, from one point of view, as seven, but from another as more than that number.* Two of these causes [profit and honour] are identical with two of the objects which have just been mentioned; but act in a different way. People get angry on account of profit and honour, not because they want to get them themselves: but because they see other people getting a larger share—some justly and some unjustly—than they themselves get. Other causes are: arrogant behaviour,* fear, superiority, contempt, or a disproportionate increase. Others, which act in a different way, are election intrigues; wilful negligence; trifling changes; and dissimilarity.

CHAPTER 3

A study of the way in which the causes of factional conflict may operate. (1) There is the kind of cause which operates intrinsically, or from reasons inherent in its own nature: of this there are seven varieties—arrogant behaviour; the desire of profit; the point of honour; the presence of some sort of superiority; fear; contempt; and the disproportionate increase of one or other element in the city. (2) There is the kind of cause which operates accidentally, and not from reasons inherent in its own nature: of this there are four varieties—election intrigues; wilful neglect; the overlooking of trifling changes; and the dissimilarity of elements in the composition of the city.

1302^b5 Among these causes it is fairly clear what influence arrogant behaviour and profit-making may exert, and in what ways they may cause factions to arise. When those who are in office behave arrogantly, and seek their personal advantage, people start factional intrigues against each other and against the constitution which permits this to happen. (Personal advantage is sometimes acquired at the expense of individuals; sometimes at that of the public.) It is also clear what influence honour exerts and how it may be a cause of faction. People form factions when they suffer dishonour themselves, and when they see others honoured. Both of these things may be unjustifiable, if the honour given or the dishonour inflicted is undeserved; both may be justifiable if they are deserved. Superiority becomes a cause of faction when someone, or some group, is in a position of strength that is too great for the city or for the strength of the general body of citizens. Such a position usually results in a monarchy, or in a 'dynastic' oligarchy.* It is for this reason that, in a number of cities, a policy of ostracism* comes to be used. Argos and Athens are examples. But it is a better policy to begin by ensuring that there shall be no such people of outstanding eminence, than first to allow them to arise and then to attempt a remedy afterwards.

1302^b21 Fear is a cause which leads to factional intrigue on the part of wrongdoers, who are afraid of punishment, and on the part of those expecting to suffer wrong, who are anxious to anticipate what they expect. At Rhodes, for example, the notables were moved to conspire against the people by alarm at the lawsuits with which they were being threatened.* Contempt is another cause of faction and insurrection. This happens in oligarchies, when those who have no share in the constitution are more numerous and consequently think themselves stronger, and in democracies, when the wealthy despise the disorder and anarchy which they see prevalent. For example, at Thebes, after the battle of Oenophyta* democracy was ruined by misgovernment. The same happened at Megara, as the result of a defeat which was caused by disorder and anarchy, at Syracuse, before Gelon became tyrant,* and at Rhodes, in the period before the rising of the notables just mentioned.

1302^{b}33 Disproportionate increase is also a cause which leads to constitutional changes. [Here we may compare the city with a body.] A body is composed of parts, and must grow proportionately if symmetry is to be maintained. Otherwise it perishes (as it will if the foot be two yards long and the rest of the body twelve inches);* or again it may sometimes change into the form of some other animal, as it will if a disproportionate increase means a change of quality as well as quantity. The same is true of a city. It, too, is composed of parts; and one of the parts may often grow imperceptibly out of proportion. The number of the poor, for example, may become disproportionate in democracies and in 'constitutional governments' [polities]. Sometimes this may be the result of accident. At Tarentum, for example, a constitutional government was turned into a democracy in consequence of the defeat and death of a number of the notables at the hands of the neighbouring Iapygian tribe, just after the Persian wars. At Argos the destruction of the 'men of the Seventh', by the Spartan king Cleomenes,* made it necessary to admit some of the serfs into the civic body. At Athens the reverses suffered on land, during the war against Sparta, depleted the numbers of the notables, under the system of compulsory service for all registered citizens. Similar changes may also happen for the same reason in democracies—though this is less likely. If the rich become more numerous, or if properties increase, democracies turn into oligarchies and 'dynasties' [or family cliques].

1303ª13 Election intrigues may lead to constitutional changes without causing factional conflict. At Heraea, for example, the fact that the results of elections were determined by intrigues led to the use of the lot being substituted for the vote. Wilful negligence, again, may be a cause; and those who are not loyal to the constitution may be allowed to find their way into the highest of the offices. Oreus, in Euboea, may serve as an example: its oligarchy was overthrown when Heracleodorus was allowed to become a magistrate, and he proceeded to turn it into a constitutional government [polity] or rather a democracy. Another cause is trifling changes. What I mean by 'trifling changes' is that a great change of the whole system of institutions may come about unperceived if small changes are overlooked. In Ambracia, for example, the property qualification for office—small to begin with—was finally allowed to disappear, on the assumption that there was little or no difference between having a small qualification and having none at all. Heterogeneity of stocks may lead to faction—at any rate until they have had time to assimilate. A city cannot be constituted from any chance collection of people, or in any chance period of time. Most of the cities which have admitted others as settlers, either at the time of their foundation or later, have been troubled by faction. For example, the Achaeans joined with settlers from Troezen in founding Sybaris, but expelled them when their own numbers increased; and this involved their city in a curse. At Thurii the Sybarites quarrelled with the other settlers who had joined them in its colonization; they demanded special privileges, on the ground that they were the owners of the territory, and were driven out of the colony. At Byzantium the later settlers were detected in a conspiracy against the original colonists, and were expelled by force; and a similar expulsion befell the exiles from Chios who were admitted to Antissa by the original colonists. At Zancle, on the other hand, the original colonists were themselves expelled by the Samians whom they admitted. At Apollonia, on the Black Sea, factional conflict was caused by the introduction of new settlers; at Syracuse the conferring of civic rights on aliens and mercenaries, at the end of the period of the tyrants, led to sedition and civil war; and at Amphipolis the original citizens, after admitting Chalcidian colonists, were nearly all expelled by the colonists they had admitted.

1303ᵇ3 (In oligarchies, as has already been noted, the ground which the masses take in justification of forming factions is that they are unjustly treated in being denied equal rights although they are actually equal. In democracies the ground taken by the notables is the injustice of their having only equal rights although they are actually superior.)

1303ᵇ7 Factional disputes also occur because of territory. This happens in cities with a territory not naturally adapted to political unity. At Clazomenae the inhabitants of the suburb of Chytrus were at discord with the inhabitants of the island; and there was a similar discord between Colophon and its seaport Notium. At Athens, again, the people are not alike; the inhabitants of the port of Peiraeus are more democratic than those of the city of Athens. Just as in war, the dividing line of a ditch, however small it may be, makes a regiment scatter in crossing, so, it seems, that every difference is apt to create a division. The greatest division is that between good and bad character; then there is the division between wealth and poverty; and there are also other divisions, some greater and some smaller, arising from other differences. Among these last we may count the division just mentioned.*

CHAPTER 4

The causes of factional conflict may be small, but the issues are great: small and personal matters may lead to large and general consequences. It may be added that revolutionary changes may also be due (1) to the growth in reputation and power of some office, or some part of the city, and (2) to an even balance of parties, resulting in a deadlock. It may also be added that force and fraud both play their part in the conduct of revolutions.

1303ᵇ17 But, though factional disputes are caused by little things, they are not about little things. The issues involved are large. Even petty quarrels attain great importance when they involve those in positions of authority. There is an example in the history of Syracuse, where a constitutional change arose as a result of two young men, who were both in office, quarrelling about a love affair. In the absence of one of the two, the other (in spite of being his colleague) seduced the affections of his friend; and the injured man, in his anger, retaliated by seducing his colleague's wife. Thereupon they drew the whole civic body into their quarrel and divided it into factions. The moral is that precautions ought to be taken at the very beginning of such disputes, and quarrels which involve those in positions of leadership and power ought to be settled at once. The error is made at the beginning; and since, as the proverb goes, 'The beginning is half of the job', a small mistake at the beginning is equal to all the mistakes made in the rest of the business. Generally speaking, disputes among the notables involve the whole city in their consequences. This may be seen from the events at Hestiaea after the Persian wars. Two brothers quarrelled about the division of an inheritance: the poorer of the two, on the ground that the other refused to declare the estate, or to disclose the amount of a treasure which their father had found, enlisted the popular party in his cause; the other, possessing a large estate, secured the aid of the wealthy. At Delphi, again, the beginning of all the later discords was a dispute which arose from a marriage. The bridegroom, interpreting as an evil omen some accident that had happened at the bride's home, on his coming to escort her away, departed without her; the bride's relations, considering themselves insulted, retaliated by putting some of the sacred treasures among his offerings during a sacrifice and then killing him for this supposed sacrilege. Similarly, at Mytilene, a dispute about the marriage of heiresses was the beginning of a host of troubles—including the war with Athens, in the course of which Paches captured the city.* Timophanes, one of the wealthier citizens, had left two daughters. A certain Dexander, who was defeated in his attempt to have them married to his sons, thereupon stirred up factional conflict, and incited the Athenians, for whom he acted as consul, to interfere. In Phocis, again, another dispute about the marriage of an heiress, in which Mnaseas the father of Mnason and Euthycrates the father of Onomarchus were concerned, was the beginning of the Sacred War in which all Phocis came to be involved. A marriage affair was also the cause of a constitutional change at Epidamnus. Someone had betrothed his daughter to another man, and was afterwards fined by the latter's father, who had entered into public office; whereupon, regarding himself as insulted, he allied himself with the disfranchised classes.

1304^{a}17 Constitutions may also be changed—in the direction of oligarchy, or democracy, or 'constitutional government' [polity]—as a result of the growth in the reputation or power of one of the public offices, or of some other element in the city. The Council of the Areopagus at Athens, for example, gained in reputation during the Persian War; and seemed for a time to be tightening the constitution. Then the mob, who served in the navy, were responsible for the victory of Salamis, and secured for Athens an empire which depended on naval power; and the effect of this was to strengthen once more the cause of democracy.* The notables of Argos, after gaining in reputation by their conduct in the battle against the Spartans at Mantinea,* attempted to suppress the democracy: at Syracuse, on the other hand, the people were responsible for the victory won in the war against Athens,* and they proceeded to turn the existing 'constitutional government' [polity] into a democracy. At Chalcis the people united with the notables to remove the tyrant Phoxus, and by the part they played immediately got a firm hold on the constitution. At Ambracia too, in much the same way, the people joined with those who had conspired against Periander in expelling the tyrant, and then changed the constitution in their own favour. Generally one should always remember, that any person or body which adds new power to the city—an individual, a board of public officials, a tribe, or generally any section or group, whatever it may be—will tend to produce faction; and the faction will either be started by people who envy the honours of those who have won success, or be due to the refusal of the latter to remain on a footing of equality when they feel themselves superior.

1304ᵃ38 Revolutions also occur when the elements in the city which are usually regarded as antagonists—for example, the rich and the common people—are equally balanced, with little or nothing of a middle class; for where either side has a clear preponderance, the other will be unwilling to risk a struggle with the side which is obviously the stronger. This is the reason why people outstanding for the excellence [of mind or character] do not, as a rule, attempt to stir up faction; they are only a few against many.

1304ᵇ5 Such, on a general view, are the springs and causes of faction and change in all constitutions. We may add that political revolutions are sometimes achieved by force, and sometimes by fraud. Force may either be used initially or at a later stage. Fraud, too, may be used at two different stages. Sometimes, by using fraud people manage at first to obtain the consent of the population for a change in the constitution; but later they keep control of affairs in the face of general dissent. This was the case with the revolution of the Four Hundred* [at Athens]: they first defrauded the people by an assurance that the Persian king would provide money for the war against Sparta, and after lying in this way they attempted to keep the constitution permanently under their control. Sometimes, however, an initial act of persuasion is followed up afterwards by a similar policy, and control is thus kept with general consent. Such, on a summary view, are the causes of change in all constitutions.

B: Particular Causes of Conflict and Change in Democracies, Oligarchies, and Aristocracies
(Chapters 5–7)

CHAPTER 5

1. Democracies. Here change tends to be caused by the policy of demagogues in attacking the rich, individually or collectively. In early times demagogues often made themselves tyrants: they no longer do so; and indeed tyrannies of every sort are becoming rare, owing, among other causes, to the increased size of cities. Democracy is liable to change from the older and more moderate forms to a new and extreme type. This is largely due to the courting of the people by eager candidates for office.

1304ᵇ19 We must now take the different constitutions separately, and study successively, in the light of these general propositions, what happens in each of the types.

1304ᵇ20 In democracies changes are chiefly due to the wanton licence of demagogues. This takes two forms. Sometimes they attack the rich individually, by bringing false accusations, and thus force them to combine (for a common danger unites even the bitterest enemies): sometimes they attack them as a class, by stirring up the people against them. The result of such action may be seen in a number of instances. At Cos democracy was overthrown by the rise of discreditable demagogues and the combination of the notables against them. The same thing happened at Rhodes, where the demagogues first introduced a system of payment [for attendance at the assembly and courts], and then withheld the sums due to the trierarchs;* the result was that the trierarchs, vexed by the suits brought against them, were compelled to combine and overthrow the democracy. At Heraclea democracy was ruined by the behaviour of demagogues soon after the colony was founded. They treated the notables unjustly, and drove them out by their conduct; but the notables gathered their forces, returned, and overthrew the democracy. At Megara,* too, democracy was ruined in a similar way. The demagogues, anxious to have an excuse for confiscating the property of the notables, drove a number of them into exile, with the result that the exiles became so numerous that they effected their return, defeated the people in battle, and established an oligarchy. The same thing happened to the democracy at Cyme, which was overthrown by Thrasymachus. A survey of changes in other cities would show that they have generally been of this character. Sometimes the demagogues, seeking to win popular favour, drive the notables to combine by the injuries they inflict upon them—by requiring [them to undertake expensive] public services, they force them to break up their estates or cripple their revenues. Sometimes they bring false accusations in the courts, in order to be in a position to confiscate the property of the wealthier citizens.

1305ᵃ7 In early times, when the same person combined the positions of demagogue and general, democracies changed into tyrannies. Most of the early tyrants were men who had first been demagogues. The reason why this was once the case, and is no longer so, is that in early times, when oratory was still in its infancy, demagogues were always drawn from the ranks of military commanders, whereas today, with the growth of the art of rhetoric, those who are good at speaking make themselves demagogues; but people of this type, since they lack experience in military matters, make no attempt at becoming tyrants—though here and there a case or two may have occurred. Another reason why tyrannies were more frequent in early times is that great offices were then entrusted to individuals. The tyranny at Miletus, for example, stemmed from the office of *prutanis*, which involved the control of many matters of importance. A further reason is the smaller size of the cities of early times. The people generally lived in the country, occupied with the daily duties of their farms; and their leaders, when they were men of military capacity, had thus the chance of establishing a tyranny. They generally did so on the strength of popular confidence; and the basis of this confidence was the hostility they showed to the wealthy. Thus at Athens Peisistratus rose to be tyrant by leading a rising against the party of the Plain.* Theagenes became the tyrant of Megara after slaughtering the cattle of the rich landlords which were grazing by the riverside. At Syracuse Dionysius* attained the position of tyrant by denouncing Daphnaeus and the rest of the rich; his enmity to them made the people put their trust in him as a good democrat.

1305ᵃ28 Changes may also take place from the traditional and 'ancestral' form of democracy to the latest and most modern form. Where the offices are filled by vote, without any property qualification, and the whole of the people has the vote, candidates for office begin to play the demagogue, and matters are brought to the point at which law itself is included in the scope of popular sovereignty. To prevent this result—or, at any rate, to diminish its full effect—the proper course is to give the vote to the separate tribes, and not to the whole of the people.

These, in the main, are the causes of all the changes in democracies.

CHAPTER 6

2. Oligarchies. Here changes are due, partly to unjust treatment of the masses, and partly to factional disputes within the governing class. Such disputes may arise (1) if a section of that class begins to play the demagogue, (2) if some of its members become impoverished and turn revolutionary, and (3) if an inner ring is formed inside the ruling body. Personal disputes may affect the stability of oligarchies; and accidental causes (e.g. a general growth of wealth, increasing the number of those eligible for office) may insensibly alter their character.

1305^a37 There are two especially obvious methods by which changes are generally brought about in oligarchies. One is the unjust treatment of the masses by the government. Any leader is then an adequate champion, especially when it so happens that the leader comes from the ranks of the governing class itself. This was the case with Lygdamis of Naxos, who afterwards made himself tyrant of the island. Where factional conflict begins outside the governing class it may take several different forms. Sometimes an oligarchy is undermined by people who, though wealthy themselves, are excluded from office. This happens when the holders of office are a very limited number, as for example at Massilia, at Istros, at Heraclea, and in other cities. Here those who had no share in office continued to cause disturbance till some share was finally given, first to the elder brothers in the family and then to the younger too. (It should be explained that in some cities father and son, and in others an elder and a younger brother, are not allowed to hold office together.) The final result was that the oligarchy at Massilia was turned into something more of the nature of a 'constitutional government' [polity]; the oligarchy at Istros ended by becoming a democracy; and the one at Heraclea, which had been in the hands of a narrow ring, was broadened to include as many as 600 members. At Cnidos, too, there was a change in the oligarchy. Here factional conflict broke out inside the ranks of the notables, because few of them were admitted to office—they followed the practice (which we have just had occasion to mention) that if a father were admitted, his son should not be eligible, and if there were several brothers in a family, only the eldest was eligible. While this faction-fighting was going on, the people took a hand; and finding a leader among the notables, they attacked and won the day—division (as it always does) leading to the fall of their enemies. There is also the case of Erythrae, which was governed oligarchically, in old times, by the clan of the Basilidae. Although they managed its affairs well, the people took offence because so few were involved in government and altered the constitution.

1305^b22 Oligarchies are disturbed from inside when their members themselves play the demagogue, for reasons of personal rivalry. There are two kinds of demagogue. One sort works on the members of the oligarchy themselves. A demagogue can arise even where these are very few in number: for example, in the days of the Thirty at Athens* Charicles and his followers gained power by courting the favour of the Thirty, and in the days of the Four Hundred* Phrynichus and his followers acted on the same lines. The other sort of demagogue is found when members of oligarchies work upon the masses. This was the case at Larissa, where the 'protectors of the citizens' paid their court to the masses because they were elected by them; and it generally happens in all oligarchies where public officials—instead of being elected on a franchise limited to those who are themselves eligible for office—are elected by those who bear arms or even the whole of the people, but with eligibility limited to the owners of large properties or the members of political clubs. (This used to be the rule at Abydus.) We may add that similar troubles also arise in oligarchies where the lawcourts are composed of people not belonging to the sovereign civic body. When this is the case, people begin to practise the tricks of the demagogue in order to secure a verdict; and this leads to factional disputes and constitutional change, as it did at

Heraclea on the Black Sea. Troubles also arise when some of the members try to make an oligarchy still more exclusive; and those who seek equality are then compelled to enlist the aid of the people.

1305ᵇ39 Another way in which oligarchies may be disturbed from inside is when their members waste their possessions in riotous living. Those who have done that want to create a revolution; and they either attempt to be tyrants themselves or set up someone else in that position. Hipparinus set up Dionysius at Syracuse in this way. At Amphipolis someone by the name of Cleotimus introduced Chalcidian settlers, and incited them after their settlement to make an attack on the rich. At Aegina, again, it was a similar cause which moved the man who conducted the transaction with Chares to attempt a change of the constitution. Sometimes these people go straight for some attempt at political change: sometimes they steal the public funds; in consequence there is faction-fighting, which may be started either by the culprits themselves or (as happened at Apollonia on the Black Sea) by those who oppose their misconduct. An oligarchy at one with itself is not easily overthrown from within. The constitution of Pharsalus may serve as an example: the governing body, restricted as it is, manages to control a large population because its members behave well towards one another.

1306ᵃ12 Oligarchies may also be undermined when people create an oligarchy within an oligarchy, that is when the members of the citizen body are few in number but even these few are not all admitted to the highest offices. This is what happened at one time in Elis. The constitution was in the hands of a small body of elders; and only a few people could be appointed to this body, because its members, of whom there were ninety in all, held office for life; moreover they were elected, much like the Spartan elders, in a way which favoured the interests of a narrow range of families.

1306ᵃ19 Changes may happen in oligarchies alike in war and in peace. They happen in war when the members of an oligarchy are compelled by distrust of the populace to employ an army of mercenaries. If a single man is entrusted with the command of these mercenaries, he frequently becomes a tyrant, as Timophanes did at Corinth; and if the command is vested in a number of people, they make themselves a governing clique. Sometimes the fear of such consequences forces an oligarchy to make use of the populace and to give them a share in the constitution. Changes happen in peace when the members of an oligarchy, under the impulse of mutual distrust, entrust the maintenance of internal security to mercenaries and a neutral arbiter—who occasionally ends as the master of both the contending factions. This happened at Larissa during the government of the Aleuad clan under Simos: it also happened at Abydus during the struggles of the clubs; one of which was the club of Iphiades.

1306ª31 Factions may also arise inside an oligarchy on matters of marriages and lawsuits, which lead to the discomfiture of one of its sections by another, and thus produce factional conflict. Some examples of factional conflicts arising from matters of marriage have already been cited;* we may also mention the overthrow of the oligarchy of the knights at Eretria by Diagoras, in resentment at an injustice he had suffered in a matter of marriage. Decisions given in lawsuits led to factional disputes at Heraclea [on the Black Sea] and at Thebes. In both cases the offence was that of adultery; and in both cases punishment was exacted (at Heraclea from Eurytion, and at Thebes from Archias) justly but in the spirit of faction—the enemies of the guilty parties carrying their resentment to the point of having them pilloried in public.

1306ᵇ3 It has also frequently happened that oligarchies have been overthrown, because they were too oppressive, by members of the governing class who resented the methods they used. This was the case, for example, with the oligarchies of Cnidus and Chios.

1306ᵇ6 Finally, constitutional change may sometimes be due to accidents. This is the case with the constitutions called 'constitutional governments' [polities], and with those forms of oligarchy where a property qualification is necessary for membership of the council and lawcourts and the holding of other offices. The qualification may have been originally fixed, on the basis of existing conditions, in a way which limited participation to the few in oligarchies, and to the middle class in 'constitutional governments'. Then, as frequently happens, there may ensue a period of prosperity, due to long peace or some other good fortune; and the result will be that the same estate must now be assessed at a value many times in excess of the old. When this is the case, the whole body of citizens comes to participate in everything—a change which may sometimes come about gradually, by small degrees and without being noticed, but sometimes may come about rapidly.

1306ᵇ16 Such are the causes of change and factional disputes in oligarchies. A general observation may be added. Both democracies and oligarchies are occasionally transformed, not into the opposite types of constitution, but into some other variety of their own type. Democracies and oligarchies which are limited by law may turn, for example, into forms which are absolutely sovereign; and the converse may equally happen.

CHAPTER 7

3. Aristocracies. Here changes are due to a policy of narrowing the circle of the government. The collapse of aristocracies—as also of 'constitutional governments' (polities), which are closely allied—is generally due to a defective balance of the different elements combined in the constitution: this may lead either to change in the direction in which the balance is tilted, or to violent reaction towards the opposite extreme. Aristocracies are particularly liable to be the victims of trifling occasions. All constitutions may be affected and undermined by the influence of powerful neighbouring cities.

1306ᵇ22 In aristocracies factional disputes may arise from the limitation of office and honours to a narrow circle. This is a cause which, as we have mentioned,* produces commotions in oligarchies; and it naturally affects aristocracies, because they too are in some sense oligarchies. In both types of constitutions, though for different reasons, the ruling class is small; and it is this common feature which will explain why an aristocracy may be regarded as a kind of oligarchy. This particularly tends to happen when there is a mass of people convinced that they are as good in character as the rulers. This was the case with those at Sparta called the Partheniae, who were the [illegitimate] sons of Spartan peers:* they conspired together but were detected, and sent out to colonize Tarentum. The same thing may happen when people of great ability, and second to none in their merits, are treated dishonourably by those who themselves enjoy higher honours—as Lysander* was by the kings of Sparta. It may happen, again, when a man of high spirit—like Cinadon, the leader of the conspiracy [in 398 BC] against the Spartan peers in the reign of king Agesilaus—is debarred from honours and office. It may happen too, when some of the ruling class become excessively poor, and others excessively rich. This happens particularly in times of war. It happened, for example, at Sparta in the time of the Messenian War. The poem of Tyrtaeus, entitled 'Good Government',* is sufficient evidence: it tells how people impoverished by the war demanded a redistribution of landed property. In addition someone who has a great position, and the capacity for a still greater, [will promote factional disputes] in order to make himself the one ruler. Pausanias,* who was general during the Persian War, is an example at Sparta; Hanno at Carthage is another.

1307ª5 But the downfall of aristocracies, and also of 'constitutional governments' [polities], is chiefly due to some deviation from justice in the constitution itself. In either case the origin of the downfall is a failure to combine different elements properly. In 'constitutional governments' the elements are democracy and oligarchy: in aristocracies they are both of these and the further element of merit; but even in the latter the real difficulty is that of combining the first two elements, which are the ones that 'constitutional governments' (as well as most of the so-called aristocracies) actually attempt to combine. The only difference between aristocracies and what are called 'constitutional governments' consists in their different ways of mixing the same two elements; and this is also the reason why the former are less secure than the latter. Constitutions where the tendency is more towards oligarchy are called aristocracies: those where the tendency is more in favour of the masses are called 'constitutional governments'. This will explain why the latter are more secure than the former. Their greater numbers give them greater strength: and people are ready to acquiesce in a government when they have an equal share of power. It is different with the wealthy. When the constitution gives them a position of superiority, they are apt to fall into arrogance and to covet even more. Generally, however, it may be said that if a constitution favours one side, it will tend to change in that direction. In each case the favoured element will proceed to increase its advantage: a 'constitutional government', for instance, will change to democracy; and aristocracy will change into oligarchy.

1307ª22 It is possible, however, that change may also go in the opposite direction. Aristocracy may change, for example, into democracy, because the poorer classes, feeling themselves unjustly treated, may divert its natural tendency into the opposite direction; and 'constitutional governments' may similarly change into oligarchies—they feel that stability is only to be found under a system of proportionate equality, on the basis of desert, by which everyone receives his corresponding due. It was a change of this nature which happened at Thurii. The first stage, due to reaction against the high property qualification required from holders of office, was a change to a lower qualification, coupled with an increase in the number of offices. Because the notables had bought up illegally the whole of the land (the oligarchical bias of the constitution enabling them to indulge their greed), [the next stage was the outbreak of civil war].* Here the masses, becoming hardened in the course of hostilities, proved stronger than the civic guard and forced those who had more land than the law allowed to relinquish their hold; [and the old aristocracy thus became a democracy]. We may add that the oligarchical bias present in all aristocratic constitutions has a general tendency to make the notables too grasping. In Sparta, for example, estates tend to pass into the hands of a narrow circle. Generally, too, the notables have too much power to do what they will, and to marry as they will. This explains the collapse of Locri, which was due to a marriage between the daughter of one of its citizens and Dionysius [of Syracuse]. This would never have happened in a democracy, or in a properly balanced aristocracy.

1307ᵃ40 A general observation which has already been made in regard to all types of constitutions—that even trifles may be the cause of changes—is particularly true of aristocracies. They are especially apt to change imperceptibly, through being undermined little by little. Once they have abandoned one of the elements of the constitution, they find it easier afterwards to alter some other feature of a little greater importance; and they end eventually by altering the whole system. This was what actually befell the constitution of Thurii. There was a law that the office of general should only be held a second time after an interval of five years. Some of the younger men showed soldierly qualities, and won a reputation with the rank and file of the guard. Despising those who were in charge of affairs, and calculating on an easy triumph, these younger men set out to abrogate the law, wishing to make it possible for generals to serve continuously, and knowing that, in that case, the people would readily elect them for one term after another. The officials charged with the duty of considering such proposals—they were called the Councillors—began by making an effort to resist the repeal of the law; but they were eventually led to agree, on the assumption that when this change had been made, the rest of the constitution would not be touched. But later when they sought to oppose other changes which were mooted, they failed to make any headway; and the whole scheme of the constitution was changed into a 'dynasty' composed of the revolutionaries.

1307ᵇ19 Constitutions generally may be undermined from without, as well as from within. This happens when they are confronted by a constitution of an opposite type, which either is their close neighbour or is powerful even if distant. It happened in the days of the Athenian and Spartan empires. The Athenians everywhere put down oligarchies; the Spartans, in turn, suppressed democracies.

The causes of changes and factional disputes in different constitutions have now been generally described.

C: Methods of Ensuring Constitutional Stability in the Three Previous Types of Constitution and More Generally (Chapters 8–9)

CHAPTER 8

Precautions should be taken against lawlessness, and especially against its petty forms. No reliance should be placed on devices intended to hoodwink the masses. A spirit of fairness should be cultivated; and something of the temper, and even some of the institutions, of democracy may therefore be advisable in oligarchies and aristocracies. To maintain a feeling of emergency may help to maintain the government. Promotions, and the award or withdrawal of honours, should be carefully handled. Watch should be kept both on private extravagance and the sudden rise of a whole social class to a new degree of prosperity. In particular, steps should be taken to prevent office from being made a source of profit. Finally, democracies will do well to spare the rich, and oligarchies to encourage and help the poor.

1307ᵇ26 It remains to treat of the methods for preserving constitutions* in general, and for each particular type. It is clear, to begin with, that to know the causes which destroy constitutions is also to know the causes which ensure their preservation. Opposite effects are brought about by opposite causes; and destruction and preservation are opposite effects.

1307ᵇ30 On this basis we may draw a number of conclusions. The first is that in constitutions where the elements are well mixed there is one thing as vitally important as any: to keep a look-out against all lawlessness, and, more particularly, to be on guard against any of its petty forms. Lawlessness may creep in unperceived, just as petty expenditures, constantly repeated, will gradually destroy the whole of a fortune. Because it is not all incurred at once, such expenditure goes unperceived; and our minds are misled by it in the same way as they are misled by the logical fallacy, 'When each is small, all are small too'. This is true in one sense, but it is not true in another. The whole or total is not small, even though the elements of which it is composed are small.*

1307^b39 This is one precaution which ought to be taken—to prevent the trouble beginning in this way. Secondly, we may lay down the rule that confidence should never be placed in devices intended to hoodwink the masses. They are always undermined by events. (We have already explained* the nature of the constitutional devices to which we are here referring.)

1308^a3 Thirdly, we have to observe that some aristocracies (and also some oligarchies) survive, not because they have stable constitutions, but because those who hold office give good treatment to those outside the constitution as well as to the members of the civic body: they do not treat those without a share in the constitution unjustly; on the contrary, they bring their leading members within the constitution; they do not wrong the ambitious among them on points of honour, or the mass of the people in matters of [money and] profit; they behave towards one another and to those who are members of the constitution in a democratic spirit.

1308^a11 The principle of equality which democrats apply to the masses is not only just but expedient when applied to those who really are 'peers'.* When, therefore, the members of the governing class are numerous, a number of democratic institutions will be expedient. It will be expedient, for instance, to restrict the tenure of office to a period of six months, and thus to enable all who belong to the class of 'peers' to enjoy their turn. A numerous class of 'peers' is already, by its nature, a sort of democracy; and that is why, as has already been noticed,* we often find demagogues emerging in such a class. When such a policy is adopted, oligarchies and aristocracies are less prone to fall into the hands of family cliques. Those who hold office with a short tenure can hardly do as much harm as those who have a long tenure; and it is long possession of office which leads to the rise of tyrannies in oligarchies and democracies. Those who make a bid for tyranny, in both types of constitution, are either the most powerful people (who in democracies are the demagogues, and in oligarchies the heads of great families), or else the holders of the main offices who have held them for a long period.

1308ª24 The preservation of a constitution may not only be due to the fact that those who would destroy it are far away; it may also, on occasion, be due to the fact that they are close at hand. When danger is imminent, people are anxious, and they therefore keep a firmer grip on their constitution. All who are concerned for the constitution should therefore create anxieties, which will put people on their guard, and will make them keep watch without relaxing, like sentinels on night-duty. They must, in a word, make the remote come near.

1308ª31 An endeavour should also be made, by legislation as well as by personal action, to guard against quarrels and factions among the notables; and watch should also be kept in advance on those who are not yet involved, before they too have caught the spirit of rivalry. Ordinary people cannot see the beginning of troubles ahead; that requires the genuine statesman.

1308ª35 Change may arise, in oligarchies and 'constitutional governments' [polities], as a result of the assessment required for the property qualification. It will tend to arise, for example, when the monetary amount of the property qualification is left unchanged but the amount of money in circulation shows a large increase. To meet this danger a comparison should regularly be made between the present sum-total of all the assessments and their sum-total in a previous year. Where the assessment is annual, the comparison should be made annually; where—as in the larger cities—the assessment is made at intervals of three or four years, the comparison should be made at those intervals. If the sum-total is then found to be many times greater (or many times less) than it was on the previous occasion when the assessments obligatory under the constitution were fixed, a law should be passed to provide for the raising (or lowering) of the qualification required. Where the total is greater than it was the assessment should be tightened by means of a proportionate increase; where it is less it should be relaxed by making it smaller. In oligarchies and 'constitutional governments' [polities] where this policy is not adopted change will be inevitable. In one case* the change will be from 'constitutional government' to oligarchy, and from oligarchy to a family clique; in the other* change will move in the reverse direction—from a 'constitutional government' to a democracy, and from an oligarchy either to a 'constitutional government' or a democracy.

1308ᵇ10 A rule which applies both to democracies and oligarchies—indeed it applies to all constitutions—is that no one should be advanced disproportionately. It is a better policy to award small honours over a period of time than to give honours rapidly. (People are easily spoiled; and it is not all who can stand prosperity.) If this rule is not followed, and if many honours are bestowed at the same time, the least that can be done is not to revoke them all at the same time, but to do so by degrees. It is also good policy to aim so to shape things, by appropriate legislation, that no one gains a position of superiority by the strength of his friends or of his wealth. Failing that, those who gain such a position should be removed from it by being sent out of the country.*

1308ᵇ20 Since people tend to become revolutionaries from circumstances connected with their private lives an office should be instituted to supervise those who live in a way that is out of harmony with the constitution—who in a democracy do not live democratically; in an oligarchy, do not live oligarchically; and so in each other type of constitution. For similar reasons watch should be kept over whatever section in the city is particularly flourishing at any moment. The remedy* is either (a) always to give the conduct of affairs and the enjoyment of office to the opposite section (I mean by this that the respectable people are opposite to the masses, and the poor to the wealthy), and thus to attempt a balance or fusion between the poor and the wealthy section, or (b) to seek to increase the strength of the middle or intervening element. Such a policy will prevent the factional disputes which arise from inequality.

1308ᵇ31 The most important rule of all, in all types of constitution, is that provision should be made—not only by law, but also by the general system of economy—to prevent the officials from being able to use their office for their own gain. This is a matter which demands attention in oligarchical constitutions, above all others. The masses are not so greatly offended at being excluded from office (they may even be glad to be given the leisure for attending to their own business); what really annoys them is to think that those who have the enjoyment of office are embezzling public funds. That makes them feel a double annoyance at a double loss—the loss of profit as well as office. If an arrangement could be made to stop people from using office as a means of private gain, it would provide a way—the only possible way—for combining democracy with aristocracy. Both the notables and the masses could then get what they desire. All would be able to hold office, as befits a democracy: the notables would actually be in office, as befits an aristocracy. Both results could be achieved simultaneously if the use of office as a means of profit were made impossible. The poor would no longer desire to hold office (because they would derive no advantage from doing so), and they would prefer to attend to their own affairs. The rich would be able to afford to take office, as they would need no subvention from public funds to meet its expenses. The poor would thus have the advantage of becoming wealthy by diligent attention to work; the notables would enjoy the consolation of not being governed by any chance comer.

1309ᵃ10 To prevent the embezzling of public money, the outgoing officers should hand over the funds [under their charge] in the presence of the whole civic body; and inventories of them should be deposited with each clan, ward, and tribe. To ensure that no profit should be made by any official in other ways, the law should provide for the award of honours to those who earn a good reputation.

1309ᵃ14 In democracies, the rich should be spared. Not only should their estates be safe from the threat of redistribution: the produce of the estates should be equally secure; and the practice of sharing it out, which has insensibly developed under some constitutions, should not be allowed. It is good policy, too, to prevent the rich, even if they are willing, from undertaking expensive, and yet useless, public services, such as the equipping of choruses for dramatic festivals, or the

provision of the expenses of torch-races, or other services of
that sort. In oligarchies, on the other hand, a good deal of
attention should be paid to the poor. They should be assigned
those offices from which profits can be made; and if a rich
man does violence against them the penalties should be heavier
than if he had been guilty of violence against members of his
own class. Nor should inheritances pass by title of bequest;
they should go by descent, and not more than one inheritance
should ever go to one person. On this system estates would be
more evenly distributed, and more of the poor might rise to a
position of affluence.

1309ª27 In matters other than property it is beneficial both
for oligarchies and for democracies to give a position of
equality, or even of precedence, to those who have a smaller
share in the constitution—in a democracy to the rich; in an
oligarchy to the poor. An exception must, however, be made
for the sovereign offices of the constitution. These should be
entrusted only, or at any rate entrusted mainly, to those who
have [full] membership in the constitution.

CHAPTER 9

*Further consideration of the methods of ensuring constitutional
stability in the three first types of constitution. In the interest of
constitutional stability, three qualities are required in the holders
of high office; their relative importance. It is always wise to
ensure that a majority of the citizen body is in favour of the
constitution. The value of the mean, and of refusing to push
political issues to an extreme: not all democratic or oligarchic
measures are calculated to ensure the permanence of democracy
or oligarchy. The cardinal importance of educating citizens to
live and act in the spirit of the constitution: this is too often
neglected, especially in extreme democracies, which encourage
the idea of 'living as one likes'.*

1309ª33 Three qualifications are necessary in those who
have to fill the sovereign offices. The first is loyalty to the
established constitution. The second is a high degree of capac-

ity for the duties of the office. The third is goodness of
character and justice, in the particular form which suits the
nature of each constitution. (If what is just varies from constitution to constitution, the quality of justice must also have its
corresponding varieties.)* Where these three qualifications
are not united in a single person, a problem obviously arises:
[how is the choice to be made?]* For instance, A may possess
military capacity, but be neither good in character nor loyal
to the constitution. B may be just in character and loyal to
the constitution, [but deficient in capacity]. How are we to
choose? It would seem that we ought to consider two
points—which quality do people on the whole have more of
and which less. Thus, for a military office, we must have
regard to military experience rather than character: people in
general have less military capacity and more honesty. For the
post of custodian of property, or that of treasurer, we must
follow the opposite rule: such posts require a standard of
character above the average, but the knowledge which they
demand is such as we all possess. A further problem may also
be raised: if someone possesses the two qualifications of
capacity and loyalty to the constitution, is there any need for
him to have the third qualification (a good character), and
will not the first two, by themselves, secure the public interest?
We may answer that those who possess these two first qualifications may lack self-control;* and just as such people fail to
serve their own interests—even though they possess self-knowl-
edge and self-loyalty—so nothing prevents some people from
being in the same position with regard to the public interest.

1309^{b}14 Generally, we may add, a constitution will tend to
be preserved by the observance of all the legal rules already
suggested, in the course of our argument, as making for
constitutional stability. Here we may note, as of paramount
importance, the elementary principle which has been again
and again suggested—the principle of ensuring that the
number of those who wish a constitution to continue shall be
greater than the number of those who do not.*

1309^{b}18 In addition to all these things, there is another
which ought to be remembered, but which, in fact, is forgotten
in perverted forms of government. This is the value of the

mean.* Many of the measures which are reckoned democratic really undermine democracies: many which are reckoned oligarchical actually undermine oligarchies. Those who think that theirs is the only form of goodness, push matters to an extreme. They fail to see that proportion is as necessary to a constitution as it is (let us say) to a nose. A nose may deviate in some degree from the ideal of straightness, and incline towards the hooked or the snub, without ceasing to be well shaped and agreeable to the eye. But push the deviation still further towards either of these extremes, and the nose will begin to be out of proportion with the rest of the face: carry it further still, and it will cease to look like a nose at all, because it will go too far towards one, and too far away from the other, of these two opposite extremes. What is true of the nose, and of other parts of the body, is true also of constitutions. Both oligarchy and democracy may be tolerable forms of government, even though they deviate from the ideal. But if you push either of them further still [in the direction to which it tends], you will begin by making it a worse constitution, and you may end by turning it into something which is not a constitution at all.*

1309^b35 It is thus the duty of legislators and statesmen to know which democratic measures preserve, and which destroy, a democracy; similarly, it is their duty to know which oligarchical measures will save, and which will ruin, an oligarchy. Neither of these constitutions can exist, or continue in existence, unless it includes both the rich and the poor. If, therefore, a system of equal ownership is introduced into either, the result will inevitably be a new and different form of constitution; and the radical legislation which abolishes riches and poverty will thus abolish along with them the constitutions [based on their presence]. Errors are made alike in democracies and oligarchies. They are made, for instance, by demagogues, in those democracies where the will of the people is superior to the law. Demagogues are always dividing the city into two, and waging war against the rich. Their proper policy is the very reverse: they should always profess to be speaking in defence of the rich. A similar policy should be followed in oligarchies: the oligarchs should profess to speak on behalf of the poor; and the oaths they take should be the opposite of those which they now take. There are cities in which their oath runs, 'I will bear ill will to the people, and I will plan against them all the evil I can.' The opinion which they ought to hold and exhibit is the very opposite; and their oaths should contain the declaration, 'I will not do wrong to the people.'

1310ª12 The greatest, however, of all the means we have mentioned for ensuring the stability of constitutions—but one which is nowadays generally neglected—is the education of citizens* in the spirit of their constitution. There is no advantage in the best of laws, even when they are sanctioned by general civic consent, if the citizens themselves have not been attuned, by the force of habit and the influence of teaching, to the right constitutional temper—which will be the temper of democracy where the laws are democratic, and where they are oligarchical will be that of oligarchy. If an individual can lack self-control, so can a city. The education of a citizen in the spirit of his constitution does not consist in his doing the actions in which the partisans of oligarchy, or the adherents of democracy, delight. It consists in his doing the actions which make it possible to have an oligarchy, or a democracy. Actual practice, today, is on very different lines. In oligarchies the sons of those in office live lives of luxury, and this at a time when the sons of the poor are being hardened by exercise, and by their daily work, and are thus acquiring the will and the power to create a revolution. In democracies of the type which is regarded as being peculiarly democratic* the policy followed is the very reverse of their real interest. The reason for this is a false conception of liberty. There are two features which are generally held to define democracy. One of them is the sovereignty of the majority; the other is the liberty of individuals. Justice is assumed to consist in equality and equality in regarding the will of the masses as sovereign; liberty is assumed to consist in 'doing what one likes'. The result of such a view is that, in these extreme democracies, each individual lives as he likes—or, as Euripides says,

For any end he chances to desire.*

This is a mean conception [of liberty]. To live by the rule of
the constitution ought not to be regarded as slavery, but
rather as salvation.*

Such, in general, are the causes which lead to the change
and destruction of constitutions, and such are the means of
ensuring their preservation and stability.

D: The Causes of Conflict and Change and the Methods of Ensuring Stability in Monarchies (Chapters 10–11)

CHAPTER 10

*The distinction, especially in origins, between kingship and
tyranny. Kingship is allied to aristocracy, and its general function is that of impartial guardianship of society; tyranny is
directed to personal interest, and it combines the more selfish
side of oligarchy with the more selfish side of democracy. In
monarchies generally, changes are caused by resentment of
arrogant behaviour; by fear; by contempt; or by a desire for
fame. Tyrannies are liable to be overthrown by the influence of
neighbouring cities of an opposite character: they may also be
destroyed by internal causes; and the causes which particularly
lead to their overthrow are hatred and contempt. Kingships are
more durable; but with the general growth of equality they are
becoming antiquated, and the form of monarchical government
now prevalent is tyranny based on force.*

1310ᵃ39 We have still, however, to treat of the causes of
destruction, and the means of preservation, when the government is a monarchy.* Generally, what has already been said
of constitutions [proper] is almost equally true of kingships
and tyrannies. Kingship is in the nature of an aristocracy.
Tyranny is a compound of the extreme forms of oligarchy
and democracy,* and that is why it is more injurious to its
subjects than any other form of government; it is composed
of two bad forms, and it combines the perversions and errors
of both. The two forms of monarchical government differ in
their very origin since they spring from opposite causes.

Kingships have grown for the purpose of helping the better classes against the populace; it is from these classes that kings have been drawn; and the basis of their position has been their own pre-eminence, or the pre-eminence of their family, in character and conduct. Tyrants, on the contrary, are drawn from the populace and the masses, to serve as their protectors against the notables, and in order to prevent them from suffering any injustice from that class. This is clear from actual events: it may safely be said that most tyrants have begun their careers as demagogues, who won the popular confidence by calumniating the notables. But though it is true that a large number of tyrannies arose in this way when cities had increased in size, there were others, of an earlier date, which arose in different ways. Some developed because kings transgressed traditional limitations, and aimed at a more despotic authority. Others were founded by people who had originally been elected to the highest offices—all the more easily because there was a habit, in ancient times, of giving long tenures to public 'craftsmen' and 'overseers'.* Others, again, arose from a practice, followed in oligarchies, of appointing a single person to supervise the chief offices. In all these ways an opportunity was created for someone who so desired to effect his purpose with ease; he had already power in his hands for a start—here as king, and there as the holder of some other high office. Pheidon of Argos and a number of others started as kings and ended as tyrants. The tyrants of Ionia and Phalaris of Agrigentum used other offices as stepping-stones. Panaetius at Leontini, Cypselus at Corinth, Peisistratus at Athens, Dionysius at Syracuse, and a number of others who became tyrants in a similar way, began as demagogues.

1310^b31 Kingship, as we have already observed, may be classified with aristocracy, since it is based on merit. The merit on which it is based may consist in personal (or family) qualities; it may consist in benefits rendered; it may consist in a combination of both of these with capacity. Those who have gained the position of king have all been men who had actually benefited, or were capable of benefiting, their cities or their peoples. Some, like Codrus* [of Athens], had saved

them from enslavement in war: others, like Cyrus* [of Persia],
had been their liberators; others, again, had settled or acquired territory, like the kings of Sparta and Macedonia, or
the Molossian kings in Epirus. It is the aim of a king to be in
the position of a guardian of society, protecting the owners
of property from any unjust treatment, and saving the bulk
of the people from arrogance and oppression. Tyranny, as
we have often noted, is just the opposite. It has no regard to
any public interest which does not also serve the tyrant's own
advantage. The aim of a tyrant is his own pleasure: the
aim of a king is the Good.* Thus a tyrant covets riches; a
king covets what makes for renown. The guard of a king
is composed of citizens: that of a tyrant is composed of
foreigners.

1311ᵃ8 Tyranny has obviously the vices both of oligarchy
and democracy. From oligarchy it derives its aim of amassing
wealth; for it is by his wealth, and by it alone, that a tyrant
has to maintain his guard and his luxury. It is also from
oligarchy that tyranny derives its habit of distrusting the
masses, and the policy, consequent upon it, of depriving them
of arms. Tyranny, too, shares with oligarchy the practice of
oppressing the common crowd, expelling it from the city, and
dispersing it in the country. From democracy it derives its
attitude of hostility to the notables, its policy of ruining them,
secretly or openly, and its habit of driving them into banishment, as the rivals and hindrances to its power. The reason
for this is that the notables are the source of conspiracies
[against tyrants]—some because they want to be rulers themselves; others because they do not want to be slaves. This
explains the advice which was offered by Periander* to [his
fellow-tyrant]—Thrasybulus, when he struck off with his stick
the outstanding ears in the cornfield. It was a hint that he
ought, from time to time, to remove outstanding citizens.

1311ᵃ22 It has already been suggested that the origins of
changes in cities with a monarchical system must be considered the same as they are in cities with regular constitutions.
Unjust oppression, fear, and contempt, are often the reasons
why subjects rebel against their monarchs. The form of unjust
oppression which most frequently leads to rebellion is arro-

gant behaviour; but the confiscation of property has sometimes the same effect. The aims [of those who rebel] are also the same in tyrannies and kingships as they are under regular constitutions. Sovereign rulers enjoy a pre-eminence of wealth and honour; and wealth and honour are objects of general desire. Attacks are in some cases delivered against the sovereign himself, and in others against his office. Attacks provoked by arrogant behaviour are directed against him personally.

1311ª33 Arrogant behaviour takes many forms; but anger is the common effect produced by all of them. Those who attack a sovereign in anger generally do so for the sake of revenge, and not for reasons of ambition. The attack on the sons of Peisistratus at Athens, by Harmodius and Aristogeiton,* was caused by the dishonour offered to the sister of Harmodius and the injury thus done to her brother. Harmodius attacked for his sister's sake; and his friend Aristogeiton joined the attack for his sake.

1311ª39 There was also a conspiracy against Periander, a tyrant in Ambracia, because he once asked his favourite, when they were carousing together, 'Aren't you yet with child by me?' The attack made by Pausanias on Philip* was due to the fact that Philip had allowed an outrage to be inflicted on him by Attalus and his circle; the attack of Derdas on Amyntas the Little was due to Amyntas' boasting that he had enjoyed his youthful favours; and the attack of the eunuch on Evagoras of Cyprus was due to a similar motive—the son of Evagoras had seduced his wife and he killed the father in resentment at the outrage. Many attacks have also been made as a result of insults offered by monarchs to the person of their subjects. The attack of Crataeus on Archelaus [of Macedonia] is an example. Crataeus had always resented his connection with Archelaus so a less serious pretext would have been sufficient. But it may be that his real reason was that Archelaus did not give him either of his daughters in marriage, in spite of having agreed to do so. Instead of keeping his promise, he gave the elder to the king of Elimeia, when he found himself hard-pressed in a war with Sirras and Arribaeus; and he gave the younger to Amyntas, his son [by a previous marriage], thinking that the result would be to pre-

vent any likelihood of a quarrel between this son and his son
by [a later marriage with] Cleopatra. But, however that may
have been, the actual beginning of the estrangement was the
chafing of Crataeus at the sexual connection between Archelaus and himself. The same sort of reason explains why
Hellanocrates of Larissa joined in the attack. When he found
that Archelaus, though he enjoyed his favours, would not
restore him to his native city, in spite of the promise he had
given that he would do so, Hellanocrates began to think that
their connection had not been due to any real passion of love,
but merely to the arrogance of pride. Python and Heraclides
of Aenus killed Cotys in revenge for the outrage which he had
inflicted on their father. Similarly, Adamas revolted against
Cotys in resentment at the outrage which he had suffered in
being emasculated, on the king's orders, during his boyhood.

1311ᵇ23 People have often been moved to anger by physical
maltreatment; and feeling themselves abused they have either
killed, or attempted to kill, even royal officers, and people
connected with the royal circle.

1311ᵇ26 In Mytilene, for example, Megacles, with the aid of
his friends, attacked and murdered the members of the Penthe-
lid family for going about and bludgeoning their fellow-
citizens with clubs; and some time afterwards Smerdis, who
had been flogged and dragged away from his wife, assassinated
[another member of the family who bore the name of] Pen-
thilus. It was for a similar reason that Decamnichus became
the leader in the attack on Archelaus [with Crataeus and
Hellanocrates as his associates], acting as the prime mover
among the conspirators. His indignation against Archelaus
was due to the fact that the king had handed him over to the
poet Euripides to be whipped—Euripides was angry with him
for the remarks he had made about his bad breath.* Many
others have taken part in assassinations or plots for similar
reasons.

1311ᵇ36 Fear is also a motive which, as we have previously
noted, operates similarly in monarchies and in constitutional
regimes as a cause of rebellion. It was fear that led the Persian
captain Artapanes to murder his master Xerxes. He was

afraid of being accused of having had Darius hung—without any orders from Xerxes—in the expectation that, unable to remember what he might have said in his cups, Xerxes would pardon the act.

1311b40 Monarchs are sometimes attacked from the motive of contempt. Sardanapalus of Assyria was killed by someone who saw him carding wool among women—assuming that what the story-tellers say is true; but if it is not true of him, it may well be true of someone else. Dionysius the Younger of Syracuse was similarly attacked by Dion* in a spirit of contempt: he saw that he was despised even by his own subjects, and was always drunk. The very friends of a single ruler will sometimes attack him because they despise him: the confidence he gives them breeds their contempt, and they are led to believe that he will notice nothing. Contempt, of a sort, is also the motive of those who think that they can seize power: they are ready to strike because they feel themselves strong, and able, in virtue of their strength, to despise any risks. This is the reason why generals attack their sovereigns. Cyrus, for instance, attacked Astyages because he despised both his capacity, which had become effete, and his habit of life, which had sunk into luxury. The Thracian Seuthes, when he was general, attacked King Amadocus for similar reasons.

1312a15 Attacks are sometimes due not to a single cause, but to a plurality of causes. Contempt, for instance, may be mingled with avarice, as it was in the attack which Mithridates made on [his father, the Persian satrap] Ariobarzanes. But rebellions caused in this way generally proceed from those who combine a hardy temper with a position of military honour in the service of their sovereign. Courage armed with power turns into hardihood; and it is this combination of courage and power which leads people to rebel, in the confidence of easy victory.

1312a21 When rebellion is due to desire for fame, we have a cause of a different character from any of those hitherto mentioned. Someone who resolves to risk rebellion out of a desire for fame behaves in a different way from those who make attempts on the lives of tyrants with an eye to great gain or high honours. People of that sort are merely moved by greed or ambition; but these will attack a ruler in the same high spirit as if they were offered the chance of some other great adventure likely to win them a name and fame among their fellows—they will want to get glory, and not a kingdom. It is true that those who are moved by such reasons are only a handful. Their action supposes an utter disregard for their own safety in the event of failure. They must have in their hearts the resolve of Dion—a resolve to which only a few can rise—when he sailed on his expedition against Dionysius the Younger with his little band of followers: 'This', he said, 'is how things stand—whatever the point I am able to reach, it is enough for me to have got so far in this undertaking. If, for instance, I perish just after getting ashore, it will be well for me to die like that.'

1312ª39 One of the ways in which a tyranny may be destroyed—and the same is true, as we have already noted, of all other forms of government—is by external causes. Another city, with an opposite form of constitution, may be stronger than a tyranny. The conflict of opposite principles will obviously lead such a city to want the destruction of the tyranny; and whenever people want to do something and have the power, they do it. This opposition of constitutions may take different forms. Democracy quarrels with tyranny in the same sort of way as, says Hesiod, 'potter quarrels with potter',* for extreme democracy is, of course, a form of tyranny. Kingship and aristocracy quarrel with tyranny, because their constitutions are the opposite of its spirit. This was the reason why Sparta suppressed most tyrannies, and why Syracuse pursued the same policy during the period in which she enjoyed a good constitution.

1312b9 Another way in which tyrannies may be destroyed is by internal causes. Those associated in a tyranny may quarrel with one another. This happened at Syracuse with the associates of Gelon,* and it has happened again in our own days with the associates of Dionysius. The tyranny established by Gelon was destroyed by Thrasybulus. He was the brother [of Gelon and of Gelon's successor] Hieron. [On Hieron's death] he flattered Gelon's son [the next heir], and ambitious to secure power for himself he seduced him into a life of pleasure.

The relatives of the heir thereupon formed a party, originally with the idea of overthrowing Thrasybulus and saving the tyranny; but in the event their supporters, feeling that the opportunity was ripe, expelled the whole of the family. The overthrow of Dionysius was due to his relative by marriage, Dion, who led an expedition against him. Dion won the support of the people and expelled Dionysius—only to perish himself.

1312ᵇ17 There are two causes which are mostly responsible for attacks on tyrannies: these are hatred and contempt. Of these hatred is something all tyrants are bound to arouse; but contempt is often the cause by which tyrannies are actually overthrown. It is a proof of this that the tyrants who have won the position by their own efforts have generally managed to retain it, while their successors proceed to lose it almost immediately. Living luxurious lives, they make themselves contemptible, and offer their assailants plenty of opportunities. Hatred must be reckoned as including anger, which produces much the same sort of effects. Anger, indeed, is often a more effective stimulus; angry men will attack with more tenacity, because their passion prevents them from stopping to calculate. There is nothing which frays men's tempers more than being subjected to abuse: this was what caused the collapse of the tyranny of Peisistratus' family,* and of many other tyrannies. Hatred can stop to calculate: you can hate your enemy without feeling pain. Anger is inseparable from pain; and pain makes calculation difficult.

1312ᵇ34 In brief, all the causes previously mentioned as tending to overthrow the unmixed and ultimate form of oligarchy, and the extreme form of democracy, must be counted as equally fatal to tyranny: indeed those forms are themselves no more than divided tyrannies.*

1312ᵇ38 Kingship is the constitution least liable to be destroyed by external causes. It therefore tends to be durable; and when it is destroyed, the causes are generally internal. Such causes may take two forms. One is dissension among the members of the royal household: the other consists in attempting to govern in a tyrannical fashion by claiming a larger prerogative without any legal restrictions. Kingships do not occur nowadays and any government of that type which emerges today is a personal government or tyranny. The reason is that kingship is a government by consent, with sovereign authority in matters of major importance, whereas [nowadays] there are many people of similar quality so that no one is outstanding enough to be fitted for the grandeur and the dignity of the office of king. There is thus no basis of consent for such a form of government; and when it is imposed, by fraud or by force, it is instantly regarded as a form of tyranny. Kingships limited to a single family are liable to be overthrown by a further cause which has still to be mentioned. Kings of this type often incur the contempt of their subjects; they lack the power of tyrants, having merely an office of honour, but they nevertheless abuse and injure [their subjects]. Their overthrow is then an easy matter. Kings cease to be kings when their subjects cease to be willing subjects, though tyrants can continue to be tyrants whether their subjects are willing or no.

The destruction of monarchical forms of government is due to these and similar causes.

CHAPTER 11

The methods of ensuring the stability of monarchies. Kingships are best preserved by a policy of moderation. There are two ways of preserving tyrannies. One way is the traditional tyrant's policy of repression, which has its analogy with the policy of extreme democracy: its three main objects are to break the spirit of subjects, to sow distrust among them, and to make them incapable of action. The other way is a policy of assimilating tyranny to kingship, by a good administration and the exercise of personal restraint; a wise tyrant will adorn his city, pay heed to public worship, honour the good, keep his own passions in check, and enlist in his favour as large a measure of social support as he possibly can. In this way he may prolong his days, and attain a state of 'half-goodness'.

1313ª18 Taking a general view of monarchical forms of government, we may say that they are all preserved by methods the converse of those which are apt to cause their destruction. Looking at them in detail, and taking kingship first, we may say that kingship is preserved by a policy of moderation. The less the area of his prerogative, the longer will the rule of a king last unimpaired: he will himself be less of a master and behave more like an equal, and his subjects, on their side, will envy him less. This is the reason for the long survival of kingship among the Molossians; and the survival of the Spartan kingship may also be attributed partly to the original division of power between the two kings, and partly to the general policy of moderation afterwards followed by Theopompus, above all in his institution of the office of Ephor.* He may be said to have strengthened Spartan kingship, in the long run, by depriving it of some of its original power; and there is a sense in which he increased rather than diminished its importance. This is the point of the answer which he is said to have given to his wife, when she asked him if he were not ashamed to be leaving his sons less power than he had inherited from his father. 'Certainly not,' he replied; 'I am leaving them a power that will last much longer.'

1313^a34 Tyrannies can be preserved in two ways,* which are utterly opposed to one another. One of them is the traditional way; and it is also the method of government still followed by the majority of tyrants. Many of its characteristics are supposed to have been originally instituted by Periander of Corinth; but many features may also be derived from the Persian system of government. These include measures previously mentioned as tending to the preservation of tyranny (so far as it can be preserved): the 'lopping off' of outstanding men, and the removal of men of spirit.* In addition it is possible: (1) to prohibit common meals, clubs, education, and anything of a like character—or, in other words, to adopt a defensive attitude against everything likely to produce the two qualities of mutual confidence and a high spirit; (2) to forbid societies for cultural purposes, and any gathering of a similar character, and to use every means for making every subject as much of a stranger as is possible to every other (since mutual acquaintance creates mutual confidence); (3) to require every resident in the city to be constantly appearing in public, and always hanging about the palace gates. (In this way they are least likely to escape notice in what they do and they will come to have a low opinion of themselves as a result of being continually in the position of slaves.) This line of policy also includes other tyrannical measures of a similar character, common in Persia and other barbarian countries. For example, a tyrant may try (4) to ensure that nothing which any of his subjects says or does escapes his notice. This entails a secret police, like the female spies employed at Syracuse, or the eavesdroppers sent by the tyrant Hieron* to all social gatherings and public meetings. (Men are not so likely to speak their minds if they go in fear of people like these; and if they do speak out, they are less likely to go undetected.) He may (5) sow mutual distrust and foster discord between friend and friend; between people and notables; between one section of the rich and another. Finally, it befits a tyrant (6) to impoverish his subjects —partly to prevent them from having the means for maintaining a civic guard; partly to keep them so busy with their daily tasks that they have no time for plotting. One example of this policy is the building of the Egyptian pyramids: another is the lavish offerings to temples made by the family of Cypselus;* a third is the erection of the temple to Olympian Zeus by the family of Peisistratus; a fourth is the additions made by Polycrates* to the Samian monuments. (All these actions have the same object: to increase the poverty of the tyrant's subjects and to curtail their leisure.) The imposition of taxes produces a similar result. We may cite the example of Syracuse, where in a period of five years, during the tyranny of Dionysius* the Elder, people were made to pay the whole of their property to the city. The same vein of policy also makes tyrants warmongers, with the object of keeping their subjects constantly occupied and continually in need of a leader.

1313^{b}29 Kings are maintained and secured by their friends but it is characteristic of tyrants to distrust them above all others, for whereas everyone wants [to overthrow tyrants], it is their friends who have most power to achieve this. The methods applied in extreme democracies are thus all to be found in tyrannies. They both encourage feminine influence in the family, in the hope that wives will tell tales of their husbands; and for a similar reason they are both indulgent to slaves. Slaves and women are not likely to plot against tyrants: indeed, as they prosper under them, they are bound to look with favour on tyrannies and democracies alike—of course the people likes to act as absolute ruler. This is the reason why, under both these forms of government, honour is paid to flatterers, in democracies to demagogues, who are flatterers of the people, and, in the case of tyrants, to those who associate with them on obsequious terms—which is the function of the flatterer. Tyranny is thus a system dear to the wicked. Tyrants love to be flattered, and nobody with the soul of a freeman can ever stoop to that; a good man may be a friend, but at any rate he will not be a flatterer. Bad men are useful for achieving bad objects; 'nail knocks out nail', as the proverb says. It is a habit of tyrants never to like anyone who has a spirit of dignity and independence. The tyrant claims a monopoly of such qualities for himself; he feels that anybody who asserts a rival dignity, or acts with independence, is threatening his own superiority and the despotic power of his tyranny; he hates him accordingly as a subverter of his own authority. It is also a habit of tyrants to prefer the company of aliens to that of citizens at table and in society; citizens, they feel, are enemies, but aliens will offer no opposition.

1314^{a}12 Such are the arts of the tyrant, and such are the means he uses in order to maintain his authority; but they plumb the depth of wrongdoing. We may regard them as all summed up under three main headings, which correspond to the three main ends pursued by tyrants. Their first end and aim is to break the spirit of their subjects. They know that a poor-spirited man will never plot against anybody. Their second aim is to breed mutual distrust. Tyranny is never overthrown until people can begin to trust one another; and this is the reason why tyrants are always at war with the good. They feel that good men are dangerous to their authority, not only because they think it shame to be governed despotically but also because of their loyalty to themselves and to others and because of their refusal to betray one another or anybody else. The third and last aim of tyrants is to make their subjects incapable of action. Nobody attempts the impossible. Nobody, therefore, will attempt the overthrow of a tyranny, when all are incapable of action.

1314ª25 We have here three principles to which the policies of tyrants may be reduced; in other words, all the activities characteristic of tyrants could be regarded as resting on these assumptions: (1) some serve to breed mutual distrust among their subjects, (2) some to make them incapable of action, and (3) some to break their spirit.

1314ª29 This is one method for the preservation of tyrannies. But there is also a second method, where the line of action followed is almost the very reverse.* We shall be able to understand the nature of this method if we go back, for a moment, to the causes which destroy kingships. We saw that one way of destroying a kingship was by making the government more tyrannical. This suggests that a way of preserving tyranny may be making it more like kingship—subject to the one safeguard that the tyrant still retains power, and is still in a position to govern his subjects with or without their consent. To surrender power as well is to surrender tyranny itself. Power must thus be retained, as an essential condition of tyranny; but otherwise the tyrant should act, or at any rate appear to act, in the role of a good player of the part of king. He must show himself, in the first place, concerned for the public funds. Not only must he refrain from expenditure in lavishing gifts which cause public discontent (and that will always arise when people toil away at their work only for others greedily to take away the proceeds and squander them on harlots, aliens, and luxury trades); he must also render accounts of his income and expenditure—a policy which a number of tyrants have actually practised. This is a method of government which will make him appear to be more of a steward than a tyrant. There is no need to fear that it will involve him in a deficit, so long as he keeps control of affairs; and if he is compelled to be absent from home he may even find that it is more to his advantage to have a deficit than it would be to leave a hoard behind him. The regents whom he appoints will be less likely, in that case, to make a bid for power; and a tyrant campaigning abroad has more reason to fear his regents than he has to fear the citizen body itself. The regents remain behind: the citizens go abroad with their ruler. Next, and in the second place, he should levy taxes, and require other contributions,* in such a way that they can be seen to be intended for the proper management of public services, or to be meant for use, in case of need, on military emergencies; and, generally, he should act in the role of a guardian, or steward, who is handling public rather than private money.

1314^b18 A tyrant should appear grave, without being harsh; and his appearance should be such that those who come into his presence will do so with awe, and not in fear. This is an aim which cannot easily be achieved if he fails to inspire respect. He should therefore cultivate military qualities, even if he fails to cultivate others, and should give the impression of military distinction. He should be personally free from any suspicion of [sexually] abusing any of his subjects, boy or girl, and all his associates should be equally free from suspicion. The women of his family should observe the same rule in dealing with other women: the arrogant behaviour of women has often been the ruin of tyrannies. In the matter of personal indulgence [in food and drink] the tyrant should be the opposite of some of the tyrants of our days, who—not content with starting at dawn and going on for days on end—actually want to be seen to do these things, in the idea that people will admire their bliss and felicity. Ideally, a tyrant should be moderate in his pleasures: if he cannot attain that ideal, he should at any rate avoid being seen. It is the drunkards, and not the sober—the drowsy, and not the vigilant—who are easily attacked and readily despised.

1314^b35 Indeed, a tyrant should do the opposite of nearly everything which we have previously described as character-istic of tyrants. He should plan and adorn his city as if he were not a tyrant, but a trustee. He should always show a particular zeal in the cult of the gods. People are less afraid of being treated unjustly by those of this sort, that is if they think that the ruler is god-fearing and pays some regard to the gods; and they are less ready to conspire against him, if they feel that the gods themselves are his friends. At the same time, the tyrant should show his zeal without falling into folly. He should also honour good men, in any walk of life; and he should do so in such a way as to make them think that they could not possibly have been honoured more by their own fellow citizens, if their fellow citizens had been free [to distribute honours themselves]. He should distribute such honours personally; but he should leave all punishments to be inflicted by the other officials or the lawcourts.

1315^a8 It is a precaution common to all forms of monarchical government [and not peculiar to tyranny] that no single person should be promoted to any great position, and if such promotion has to be made, it should be shared by a number of persons, who will then keep a watch upon one another. But if, after all, a single person must needs be promoted to some great position, he should never be someone of bold spirit: tempers of that sort are the quickest to strike in all fields of action. If, on the other hand, a decision is taken to remove someone from a position of power, the removal should be gradual, and he should not be deprived of all his authority at a single blow. A tyrant should abstain from every form of arrogant behaviour, and from two forms above all others—the infliction of physical chastisement, and [sexual] abuse of the young. He should show a particular caution of behaviour when he is dealing with someone of sensitive honour. Arrogance in matters of money is resented by those who care about money; but it is arrogance in matters affecting honour which is resented by men of honour and virtue. A tyrant should therefore abstain from such acts; or, at the very least, he should make it clear that when he inflicts any punishment, he is doing so not from arrogance but in a spirit of paternal discipline, and when he indulges himself with the young, he is doing so not in the licence of power but because he is genuinely in love. In all such cases, too, he should atone for the dishonours which he appears to inflict by the gift of still greater honours.

1315^a24 Attempts at assassination are most dangerous, and need most watching, when they are made by those who are not concerned about escaping with their lives after the deed is done. For this reason special precautions ought to be taken against any who feel that either they themselves, or others for whom they care, are being subjected to abuse. Those who are acting in hot blood take little heed to themselves: witness the saying of Heraclitus, 'It is hard to fight against heat of the spirit, for it is willing to pay the price of life.'*

1315ᵃ31 Given that a city is composed of two sections—the poor and the rich, both of these should, if possible, be induced to think that it is the tyrant's power which secures them in their position, and prevents either from suffering injury at the hands of the other. If, however, one of the sections is stronger than the other, the tyrant should attach that section particularly to his side. There will be no need, if he has its support, to resort to such measures as the emancipation of slaves or the disarming of citizens. Either section, if added to the power which he already possesses, will be strong enough to defeat any attempt against his position.

1315ᵃ40 It is unnecessary to treat such matters as these in detail. The general aim is sufficiently evident. He should appear to his subjects not as a tyrant, but as a steward and king of his people. He should show himself a trustee, not as one intent on his own interest; he should seek the society of the notables, and yet court the favour of the masses. This will ensure, first, that his rule will be a nobler and a more enviable rule, that his subjects will be people of a better sort, free from humiliation, and that he himself will cease to be an object of hatred and fear. It will ensure, secondly, that his rule will be more lasting, and that he will himself attain a habit of character, if not wholly disposed to goodness, at any rate half-good—half-good and yet half-bad, but at any rate not wholly bad.

E: The Chronology of Tyrannies and Criticisms of Plato's Account of Constitutional Change (Chapter 12)

CHAPTER 12

The first part of this chapter explains that tyrannies, in the past, have been generally short-lived. The rest contains a criticism of Plato's account, in the Republic, of the causes of constitutional change. The criticism is partly concerned with Plato's attempt to give a mathematical explanation of change and corruption in the ideal city, and partly with its failure (1) to explain at all the cause of change in tyrannies and (2) to explain satisfactorily the causes of changes in oligarchies.

1315ᵇ11 Yet no constitutions are so short-lived as oligarchy and tyranny.* The tyranny of longest duration was that of Orthagoras and his descendants* at Sicyon, which lasted for a century. The reason for its permanence was the moderation of their behaviour towards their subjects, and their general obedience to rules of law: Cleisthenes [one of the later tyrants at Sicyon] was too much of a soldier to be despised, and the dynasty generally courted the favour of its subjects by the attentions it paid them. It is recorded of Cleisthenes that he awarded a crown to the judge who gave a verdict against him [in the games]; and there are some who say that the seated figure in the public square at Sicyon is a statue of the judge who gave this verdict. There is a [similar] story that Peisistratus, the tyrant of Athens, once allowed himself to be summoned as defendant in a case before the Areopagus.

1315ᵇ22 The second tyranny in point of length was that of the family of Cypselus* at Corinth, which lasted seventy-three years and a half: Cypselus himself was tyrant for thirty years, Periander for forty years and a half, and Psammetichus the son of Gorgus for three. The causes of this long duration were the same as at Sicyon: Cypselus courted the favour of his subjects, and dispensed with a bodyguard during the whole of his reign; Periander proved himself a soldier, if he also proved a despot.

1315ᵇ29 The third tyranny in point of length was that of the family of Peisistratus* at Athens; but this was not continuous. Peisistratus was expelled twice during the course of his reign, and was only tyrant for seventeen years in a period of thirty-three: his sons between them ruled for eighteen years; and the whole reign of the family was thus confined to a period of thirty-five years.

1315ᵇ34 The most durable of the other tyrannies was that of Hieron and Gelon* at Syracuse. But it, too, was comparatively brief, and only lasted for eighteen years altogether; Gelon was tyrant for seven years and died in the eighth year of his reign: Hieron ruled for ten years: Thrasybulus was expelled after ruling for ten months. Tyrannies generally have all been quite short-lived.*

1315ᵇ40 We have now considered all (or almost all) the causes which lead to the destruction and the preservation of constitutions and monarchies. We may note, in conclusion, that the subject of constitutional change is treated by 'Socrates' in the *Republic*;* but the treatment is defective. In the first place, he fails to mention specifically the cause of the change peculiar to his own first and ideal constitution. He says that the cause is that nothing abides, and that everything changes in a given period; and he goes on to say that the source [of such general change] is to be found in a system of numbers, 'in which the root ratio of 4 to 3, wedded to 5, furnishes two harmonical progressions'* (he adds words to the effect that this happens when the arithmetical value of the diagram is cubed). The implication here is that the reproduction of the species sometimes issues in people of poor quality, who are beyond the reach of education. This implication, in itself, is perhaps not incorrect: there may be some who cannot possibly be educated or made into good men. But why should this be a cause of change peculiar to the ideal city which he describes, rather than one common to all cities, and indeed to all things that come into existence?* There is a further point. Can the passage of time, which, he says, causes all things to change, explain how things which did not begin simultaneously should simultaneously undergo change? Does a thing which came into existence on the day before the turn of the tide change simultaneously [with things of an earlier origin]?

1316ª17 Again, we may ask why the ideal city should turn into a city of the Spartan type. Constitutions change, as a rule, more readily into an opposite than into a cognate form. The same argument also applies to the other changes mentioned by 'Socrates', when he depicts the Spartan type as changing into oligarchy, oligarchy into democracy, and democracy into tyranny. The very reverse may equally happen: democracy, for example, can change into oligarchy, and indeed it can do so more easily than it can change into monarchy.

1316ª25 When it comes to tyrannies, he never explains whether they do, or do not, change, nor, if they do, why they do so, or into what constitution they change. The reason for this omission is that any explanation would have been difficult. The matter cannot be settled along the lines of his argument; for on those lines a tyranny would have to change back into the first and ideal constitution, in order to maintain continuity in the revolving cycle of change. Actually, however, one tyranny may change into another, as the tyranny at Sicyon changed from that of Myron to that of Cleisthenes; a tyranny may equally change into oligarchy, like the tyranny of Antileon at Chalcis; it may also turn into democracy, like the tyranny of Gelon at Syracuse; or it may change into aristocracy, as happened to the tyranny of Charilaus at Sparta, and as also happened at Carthage. Again, there are cases where the change has been from oligarchy to tyranny.* This was what happened to most of the ancient oligarchies in Sicily: for instance, the oligarchy at Leontini was succeeded by the tyranny of Panaetius, the one at Gela by the tyranny of Cleander, and the one at Rhegium by the tyranny of Anaxilaus. The same thing has also happened in a number of other cities.

1316ª39 It is strange to suppose that the change [of the Spartan type of constitution] into oligarchy is merely due to the fact that the officials turn money-lovers and profit-makers, and not because those who are greatly superior in wealth think it unjust for those without property and those who have property to be given equal shares in the city.* Actually, in a number of oligarchies, profit-making is forbidden, and there are specific laws to the contrary. On the other hand, at Carthage, although it is democratically governed, profit-making is common*—and yet the constitution has never yet changed its character. It is also absurd to say that an oligarchical city is two cities—one of the rich and one of the poor [551d]. Why should it be affected more than the Spartan type, or more than any other type where all are not equal in property or on the same level of merit? Without anyone having become any poorer than he was previously, oligarchies none the less turn into democracies if the poor become the majority. Conversely, democracies change into oligarchies if the wealthier classes are stronger than the masses, and take an active interest in affairs while the latter pay little attention.

1316**b**14 There are thus a number of causes which may produce a change from oligarchy to democracy; but he confines himself to one [555d]—extravagance, leading to debt, and ending in poverty—a view which assumes that all, or most, are rich to begin with. This is not the truth of the matter. What is true is that when any of the leading men lose their property, they become revolutionaries. But when this happens to any of the others there is no untoward consequence; and any change that may ensue is no more likely to be a change to democracy than it is to be a change to some other form of constitution. There is also a further point. To have no share in honours and office, or to suffer injustice or abuse, is sufficient to cause factional disputes and constitutional changes, even if there has been no squandering of property through that licence to 'do as you like' which is caused, in his view, by an exaggerated sense of liberty.

Though there are many varieties of oligarchy and democracy, 'Socrates' discusses their changes as if there were only one form of either.

BOOK VI
METHODS OF CONSTRUCTING DEMOCRACIES AND OLIGARCHIES WITH A SPECIAL VIEW TO THEIR GREATER STABILITY

A: The Construction of Democracies (Chapters 1–5)

CHAPTER 1

The varieties of democracy: they are due to two causes—the different characters of the populace, and the different combinations of democratic institutions, in different democracies.

1316ᵇ31 We have discussed* the number and nature of the varieties to be found (*a*) in the deliberative body, which is the sovereign element in the constitution, (*b*) in the system of offices, and (*c*) in judicial bodies; and we have discussed the form of each institution that is appropriate to each kind of constitution. We have also dealt with the circumstances and the causes which lead to the destruction and preservation of the different constitutions.*

1316ᵇ36 Since democracy and the other types of constitution each take a number of forms, we must consider what still remains to be said about each form, and, more especially, what mode of organization is appropriate and advantageous to each. We must also investigate the possible combinations of these various modes of organization for the effect of such combinations is to make constitutions overlap with each other—to make aristocracy, for instance, have an oligarchic character, or constitutional government [polity] more democratic. The possible combinations—which have not received the consideration they deserve—may be illustrated by examples. The deliberative body and the method of electing the officials may be arranged on an oligarchical basis, while the judicial bodies are constituted on an aristocratic basis. The judicial bodies and the deliberative body may be constituted on an oligarchical basis, while the method of electing the officials is arranged on an aristocratic basis. Other ways may also be followed for getting at the same result—that the elements of a constitution should not all have the same character [as that constitution].

1317ª10 We have already explained* which form of democracy is appropriate to what type of city; which form of oligarchy agrees with which sort of population; and which of the other constitutions is to the advantage of which peoples. But it is not enough to ascertain which form of constitution is best for each city. We have also to ascertain the proper way of constructing these, and other forms. We must treat the problem succinctly; but if we begin with democracy, we shall, in dealing with it, also be learning to understand its opposite, which is commonly termed oligarchy. For the purposes of this inquiry we have to take into account all the attributes of democracy, and every feature generally held to be characteristic of democratic constitutions. Combinations of these attributes account for the origin of different types of democracy and explain both why there is more than one type, and why the types vary.

1317ª22 There are two reasons why there are several forms of democracy. One has already been mentioned.* Different peoples differ in character. Here you may have a populace of farmers; there you may have one of mechanics and day-labourers. If you add the first of these groups to the second and then add in the third, you have a constitution which differs, not just in being better or worse, but in being a quite different form of democracy. It is, however, the second reason we are now discussing: this is that [different] combinations of the features which characterize democracy and are supposed to be its attributes produce different forms of democracy. One variety of democracy will have fewer of these features; a second will have more; a third will have them all. Studying each of these [attributes of democracy] not only helps in constructing whatever variety one may happen to want: it also helps the reform of existing ones. Those engaged in building a constitution often seek to bring together all the features which fit their basic principle. But this is an error, as we have already noted* in discussing the destruction and preservation of constitutions.

Let us now consider the postulates, the character, and the aims of democratic constitutions.

CHAPTER 2

The underlying idea of democracies is liberty. Liberty as conceived in democracies is twofold; in one form it means that all have a term of office and the will of all prevails; in the other it consists in 'living as you like'. The institutions involved by this idea, in the spheres of the executive, the judicature, and the deliberative; the payment of the people for political services, and the democratic objection to any long tenure of office. On the other hand, it is to be noted that a specially typical form of democracy (the agricultural or 'peasant' form?) may be based on an idea of justice which involves a general and all-round system of equality—i.e. a system which does not favour the poorer class.

1317^a40 The underlying principle of the democratic type of constitution is liberty. Indeed it is commonly held that liberty can only be enjoyed in this sort of constitution, for this, so they say, is the aim of every democracy. Liberty in one of its forms consists in the interchange of ruling and being ruled.* The democratic conception of justice consists in arithmetical equality, rather than proportionate equality on the basis of desert. On this conception of justice the masses must necessarily be sovereign and the will of the majority must be ultimate and must be the expression of justice. The argument is that each citizen should be in a position of equality; and the result which follows in democracies is that the poor are more sovereign than the rich, for they are in a majority, and the will of the majority is sovereign. This then is one mark of liberty, which all democrats agree in making the defining feature of their sort of constitution. Another mark is 'living as you like'. Such a life, they argue, is the function of the free man, just as the function of slaves is not to live as they like. This is the second defining feature of democracy. It results in the view that ideally one should not be ruled by any one, or, at least, that one should [rule and] be ruled in turns. It contributes, in this way, to a general system of liberty based on equality.

1317^b17 Such being the idea of democracy, and the principles on which it is founded, its characteristic features are the following: the election of officers by all, and from all; the system of all ruling over each, and each, in his turn, over all; the method of appointing by lot to all offices—or, at any rate, to all which do not require some practical experience and professional skill; the practice of having no property qualification—or, at any rate, the lowest possible qualification —for office; the rule that, apart from the military offices, no office should ever be held twice by the same person—or, at any rate, only on few occasions, and those relating only to a few offices; the rule that the tenure of every office—or, at any rate, of as many as possible—should be brief; the practice of having courts, composed of all the citizens or of persons selected from all, and competent to decide all cases—or, at any rate, most of them, and those the greatest and most important, such as the audit of official accounts, constitutional issues, and matters of contract; and the rule that the popular assembly should be sovereign in all matters—or, at any rate, in the most important, and conversely that the officials should be sovereign in none—or, at any rate, in as few as possible.

1317^b31 Among the public offices the one most popular in democracies is the Council,* wherever there are not adequate means for paying all the citizens to attend the assembly. If there are adequate means, the Council itself is deprived of its power; and the people, once provided with pay, begin to take everything into their hands, as has already been noticed in the previous section of our inquiry.* This system of payment is a further attribute of democracy. The ideal is payment for all functions—for the assembly, for the courts, and for those who hold office; but, failing this, there will at any rate be payment for attending the courts, the council, and the stated meetings of the popular assembly, and also for serving on any board of officials whose members are required to have a common table. (It may be remarked that while oligarchy is characterized by good birth, wealth, and culture, the attributes of democracy would appear to be the very opposite—low birth, poverty, and vulgarity.)* Another attribute of democracy is to dispense with all life-offices—or at least to curtail the powers of any such offices, if they have been left surviving from some earlier epoch of change—and to make appointments to any life-office depend on the use of the lot and not on election.

1318ª3 These are the attributes common to democracies generally. But the form of democracy and the sort of populace which is generally held to be specially typical, arises from the conception of justice which is recognized as being demo-cratic—that of equality for all on an arithmetical basis. There would be equality if the poorer class exercised no greater authority than the rich, or, in other words, if sovereignty was not exercised by the poorer class alone, but was equally vested in all the citizens on a numerical basis.* If that was the case one really could believe that equality—and liberty—was achieved by their constitution.

CHAPTER 3

How is equality to be secured in democracies? Should the basis of equality be the amount of property owned or should it be the numbers of people concerned? It may be suggested that property and numbers should both be taken into account, and that sovereignty should rest with the will of a majority of persons who are also the owners of a majority of property.

1318ª11 This raises the question, 'How is such equality actually to be secured?' [Suppose, for example, there are 500 large owners and 1,000 small owners.] Should the assessed properties of the citizens be divided so that those of the 500 [are equal in total value to those of] the 1,000, and should the 1,000 and the 500 have equal [voting] power?* Or, alterna-tively, should equality of this sort be calculated on some other system—a system, for example, by which properties are di-vided into blocks, as before, but equal numbers of representa-tives are then selected from the 500 and from the 1,000, and the representatives so selected are given control of the elections and the lawcourts?* Now is a constitution so based the one most in accordance with justice, as justice is conceived in democracies? Or is a constitution based on numbers more truly in accordance with justice? Democrats reply by saying that justice consists in the will of a majority of persons. Oligarchs reply by saying that it consists in the will of those with greater wealth, and that decisions should be taken on the basis of weight of property. Both of these answers involve inequality and injustice. If justice is made to consist in the will of the few, tyranny is the logical result; for according to the oligarchical conception of justice, a single person who owns more than all the other owners of property put together will have a just claim to be the sole ruler. If, on the other hand, justice is made to consist in the will of a numerical majority, that majority will act unjustly, as we have already noted,* and confiscate the property of the rich minority.

1318ᵃ27 We have to ask, in the light of the definitions of justice propounded by both sides, 'What is the sort of equality to which both sides can agree?' Both sides affirm that the will of the major part of the citizens should be sovereign. We may accept that statement; but we cannot accept it without modification. Since there are two classes which compose the city —the wealthy class, and the poor, we may attribute sovereignty, accordingly, to the will of both these classes, or that of a majority [in each]. Suppose, however, that the two classes are resolved on conflicting measures. In that case we may attribute sovereignty to the will of a majority of those who are also the owners of a majority of property.* Suppose, for example, that there are 10 in the wealthy class, and 20 in the poor; and suppose that 6 of the 10 have come to one decision while 15 of the 20 have come to another. This means that 4 of the wealthy class agree with [the majority of] the poorer class, and again, that 5 of the poorer class agree with [the majority of] the wealthy class. In that case sovereignty should rest with the will of that side whose members, on both of its elements being added together, have property in excess of that belonging to the members of the other. If the two sides turn out to be equal the difficulty is the same as that which arises today when a popular assembly or a lawcourt is equally divided. The matter has to be settled by lot, or some other similar method has to be used.

1318ᵇ1 To find where truth resides, in these matters of equality and justice, is a very difficult task. Nevertheless it is an easier task than that of persuading men to act justly, if they have power enough to secure their own selfish interests.

The weaker are always anxious for equality and justice. The strong pay no heed to either.

CHAPTER 4

(a) *The agricultural form of democracy. It needs, in the interest of stability, a balance between the mass of the people, on the one hand, and the propertied classes, on the other. That balance may be secured (1) by allowing the whole civic body to take part in electing officials, to call them to account, and to sit in the lawcourts, and (2) by allowing only the propertied classes to hold the more important offices. Methods may also be used for encouraging the growth of an agricultural population. (b) The pastoral form of democracy. (c) The form based on a populace of mechanics, shopkeepers, and day-labourers. This last form is too often connected with the policy of giving citizenship indiscriminately to all and sundry: it is a wiser policy to stop short at the point at which the strength of the masses just exceeds the combined strength of the upper and middle classes. Other policies which may also be followed in this form of democracy.*

1318ᵇ6 Of the four varieties of democracy the best, as has already been noted in the previous section of our inquiry,* is the one that comes first in the order of classification. It is also the oldest of all the varieties. But the reason why it comes first is connected with the grading of the different kinds of populace. The best kind of populace is one of farmers, so, where the bulk of the people live by arable or pastoral farming, there is no difficulty in constructing a democracy. Such people, since they do not have a great amount of property, are busily occupied; and they have thus no time for attending the assembly. Because they [do not]* have the necessities of life, they stick to their work, and do not covet what does not belong to them; indeed they find more pleasure in work than they do in politics and government—unless there are large pickings to be got from having a finger in government. The masses covet profits more than they covet honours; an indication of this is that they put up with the old-time tyrannies, and still continue to tolerate oligarchies if only they are allowed to get on with their work and are not robbed of their earnings. That way they either become rich, or, at any rate, cease to be poor. Any craving which the masses may feel for position and power will be satisfied if they are given the power to elect officials and to call them to account. Indeed there are some democracies where the mass of the people are content with a system under which they do not take part in the election of officials (some of their number are selected in turn for this purpose, as happened in Mantinea), but the people has the sovereign power of deliberation. Such a system must still be considered as a system of democracy, and it was such at Mantinea.

1318^{b}27 For these reasons it is both advantageous and the general practice for the variety of democracy we mentioned earlier to have the following arrangements: all the citizens take part in the election of officials, call them to account, and sit in the lawcourts, but the most important offices are filled by election, and confined to those who can satisfy a property qualification. The greater the importance of an office, the greater the property qualification that is required. Alternatively, no property qualification may be required for any office, but only men of capacity are actually appointed. A city which is governed in this way will be sure to be well governed (its offices will always be in the hands of the best of its members, with the people giving its consent and bearing no grudge against persons of quality); and the men of quality and the notables will be sure to be satisfied, under a system which at once preserves them from being governed by other and inferior persons and ensures (because others are responsible for calling them to account) that they will themselves govern justly. To be kept in such dependence, and to be denied the power of doing just as one pleases, is an advantage, since the power to act at will leaves no defence against the evil that is present in every human being. The outcome will be what is most beneficial in any constitution: government will be conducted by men of quality, and they will be free from misconduct, while the masses will not be disadvantaged.

1319^{a}4 It is evident that this form of democracy [based on a farming populace] is the best; and the reason is also evident—

that the populace on which it is based is of a particular kind. In the creation of such a populace some of the laws which were generally current in earlier ages will always be of service —laws, for example, forbidding absolutely the acquisition of property in land beyond a certain amount, or, at any rate, forbidding it within a fixed distance from the town or the citadel. There used also to be laws, in a considerable number of cities, prohibiting the sale of the land originally allotted to one's family; there is also the law [at Elis], attributed to Oxylus, which prohibits, in effect, the raising of a mortgage on a certain proportion of anyone's estate. As things are, the situation needs to be corrected and a law like that of Aphytis should be adopted as a corrective, and as likely to help in securing the object we have in view. The people of Aphytis, although they combine a large population with a small territory, are all engaged in farming. The reason is that estates are not assessed as single units. Estates are divided, for purposes of assessment, into a number of sections; and the sections are small enough to ensure that even the poorer landowners will show an assessment exceeding the amount required [as a qualification for participation in politics].*

1319ª19 Next to a populace of farmers, the best sort is a pastoral populace living by its herds and flocks. Many of their characteristics are similar to those of farmers; but with their robust physique, and their capacity for camping out in the open, they are specially trained and hardened into a good condition for war. The other kinds of populace which form the basis of the other varieties of democracy, are almost without exception of a much poorer character. They lead a poor sort of life: and none of the occupations followed by a populace which consists of mechanics, shopkeepers, and day-labourers, leaves any room for excellence. Revolving round the market-place and the city centre, people of this class generally find it easy to attend the sessions of the popular assembly—unlike the farmers who, because they are scattered through the countryside, neither see so much of each other nor feel the need for meetings of this sort. When there is also the further advantage of a countryside which lies at a considerable distance from the city, it is easy to construct a good democracy or 'constitutional government' [polity]. The mass of the people are then compelled to fix their abode on their lands; and even if there is still a mob left which lives round the market-place, a rule will have to be made, where the constitution is democratic, that there shall be no meetings of the popular assembly without the people from the country.

It has now been shown how the first and best variety of democracy ought to be constructed. It is also clear, from what has been said, how the other varieties should be constituted. They should deviate in successive stages, and by excluding, at each stage, a progressively inferior class.*

1319ᵇ1 The last variety, which includes all classes alike, is one that cannot be borne by all cities, and can hardly itself endure, unless it is properly constituted so far as its laws and customs are concerned. The causes which lead to the destruction of this as of other forms of government have already been, in the main, described.* In attempting its construction the leaders of popular parties usually follow the policy of seeking to strengthen the populace by simply increasing its numbers to the utmost possible extent. Citizenship is given not only to the lawfully born, but also to the illegitimate and to those who have only one citizen parent, whether that parent be father or mother. Of course, this whole element suits the kind of democracy we are discussing. But, although this is the policy of construction usually followed by demagogues, they ought to increase numbers only to the point at which the masses exceed [in number] the notables and the middle class. They should never go beyond this point. Any greater proportion will at once disturb the balance of the constitution; and it will also incite the notables still more against democracy—a situation which caused the faction-fighting in Cyrene. A small evil may be overlooked; but an evil which grows to large dimensions is always before one's eyes.

1319ᵇ19 Other measures which are also useful in constructing this last and most extreme type of democracy are measures like those introduced by Cleisthenes at Athens, when he sought to advance the cause of democracy, or those which were taken by the founders of popular government at Cyrene. A number of new tribes and clans should be instituted by the side of the old; private cults should be reduced in number and conducted at common centres; and every contrivance should be employed to make all the citizens mix, as much as they possibly can, and to break down their old loyalties. All the measures adopted by tyrants may equally be regarded as congenial to democracy. We may cite as examples the licence allowed to slaves (which, up to a point, may be advantageous as well as congenial), the licence permitted to women and children, and the policy of conniving at the practice of 'living as you like'. There is much to assist a constitution of this sort, for most people find more pleasure in living without discipline than they find in a life of temperance.

CHAPTER 5

Besides constructing democracies on a sound basis, it is also necessary to ensure their permanence. The true policy is not one which guarantees the greatest possible amount of democracy, but one which guarantees its longest possible duration. Moderation is therefore advisable. On the one hand, the rich should not be alienated by a policy of confiscating their riches, and the system of payment for political services should be kept within modest bounds; on the other hand, measures should also be taken to improve the lot of the common people by a system of social services, both public and private.

1319ᵇ33 For the legislator and for those who would found a constitution of this type the work of construction is neither the only task, nor the most important one. The maintenance of a constitution is what really matters;* after all it is not difficult to keep any kind of constitution in being for two or three days. Legislators should therefore direct their attention to the causes which lead to the preservation and the destruction of constitutions—a theme which has already been treated—and on that basis they should devote their effort to creating stability. They must be on their guard against all destructive elements and must establish written and unwritten laws, which include, above everything else, all those features which tend to preserve constitutions; they must believe that

the genuinely democratic and the genuinely oligarchic policies
are not those which ensure that the city will have the greatest
possible amount of democracy or oligarchy, but those which
ensure that it will do so for the longest period of time. The
demagogues of our own day, zealous to please the peoples of
their cities, cause a large amount of property to be confiscated
to public use by means of the lawcourts. Those who care for
the well-being of their constitution should labour to correct
such practices. They should have a law passed which prevents
the fines imposed in lawcourts from becoming public property
or being paid into the treasury, and makes them, instead,
temple property. Wrongdoers would not, in that case, be any
more heedless than they are now (they would still have to pay
the same fine), and the mob, having nothing to gain, would
be less inclined to vote against defendants. Public prosecutions
should also be made as few as possible; and heavy fines
should be used to deter prosecutors from bringing them at
random. Such prosecutions are usually brought against notables only, and not against those who belong to the popular
party; but the proper policy, wherever it can be pursued, is to
keep all citizens alike attached to the constitution, or at any
rate, failing that, to prevent them from regarding those in
authority as their enemies.

1320ª17 Extreme democracies generally have large populations and it is difficult to get the citizens to attend the
assembly without a system of payment. Such a system bears
hardly on the notables—unless sufficient revenues are in hand
to pay its cost. The necessary funds have to be procured by a
tax on property, by confiscation, and by means of corrupt
lawcourts; and these are all methods which have led in the
past to the overthrow of many democracies. So, unless there
are sufficient revenues already in hand, the meetings of the
assembly should be infrequent, while the lawcourts, although
they may have a large membership, should meet on only a
small number of days. This has two advantages: in the first
place, the wealthier classes will cease to fear the expenditure
involved—the more if it is only the poor, and not also the
well-to-do, who are allowed to receive pay; and secondly, the
cases before the courts will be much better decided, as the rich

(who do not care to be absent from their business for days together, but do not mind a short absence) will now be willing to attend.

1320ᵃ29 When, on the other hand, there are sufficient revenues [to defray the cost of a system of payment], the policy nowadays followed by demagogues should be avoided. It is their habit to distribute any surpluses among the people; and the people, in the very act of taking them, ask for the same again. To help the poor in this way is like trying to fill a leaky jar. Yet it is the duty of a genuine democrat to see to it that the masses are not excessively poor. Poverty is the cause of the defects of democracy. That is the reason why measures should be taken to ensure a permanent level of prosperity. This is in the interest of all classes, including the prosperous themselves; and therefore the proper policy is to accumulate any surplus revenue in a fund, and then to distribute this fund in block grants to the poor. The ideal method of distribution, if a sufficient fund can be accumulated, is to make such grants sufficient for the purchase of a plot of land: failing that, they should be large enough to start men in commerce or agriculture.* If such grants cannot be made to all the poor simultaneously, they should be distributed successively, by tribes or other divisions: and meanwhile the rich should contribute a sum sufficient to provide the poor with payment for their attendance at the obligatory meetings of the assembly, but should be exempted from rendering useless public services.*

1320ᵇ4 It is by a policy of this sort that the Carthaginians have secured the goodwill of the people. They regularly send some of the populace to the dependent cities, and thus enable them to become prosperous. It is also possible for notables who are men of feeling and good sense each to take responsibility for a section of the poor and to give them the means of starting in new occupations. The example of the citizens of Tarentum may also be commended for imitation: the well-to-do share with the poor the use of their property and thereby conciliate the goodwill of the masses. The Tarentines have also divided all offices into two classes—one with appointments made by election, and the other with appointments made by lot—with the intention that the latter will give the

people a share in office, while the former will help to ensure a
better administration. The same result may also be achieved
by dividing the members of each board of officials into two
classes—an elected class, and a class appointed by lot.

We have now explained how democracies should be constructed.

B: The Construction of Oligarchies (Chapters 6–8)

CHAPTER 6

*The best sort of oligarchy will correspond to the best, or
agricultural, sort of democracy: it will require a moderate
property qualification for the holding of any office. The last
form of oligarchy, answering to the last, or 'extreme', form of
democracy, needs the greatest vigilance. Generally, while democracies rely on quantity or numbers, oligarchies ought to rely on
the quality of their organization.*

1320ᵇ18 From these considerations it is fairly clear how
oligarchies ought to be constituted. Our account of each
variety of oligarchy should be based on a consideration of
opposites—that is to say, each should be compared with the
variety of democracy opposed to it.* The best balanced of
oligarchies comes first; it is closely akin to what is called
'constitutional government' [polity]. In an oligarchy of this
type there should be two separate assessment rolls, a higher
and a lower. Entry in the lower roll should qualify men for
appointment to the indispensable offices; but entry in the
higher should be required for appointment to the more important ones. On the other hand, any person who acquires
sufficient property to be put on an assessment roll should be
allowed to share in the constitution; thus, by means of the
assessment, a sufficient number of the people at large will be
admitted to ensure that those with a share in the constitution
are stronger than those without. The persons newly admitted
should always be drawn from the better sections of the
people.

1320ᵇ29 The next succeeding variety of oligarchy should be constructed on similar lines to the first, but with some little tightening [of the qualifications required for office]. The variety of oligarchy which corresponds to extreme democracy is most in the nature of a ruling clique and most akin to tyranny; and, as it is worst of all, it requires all the greater vigilance. A man with a healthy physique or a ship suited for navigation, with a good crew on board, can survive a number of mistakes without being destroyed; but a man of sickly physique, or a ship badly jointed and poorly manned, cannot survive even a slight mistake. Just the same is true of constitutions: the worst need the greatest vigilance. In democracies the size of the population is generally the saving factor; it serves in place of a system of distributive justice on the basis of merit. The opposite obviously goes for oligarchy: it must seek security by the quality of its organization.

CHAPTER 7

Military factors have an important bearing on oligarchies. A cavalry force is favourable to a strict form of oligarchy; on the other hand, light-armed troops and naval forces are favourable to democracy. It is a wise policy for an oligarchy to train its own members to serve as light-armed troops. Oligarchies will also do well to give the masses some share in the government, and to require their more important officials to perform unpaid public services. In a word, they should direct themselves by the idea of public service rather than by that of private profit.

1321ª5 Just as there are four chief divisions of the mass of the population—farmers, mechanics, shopkeepers, and day-labourers—so there are also four kinds of military forces*—cavalry, heavy infantry, light-armed troops, and the navy. Where a territory is suitable for the use of cavalry, there conditions are favourable for the construction of a strong oligarchy: the inhabitants of such a territory need a cavalry force for security, and it is only those with large means who can afford to breed and keep horses. Where a territory is suitable for the use of heavy infantry, the next variety of oligarchy is natural; service in the heavy infantry is a matter for the well-to-do rather than for the poor. Light-armed troops and the navy are wholly on the side of democracy; and at present, where light-armed troops and naval forces are numerous, the oligarchical side is generally worsted in any factional dispute. This situation should be met, and remedied, by following the practice of some military commanders, who combine an appropriate number of light-armed troops with the cavalry and heavy infantry. The reason why the masses can defeat the wealthier classes, in factional disputes, is that a light-armed and mobile force finds it easy to fight with a force of cavalry and heavy infantry. An oligarchy which builds up a light-armed force exclusively from such people is thus only building up a challenge to itself. Given that there is a distinction between age groups (that is, between those who are older and those who are younger), the oligarchs should see that their sons while still young are instructed in the work of agile, lightly armed fighters. Then, when they are promoted from among the boys, they will themselves be able to perform these tasks, in actual practice.

1321ª26 There are various ways in which an oligarchy may give the masses some place in the civic body. One way, which has already been mentioned, is for a place to be granted to anyone who acquires sufficient property to put him on the assessment roll, or, as in Thebes, to those who have not followed any mechanical occupation for a number of years. Alternatively, it is possible to follow the practice of Massilia and compile a list of all who are worthy of a place, whether or not they are at the time members of the civic body.

1321ª31 The most important offices, which must necessarily be held by full citizens, should involve the duty of performing public services at one's own expense. This will have the effect of making the people willing to acquiesce in their own exclusion from such offices, and it will make them ready to tolerate officials who pay so heavy a price for the privilege. These higher officials may also be properly expected to offer magnificent sacrifices on their entry into their office, and to erect some public building during its course. The people—sharing in these entertainments, and seeing their city decorated with votive ornaments and edifices—will readily tolerate the continuance of the constitution; and the notables will have their reward in visible memorials of their own outlay. But it is not this policy which is pursued by the oligarchs of our days. Their policy is the very opposite; they covet profit as well as honour: and from this point of view oligarchy may well be described as democracy 'writ small'.

1321ᵇ1 This may suffice as an account of the methods which ought to be followed in constructing democracies and oligarchies.

CHAPTER 8

A study of the best modes of organizing the executive offices in cities generally. A first list of the six indispensable offices which are required for the performance of the minimum functions of a city. A second list of the four more important offices, which are concerned with more important functions and require greater capabilities, military command, the control of finance, the preparation of business for the deliberative body, and the direction of public worship. A final classification of all offices under a number of heads, according to the general character of their functions.

1321ᵇ4 This leads us on naturally to consider the right distribution of the executive offices, and to examine their number, their nature, and the functions proper to each—a subject which has already been treated in a previous passage.* No city can exist at all in the absence of the indispensable offices; a city cannot be properly governed in the absence of those which ensure good organization and order. Furthermore, there should be fewer offices in small and a greater number in large cities, as indeed we have already noted; and accordingly we must not omit to consider which offices can be conjoined, and which ought to be kept separate.

1321ᵇ12 Among the indispensable offices the first is the office charged with the care of the market-place. This requires an official for the supervision of contracts and the maintenance of good order. Buying and selling are needed in all cities equally, for the mutual satisfaction of wants; they are also the readiest means for the attainment of self-sufficiency, which is generally regarded as the chief object of men's coming together under a common constitution.

1321ᵇ18 A second function, which follows on this first, and is closely connected with it, is the superintendence of private and public property in the city centre, with a view to good order; the maintenance and repair of derelict buildings and roads; the superintendence of boundaries, with a view to the prevention of disputes; and other similar matters demanding public attention. The one who holds this office is generally called the city warden; it involves a number of functions and in more populous cities these may be assigned to different officials, such as repairers of the walls, superintendents of the fountains, and controllers of the harbour.

1321ᵇ27 The third indispensable office is closely akin to the second. Its functions are just the same; but they are exercised outside the city, and in the countryside. The holders of this office are sometimes called country wardens, and sometimes forest wardens.

1321ᵇ30 Besides these three first offices, with their respective functions, there is a fourth for receiving and holding the public revenues, and for distributing them among the several departments. The holders of this office go by the name of receivers of accounts, or treasurers.

1321ᵇ34 The fifth office deals with the registration of private contracts and court decisions: indictments have also to be deposited with it, and preliminary proceedings begun before it. In a number of cities this office is divided into departments, though in some places a single officer (or board of officers) remains in general control of the whole. The holders of the office go by the name of 'sacred recorders', 'supervisors', 'recorders', or other similar titles.

1321ᵇ40 We now come to an office which follows naturally on the fifth, but which is also, in itself, at once the most indispensable and the most difficult of all offices. This is the office which deals with the execution of sentences on offenders; with the recovery of debts due to the city from persons whose names are posted on the public lists; and with the custody of prisoners.* It is a difficult office, because it involves a good deal of ill feeling; and unless it affords opportunities for making considerable gains, people either shrink from it or, if they accept it, are loath to discharge its duties with the rigour the law demands. But it is, none the less, an indispensable office. There is no benefit in bringing cases before courts of justice if these have no effective conclusion; and if men cannot share a common life without a system for deciding cases, neither can they do so without a system for enforcing such decisions. For these reasons it is better that there should not be a single office to discharge these responsibilities but that there should be different officials for the different courts; and an attempt should be made, in the same sort of way, to distribute the duty of posting up names on the list of public debtors. In addition, the various boards of officials might give some help in enforcing decisions. In particular, incoming boards might enforce the decisions of their predecessors; or if this be impossible, and penalties have to be inflicted and enforced by those currently in office, the enforcement of a penalty might be left to a different board from that which inflicts it—for instance, the city wardens might enforce any penalty inflicted by the market inspectors, and other offices might, in turn, enforce any penalty they had inflicted. The less the ill feeling which attaches to the enforcement of penalties, the more effective will such enforcement be. When the same body of persons which inflicts a penalty also enforces the penalty, that body is doubly disliked; but when one and the same set of officers has to enforce every penalty, it will incur general enmity.

1322ª19 In a number of cities the office responsible for the custody of prisoners is combined with that responsible for the execution of sentences, as happens, for example, with the Eleven at Athens.* This suggests that it may be best to make it a separate office, and then to apply to that office the same devices as in the enforcement of penalties. The office of the gaoler is as indispensable [as that for enforcing penalties]; but it is an office which the good particularly shun, and which cannot safely be given to the bad (who are more in need of a gaoler themselves than capable of acting as gaolers to others). We may therefore conclude that the superintendence of gaols should not be assigned to a board appointed for that one

purpose, or left permanently to any one board. It is a duty
which should be undertaken by different and successive sections—sections partly drawn (in cities where young men are
given some training in military and police duties) from the
younger citizens, and partly from the boards of officials.

1322ª29 These offices must be ranked first, as being the most
indispensable. Next in order come a number of other offices,
which are also indispensable, but of a higher order of importance. They are offices which require a large experience and a
high degree of fidelity. We may count among them, first and
foremost, the offices charged with the defence of the city, and
any others intended for military purposes. In peace as well as
in war there must be persons to superintend the defence of the
city's gates and walls, and to inspect and drill its citizens.
Some cities have a number of different offices to deal with
these various duties, others have only a few, and in small
cities there may be only a single office to deal with them all.
The holders of these offices are commonly called generals or
commandants. Where there are separate forces of cavalry,
light-armed troops, archers, and marines, each of them is
sometimes placed under a separate command; and the officer
commanding is then termed admiral, or general of horse, or
general of the light forces. Their subordinate officers, in turn,
are termed naval captains, captains of horse, and company
commanders; and corresponding titles are given to the officers
commanding smaller sections. The whole of this organization
forms a single department—that of military command.

1322ᵇ6 From the organization of military command, as it
has just been described, we may next turn to the organization
of finance. Several of the offices of a city, if not all, handle
large amounts of public money. There must accordingly be a
separate office for finance which receives and audits the
accounts of other offices, and is only concerned with this one
function. The holders of this office go by different names
in different places—auditors, accountants, examiners, or
advocates.

1322ᵇ12 Besides the various offices already mentioned, there
is another which controls, more than any other office, the
whole range of public affairs. The office in question often has

both the power of introducing matters [to the assembly] and of bringing them to completion, or, where the people itself is in control, it presides over the assembly; for there must be a body to act as convener to the controlling authority of the constitution. The holders of this office are in some cities called Preliminary Councillors,* because they initiate deliberation; but where there is a popular assembly, they are called the Council.

1322^b17 These are pretty well all the main political offices. But there is also another province of affairs, which is concerned with the cult of the civic deities; and this requires officers such as priests and custodians of temples—custodians charged with the maintenance and repair of fabrics and the management of any other property assigned to the service of the gods. Occasionally (for example, in small cities) the whole of this province is assigned to a single office; in others it may be divided among a number of offices, and apart from priests there may also be the superintendents of sacrifices, the guardians of shrines, and the stewards of religious property. Closely related to these various offices there may also be a separate office, charged with the management of all public sacrifices which have the distinction of being celebrated on the city's common hearth, and, as such, are not legally assigned to the priests. The holders of this office are in some cities called *archōn*, in others king,* and in others *prutanis*.

1322^b29 The offices required in all cities may be summarily classified on the basis of their various functions.* First, there are the functions connected with public worship, military matters, revenue and expenditure, the market-place, the city centre, the harbours, and the countryside. Then there are the functions connected with the lawcourts, the registration of contracts, the enforcement of penalties, the custody of prisoners, and the reviewing, scrutiny, and audit of the accounts of officials. Finally, there are the functions connected with deliberation on public affairs. In addition there are offices peculiar to certain cities which have a more leisured character and a greater degree of prosperity, and concern themselves with good discipline—offices for the supervision of women; for enforcing obedience to law for the supervision of children;

and for the control of physical training. We may also include the office for the superintendence of athletic contests and dramatic competitions and all other similar spectacles. Some of these offices—those for the supervision of women and children, for example—are clearly out of place in a democracy: the poor man, not having slaves, is compelled to use his wife and children as attendants. There are three sorts of offices concerned with the conduct of the elections made by the electoral body to the highest offices. The first is the Guardians of the Law; the second, the Preliminary Councillors; and the third, the Councillors. The first is appropriate to aristocracy; the second to oligarchy; the third to democracy.

We have now given a sketch, in outline, of almost every kind of office, but . . .

BOOK VII
POLITICAL IDEALS AND
EDUCATIONAL PRINCIPLES

A: Political Ideals: The Nature of the Highest Good and of the Best and Happiest Life (Chapters 1–3)

CHAPTER 1

The three 'goods'—external goods; goods of the body; and goods of the soul. The primacy of the goods of the soul is attested by experience and evinced by philosophy: the possession of such goods—courage, wisdom, and the other virtues—depends not on fortune but on ourselves; and it is, for cities as well as for individuals, the condition and the cause of the best and happiest life. We thus come to the conclusion that 'the best way of life, both for cities and for individuals, is the life of goodness, duly equipped with such a store of requisites—i.e. external goods and goods of the body—as makes it possible to share in the activities of goodness'.

1323ª14 Anyone who is going to make a proper inquiry about the best form of constitution must first determine what mode of life is most to be desired.* As long as that is obscure, the best constitution must also remain obscure. It is to be expected that, provided that nothing extraordinary happens, those who live under the constitution that is best for those in their circumstances* will have the best way of life. We must therefore, first of all, find some agreed conception of the way of life which is most desirable for all men and in all cases; and we must then discover whether or not the same way of life is desirable in the case of the community as in that of the individual.

1323ª21 Assuming that our extensive discussions of the best way of life in works intended for the general public* are adequate, we should make use of them here. There is one classification of goods which it is certain that no one would challenge. This is the classification of these elements into three groups: external goods; goods of the body; and goods of the soul.* These all belong to the happy man. No one would call a man happy who had no particle of courage, temperance, justice, or wisdom;* who feared the flies buzzing about his head; who abstained from none of the extremest forms of extravagance whenever he felt hungry or thirsty; who would ruin his dearest friends for the sake of a quarter of an obol; whose mind was as senseless, and as much deceived, as that of a child or a madman. These are all propositions which would be accepted by nearly everybody as soon as they are stated, but people differ about the amount [of each different kind of good that is required] and about their relative superiority. So far as goodness [of mind and character] is concerned any amount is regarded as adequate; but wealth and property, power, reputation, and all such things, are coveted without limit.* In answer to these people we shall say: 'The facts themselves make it easy for you to assure yourselves on these issues. You can see for yourselves that the goods of the soul are not gained or maintained by external goods. It is the other way round. You can see for yourselves that the happy life—no matter whether it consists in pleasure, or goodness, or both—belongs more to those who have cultivated their character and mind to the uttermost, and kept acquisition of external goods within moderate limits, than it does to those who have managed to acquire more external goods than they can use, and are lacking in the goods of the soul.' But the problem can also be easily solved if we consider it theoretically.

1323^{b}7 External goods, like all other instruments, have a necessary limit of size. Indeed everything which is useful is useful for some purpose; and any excessive amount of such things must either cause its possessor some injury, or, at any rate, bring him no benefit. But with goods of the soul, the greater the amount of each, the greater is its usefulness—if indeed it is proper to predicate 'usefulness' at all here, and we ought not simply to predicate 'value'.* In general terms, we are clearly entitled to lay down that the best state of one thing is superior to the best state of another, to the same degree that the things of which they are states differ.* If, therefore, the soul is a thing more precious—intrinsically as well as in relation to us—than either our property or our body, the best state of the soul must necessarily bear the same relation to the best state of either our property or our body. Let us add that it is for the sake of the soul that these other things are desirable, and should accordingly be desired by everyone of good sense—not the soul for the sake of them.

1323ᵇ21 We may therefore join in agreeing that the amount of happiness which falls to each individual man is equal to the amount of his goodness and his wisdom, and of the good and wise acts that he does. God himself bears witness to this conclusion. He is happy and blessed; but he is so in and by himself, by reason of the nature of his being, and not by virtue of any external good.* This will explain why there must always be a difference between being happy and being fortunate. Accident and chance are causes of the goods external to the soul; but no man can be just and temperate merely from chance or by chance.*

1323ᵇ29 The next point, which is based on the same general train of reasoning, is that the best city is the one which is happy and 'does well'. To do well is impossible unless you also do fine deeds; and there can be no doing fine deeds for a city, any more than there can be for an individual, in the absence of goodness and wisdom.* The courage of a city, and the justice and wisdom of a city, have the same force, and the same character, as the qualities which cause individuals who have them to be called just, wise, and temperate.

1323ᵇ36 These observations may serve, at any rate so far as they go, as a preface to our argument. They deal with matters on which it is impossible not to touch; but it is equally impossible to develop here the whole of the argument which is involved. That is a matter for another and different branch of study. Here it may be sufficient to take this much as established: the best way of life, for individuals separately as well as for cities collectively, is the life of goodness duly equipped with such a store of requisites as makes it possible to share in the activities of goodness. This may conceivably be challenged; but we must leave the matter there—so far as our present inquiry is concerned—and defer to a later occasion any attempt to answer the arguments of those who refuse to accept our views.

CHAPTER 2

Assuming that the best way of life, alike for the city and for the individual, is the life of goodness, we may go on to raise the question whether the life of goodness consists more in external action, or more in internal development. So far as cities are concerned, we are presented with a choice between (a) the life of politics and action, which issues in the assumption of authority over other cities, and (b) the life of the self-contained city, engaged in developing its own resources and culture. The former ideal is illustrated by Sparta, and by other military and imperialist cities; but it raises doubts in the mind when one reflects on the ethics of conquest and the claims of liberty. The conclusion which suggests itself is that while a city should put itself in a position to maintain its own independence, military activity is only a means to the highest good, which is to share in a good life and the happiness of that life.

1324ᵃ5 It remains to discuss whether the happiness of the city is the same as that of the individual, or different. The answer is clear: all are agreed that they are the same. Those who believe that the well-being of the individual consists in his wealth, will also believe that the city as a whole is happy when it is wealthy. Those who rank the life of a tyrant higher than any other, will also rank the city which possesses the largest empire as being the happiest city. Anyone who grades individuals by their goodness, will also regard the happiness of cities as proportionate to their goodness.

1324ᵃ13 Two questions arise at this point which both need consideration. The first is, 'Which way of life is the more desirable: to join with other citizens and share in the city's activity, or to live in it like an alien, released from the ties of the political association?'* The second is, 'Which is the best constitution and the best way of organizing a city—no matter whether we assume that it is desirable for all to have a share in the city, or regard it as desirable for the majority only?'

1324ᵃ19 This second question—unlike the first, which raises the issue of what is good for the individual—is a matter for political thought and political speculation; and as we are now engaged on a discussion which belongs to that field, we may regard it as falling within the scope of our present inquiry—as the other question can hardly be said to do. There is one thing clear about the best constitution: it must be a political organization which will enable anyone to be at his best and live happily. But if that is clear, there is another point on which opinions diverge. Even those who agree in holding that the good life is most desirable are divided upon the issue, 'Which way of life is the more desirable? The way of politics and action? Or the way of detachment from all external things—the way, let us say, of contemplation, which some regard as the only way that is worthy of a philosopher?'* Here, we may say, are the two ways of life—the political and the philosophic—that are evidently chosen by those who have been most eager to win a reputation for goodness, in our own and in previous ages. It is a matter of no small moment on which of the two sides truth lies: for whether individuals or cities are in question, wisdom must aim at the higher mark.

1324^{a}25 There are some who regard it as the height of injustice to exercise despotic rule over one's neighbours. Ruling over them constitutionally does not, they believe, involve this injustice but it does interfere with one's own well-being. Others again take an opposite view: they hold that the practical and political life is the only life for a man: they believe that a private life gives no more scope for action in any of the fields of goodness than the life of public affairs and political interests. This is the position adopted by some of them, but others argue that the despotic and tyrannical form of constitution is the only one which gives happiness; and indeed there are cities where the exercise of despotic authority over neighbouring cities is made the standard to which both constitution and laws must conform.*

1324^{b}5 It is for this reason that, although in most cities, most of the laws are only a miscellaneous heap of legislation, where they are directed, in any degree, to a single object, that object is always conquest. In Sparta, for instance, and in Crete the system of education and most of the laws are framed with a general view to war.* Similarly all the barbarian peoples which are strong enough to conquer others pay the highest honours to military prowess; as witness the Scythians, the Persians, the Thracians, and the Celts. Some of these nations even have laws for the definite encouragement of military qualities: Carthage, for instance, is said to decorate its soldiers with an armlet for every campaign they go on. Macedonia, again, had once a law condemning those who had never killed an enemy to wear a halter instead of a belt. It was a custom among the Scythians that a man who had never killed an enemy was not entitled to drink from the loving-cup passed round at a certain festival. The Iberians, who are a warlike people, have a similar custom: they place a circle of pointed stones round the tombs of the dead, one for each enemy they have killed.

1324^b20 There are many institutions of this kind, which vary from people to people—some of them sanctioned by laws, and some of them matters of custom. Yet it cannot, perhaps, but appear very strange, to anyone ready to reflect on the matter, that it should be the function of a statesman to be able to lay plans for ruling and dominating neighbouring cities whether or not they give their consent. How can something which is not even lawful* be proper for a statesman or lawmaker? (It is unlawful to rule without regard to the justice or injustice of what you are doing—one may be a conqueror without acting justly.) There is no profession in which we can find a parallel for statesmanship of this type. Doctors and pilots are never expected to use coercion or cajolery in handling their patients or crews. But when it comes to politics most people appear to believe that mastery is the true statesmanship; and they are not ashamed of behaving to others in ways which they would refuse to acknowledge as just, or even expedient, among themselves. For their own affairs, and among themselves, they want an authority based on justice; but when other people are in question, their interest in justice stops. It would be curious if there were not some elements which are meant by nature to be subject to control as well as some which are not. If that is the case any attempt to establish control should be confined to the elements meant for control, and not extended to all.* One does not hunt men to furnish a banquet or a festival: one hunts what is meant to be hunted for that purpose; and what is meant to be hunted for that purpose is any wild animal meant to be eaten. It is possible to imagine a solitary city which is happy in itself and in isolation. Assume such a city, living somewhere or other all by itself, and living under a good system of law. It will obviously have a good constitution; but the scheme of its constitution will have no regard to war, or to the conquest of enemies, who, upon our hypothesis, will not exist.

1325^{a}5 It is clear, then, from the course of the argument, that if military pursuits are one and all to be counted good [they are good in a qualified sense]. They are not the chief end of man, transcending all other ends: they are means to his chief end. The task of a good lawgiver is to see how any city or race of men or society with which he is concerned, may share in a good life and in whatever form of happiness is available to them. Some of the laws enacted will vary according to circumstances. If a city has neighbours, it will be the duty of its legislator to see what modes of [military] training should be adopted to match their different characters, and, how appropriate measures may be taken to deal with each of them. But the problem here raised—which is that of the end at which the best constitution should aim—may well be reserved for consideration at a later stage.*

CHAPTER 3

From discussing the relative claims of external action and internal development in their bearing on cities, we may now turn to discuss them in their bearing on the individual. Is it better for him to follow the way of political action, with his life wrapped up in that of the city, or to follow the more solitary way of thought and contemplation? It may be argued that the activity of political management of equals, in a free society, is something higher and finer than the activity of managing slaves; and it may also be argued that true happiness, by its nature, connotes activity. On the other hand, the permanent management of others, whatever its basis may be, is not a desirable object; and even if happiness means activity, thought is an activity as much

as action itself, and it may even be more of an activity than
action is. The self-contained individual—like the self-contained
city—may be busily active: the activity of God and the universe
is that of a self-contained life.

1325ª16 We must now consider the views of those who are
agreed in accepting the general principle that a life of goodness
is most desirable, but divided in their opinion about the right
way of living that life. Two different schools of opinion have
thus to be discussed.* One is the school which eschews political office, distinguishing the life of the individual freeman
from that of the politician, and preferring it to all others. The
other is the school which regards the life of the politician as
best; they argue that those who do nothing cannot be said to
'do well', and they identify happiness with active 'well-doing'.
Both of these schools are right on some points and wrong on
others. The first school is right in holding that the life of a
free individual is better than that of the master of any number
of slaves. There is nothing very dignified in managing slaves,
when they are acting in that capacity; and giving orders about
menial duties has nothing fine about it. On the other hand, it
is wrong to regard every form of authority as so much
'mastery'. Ruling over freemen differs as much from ruling
over slaves as that which is by nature free differs from that
which is by nature servile. But enough has already been said
on that theme in the first book. It is also a mistake to praise
inaction in preference to action. Happiness is a state of
activity; and the actions of just and temperate men bring
many fine things* to fulfilment.

1325ª34 The conclusion to which we have just come may
possibly be interpreted to mean that sovereign power is the
highest of all goods, because it is also the power of practising
the greatest number of the highest and best* activities. It
would follow on this that a man who is able to wield authority
should never surrender it to his neighbour; on the contrary,
he should wrest it from him. A father should pay no regard to
his children, children none to their father, and friends of any
kind none to their friends: no man should think of another
when it comes to this cardinal point: all should act on the

principle, 'The best is the most desirable': and 'to do well is
the best'. There might be truth in such a view if it were really
the case that those who practised plunder and violence did
attain a supremely desirable object. But it is perhaps impossible that they should; they are rather making a false assumption, for it is not possible [for a ruler] to do fine deeds unless
he has a degree of pre-eminence over [those he rules] as great
as a husband has over his wife, or a parent over his children,
or a master over his slaves. It follows that the transgressor
can never achieve any subsequent gain which will equal the
loss of goodness already involved in his transgression.*

1325^{b}7 Among those who are like one another it is a just
and fine thing that office should go on the principle of
rotation, for that is to treat people equally and alike. But that
equals should be given unequal shares, and those who are
alike treated in ways that are not alike, is contrary to nature;
and what is contrary to nature is not a fine thing. If, of course,
someone emerges who is superior to others in goodness and in
capacity for actually doing the best, it is a fine thing to follow
him, and just to obey him. Goodness by itself is not enough: there
must also be a capacity for being active in doing good.

1325^{b}14 If we are right in our view, and happiness should be
held to consist in 'well-doing', it follows that the life of action
is best, alike for every city as a whole and for each individual
in his own conduct. But the life of action need not be, as is
sometimes thought, a life which involves relations to others.
Nor should our thoughts be held to be active only when they
are directed to objects which have to be achieved by action.
Thoughts with no object beyond themselves, and speculations
and trains of reflection followed purely for their own sake,
are far more deserving of the name of active. 'Well-doing' is
the end we seek: action of some sort or other is therefore our
end and aim; but, even in the sphere of outward acts, action
can also be predicated—and that in the fullest measure and
the true sense of the word—of those who, by their thoughts,
are the prime authors* of such acts. Cities situated by themselves, and resolved to live in isolation, need not be therefore
inactive. They can achieve activity by sections: the different
sections of such a city will have many mutual connections.

This is also, and equally, true of the individual human being.
If it were not so, there would be something wrong with God
himself and the whole of the universe, who have no activities
other than those of their own internal life.

It is therefore clear that the same way of life which is best
for the individual must also be best for the city as a whole
and for all its members.

B: The Population, the Territory, the Natural Endowment of the Inhabitants, the Social Structure, and the Physical Planning of an Ideal City (Chapters 4–12)

CHAPTER 4

1. The population, in *size and quantity, must be neither too
large nor too small for the discharge of its civic function. The
size of the population is therefore determined and limited by the
nature of the civic function; and a great population is not an
index of civic greatness. A very populous city will find it
difficult to achieve self-sufficiency. A city, like a ship, must be
neither too large nor too small for the business it has to do. In
order to do civic business properly, the citizens should know one
another personally; and we may thus define the optimum number
of the population as 'the greatest surveyable number required
for achieving a life of self-sufficiency'.*

1325^{b}33 The points we have just made about these topics
will serve as an introduction. We have already investigated
other forms of constitution. So we may now embark on the
rest of our theme by asking 'What are the necessary presuppo-
sitions for the construction of a city which will be just as one
would desire?' The best constitution cannot, of course, come
into being unless it is equipped with the appropriate resources.
We must therefore assume everything as we would wish it to
be, though nothing we assume must be impossible. These
conditions include, among others, a citizen body and a territory. All producers—weavers, for instance, or shipwrights—
must have the materials proper to their particular work; and

the better prepared these materials are, the better will be the products of their skill. In the same way, the statesman and the lawmaker must have their proper materials, and they must have them in a condition which is suited to their needs. The primary factor necessary, in the equipment of a city, is the human material; and this involves us in considering the quality, as well as the quantity, of the population naturally required. The second factor is territory; and here too we have to consider quality as well as quantity. Most people think that the happiness of a city depends on its being great. They may be right; but even if they are, they do not know what it is that makes a city great or small. They judge greatness in numerical terms, by the size of the population; but it is capacity, rather than size, which should properly be the criterion. Cities, like other things, have a function to perform; and the city which shows the highest capacity for performing the function of a city is therefore the one which should be counted greatest. In the same way Hippocrates would naturally be described as 'greater' (not as a man, but as a doctor) than somebody who was superior in point of bodily size. But even if it were right to judge a city by the size of its population, it would still be wrong to judge in the light of some mere chance total. We have to remember that cities will very likely contain a large number of slaves, resident aliens, and foreigners. If we judge a city by the standard of its population, we ought to limit the population to those who are members of the city and essential elements in its composition. An outstanding number of these may be evidence of a great city; but a city which sends into the field a large force of mere mechanics, and can only raise a handful of heavy-armed infantry, cannot possibly be great, for a great city is not the same as a populous city.

1326ª25 There is a further consideration. Experience shows that it is difficult, if not indeed impossible, for a very populous city to enjoy good government. Observation tells us that none of the cities which have a reputation for being well governed are without some limit of population. But the point can also be established on the evidence of the words themselves. Law [*nomos*] is a system of order [*taxis*]; and good government [*eunom-ia*] must therefore involve a general system of orderliness [*eu-tax-ia*]. But an unlimited number cannot partake in order. That is a task for the divine power which holds together the whole [of this universe], for fineness of form* generally depends on number and magnitude. We may therefore conclude that the finest city will be one which combines magnitude with the principle just mentioned.* But we may also note that cities, like all other things (animals, plants, and inanimate instruments), have a definite measure of size. Any object will lose its power of performing its proper function if it is either excessively small or of an excessive size. Sometimes it will wholly forfeit its nature; sometimes, short of that, it will merely be defective. We may take the example of a ship. A ship which is only 6 inches in length, or is as much as 1,200 feet long,* will not be a ship at all; and even a ship of more moderate size may still cause difficulties of navigation, either because it is not large enough or because it is excessively large. The same is true of cities. A city composed of too few members is a city without self-sufficiency (and the city, by its definition, is self-sufficient). One composed of too many will indeed be self-sufficient in the matter of material necessities (as a nation may be) but it will not be a city, since it can hardly have a constitution. Who can be the general of a mass so excessively large? And who can be its herald, unless he has Stentor's voice?*

1326^b7 The initial stage of the city may therefore be said to require such an initial amount of population as will be self-sufficient for the purpose of achieving a good way of life in the shape and form of a political association. A city which exceeds this initial amount may be a still greater city; but such increase of size, as has already been noticed, cannot continue indefinitely. What the limit of increase should be is a question easily answered if we look at the actual facts. The activities of a city are partly the activities of its governors, and partly those of the governed. The function of governors is to issue commands and give decisions. Both in order to give decisions in matters of disputed rights, and to distribute the offices of government according to the merit of candidates, the citizens of a city must know one another's characters. Where this is not the case, the distribution of offices and the giving of decisions will suffer. Both are matters in which it is wrong to operate by guesswork; but that is what obviously happens where the population is over-large. Another thing also happens under these conditions. Foreigners and resident aliens readily assume a share in the constitution: it is easy for them to go undetected among the crowd.*

1326ᵇ22 These considerations indicate clearly the optimum standard of population. It is, in a word, 'the greatest surveyable number required for achieving a life of self-sufficiency'. Here we may end our discussion of the proper size of the population.

CHAPTER 5

2. The territory should also be of a moderate size—no more, and no less, than will enable the citizens to live a life of leisure which combines temperance and liberality. Like the population, it should be 'surveyable'. This will enable the defence of the city to be properly planned, and will ensure the proper relation of the central city to the surrounding country for economic as well as for military purposes.

1326ᵇ26 Similar considerations apply also to the matter of territory. So far as the character of the land is concerned, everybody would obviously give the preference to a territory which ensures the maximum of self-sufficiency; and as that consists in having everything, and needing nothing, such a territory must be one which produces all kinds of crops. So far as extent and size are concerned, the territory should be large enough to enable its inhabitants to live a life of leisure which combines liberality with temperance. Whether this standard is right or wrong is a question we shall have to examine more closely at a later stage of the argument,* when we come to consider the general problem of property and the possession of means, and to examine the relation which ought to exist between possession and use. This is a much disputed matter; and people tend to conduct their lives in a way that runs to one or other of two extremes—miserliness or extravagance.

1326ᵇ39 As for the general lie of the land, it is easy to make the suggestion (though here a number of questions arise on which the advice of military experts ought to be taken) that the territory of a city should be such that it is difficult for enemies to attack, and easy for its inhabitants to make sorties. What was said above of the population—that it should be such as to be surveyable—is equally true of the territory. A territory which can be easily surveyed is also a territory which can be easily defended. The ideal position of the central city should be determined by considerations of its being easy of access both by land and by sea. One requirement is that already mentioned: it should be a common centre for the dispatch of aid to all points in the territory. Another is that it should also be a convenient centre, for the transport of food supplies, of timber for building, and of raw materials for any other similar industry which the territory may possess.

CHAPTER 6

It is a question much debated whether the territory of a city should have a close connection with the sea. Some argue that maritime connections mean the introduction of a crowd of undesirable aliens; but on the other hand there are reasons, both of military security and of economic supply, which make such connections valuable. A city should not be a market-place for the world, but it ought to secure its own market; and a certain amount of naval power is also desirable—though the oarsmen required as the basis of such power should not be citizens, but serfs and labourers.

1327ª11 It is a hotly debated question whether connection with the sea is to the advantage, or the detriment, of a well-ordered city. There are some who maintain that the introduction of strangers, who have been born and bred under other laws, and the consequent increase of population, is prejudicial to good order. They argue that such an increase is inevitable when numbers of merchants use the sea for the export and import of commodities; and they regard it as inimical to good government. On the other hand, and if only this increase can be avoided, there can be no doubt that it is better, in the interest both of security and of a good supply of material necessities, for the city and territory of a city to be connected with the sea. In order to enjoy security, and to meet enemy attacks more easily, a city should be capable of being defended by sea as well as by land. And if it has the use of both elements, it will be in a better position to inflict losses on its assailants, by acting on one or the other, even when it cannot do so on both. Similarly, in order to procure supplies, it is essential that a city should be able to import commodities which it does not itself produce, and to export the surplus of its own products. It should act as a merchant for itself—but not as a merchant for others. Cities which make themselves market-places for the world only do it for the sake of revenue; and if a city ought not to indulge in this sort of profit-making, it follows that it ought not to be a trading centre of that kind. We see from the practice of our own times that territories and cities often have ports and harbours which are conveniently placed in relation to the main city—they do not encroach on the town but are not too far from it, and can thus be commanded by connecting walls and other such fortifications. Any advantage which can be derived from connection with ports and harbours will obviously be secured by these methods; any disadvantage which may threaten can easily be met by legislation which states and defines those who may, or may not, have dealings with one another.

1327ᵃ40 A certain amount of naval power is obviously a great advantage. A city must not only be formidable to its own citizens and to certain of its neighbours but must also be in a position to assist them by sea as well as by land. The actual size and amount of such power must be determined by the city's way of life. If it prefers to pursue a life of leadership, and of active relations with other cities,* naval power must be commensurate with the activities which are involved. The large population which results from a crowd of naval oarsmen is a consequence which need not follow: there is no need for such people to be part of the citizen body. The marines belong to the class of full freemen: they count as part of the infantry, and are in control and command on shipboard. But if there are masses of serfs and farm-workers ready to hand, it should always be possible to draw an abundant supply of sailors from this source. We may observe that this policy is actually followed, at the present day, in a number of cities. It is followed, for instance, at Heraclea [on the Black Sea], which fits out a considerable number of triremes with a citizen body more moderate in size than those of other cities.

This may suffice by way of conclusions about territory, harbours, towns, the sea, and naval power.

CHAPTER 7

3. The natural endowment *proper to the citizens of our city is suggested by a comparison of three peoples—the people of the colder regions of Europe; the people of Asia; and the Greek people. The first has high spirit, but less skill and intelligence: the second has skill and intelligence, but little spirit: the Greeks combine both sets of qualities. The legislator will naturally prefer the mixed endowment; and he will not, as Plato does, attach too great an importance to the factor of high spirit—valuable as that factor is in its sphere.*

$1327^{b}18$ We have already discussed the proper standard for determining the number of citizens. We have now to consider what sort of natural endowment they ought to have.* We may get some idea of what this endowment should be if we take a general view, which not only embraces the Greek cities of standing and reputation, but also includes the non-Greek peoples in their distribution throughout the whole of the habitable world. The peoples of cold countries generally, and particularly those of Europe, are full of spirit, but deficient in skill and intelligence; and this is why they continue to remain comparatively free, but attain no political development and show no capacity for governing others. The peoples of Asia are endowed with skill and intelligence, but are deficient in spirit; and this is why they continue to be peoples of subjects and slaves.* The Greek stock, intermediate in geographical position, unites the qualities of both sets of peoples. It possesses both spirit and intelligence, for which reason it contin-ues to be free, to have the highest political development, and to be capable of governing every other people—if only it could once achieve political unity.* The same sort of difference is found among the Greek peoples themselves. Some of them are of a one-sided nature: others show a happy mixture of spirit and intelligence.

1327ᵇ36 It is clear that the sort of people which a legislator can easily guide into the way of goodness is one with a natural endowment that combines intelligence and spirit. As for the attitude which some require in their guardians—to be friendly disposed to all whom they know, and stern to all who are unknown*—spirit is the faculty of our souls which issues in love and friendship; and it is a proof of this that when we think ourselves slighted our spirit is stirred more deeply against acquaintances and friends than ever it is against strangers. This explains why Archilochus, when he is complaining of his friends, is naturally led to address his spirit, and to say to it

> Verily thou wert wounded in the house of thine own friends.*

This faculty of our souls is also the source for us all of any power of commanding and any feeling for freedom. Spirit is a commanding and an unconquerable thing. But it is wrong to say that one should be harsh to those who are unknown. One ought not to be harsh to anybody; and magnanimous people, as a matter of fact, are not of a stern disposition—except when they have to deal with wrongdoers. Even then they are likely to show still greater sternness, as we have just had reason to notice, if those by whom they think themselves wronged are their own acquaintances. This is only what might be expected. We feel, in such a case, that those whom we regard as under an obligation to repay us for our services are adding insult to injury, and ingratitude to wrongdoing.

> Stern is the strife between brethren,

as one of our poets says; and as another also says,

> Those who have loved exceedingly can hate
> As much as they have loved.*

Such, in general terms (for the degree of precision required in

1327^b36

a theoretical discussion is not as great as is needed in dealing
with the data of sense-perception), are the conclusions which
we have reached about (1) the right size of the citizen body,
and the proper character of its natural endowment; and (2)
the right size of the territory, and the proper character of its
soil.

CHAPTER 8

*4. The social structure. We must begin by making a distinction
between 'integral parts' and 'necessary conditions'. The integral
parts of a city are the full citizens who share actively in the full
good life of the city: the necessary conditions are the ancillary
members who make it possible for the full citizens to share in
that life. Including together both 'parts' and 'conditions', we
may enumerate six services which must be supplied by the social
structure of the city: the service of agriculture; the service of
arts and crafts; the service of defence; the service of landownership; the service of public worship; and the service of political
deliberation and civil jurisdiction.*

1328ᵃ21 In the city, as in other natural compounds,* the
conditions which are necessary for the existence of the
whole are not parts of the whole system which they serve.
The conclusion which clearly follows is that we cannot
regard the elements which are necessary for the existence of
the city, or of any other association forming a single whole,
as being 'parts' of the city or of any other such association.*

1328ᵃ26 There must be some one thing which is common to
all the members, and identical for them all, though their
shares in it may be equal, or unequal. The thing itself may be
various—food, for instance, or a stretch of territory, or anything else of the kind. Now there is nothing joint or common
to the means which serve an end and the end which is served
by those means—except that the means produce and the end
takes over the product. Take, for example, the relation in
which building tools, and the workmen who use them, stand
to the result produced by their action. There is nothing in

common between the builder and the house he builds: the builder's skill is simply a means, and the house is the end. Thus, while cities need property, property is not a part of the city. It is true that property includes a number of animate beings,* as well as inanimate objects. But the city is an association of equals; and its object is the best and highest life possible. The highest good is happiness; and that consists in the actualization and perfect practice of goodness. But, as things happen, some may share in it fully, but others can only share in it partially or cannot even share at all. Obviously this is the reason why there are different kinds and varieties of cities, and a number of different constitutions. Pursuing this goal in various ways and by various means, different peoples create for themselves different ways of life and different constitutions.*

1328^b2 We must inquire how many elements are necessary for the existence of the city. These will, of course, include what we have called the 'parts' of the city as well as what we have termed its 'conditions'. We must first determine how many services a city performs; and then we shall easily see how many elements it must contain.* The first thing to be provided is food. The next is crafts; for life requires many tools. The third is arms: the members of a city must bear arms in person, partly in order to maintain their rule over those who disobey, and partly in order to meet any threat of external aggression. The fourth thing which has to be provided is a certain supply of property, alike for domestic use and for military purposes. The fifth (but really first) is an establishment for the service of the gods, or, as it is called, public worship. The sixth thing, and the most vitally necessary, is a method of deciding what is demanded by the public interest and what is just in men's private dealings. These are the services which every city may be said to need. A city is not a mere casual group. It is a group which, as we have said, must be self-sufficient for the purposes of life; and if any of these services is missing it cannot be totally self-sufficient. A city should accordingly be so constituted as to be competent for all these services. It must therefore contain a body of farmers to produce the necessary food; craftsmen; a military force; a

propertied class; priests; and those who decide necessary issues
and determine what is the public interest.

CHAPTER 9

*The question arises whether each of the necessary services
should be performed by a separate social class, or whether some
of them may be combined—and, if so, which. We may answer
that (1) the first two services—agriculture, and the arts and
crafts—cannot be rendered by the full citizens, because their
life needs leisure, and (2) three of the other services—defence,
public worship, and the service of deliberation and jurisdiction—
should, from one point of view, be combined in the hands of the
same people, but, from another, be discharged by different
people. This last result can be achieved if (a) all full citizens are
concerned with all these three services at some time or other of
their lives, but (b) the younger citizens are set to render the
service of defence, the middle-aged to render the service of
deliberation and jurisdiction, and the aged to render the service
of public worship. The effect will be that each citizen will be
concerned with each of these three services, but will be concerned
with each at a different period of his life. The remaining
service—that of landownership—should be assigned to the whole
body of full citizens (which is the contrary of Plato's view in the
Republic, where the full citizens are debarred from the ownership of land).*

1328^b24 Now that these points have been determined, it
remains to consider whether everyone should share in the
performance of all these services? (That is a possibility: the
same people may all be engaged simultaneously in farm work,
the practice of arts and crafts, and the work of deliberation
and jurisdiction.) Or should we assume different people for
each of the different services? Or, again, should some of the
services be assigned to different sets of people, and others be
shared by all? The system is not the same in every constitution,
for, as we have noted,* it is possible for all to share in all
functions, and also for all not to share in all but for [only]
some people to share in some of them. These alternatives lead

to the different constitutions: in democracies everyone shares in all functions, while the opposite practice is followed in oligarchies. Here we are concerned only with the best constitution. Now the best constitution is that under which the city can attain the greatest happiness; and that, as we have already stated,* cannot exist without goodness. Upon these principles it clearly follows that in a city with the best possible constitution—a city which has for its members people who are absolutely just, rather than ones who are merely just in relation to some particular standard—the citizens must not live the life of mechanics or shopkeepers, which is ignoble and inimical to goodness. Nor can those who are to be citizens engage in farming: leisure is a necessity, both for growth in goodness and for the pursuit of political activities.

1329ª2 On the other hand, a military force and a body to deliberate on matters of public interest and to give decisions in matters of justice are both essential, and are evidently 'parts' of the city in a special sense. Should they be kept separate? or should both functions be given to one and the same set of people? The obvious answer is that from one point of view they should be given to the same people, but from another point of view they ought to be given to different ones. Either function requires a different prime of life: one needs wisdom while the other needs strength; from this point of view they ought to go to different people. But those who are strong enough to use force (or to prevent it from being used) cannot possibly be expected to remain in subjection; and from this point of view the two functions should go to the same people. After all those who have military power also have the power to determine whether or not the constitution will survive. The only course thus left to us is to vest these constitutional powers in one set of the people—that is, in both age-groups—but not at the same time. The order of nature gives strength to youth and wisdom to years; and it is prudent to follow that order in distributing powers among both age-groups. It is just, as well as prudent; for distribution on such a basis is in proportion to desert.

1329ª17 Property must also belong to these people, for the citizens must have a supply of property and these are citizens.

The class of mechanics has no share in the city; nor has any other class which is not a 'producer' of goodness. This conclusion clearly follows from the principle [of the best city]. That principle requires that happiness should go hand in hand with goodness, and in calling a city happy we should have regard, not just to a part of it, but to all the citizens.* A further argument is provided for the view that property ought to belong to citizens, if we consider that the farm-workers ought to be slaves or barbarian serfs.

1329ᵃ27 Of the elements which we enumerated, only the priesthood is left. The plan on which it ought to be based is clear. Nobody belonging to the farming or the mechanic class should be made a priest. The cult of the gods should be undertaken by citizens. Now the citizen body has been divided into two sections, the military and the deliberative. Moreover, it is appropriate for the service of the gods and the relaxation which it brings to be assigned to those who have given up [these tasks] through age. It is to these people, therefore, that the priestly offices should be assigned.

1329ᵃ34 This completes our survey of the factors without which a city cannot exist, and those which constitute 'parts' of the city. Farm-workers, craftsmen, and the general body of day-labourers, must necessarily be present in cities, while the military force and the deliberative body are parts of the city. Each of these is a separate element—the separation being permanent in some cases, and by turns in others.

CHAPTER 10

A system of classes, we may note in passing, appeared at an early date in Egypt and Crete. The system of common meals (suggested later in Chapter 12) may also be found in ancient Crete; and it appeared even earlier in south Italy. This leads us to note that institutions generally have been invented again and again, in the course of time, in a number of different places. Returning to the subject of landownership, the land should not be entirely owned in common—though some of it may be, in order to provide for a system of common meals and for the needs of public worship. On this basis we may suggest (1) that

*some of the land should be publicly owned, for the purpose of
such provision, but (2) that the rest should be privately owned,
and each owner should have two plots—one near the central
city, and one on the frontier. The cultivation of all the land
should be assigned to slaves or serfs.*

1329ª40 It does not appear to be a new or even a recent
discovery in the theory of the constitution that cities ought to
be divided into classes, and that the military class and the
farming class should be separate. Even today this is still the
case in Egypt, as it is also in Crete: the practice began in
Egypt, so it is said, with the legislation of Sesostris, and it
began in Crete with that of Minos. The institution of common
meals also appears to be ancient. It started in Crete with the
reign of Minos; but it goes back farther still in southern Italy.
The chroniclers of those parts tell of a legendary King of
Oenotria, by the name of Italus, from whom the Oenotrians
(changing their previous name) came to be known as 'Italians',
and who gave the name of 'Italy' to the projection of Europe*
which lies to the south of a line drawn from the bay of
Scylacium to that of Lametus—two bays which are only half
a day's journey from one another. According to the chroniclers, this Italus turned the Oenotrians from a pastoral into
an agricultural people; and besides enacting other laws he
instituted, for the first time, a system of common meals. That
is why some of his descendants still maintain the institution of
common meals along with some of his laws. Towards Tyrrhe-
nia, there lived the Opici, who were formerly (and indeed still
are) surnamed Ausonians; towards Iapygia and the Ionian
gulf, in the territory known as Siritis, there lived the Chonians,
who were also of Oenotrian origin. It was thus in this region
that the system of common meals originated. The division of
the body politic into classes, on the other hand, originated in
Egypt: the reign of Sesostris is long anterior to that of Minos.
Accordingly we must also believe that most other institutions
have been invented in the course of the years on a number of
different occasions—indeed an indefinite number.* Necessity
itself, we may reasonably suppose, will steadily be the mother
of indispensable inventions: on that basis, and with these once

provided, we may fairly expect that inventions which make for the adornment and graces of life will also steadily develop; and this general rule must be held to be true in constitutional matters as well as in other spheres. The history of Egypt attests the antiquity of all such institutions. The Egyptians are generally accounted the oldest people on earth; and they have always had a body of law and a constitutional system. We ought, therefore, to make proper use of what has already been discovered, and confine ourselves to seeking what has hitherto been omitted.

1329^b36 It has already been stated that the land should belong to those who bear arms and to those who share in the constitution. It has also been explained why the farm-workers should be separate from these two classes; what the extent of the territory should be; and what kind of land it should have. We have now to discuss the distribution of the land and to determine who should farm it and what sort of people these should be. On our view, property ought not to be owned in common, as some writers have maintained—though it ought to be used in common and as friends treat their belongings,* but none of the citizens should go in need of subsistence. The institution of common meals is generally agreed to be for the advantage of all well-ordered cities; and we shall explain, at a later point,* why we share this view. All citizens should share in these but it is difficult for the poor to contribute their allotted quota from their own resources, when they have also to provide simultaneously for the rest of the family expenditure. Moreover, expenditure on public worship is also a common charge on the city.

1330^a9 It is thus necessary for the territory of our city to be divided into two parts, one of which will be public property, while the other will belong to private owners. Each of these parts should again be divided into two sections. One section of the public property should be allocated to the service of the gods, and the other to the expenses of the system of common meals. The land which belongs to private owners should be so divided that one section lies on the frontiers, and the other is near the city—each individual receiving a plot in either section,* and all thus sharing an interest in both. This arrangement combines equality with justice; and it produces more solidarity in the face of border wars. In the absence of such an arrangement, some of the citizens will think little of [incurring] the enmity of a neighbouring city, while others will think of it only too much, and more than honour can justify. This will explain why some cities have laws which prohibit citizens on the frontier from joining in deliberations about hostilities with neighbouring cities; the reason is that because of their personal interest they cannot exercise their judgement properly.

1330ª23 The territory of the city must be distributed in the way we have suggested. The class which farms it should ideally, and if we can choose at will, be slaves—but slaves not drawn from a single stock, or from stocks of a spirited temperament. This will at once secure the advantage of a good supply of labour and eliminate any danger of revolutionary designs. Failing slaves, the next best class will be one of serfs who are of barbarian origin and whose character is like that just described. The farm-hands employed on private estates should belong to the owners of those estates: those who are employed on public property should belong to the public. How the slaves who till the soil should be treated, and why it is wise to offer all slaves the eventual reward of emancipation, is a matter which we shall discuss later.*

CHAPTER 11

5. The planning of the central city. This should be determined mainly by (a) considerations of health (which require a good exposure and a good water-supply), and (b) considerations of defence (which affect the internal layout of the city and raise the vexed question of fortifications). Other considerations which affect the planning of the city are (c) convenience for political activities, and (d) beauty of appearance.

1330ª34 The city itself, as we have already noticed, should be, so far as circumstances permit, a common centre, linked to the sea as well as the land, and equally linked to the whole of the territory. Internally, and in its own layout, we ought to plan the ideal of our city with an eye to four considerations.

The first, as being the most indispensable, is health. Cities which slope towards the east, and are exposed to the winds which blow from that quarter, are the healthiest: the next best aspect, which is healthy in the winter season, is one sheltered from the north wind. Two other considerations to be borne in mind are matters of the city's convenience for political and military activities. For the purpose of military activities it should be easy for its inhabitants to make sorties, but difficult for any enemies to approach or blockade. It should also have, if possible, a natural supply of waters and streams, but if there is no such supply, a substitute has been found in the construction of large and bountiful reservoirs of rain-water, which will not fail even when the inhabitants are cut off by the pressure of war from the territory round their city. Due regard for the health of the inhabitants not only means that their place of abode should be in a healthy locality and should have a healthy exposure: it also means that they should have the use of good water. This is a matter which ought not to be treated lightly. The elements we use most and oftenest for the support of our bodies contribute most to their health; and water and air have both an effect of this nature. It should therefore be laid down, in all prudently conducted cities, that if all the streams are not equally wholesome, and the supply of wholesome streams is inadequate, the drinking-water ought to be separated from the water used for other purposes.

1330^{b}17 In the planning of strongholds there is no one policy which is equally good for all constitutions. A citadel [or acropolis] suits oligarchies and monarchies; a level plain suits democracy; neither suits an aristocracy, for which a number of strong places is preferable. The arrangement of private houses is generally considered to be more sightly, and more convenient for peacetime activities, when it is regularly planned [i.e. with straight streets] in the modern style introduced by Hippodamus.* For reasons of military security, however, the very reverse is preferable—they should follow the old-fashioned manner, which made it difficult for strangers to make their way out and for assailants to find their way in. The two methods of arrangement should accordingly be com-

bined; and this may be done by adopting the system which
vine-growers follow in planting their 'clumps' of vines. In this
way regular planning will be confined to certain sections and
districts, and not made to cover the whole of the city. This
will conduce at once to security and to elegance.

1330^{b}32 So far as walls are concerned, those who argue that
cities which lay claim to military excellence ought to do
without them have singularly antiquated ideas—all the more
as it is plain to the eye that cities which prided themselves on
this point are being refuted by the logic of fact.* When the
question at issue is one of coping with an enemy city of a
similar character, which is only slightly superior in numbers,
there is little honour to be got from an attempt to attain
security by the erection of a barrier of walls. But it sometimes
happens—and it is always possible—that the superiority of
the assailants may be more than a match for ordinary human
courage and even for the courage which only a few can
display; and then, if a city is to avoid destruction, and to
escape from suffering and humiliation, the securest possible
barrier of walls should be deemed the best of military methods
—especially today, when the invention of catapults and
other engines for the siege of cities has attained such a high
degree of precision. To demand that a city should be left
undefended by walls is much the same as to want to have the
territory of a city left open to invasion, and to lay every
elevation level with the ground. It is like refusing to have
walls for the exterior of a private house, for fear they will
make its inhabitants cowards. We have also to remember that
a people with a city defended by walls has a choice of
alternatives—to treat its city as walled, or to treat it as if it
were unwalled—but a people without any walls is a people
without any choice. If this argument be accepted, the conclusion will not only be that a city ought to be surrounded by
walls; it will also be that the walls should always be kept in
good order, and be made to satisfy both the claims of beauty
and the needs of military utility—especially the needs revealed
by recent military inventions. It is always the concern of those
on the offensive to discover new methods by which they may
seize an advantage; but it is equally the concern of those on

the defensive, to search and think out other inventions in
addition to those which have already been made. An assailant
will not even attempt to make an attack on those who are
well prepared.

CHAPTER 12

*The common meals maintained in the city should take place in
the temples; and the temples should be placed on a commanding
site, with the 'Free Square' at its foot for the recreations of the
older citizens. There should also be a separate 'Market Square',
with the courts of law for business matters adjacent to it. In
the countryside the common eating-places should be connected
with the guard-houses of the militia, and there should be a
number of country temples.*

1331ᵃ19 If we assume that the citizens should be distributed
in eating-places [for the common meals], and the walls should
be dotted with guard-houses and towers at convenient intervals, the idea will naturally occur that some of the eating-
places should be established in these guard-houses. This will
be one combination. The principal common eating-places of
those in office may be associated with the buildings devoted
to public worship, on some convenient and common site—except for such temples as are required by law, or by a rule of
the Delphic oracle, to be kept distinct and separate. This site
should be on an eminence, conspicuous as a seat of goodness,
and strong enough to command the adjacent quarters of the
city. Below this site provision should be made for a public
square, of the sort which is called in Thessaly by the name of
the Free Square. This should be clear of all merchandize; and
no mechanic, or farmer, or other such person, should be
permitted to enter, except on the summons of the magistrates.
The place would be all the more pleasant if exercise grounds
for the older men were included in its plan. The arrangements
for exercise (like those for the common meals) should be
different for different age-groups; and if this plan be followed
some of those in office should stay with the younger men
[near their guard-houses] while the older men should remain

[in the public square] with the other officials. To be under the eyes of office-holders will serve, above anything else, to create a true feeling of modesty and the fear of shame which should animate freemen. The market-place for buying and selling should be separate from this public square and at a distance from it: it should occupy a site easily accessible for all commodities which are imported by sea or come from the city's own territory.

1331^b4 Since one section of the population is that of the priests, it is fitting that the common meals of the priests should be arranged to take place near the temple buildings. The proper place in which to establish the officials who deal with contracts, indictments in lawsuits, summonses into court, and other business of that sort—and, we may also add, those concerned with the superintendence of the market square and the duties of 'city superintendence'—will be near some square or general centre of public resort. The place which suits this requirement is by the market-place, where the necessary business of life is done. The public square, on its higher ground, is assigned on our plan to leisure: the market square belongs to the necessary activities. Arrangements in the country should copy those we have described. There, too, the various officials—who are sometimes termed forest wardens, and sometimes rural inspectors—should have guard-houses and eating-places in connection with their duties; and the country should be studded with temples, some of them dedicated to the gods and others to heroes.

1331^b18 But it would be a waste of time to linger here over details and explanations. It is easy enough to theorize about such matters: it is far less easy to realize one's theories. What we say about them depends on what we wish; what actually happens depends upon chance. We may therefore dismiss, for the present, any further study of these issues.

C: The General Principles of Education
(Chapters 13–15)
CHAPTER 13

1. The end and the means. For the attainment of well-being, or happiness, it is necessary to know the right end as well as to choose the right means. (a) So far as the end is concerned, happiness has been defined in the Ethics, *as 'the complete actualization and practice of goodness, in an absolute rather than a conditional sense'. The point of the words 'in an absolute sense' is that goodness must not be handicapped (in which case the manner of its energy will only be 'conditional'), but must go into action furnished with the proper advantages of health, wealth, and general equipment. In order, therefore, to be in a position to attain the end of happiness, a city must start with the proper advantages—which is a matter of good fortune rather than of man's art; in order actually to attain it, a city (i.e. its members) must achieve 'the actualization and practice of goodness'—and this belongs to the realm of human knowledge and purpose, where the art of the legislator can operate. We thus turn to consider means. (b) There are three means by which the members of a city may achieve goodness—nature; habit; and reason. Nature has already been considered in Chapter 7: we have now to discuss habit and reason; and here we enter the domain of education and legislative art.*

1331ᵇ24 We have now to speak of the constitution itself;* and here we have to explain the nature and character of the elements required if a city is to enjoy a happy life and possess a good constitution. There are two things in which well-being always and everywhere consists. The first is to determine aright the aim and end of your actions. The second is to find out the actions which will best conduce to that end. These two things—ends and means—may be concordant or discordant. Sometimes the aim is determined aright, but there is a failure to attain it in action. Sometimes the means to the end are all successfully attained, but the end originally fixed is only a poor sort of end. Sometimes there is failure in both respects: in medicine, for example, one may fail both to judge correctly what a healthy body should be like and to discover the means that produce the object which one actually has in view. When using any kind of skill or practical knowledge one ought to be in control of both these things, that is, of the end itself and also of the actions which conduce to the end.

1331ᵇ39 Obviously everyone aims at the good life, or happiness, but some have the capacity to attain it, whereas others, as a result of some chance or something in their own natural endowment, do not. A certain amount of equipment is necessary for the good life, and while this amount need not be so great for those whose endowment is good, more is required for those whose endowment is poor. Others, again, start wrong from the outset; and though they have the power of attaining happiness they seek it along the wrong lines. Here, and for the purposes of our inquiry, it is obviously necessary to be clear about the nature of happiness. The object we have in view is to discover the best constitution. The best constitution is that under which the city is best constituted. The best constituted city is the city which possesses the greatest possibility of achieving happiness.

1332ᵃ7 It has been argued in the *Ethics* (if the argument there used is of any value) that happiness is 'the complete actualization and practice of goodness, in an absolute rather than a conditional sense'.* By 'conditional' I mean 'unavoidable' and by 'absolute' I mean 'possessing [intrinsic] value'. Consider, for example, the case of just actions. To inflict a just penalty or punishment is indeed an act of goodness; but it is also an act which is necessary, and it has value only as being necessary. (It would be better if neither individuals nor cities ever needed recourse to any such action.) Acts done with a view to bestowing honours and wealth on others are acts of the highest value in the absolute sense. Acts of the first kind undo evils: acts of the second kind have an opposite character—they are the foundations and origins of good things. Similarly, while a good man would handle well the evils of poverty, sickness, and the other mishaps of life, the fact remains that happiness consists in the opposites [of these evils].* The truly good and happy man, as we have stated elsewhere in our arguments on ethics,* is one for whom, because of his goodness of character, the things which are absolutely good are good [in practice]. It is plain that his use of such goods must be good and valuable in the absolute sense. But this leads people to think that external advantages are the causes of happiness. One might as well say that a well-executed piece of fine harp-playing was due to the instrument, and not to the skill of the artist.

1332ª28 It follows from what has been said that some elements of the city should be 'given', or ready to hand, and the rest should be provided by the art of the legislator. Thus we pray that the establishment of the city be blessed with fortune, in matters where fortune is sovereign (for we hold that she is sovereign). But the goodness of the city is not the work of fortune; it requires knowledge and purpose. A city is good in virtue of the goodness of the citizens who have a share in its constitution. In our city all the citizens have a share in the constitution. We have therefore to consider how a man can become good. Even if it is possible for all to be good [collectively], without each being good individually, the latter is preferable, for if each individual is good it will follow that all [collectively] are good.

1332ª38 There are three means by which individuals become good and virtuous. These three are nature, habit, and reason. So far as nature is concerned, we must start by being men—and not some other species of animal—and men too who have certain qualities both of body and soul. There are, indeed, some qualities which it is no help to have had at the start. Habits cause them to change: implanted by nature in a neutral form, they can be modified by the force of habit either for better or worse.

1332ᵇ2 Animate beings other than men live mostly by natural impulse, though some are also guided to a slight extent by habit. Man lives by reason too; and he is unique in having this. It follows that these [three powers of man] must be tuned to agree: men are often led by reason not to follow habit and natural impulse, once they have been persuaded that some other course is better. We have already determined, in an earlier chapter,* the character of the natural endowment which is needed for our citizens, if they are to be easily moulded by the art of the legislator. The rest is entirely a matter of education; they will learn some things by habituation and others by listening [to instruction].

CHAPTER 14

2. Education and citizenship; education for leisure, and education of character. The system of education which is appropriate

to a city depends on the way in which rulers and ruled are
distinguished from one another. In our city the young must
learn to obey a free government of which they will eventually be
members; and in doing so they will also be learning to govern
when their turn comes. In thus learning generally 'the virtue of
the good citizen', they will also be learning 'the virtue of the
good man'; for the two virtues, as has been argued before (in
Book III, ch. 9), are here fundamentally the same. In planning
the system of education which will produce the good man and
citizen, we must distinguish the different parts of the soul—the
part which has reason (in its turn divided into a practical and
speculative part), and the part which has simply the capacity for
obeying reason. We must also distinguish the different parts or
aspects of life—action and leisure; war and peace. Education
must regard all the different parts of the soul and the different
parts or aspects of life. The laws of Sparta have been much
praised but they are fundamentally defective because they are
directed towards victory in war and the subjugation of other
peoples. In reality cities, like individuals, should devote them-
selves chiefly to that aspect of life which is concerned with
peace and leisure.

1332ᵇ12 As all political associations are composed of rulers
and ruled, we have to consider whether different people
should be rulers and the ruled or whether the same people
[should occupy these roles] throughout their lives. The system
of education will necessarily vary according to the answer we
give. We may imagine one set of circumstances in which it
would be obviously better that the one group should once
and for all be rulers and one group should be ruled. This
would be if there were one class in the city surpassing all
others as much as gods and heroes are supposed to surpass
mankind—a class so outstanding, physically as well as mentally, that the superiority of the rulers was indisputably clear
to those over whom they ruled. But that is a difficult assumption to make; and we have nothing in actual life like the gulf
between kings and subjects which the writer Scylax describes
as existing in India. We may therefore draw the conclusion,
which can be defended on many grounds, that all should

share alike in a system of government under which they rule and are ruled by turns. In a society of peers equality means that all should have the same [privileges]: and a constitution can hardly survive if it is founded on injustice. Along with those who are ruled there will be all those [serfs] from the countryside who want a revolution; those who belong to the citizen body cannot possibly be sufficient in number to overcome all these.* On the other hand, it cannot be denied that there should be a difference between governors and governed. How they can differ, and yet share alike, is a dilemma which legislators have to solve. This is a matter we have already discussed.*

1332ᵇ35 Nature, we have suggested, has provided us with the distinction we need. She has divided a body identical in species into two different age-groups, a younger and an older, one of them meant to be ruled and the other to rule. No one in his youth resents being ruled, or thinks himself better [than his rulers]; especially if he knows that he will redeem his contribution on reaching the proper age. In one sense, therefore, it has to be said that rulers and ruled are the same; in another, that they are different. The same will be true of their education: from one point of view it must be the same; from another it has to be different, and, as the saying goes, one who would learn to rule well, must first learn to be ruled. Ruling, as has already been said in our first part,* takes two forms, one for the benefit of the rulers, the other for the benefit of the ruled. The former is what we call 'despotic'; the latter involves ruling over freemen.

1333ᵃ6 Some of the duties imposed [on the free] differ [from those of slaves] not in the work they involve, but in the object for which they are to be done. This means that a good deal of the work which is generally accounted menial may none the less be the sort of work which young freemen can honourably do. It is not the inherent nature of actions, but the end or object for which they are done, which makes one action differ from another in the way of honour or dishonour.*

1333ᵃ11 We have said that the excellence of the citizen who is a ruler is the same as that of the good man and that the same person who begins by being ruled must later be a ruler.*

It follows on this that the legislator must labour to ensure that his citizens become good men. He must therefore know what institutions will produce this result, and what is the end or aim to which a good life is directed.

1333ª16 There are two different parts of the soul. One of these parts has reason intrinsically and in its own nature. The other has not; but it has the capacity for obeying such a principle. When we speak of a man as being 'good', we mean that he has the goodnesses of these two parts of the soul. But in which of the parts is the end of man's life more particularly to be found? The answer is one which admits of no doubt to those who accept the division just made. In the world of nature as well as of art that which is worse always exists for the sake of that which is better.* The part which has reason is the better part. But this part is in turn divided, on the scheme which we generally follow, into two parts of its own. Reason, according to that scheme, is partly practical, partly speculative.* It is obvious, therefore, that the part of the soul which has this principle must fall into two corresponding parts. We may add that the same goes for the activities [of those parts]. It follows that those who can attain all the activities possible, or two of those activities, will be bound to prefer the activity of the part which is in its nature better. All of us always prefer the highest we can attain.

1333ª30 Life as a whole is also divided into action and leisure, war and peace; and actions are divided into those which are [merely] necessary, or useful, and those which have value [in themselves]. The same [pattern of] choice applies to these as applies to the parts of the soul and their different activities—war for the sake of peace; work for the sake of leisure; and acts which are merely necessary or useful for the sake of those which are valuable in themselves. The legislation of the true statesman must be framed with a view to all of these factors: it must cover the different parts of the soul and their different activities and should be directed more to the higher than the lower, and rather to ends than means. The same goes for the different parts or ways of life and for the choice of different activities. It is true that one must be able to engage in work and in war; but one must be even more able to lead a life of leisure and peace. It is true, again, that one must be able to do necessary or useful acts; but one must be even more able to do deeds of value. These are the general aims which ought to be followed in the education of childhood and of the stages of life which still require education.

1333ᵇ5 The Greek cities of our day which are counted as having the best constitutions, and the legislators who framed their constitutions, have plainly not drawn up their constitutional arrangements with a view to the highest goal, nor have they directed their laws and systems of education to all the virtues. On the contrary, there has been a vulgar decline into the cultivation of qualities supposed to be useful and of a more profitable character. A similar spirit appears in some of our recent writers who have adopted this point of view. They praise the constitution of Sparta, and they admire the aim of the Spartan legislator in directing the whole of this legislation to the goal of conquest and war. This is a view which can be easily refuted by argument, and it has now been also refuted by the evidence of fact. Most people are believers in the cause of empire, on the ground that empire leads to a large accession of material prosperity. It is evidently in this spirit that Thibron, like all the other writers on the constitution of Sparta, lauds its legislator for having trained men to meet danger and so created an empire. Today the Spartans have lost their empire; and we can all see for ourselves that they are not a happy community and that their legislator was not a good one. It is indeed a strange result of his labours: here is a people which has stuck to his laws and never been hindered in carrying them out, and yet it has lost the ability to live in a way that has real value. In any case the partisans of Sparta are in error about the type of government for which the legislator should show a preference. Ruling over freemen is a finer thing and one more connected with goodness, than ruling despotically.

1333ᵇ29 There is another reason why a city should not be considered happy, or its legislator praised, when its citizens are trained for victory in war and the subjugation of neighbouring cities. Such a policy involves a great risk of injury. It obviously implies that any citizen who can do so should make it his object to rule his own city.* This is exactly what the Spartans accuse their King Pausanias of having attempted to do—and this although he already held an office of such great dignity. We may justly conclude that none of these arguments and none of these systems of law is statesmanlike, or useful, or right.

1333^{b}37 The same things are best both for individuals and for communities; and it is these which the legislator ought to instil into the minds of his citizens. Training for war should not be pursued with a view to enslaving people who do not deserve such a fate. Its objects should be these—first, to prevent us from ever becoming enslaved ourselves; secondly, to put us in a position to exercise leadership—but leadership directed to the interest of those who are ruled, and not to the establishment of a general system of slavery; and thirdly, to enable us to make ourselves masters of those who naturally deserve to be slaves. In support of the view that the legislator should make leisure and peace the cardinal aims of all legislation bearing on war—or indeed, for that matter, on anything else—we may cite the evidence of actual fact. Most of the cities which make war their aim are safe only while they are fighting. They collapse as soon as they have established an empire, and lose their edge like iron, in time of peace. The legislator is to blame for having provided no training for the proper use of leisure.

CHAPTER 15

If leisure is thus of major importance, we may go on to notice that its enjoyment demands certain conditions, or, in other words, requires certain virtues—especially the virtues of wisdom and temperance. This will explain why a training such as the Spartan, which encourages only the virtue of courage, is defective and breaks down in practice ... Reverting now to the means of education—training in habits and the training of reason—we must inquire, 'Which of them should first be employed?' The answer is that the training of reason should, from the very first, be kept in view as the ultimate aim; but the training which ought to be given first is that of the part of the soul which has the capacity for obeying reason, and we must therefore begin by providing for the training of this part in habits. But even prior to the training of this part of the soul, there is a physical problem to be considered—the problem of ensuring a good physique which will be a good servant of the soul.

1334ᵃ11 The final end of human beings is the same whether they are acting individually or acting collectively; and the standard followed by the best man is thus the same as the standard followed by the best constitution. It is therefore evident that the qualities required for the use of leisure must belong [to the city as well as the individual]; for, as we have repeatedly argued, peace is the final end of war, and leisure the final end of work.* The good qualities required for the use of leisure and the cultivation of the mind are twofold. Some of them are operative during leisure itself: some are operative while we are at work. A number of necessary conditions must be present, before leisure is possible. This is why a city must possess the quality of temperance, and why, again, it must possess the quality of courage and endurance. 'There's no leisure for slaves', as the proverb goes, and those who cannot face danger courageously become the slaves of those who attack them. The quality of courage and endurance is required for work: wisdom is required for leisure: temperance and justice are qualities required for both times—though they are particularly required by those who enjoy peace and leisure. War automatically enforces temperance and justice: the enjoyment of prosperity, and leisure accompanied by peace, is more apt to make people overbearing. A great deal of justice and a great deal of temperance is therefore required in those who appear to be faring exceptionally well and enjoying all that is generally accounted to be happiness, like those, if there are any, who dwell in 'the happy isles' of which poets sing; and the greater the leisure which these people enjoy, when they are set among an abundance of blessings, the greater too will be their need of wisdom, as well as of temperance and justice.

1334ᵃ35 We can now understand why a city which seeks to

achieve happiness, and to be good, must share in these virtues. If some shame must always attach to anyone who cannot use properly the goods of life, a special measure of shame must attach to those who cannot use them properly in times of leisure—to those who show themselves good in work and war, but sink to the level of slaves in times of peace and leisure.

1334ª40 Excellence must not be sought by a training such as the Spartan. The Spartans are like the rest of the world in their view of the nature of life's highest goods: they only differ from others in thinking that the right way of getting them is to cultivate a particular kind of excellence. Regarding external goods as higher than any others, and the enjoyment they give as greater than that derived from the general cultivation of excellence, [they cultivate only the single excellence which they consider useful as a means to securing those goods. But it is the whole of excellence which ought to be cultivated, and cultivated]* for its own sake, as our argument has already shown. That still leaves us, however, with the problem, 'How, and by what means, is a general excellence to be achieved?'

1334ᵇ6 We have already explained that there is need for natural endowment, habit, and reason.* So far as the first of these is concerned, we have already determined* the character of the endowment which our citizens should have. It remains to consider whether training in habit or training in reason ought to come first. The two modes of training must harmonize with one another to the highest degree; reason may fail to arrive at the best principle and one may likewise be led astray by habit. The following points, at any rate, are evident. First, in human life (as in all life generally), birth has a first beginning, but the end attained from such a beginning is only a step to some further end. Reason and thought is the ultimate end of our nature. It is therefore with a view to these that we should regulate, from the first, the birth and the training in habits [of our citizens]. Secondly, as soul and body are two, so there are also two parts of the soul, the irrational and the rational; and there are also two corresponding states of these parts—appetite and thought. By birth, the body is prior to the soul, and the irrational part of the soul to the rational. This is proved by the fact that anger, will, and desire are visible in children from their very birth; while reasoning and thought naturally appear, as they grow older. The conclusion which follows is obvious. Children's bodies should be given attention before their souls; and their appetites should be the next part of them to be regulated. But the regulation of their appetites should be intended for the benefit of their minds —just as the attention given to their bodies should be intended for the benefit of their souls.

D: The Early Stages of Education (Chapters 16–17)

CHAPTER 16

1. The regulation of marriage is the first necessity, if we are to ensure a good physique for our future citizens. The age at which husband and wife marry affects the physique of their offspring; and on physical grounds it may be suggested that the husband should be older than the wife, and the man of 37 should marry the woman of 18. The husband's physique should not be spoiled by over-exercise or the reverse; the wife should take regular exercise during pregnancy. If the size of the family has to be limited, it will be necessary to consider means such as the exposure of infants and the procuring of miscarriages. The age at which procreation should cease, and the treatment of adultery.

1334ᵇ29 If we assume that the legislator ought, for a start, to see that the children who are brought up have the best possible physical endowment, it follows that his first attention must be devoted to marriage; and here he will have to consider what the ages of the partners should be, and what qualities they ought to possess. In dealing with this form of association the legislator must take into account both the partners themselves and the length of time for which they will live, so that they may arrive simultaneously at the same stage of sexual life. There should be no divergence of physical power, with the husband still able to beget but the wife unable to conceive, or the wife still able to conceive and the husband unable to beget—that is apt to cause conflicts and differences between them. The legislator should then consider when children will succeed to their parents' estates. On the one hand, there should not be too much of a gap: in that case fathers will not get the benefit of their children's gratitude while the children will not benefit from their fathers' assistance; and yet, on the other hand, they should not be too close. That, too, leads to considerable difficulties: it makes children treat parents with less respect, feeling that they are almost contemporaries, and it readily leads to quarrels about the management of the household. Then—and here we return to the point from which we have just digressed—the legislator has to ensure that the physical endowment of the children who are born is suitable for his purposes.

1335ᵃ6 Now all these objects may be secured at once by a single policy. The period of procreation finally ends, as a rule, at the age of 70 for men, and the age of 50 for women; and the beginning of their union should therefore be fixed at such an age as to ensure that they reach this point of their lives at the same time. The union of young parents is bad for the procreation of issue. In the whole of the animal world the offspring of young parents have imperfections. They tend to be of the female sex, and they are diminutive in figure. The same must therefore happen among human beings. There is evidence of this: in all the cities where it is the custom for men and women to marry young, the inhabitants are imperfectly developed and small of stature. We may add that young mothers have harder labours and die more often in childbirth. This was the reason, according to some accounts, for the response once given by the oracle to the people of Troezen.* It had no relation to the cultivation of crops, but referred to the large mortality caused by the marriage of girls at too early an age. It also conduces to sexual restraint if the daughters of a family are not married early: young women are supposed to be more intemperate when once they have had experience of sexual intercourse. The physique of men is also supposed to be stunted in its growth, when intercourse is begun before the seed has finished its growth. (The seed, too, has its own period of growth—a period which it observes exactly, or with only a slight variation, in the course of its development.)

1335ᵃ28 Women should therefore marry about the age of 18, and men at 37 or thereabouts.* If these ages are observed, union will begin while the bodies of both the partners are still in their prime, and it will end for both simultaneously with the simultaneous ending of their power of procreation. The succession of children to parents will also be as it should be. If reproduction, as we may reasonably expect, begins immediately [after marriage], children will be ready to take over in the beginning of their own prime, and just at the time when the period of the father's vigour has come to an end with the attainment of the age of 70.

1335ᵃ35 We have now discussed the proper ages for marriage. In regard to the proper season of the year, it is best to follow the sensible practice, which is observed by the majority of people today, of fixing winter as the time for men and women to set up house together. Married couples should also study for themselves the lessons to be learned from doctors and natural philosophers about the bringing of children into the world. Doctors can tell them all they need to know about the times of good physical condition: natural philosophers can tell them about favourable winds (for instance, they hold that the north wind is better than the south).

1335ᵇ2 What physical characteristics in the parents are likely to be of most benefit to their offspring? That is a theme to which closer attention will have to be paid when we come to treat of the management of children; but some general indication may be given here. The athlete's physical condition neither produces a good condition for the purposes of civic life, nor does it encourage health and the procreation of children. The condition of valetudinarians and those unfit for any exertion is equally unfavourable. The best condition is one which comes midway between these. Some amount of exertion must therefore go to its making. But the exertion must not be violent or specialized, as is the case with the athlete; it should rather be a general exertion, directed to all the activities of a freeman.

1335ᵇ11 Wives, as well as husbands, need the physical qualities of which we have just been speaking. Pregnant mothers should pay attention to their bodies: they should take regular exercise, and follow a nourishing diet. The legislator can easily lead them to a habit of regular exercise if he requires them to make some daily pilgrimage for the purpose of worshipping at the shrines of the goddesses who preside over childbirth. Their minds, unlike their bodies, should be kept free from exertion; for children evidently draw on the mother who carries them in her womb, just as plants draw on the soil.*

1335^{b}19 The question arises whether children should always be reared or may sometimes be exposed to die. There should certainly be a law to prevent the rearing of deformed children. On the other hand, if the established social customs forbid the exposure of infants simply to keep down the number of children, a limit must be placed on the number who are born. If a child is then conceived in excess of the limit so fixed, a miscarriage should be induced before sense and life have begun in the embryo. (Whether it is right or wrong to induce a miscarriage will thus depend on whether sense and life are still to come, or have already begun.)

1335^{b}26 We have now determined the ages at which men and women should begin their married life. It remains to determine the length of time for which they should render public service* by bringing children into the world. The offspring of elderly men, like that of very young men, tends to be physically and mentally imperfect; and the children of old age are weakly. We may therefore fix the length of time for which procreation lasts by reference to the mental prime. This comes for most men—as some of the poets, who measure life in seven-year periods, have suggested—about the age of 50. Men may therefore be released from the service of bringing children into the world when they are four or five years above this age; and from that time forward we must regard them as indulging in intercourse for reasons of health, or for some similar cause.

1335^{b}38 For husband and wife to be detected in the commission of adultery—at whatever time it may happen, and in whatever way, during all the period of their being married and being called husband and wife—must be made a matter of disgrace. But to be detected in adultery during the very period of bringing children into the world is a thing to be punished by a stigma of infamy proportionate to such an offence.

CHAPTER 17

2. The nursery and the infant school. The first stage: the diet of the infant; the proper use of its limbs; the inuring of children to cold. The second stage, to the age of 5: games and stories; young children should be protected from bad company, and safeguarded from hearing indecent language or seeing indecent pictures; generally, they should be saved from an early familiarity with anything low, since early impressions go deep. The third stage, from the age of 5 to that of 7: children of this age should watch other children doing the work they will have to do later themselves.

After the age of 7 education will fall into two periods—the first from the age of 7 to that of puberty: the second from the age of puberty to the age of 21. Should there be a code of regulations, and should the care of children be managed by the city or privately?

1336^a3 When children are born, the sort of nourishment which they are given can be expected to make a great difference to their physical powers. On any consideration of the matter, and whether we look to the animal world or to the example of those tribal peoples who make it their aim to produce a bodily condition fit for war, it is evident that a diet abounding in milk is best suited to the physical development of children; and the less wine they are given the better, if they are to escape diseases. It is also good to encourage every sort of physical movement which ones so young can make; but in order to prevent any distortion of their soft limbs, some tribal peoples still use mechanical appliances which keep their bodies straight. It is good to habituate children to the endurance of cold from their earliest infancy; and this is a practice which greatly conduces to their general health, as well as hardening them in advance for military service. This will explain why some barbarian peoples have the habit of plunging their children at birth into a cold river, or (like the Celts) of making them go lightly clad. Wherever it is possible to implant a habit in children, it is best to begin the process of habituation in their earliest years, and then to increase it gradually. The physical constitution of children, owing to their natural warmth, is well adapted for training in the endurance of cold.

1336ª21 The earliest years will best be handled in the ways we have just described, and in other similar ways. The next stage of the child's life, which lasts to the age of 5, is one which cannot be set any lessons, or put to any compulsory tasks, for fear of hindering its growth. But it is a stage which needs some practice in movement, to prevent the body from becoming limp; and this should be provided by games, as well as in other ways. The games should be neither laborious nor undisciplined, but such as become a freeman. Care should also be taken by the officers in charge (who are generally termed the superintendents of education) to determine the sort of tales and stories which children of this age ought to be told. All these things should prepare the way for the occupations of later years; and even the games of children should be for the most part mimicries of what will later be earnest. Those who, in their *Laws*,* prevent children from straining their lungs and sobbing are wrong to forbid [this sort of thing]. It helps the growth of children: it is, in its way, a sort of physical exercise; and just as holding the breath gives adults strength for exertion, so straining the lungs has the same effect in children.

1336ª39 The superintendents of education must exercise a general control over the way in which children pass their time. In particular, they must be careful that very little of their time is passed in the company of slaves. The stage of life through which children pass down to the age of 7 is bound to be one of home training; and, young as they are, they will be likely to contract slave-like habits from what they hear or see. It should therefore be a primary duty of the legislator to exorcize the use of bad language everywhere in our city. The use of bad language leads to similar kinds of behaviour. The young, especially, should be kept free from hearing, or using, any such language. Those who are found talking or acting in any of the prohibited ways must be punished accordingly. The younger freemen who are not yet allowed to recline at the common tables,* must be subjected to corporal punishment and other indignities; and men of an older age should pay the penalty for behaving like slaves by undergoing indignities of a slave-like character.

1336^b12 If talk of this kind is proscribed, it is obvious that we must also prevent the young from seeing indecent pictures and [hearing] indecent speeches.* It should therefore be the duty of those in office to prohibit all statuary and painting which portrays any sort of indecent action. An exception may, however, be made for the festivals of deities where even the use of scurrility is licensed by the law. (But here, we may note, the law also allows men who have reached a proper maturity to worship the gods on behalf of their wives and children as well as for themselves.)* Legislation should forbid the young from attending iambics* or comedies, until they have reached the age when they are allowed to share in the practice of reclining and taking wine [at the common tables]. By that time their education will have made them all immune from the evil effects of such performances.

1336^b22 We have now given a cursory account of this question. We must give it our attention, and settle it in more detail, at a later stage, when we have gone into the arguments for and against [such legal control], and discussed the form which it ought to take. Here we have only touched on the issue so far as the occasion immediately requires. Perhaps there is point in the remark of Theodorus, the tragic actor, that he had never yet allowed any other actor, however poor he might be, to make his entrance before he did, because (as he put it) 'spectators get fond of those they hear first'. This is a fate which is apt to befall us not only when we are dealing with people, but also when we are dealing with things: we always prefer what we come across first. The young must therefore be kept from an early familiarity with anything that is low, and especially anything that may suggest depravity or malice.

1336ᵇ35 When the first five years are safely over, children should then spend the next two years, down to the age of 7, in watching others at work on the lessons which they will afterwards have to learn themselves.

1336ᵇ37 There should be two different periods of education—the first from the age of 7 to that of puberty; the second from puberty to the age of 21. Those who divide man's life into seven-year periods are on the whole right. But the divisions which we ought to follow are those made by nature herself. The purpose of education, like that of every kind of art, is to make good nature's deficiencies. Three subjects here suggest themselves for our consideration. The first is whether there ought to be some code of regulations concerning children. The second is whether the care of children should be a matter for the city, or should be conducted on a private basis, as it still is, even today, in the great majority of cases. The third question which we have to consider is what this code of regulations should be.

BOOK VIII
THE TRAINING OF YOUTH

A: The General Scheme of Training (Chapters 1–3)

CHAPTER 1

Legislation is needed to regulate education, both for political and for moral reasons. There should be a uniform system for all, and it should be a system of public education.

1337ª11 All would agree that the legislator should make the education of the young his chief and foremost concern.* After all, the constitution of a city will suffer if this does not happen. The form of education must be related to each form of constitution. The type of character appropriate to a constitution tends to sustain that constitution as well as to bring it into being. The democratic type of character creates and sustains democracy; the oligarchical type creates and sustains oligarchy; and in every case the best type of character will always tend to produce a better form of constitution. What is more, every capacity, and every form of art, requires as a condition of its exercise some measure of previous training and some amount of preliminary habituation, so the same must clearly go for acts embodying goodness of character.

1337ª21 The city as a whole has a single end. Evidently, therefore, the system of education must also be one and the same for all, and the provision of this system must be a matter of public action. It cannot be left, as it is at present, to private enterprise, with each parent making provision privately for his own children, and having them privately instructed as he himself thinks fit. Training for an end which is common should also itself be common. We must not regard a citizen as belonging just to himself: we must rather regard every citizen as belonging to the city, since each is a part of the city;* and the provision made for each part will naturally be adjusted to the provision made for the whole. Here the

Spartans are to be praised. They pay the greatest attention to the training of the young; and they pay attention collectively, and not in their private capacity.

CHAPTER 2

The absence of any clear view about the proper subjects of instruction: the conflicting claims of utility, moral discipline, and the advancement of knowledge. Some subjects should be taught because of their utility; but the teaching of such subjects should never go so far as to produce a 'mechanical bias', and even the more liberal subjects should not be studied too professionally.

1337ª33 It is now evident both that there ought to be laws to regulate education and that education ought to be conducted by the city. But we have to consider what education should be given, and the methods by which it should be given. At present opinion is divided about the subjects of education. All do not share the same opinion about what should be learned by the young, with a view to goodness or to the best life; nor is opinion clear whether education should be directed mainly to the understanding, or mainly to moral character. If we look at actual practice, the result is confusing; it throws no light on the problem whether there should be training in those pursuits which are useful in life, or those which make for goodness, or those which go beyond the ordinary run [of knowledge]. Each sort of study receives some votes in its favour. There is, for example, a total absence of agreement about the studies which make for goodness. To begin with, those who honour goodness do not all have the same conception of goodness; so it is hardly surprising that they should also differ about the right methods of practising it.

1337ᵇ4 There can be no doubt that such useful subjects as are really necessary ought to be part of the instruction of children. But this does not mean the inclusion of every useful subject. Occupations are divided into those which are fit for freemen and those which are unfit for them; and clearly children should take part in useful occupations only to the extent that they do not turn those taking part in them into 'mechanical' types. The term 'mechanical' [*banausos*] should properly be applied to any occupation, art, or instruction which is calculated to make the body, or soul, or mind of a freeman unfit for the pursuit and practice of goodness. We may accordingly apply the word 'mechanical' to any art or craft which adversely affects men's physical fitness, and to any employment which is pursued for the sake of gain; these preoccupy and debase the mind. Much the same may also be said of those branches of knowledge which are fit for a freeman. It is not out of keeping with a freeman's character to study these up to a certain point; but too much concentration upon them, with a view to attaining perfection, is liable to cause the same evil effects that have just been mentioned. A good deal depends on the purpose for which acts are done or subjects are studied.* Doing these to satisfy a personal need, or to help a friend, or to attain goodness, is not unfitting for a freeman; but the very same act, when done repeatedly at the instance of other people, may be counted menial and servile.

CHAPTER 3

There are four subjects of instruction to be considered—reading and writing; drawing; gymnastics; and music. The first two have an element of utility: the third promotes the moral virtue of courage: the purpose of the fourth is not so clear, but it may be argued that it serves to promote the proper use of leisure. This leads us to note the distinction between (1) work, (2) play or relaxation, and (3) the use of leisure. The real purpose of music is to be found in the cultivation of leisure; and drawing too, while it has its utility, may also serve to give the young an observant eye for beauty of form and figure.

1337ᵇ23 The studies now generally established as parts of the curriculum may be regarded, as has already been said, from two different points of view.* There are some four subjects which are usually included in education. They are reading and writing, physical training, and music; and some would also add drawing. Reading and writing together with drawing are generally regarded as useful for the practical purposes of life in a number of different ways. Physical training is commonly thought to foster courage. But there is a doubt about music. At present, indeed, it is mainly studied as if its object were pleasure; but the real reason which originally led to its being made a subject of education is that our very nature (as we have often remarked) seeks the power, not only to work in the right way but also to use leisure well; indeed leisure, as we would once more repeat,* is the basis of everything. It is true that work and leisure are both necessary; but it is also true that leisure is preferable, and is more of an end. We must consider, therefore, what we should do to occupy our leisure. It cannot be playing, since play would then be the end for the sake of which we live. That is an impossibility. Play is a thing to be chiefly used in connection with work. Those who labour need relaxation; and play exists for the purpose of relaxation. Work involves labour and exertion. We may therefore conclude that play should be admitted into our city at the proper times, and should be applied as a kind of medicine. The effect which play produces in the mind is one of relief from exertion; and the pleasure it gives provides relaxation. Leisure of itself, so it seems, involves pleasure, happiness, and well-being. This is the condition, not of those who are at work, but of those who are at leisure. Those who work do so with a view to some end which they regard as still unattained. But happiness is an end; and all men think of it as accompanied by pleasure and not by pain. It is true that all do not conceive this pleasure in the same way. Different people conceive it differently, according to their own personality and disposition. But the highest pleasure, derived from the noblest sources, will be that of the man of greatest goodness.

1338ᵃ9 It is clear, therefore, that there are some branches of learning and education which ought to be studied with a view to living a life of leisure. It is clear, too, that these forms of education and of learning are valued for their own sake, while those studied with a view to work should be regarded merely as matters of necessity and valued as means to other things. This will explain why our forefathers made music a part of education. They did not do so because it was necessary: it is nothing of the sort. Nor did they do so because it is useful, as reading and writing are useful for money-making, for household management, for the acquisition of knowledge, and for many political activities. Drawing may be held to be useful in helping us to judge more correctly the works of different craftsmen. Nor is music, like physical training, useful in improving health and strength: it has no visible effect upon either. We are thus left with its value for living a life of leisure. This is evidently the reason for its being introduced into education: it ranks as one of the ways in which a freeman should pass his time. This is the meaning of the lines in Homer, beginning,

> Such are they who alone should be called to the bountiful banquet

and continuing (after a mention of various guests) with the words:

> With them call they a minstrel, to pleasure all men with his music.

Again, in another passage, Odysseus is made to say that music is the best of pastimes when men are all merry, and

> They who feast in the hall lend their ears to the minstrel in silence,
> Sitting in order due.*

1338ª30 We may take it as evident, from what has been said, that there is a kind of education in which parents should have their sons trained not because it is necessary, or because it is useful, but simply because it befits a freeman and is good in itself. Whether this kind of education is confined to a single subject, or includes a number of subjects; what the subjects are, and how they should be studied—all this must be left for further discussion.* But we have already reached a point at which we are entitled to say that the evidence of tradition supports our general view. This is shown by the old-established subjects of study; and the example of music is sufficient to make it clear. We are also entitled to say that some of the useful subjects—for example, reading and writing—ought to be taught to children, not only because they are useful, but also because, by their means, many other kinds of learning become possible. Similarly the object of instruction in drawing is not so much to save people from making mistakes in their private purchases, or from being deceived in the buying and selling of articles; it is rather to give them an observant eye for beauty of form and figure. To aim at utility everywhere is utterly unbecoming to the high-minded* and to those who have the character of freemen.

1338ᵇ4 In educating children we must clearly make use of habit before reason, and we must deal with the body before we deal with the mind. We must therefore begin by putting them into the hands of physical instructors and games masters. The former is concerned with the proper condition of the body: the latter with what it can do.

B: Physical Training, or Gymnastics (Chapter 4)

CHAPTER 4

There are dangers in over-athleticism, and defects in the Spartan system of education: courage is not the only virtue, and a training meant to produce toughness is one-sided and ineffective, even in the matter of fostering true courage. The right policy in regard to physical training is to avoid an excessive early training, which stunts the proper development of the body. Light exercises till the age of puberty, followed by a period of three years spent in study, which should be followed in turn by a period of hard exercise and strict diet—this is the best system. The young should not be made to work hard with body and mind simultaneously.

1338ᵇ9 Among the cities which are generally regarded as paying the greatest attention to the training of youth, there are some which create an athletic habit of body at the cost of impairing both the appearance of the body and its growth. The Spartans have not made this particular error; but they give the young a savage character by imposing rigorous exercises, on the assumption that this is the best way of fostering courage. It is, however, a mistake, as we have repeatedly said, to direct the training of youth exclusively, or mainly, to this one end; and even if courage were the main object, the Spartans are wrong in their way of encouraging it. Both in the animal world, and among tribal peoples, courage is always found, as observation will show us, not in association with the greatest ferocity, but in connection with a gentler and more lion-like temperament. There are, it is true, many tribal peoples which are ready enough to indulge in killing and cannibalism. Among the peoples on the coast of the Black Sea, the Achaeans and Heniochi are of this sort, and some of the inland peoples are equally or even more savage; they are peoples of bandits—but they have no real courage. Even the Spartans themselves, as we know from experience, were superior to others only so long as they were the only people who assiduously practised the rigours of discipline; and nowadays they are beaten both in athletic contests and in actual war. Their previous superiority was not due to the particular training which they gave to their youth: it was simply and solely due to their having some sort of discipline when their antagonists had none at all. Nobility of character, rather than ferocity of temper, should take pride of place. It is not wolves, or other savage animals, that will fight a good fight in the presence of a noble danger, but the good man. To let youth run wild in savage pursuits, and to leave them untrained in the disciplines they really need, is really to degrade them into vulgarity. It is to make them serve the statesman's purposes in one respect, and one only; and even there, as our argument shows, it is to make them of less service than those who have been differently trained. We must not judge the Spartans on the grounds of their former achievement, but on the grounds of their present position. The Spartan training has now to face rivals. Formerly it had none.

1338^{b}38 There is general agreement about the necessity of physical training, and about the way in which it ought to be given. Till the age of puberty the exercises used should be light, and there should be no rigorous dieting or violent exertion, such as may hinder the proper growth of the body. The effects of these practices are strikingly evident. In the lists of Olympic victors there are only two or three cases of the same person having won in the men's events who had previously won in the boys'; and the reason is that early training, and the compulsory exercises which it involved, had resulted in loss of strength. After that age is reached, the next three years may be spent in other studies; and then the next period of development may properly be given to hard exercise and strict diet. It is not right to do work with the mind and the body at the same time. The two different sorts of work tend naturally to produce different, and indeed opposite, effects. Physical work clogs the mind; and mental work hampers the body.

C: The Aims and Methods of Education in Music (Chapters 5–7)

CHAPTER 5

There are three possible views about the purpose of education in music—(1) that it serves for amusement and relaxation; (2) that it serves as a means of moral training; (3) that it serves as a means to the cultivation of the mind. Amusement cannot be the aim: if it were, we should not want to have children taught to play music themselves; we should be content to let them get amusement by listening to the playing of others. But the same would be true if moral training or the cultivation of the mind were regarded as the purpose of music. We may therefore leave aside for the moment the question whether children should play themselves and turn back to consider independently the place of music in education. The pleasure music produces may serve the purpose of amusement as well as that of cultivation of the mind and the right use of leisure. But music may also serve the purpose of moral training. It can supply 'images' of the virtues, and by inducing us to take pleasure in these 'images' it can induce us to take pleasure in the virtues themselves.

1339ª11 Some questions concerning music have already been raised at an earlier stage of our argument; but it will be well to pick up the thread again here, and to pursue the matter further.* We may thus provide something in the nature of a preface to the considerations which would naturally be advanced in any full view of the subject. It is difficult to define the exact effects of music; and it is equally difficult to define the purpose for which it ought to be studied. Some would hold that the purpose of music, like that of sleeping or drinking, is simply amusement and relaxation. Sleep and drink are not in themselves good things; but they are at any rate pleasurable things, and, as Euripides says,* they 'give us rest from care'. It is on this ground that music is sometimes ranked with them both, and that sleep and drink and music (to which dancing may also be added) are all treated in just the same way. Another possible view is that music should be regarded as something of an influence making for goodness, inasmuch as it has the power of giving a tone to our character (just as physical training can give a tone to our bodies) by habituating us to feel pleasure in the right sort of way. There is still a third possible view—that music has some contribution to make to a cultivated way of living* and to the growth of wisdom.

1339ᵃ26 It is clear that amusement is not the object with a view to which the young should be educated. Learning is not a matter of amusement. It is attended by effort and pain. On the other hand, it is also true that a cultivated way of living is not a thing which is proper for children or the young of a tender age. Those who are themselves still short of their own end cannot yet cope with the ultimate end. Perhaps the serious studies of children are means to the amusement which they will be able to enjoy when they reach their full growth as adults. But if that view be taken, why (we may ask) should children be taught to play music themselves? Why should they not follow the example of the Persian and Median kings, and get their pleasure and instruction through listening to others making music? Those who make it an occupation and a profession are bound to attain a better result than those who only practise it long enough just to learn. We may add that if children are to be made to work away at musical performances, they ought equally to be made to work at the business of cooking—which is absurd.

1339ᵃ41 The same problem arises if we look at music as a power which can improve character. Here, too, we may ask,

'Why should children learn to perform themselves, and why should not listening to the music of others be enough to give them the power of enjoying and appreciating music in the right sort of way?' The Spartans act on that principle: they do not learn to play; but, so it is said, they are able to appreciate properly the difference between good and bad tunes. The same is true if we take the third view about music, and hold that it ought to be used to promote a way of living that is both pleasant and worthy of a freeman. Why, for this purpose, should we learn ourselves, instead of drawing on the services of others? Here we shall do well to remember the conception we hold of the gods. The Zeus of our poets does not sing, or play on the harp. We are apt to regard as vulgar [banausos] those who do otherwise, and we think of them as behaving in a way in which a man would not behave unless he were drunk or jesting.

1339ᵇ10 This, however, is perhaps a matter for later consideration. We must first inquire 'Should music be included in education, or should it not?' and 'Which of the three effects previously distinguished does it have?' 'Does it contribute to education, or to amusement, or to a cultivated way of living?' There are reasons for connecting it with all three; for it evidently embraces elements common to all. For example, amusement is intended to produce relaxation; and relaxation, which is in its nature a remedy for the pain produced by exertion, must necessarily be pleasant. Similarly, again, it is generally agreed that a cultivated way of living must include pleasure, as well as nobility, since these are both part of the happy life. Now we all agree that music, whether instrumental or accompanied by the voice, is one of the greatest of pleasures. At any rate we can cite the testimony of the poet Musaeus:*

> Song is to mortals the sweetest;

and here we may see the reason why people very naturally enlist the aid of music for their social parties and pastimes—it has the power of gladdening their hearts. We may therefore conclude that this is one of the reasons why children ought to be educated in music. All innocent pleasures have a double use: they not only help us to achieve our end,* but they also serve us as a means of relaxation. It is seldom that people attain their end. But they can often relax, and indulge themselves in amusements (not so much with a view to something beyond, but just for pleasure); and it may therefore be well that they should rest and relax for a while in the pleasures which come from music.

1339^b**31** People fall, it is true, into a way of making amusements the end of their life. The reason for their doing so is that the end of life would seem to involve a kind of pleasure. This kind of pleasure is not the ordinary, but in their search for it people are apt to mistake ordinary pleasure for it; and they do so because pleasure generally has some sort of likeness to the ultimate end of their activity. This end is desirable just for itself, and not for the sake of any future result; and the pleasures of amusement are similar—they are not desired for the sake of some result in the future, but rather because of something which has happened in the past, that is to say, the exertion and pain [which have already been undergone]. This, it may reasonably be held, is the cause which induces people to seek happiness from pleasures of this sort.

1339^b**40** Pleasure is not the only reason for having recourse to music. Another reason is its utility in furnishing relaxation. This is how the case for it seems to stand. But we have to inquire whether it does not possess a natural character which is of higher value than the uses hitherto mentioned. Perhaps there is more in question than our sharing in the common pleasure which everyone senses in music—a pleasure, indeed, which is natural, and which explains why the use of music appeals to all ages and all types of character—and perhaps we ought to consider whether music has not also some sort of bearing on our characters and our souls. It will clearly have such a bearing if our characters are actually affected by music. That they are so affected is evident from the influence exercised by a number of different tunes, but especially by those of Olympus.* His tunes, by general consent, have an inspiring effect on the soul; and a feeling of inspiration is an affection of the soul's character. We may add that, in listening to imitative [music],* everyone is moved to feelings of sympathy, quite apart from the effects of rhythm and melody.

1340ᵃ14 Since music belongs to the category of pleasures, and since goodness consists in feeling delight where one should, and loving and hating aright, we may clearly draw some conclusions.* First, there is no lesson which we are so much concerned to learn, and no habit which we are so much concerned to acquire, as that of forming right judgements on, and feeling delight in, fine characters and good actions. Next, rhythm and melodies provide us with images of states of character, which come closer to their actual nature than anything else can do—images of anger and of calm, of courage and of temperance, and of their opposites, images, in fact, of every state of character. This is a fact which is clear from experience; to listen to these images is to undergo a real change of the soul. Now to acquire a habit of feeling pain or taking delight in an image is something closely allied to feeling pain or taking delight in the actual reality. For example, if someone finds delight in looking at the image of some object purely on the ground of its form, he will also be bound to find pleasure in looking at the actual object whose image he now sees. It is true that the objects of some of the senses, such as touch and taste, cannot furnish any resemblance to states of character. Objects of sight may do so, but only to a slight extent. There are indeed shapes and figures which bear a resemblance to states of character, but the resemblance is not great; and [we have to remember that] everyone shares this sense.* Moreover, the shapes and colours [presented by visual art] are not representations of states of character: they are merely indications. And they are indications which can only be given by depicting the body when under the influence of some emotion. But in so far as there is any difference between the effects of looking at different works of art, the young should be discouraged from looking at the works of Pauso, and encouraged to study the works of Polygnotus and any other painter or sculptor who depicts moral character.*

1340ᵃ38 With musical compositions, however, the case is different. They involve representations of states of character themselves. This is an evident fact. In the first place, the nature of the modes varies; and listeners will be differently affected according as they listen to different modes.* The effect of some will be to produce a sadder and graver temperament; this is the case, for example, with the mode called the Mixolydian. The effect of others (such as the soft modes) is to relax the tone of the mind. Another mode is specially calculated to produce a moderate and collected temperament; this is held to be the peculiar power of the Dorian mode, while the Phrygian mode is held to give inspiration and fire. Those who have studied this kind of education do well to make these points, for the evidence by which they support their theories is derived from actual facts. The same goes for the various rhythms: some have a more steady character while others have a lively quality; and these last may again be divided, according as they move with a more vulgar rhythm or move in a manner more suited to freemen.

1340^{b}10 What we have said makes it clear that music possesses the power of producing an effect on the character of the soul. If it can produce this effect, it must clearly be made a subject of study and taught to the young. We may add that the teaching of music is congenial to the natural character of youth. Owing to their tender years, the young will not willingly tolerate any unsweetened fare; and music, by its nature, has a quality of sweetness. Nor is that all. The modes and rhythms of music have an affinity [with the soul], as well as a natural sweetness. This explains why many thinkers connect the soul with harmony—some saying that it is a harmony, and others that it possesses the attribute of harmony.*

CHAPTER 6

We return to the question, 'Should children be taught to play themselves?' To judge any performance well, you ought to be able to perform yourself; and the answer to the question is therefore 'Yes'—provided that the performance of music is not carried to professional lengths. Three inquiries thus suggest themselves: (1) what is the length to which the performance of music should be carried; (2) what sorts of melodies and rhythms should children learn to play; and (3) what instruments should they use? In regard to the first of these questions, we may say that difficult compositions should not be attempted, and the point to which children should go in learning to play themselves is the point at which they begin to be able to appreciate good melodies and rhythms. In regard to the last of the three questions, we may deprecate the use of the flute or similar instruments. We may also deprecate any attempt at professional skill and any entering for competitions, which tends to have a vulgarizing effect.

1340ᵇ20 It remains to answer the question, which has already been raised, whether children ought to learn music by actually singing and playing. It is clear that it makes a great difference to the acquisition of an aptitude if one has taken part in performances. It is difficult, if not impossible, for those who have never taken part in performances to become good judges of others. Children, too, should always have something to keep them occupied; and the rattle of Archytas* (which parents give to children in order to divert their attention and stop them from breaking things in the house) must be counted an admirable invention. Young things can never keep quiet: so a rattle suits children in infancy, while education serves as a rattle for older children.

1340ᵇ31 These considerations make it plain that a musical education should include some share in its actual performance. There is no difficulty in determining what is suitable or unsuitable for the different ages of growth or in answering the objection that this is a vulgar 'mechanical' kind of occupation. We must begin by noting that the purpose for which the young should join in the actual performance of music is only that they should be able to judge [musical performances]. This means that they ought to practise execution in their earlier years; but it also means that they ought to be released from it at a later age, when the education they have received in their youth should have made them able to judge what is good and to appreciate music properly. The censure which is sometimes passed on music—that it produces a professional or mechanical turn of mind—may be easily answered if we pause to ask a few questions. What, in the first place, is the point up to

which those who are being trained with a view to excellence
of a citizen should continue to join in actual performances?
Secondly, what is the quality of the melodies and rhythms in
which they ought to be instructed? Thirdly, in what sorts of
instruments should they be trained? (For that, too, is likely to
make a difference.) If we answer these questions we shall also
be able to answer the censure. After all, nothing prevents
some kinds of music from having the effect we have
mentioned.*

1341ᵃ5 We may take it for granted that the study [of music]
should neither impede the activities of later years, nor produce
a vulgar mechanical kind of body which is ineffective for the
purposes of the period of military and civic training—ineffective, initially, in bodily exercise, and afterwards in the acquisition of knowledge. The study of music might follow these
lines if two conditions were observed—first, that pupils were
not set to work on the sort of performances which belong to
professional competitions; secondly, that they were not made
to attempt the extraordinary and extravagant feats of execution which have recently been introduced into competitions,
and have thence passed on into education. Even so, performances should be carried only to the point at which students
begin to be able to appreciate good melodies and rhythms,
and are not content merely to enjoy that common element in
music* which is felt by some of the animals and by nearly all
slaves and children.

1341ᵃ17 The nature of the instruments which should be used
may also be inferred from what has just been said. Flutes
should not be used in musical education; and we ought to
avoid any other instrument which requires professional skill,
such as the harp and all other such instruments. The instruments which ought to be used are those that will produce
good listeners* in music or in other forms of education. A
further argument against the flute is the fact that it does not
express a state of character, but rather a mood of religious
excitement; and it should therefore be used on those occasions
when the effect to be produced on the audience is the release
of emotion [katharsis], and not instruction. Another reason
against the use of the flute in education is the fact that flute-

playing prevents the player from using words.* Our ancestors were therefore right in debarring the use of the flute to youths and freemen—although they had in earlier days encouraged it. This came about as follows: wealth gave them increased leisure and a higher appetite for general excellence, while their achievements both before and after the Persian wars elated their pride; they were anxious only to explore fresh fields and thus seized indiscriminately on every kind of study; so they introduced flute-playing into education. Even in Sparta the leader of a chorus is reported to have played the flute for his dancers personally; but at Athens flute-playing attained such vogue that most freemen joined in—witness the tablet erected in honour of Ecphantides* by Thrasippus, who had equipped a chorus of dancers. At a later date, when people were better able to judge what really conduced to excellence, and what had the opposite effect, a larger experience of flute-playing led to its final rejection. Many of the older instruments were also included in the rejection—the péctis, the barbitos, and similar instruments calculated merely to please the audience; and, along with them, heptagons, triagons, sambukai,* and all other instruments merely requiring manual dexterity. There is wisdom in the myth of the ancients about the flute. Athene, it tells us, invented the flute—and then threw it away. There is some point, too, in the rest of the story—that she threw it away in disgust at the ugly look of her face when she was playing upon it. But Athene is the goddess to whom we ascribe the gift of knowledge and skill in the arts; and it seems more likely that she threw it away because the study of flute-playing has nothing to do with the mind.

1341ᵇ8 Both in regard to the instruments used, and the degree of proficiency sought, we may accordingly reject any professional system of instruction. By that we mean any system intended to prepare pupils for competitions. On such a system the player, instead of treating music as a means to his own improvement, makes it serve the pleasure—and that a vulgar pleasure—of the audience to which he is playing. That is why we regard his performance as something improper in a freeman, and more suited to a hired labourer. The players themselves may also become vulgar in the process. The standard by which they fix their aim is a bad standard:* the commonness of the audience tends to debase the quality of the music; this affects not only the character of the artists, playing as they do with the audience in mind, but also their bodies because of the movements they make.

CHAPTER 7

In regard to the second question—what sort of melodies and rhythms should children learn to play?—there is this to be said. Melodies can be divided into (1) those which are expressive of character, (2) those which stimulate to action, and (3) those which produce inspiration. The benefits which may be derived from music can also be stated under three heads—(1) education, (2) release of emotion, and (3) cultivation of the mind, with which we may also link relaxation and recreation. The relation of the different sorts of melodies to the different benefits: the melodies suitable for producing the benefit of release of emotion. The adaptation of melodies to different sorts of audiences—the educated and the uneducated. The character of the different modes, especially the Dorian and Phrygian, and the different effects which they produce. The different ages of life best suited by different sorts of music.

1341ᵇ19 It remains to consider the different modes and rhythms; to determine whether they should all be used, or a distinction should be made among them; and to decide whether we should apply the same distinction, or a different one, to those who are practising music with a view to education.* Music is produced, as we may easily observe, by the two means of melody and rhythm; and we ought therefore to know what influence is exercised on education by each of these means, and whether we ought to prefer music with good melody to music in good rhythm. But we believe that there is a good deal of truth in the observations made on these matters by some of the musicians of our day, and also by some of those, on the philosophical side, who have experience of the general subject of musical education. We shall therefore refer anyone who desires a precise treatment of each subject to these authorities and confine ourselves here to sketching general outlines and laying down, much as a law does, the broad rules to be followed.

1341ᵇ32 We accept the classification of melodies, which is made by some of our philosophic thinkers, into those which are expressive of character, those which stimulate to action, and those which produce inspiration; and we note that these thinkers would also make the nature of the musical modes correlative to that of these classes, with each different mode corresponding to each different class of melody. On the other hand, we hold that music should not be pursued for the sake of any single benefit, but for several. It should be pursued for the sake of education and for the release of emotion [*katharsis*] (the sense of that term will be explained more clearly in our lectures on poetics, but may be left to speak for itself at the moment): a third is to live in a cultivated way, that is with a view to recreation and relaxation from strain.* It is clear that all the modes should be used, but not all in the same sort of way. When education is the object in view, the modes which ought to be used are those which express character best: when it is a question of listening to the performance of others, we may also admit the modes which stimulate people to action or provide them with inspiration. Any affection which strongly moves the souls of several people will move the souls of all, and will only differ from person to person with a difference of degree. Pity, fear, and inspiration are such affections. The feeling of being possessed by some sort of inspiration is one to which some people are particularly liable. These people, as we can observe for ourselves, are affected by religious melodies; and when they come under the influence of melodies which fill the soul with religious excitement they are calmed and restored as if they had undergone a medical treatment and purging.* The same sort of effect will also be produced on those who are specially subject to feelings of fear and pity, or to feelings of any kind; indeed it will also be produced on the rest of us, in proportion as each is liable to some degree of feeling; and the result will be that all alike will experience some sort of purging, and some release of emotion accompanied by pleasure. We may add that melodies designed to purge the emotions are likewise also a source of innocent delight to us all.

1342ᵃ16 We may go on to argue that these are the modes and melodies which competitors in musical contests ought to be required to use. But there are two different kinds of audiences. One is an audience composed of the free and educated; the other is the common audience composed of mechanics, hired labourers, and the like. There should therefore be contests and festivals to provide relaxation for this second kind of audience. Just as the souls of its members are distorted from their natural state, so there are musical modes which are correspondingly perverted, and melodies which are similarly strained and over-coloured. A man derives pleasure from what suits him best; and we must therefore permit musicians who are competing before this kind of audience to use the corresponding kind of music.

1342ᵃ28 For education, as we have already noted, the melodies and modes which ought to be used are those expressive of character. The Dorian, as we have already observed, is one of these modes; but we must also adopt any of the other modes which we find recommended by those who have been concerned in philosophical studies and musical education. 'Socrates', in the *Republic,* makes the error of selecting the Phrygian mode as the only one to be kept along with the Dorian; and his error is the more striking, as previously, in dealing with instruments, he rejected the use of the flute.* Actually the effect of the Phrygian as a mode corresponds to that of the flute as an instrument: the effect of both is religious excitement and general emotion. We can see from poetry that this is so. Dionysiac frenzy, and all such agitations of the mind, are expressed by the flute more than by any other instrument. Similarly, in the matter of modes, we find that melodies which are in the Phrygian mode are the vehicle suitable for such states of mind. For example the dithyramb* is generally agreed to be Phrygian in character. Many instances attesting to this are cited by experts in the art of music. The case of Philoxenus is one. He attempted, but failed, to compose a dithyramb, entitled 'The Mysians', in the Dorian mode; and he was driven by the very nature of this

theme to fall back on the Phrygian mode as the more appropriate. The Dorian mode is generally agreed to be the gravest
and the most expressive of a manly character. What is more,
it is our view that the mean, which lies midway between
extremes, is preferable and ought to be followed. The Dorian
mode stands to other modes in the position of the mean. It is
therefore Dorian melodies which suit the young best as a
means of education.

1342^b17 There are two kinds of aim—the possible, and the
proper; and every individual should concern himself particularly with what is possible and proper. This is determined for
him by his age. Those who have lost their vigour through age
find it difficult to sing in high-pitched modes; and nature
herself supplies the lower and softer modes for such people.
There is therefore justice in the censure which some musicians
pass upon 'Socrates' for rejecting the lower and softer modes
as instruments of education,* on the ground that they are
connected with drinking—an argument which is not founded
on the effect of drink (which is mainly one of inspiring a
frenzy of intoxication), but as lacking vigour. So, for the sake
of the years to come and the days of old age, the lower and
softer modes and melodies must also be used. We must also
include any mode which is proper to the age of youth by
virtue of combining the attraction of beauty with some instruc-
tive power. This is a combination which the Lydian mode
would seem particularly to present. There are thus three
standards to which education in music should conform—the
mean, the possible, and the proper.*

EXPLANATORY NOTES

BOOK I

CHAPTER 1

1252ª *every city (polis) is a species of association*: for an account of the Greek *polis* or city-state see Introduction, pp. xvii–xix 'Association' serves here and elsewhere as a translation of *koinōnia*. This term, which plays a key role in Aristotle's political vocabulary, means literally 'a sharing' and is often translated as 'partnership' or as 'community'. In defining the *polis* or city-state as *koinōnia* Aristotle implies that it is to be seen as a shared enterprise undertaken by the citizens.

all men do all their acts with a view to achieving something which is, in their view, a good: it is a standard doctrine with Aristotle that all our deliberate acts are directed to some good. See, for example, *NE* I. I, 1094ª1–2. It is of course possible to be mistaken in our conception of the good and thus to direct our acts to ends which are in fact bad.

It is a mistake to believe . . . a number of slaves: Aristotle may here be thinking of Plato, *Statesman* 258e–259d. The idea that these forms of rule differ in kind (and not just in the number of subjects) is the central theme of much of this Book and prepares the way for later discussions of different forms of constitution.

statesman: *politikos*, i.e. one who concerns himself with the public affairs of the city or *polis*.

this is a view which cannot be accepted as correct: the city or *polis*, as Aristotle sees it, is an association of free and equal citizens. So the *politikos* who handles its affairs is only the first among equals. In this he differs both from the monarch whose subjects are not his equals and from the master of a household who rules over slaves. See below, I. 7 and 12, III. 6.

a compound: *suntheton* (from the same root as our word 'synthesis') is a whole made up of parts, as opposed to a mere collection or heap. As applied to the city this is significant because it implies that the city has an identity of its own and is not simply a collection of individuals. As becomes clear in Book III it is the constitution which gives the city its unity and thus stands to the citizens in much the same relation as that in which the form of a house stands to the bricks of which the house is made. See *Metaphysics* VII. 15, 1041^{b}11–33.

CHAPTER 2

1252^a *if we begin at the beginning and consider things in the process of their growth*: in the previous chapter Aristotle proposed to study the city or *polis* analytically by examining its simplest elements. In this chapter he identifies the household as the simplest form of association and argues that out of it there naturally grows first the village and then the *polis*. It is not clear whether Aristotle sees this sequence as an historical process (i.e. whether he thinks that at one time people lived in isolated households, that they then coalesced into villages, and finally formed the *polis*). Some readers hold that this cannot be his view because his general position that life in the *polis* is natural to human beings implies that there must always have been at least a rudimentary form of *polis*. But the claim that life in the *polis* is natural does not imply that human beings must always live in a *polis*, only that they have a tendency to live in this way and can achieve a good life only if they do so. Some of the phrases in this chapter clearly imply that there have been times when people lived in scattered households without any form of political organization.

1252^b *the Delphic knife*: clearly a knife designed to serve a number of different purposes but which is not ideal for any of them. Nothing more appears to be known of it.

Among barbarians ... the female and the slave occupy the same position: Aristotle here assumes his own theory of natural slavery (see Ch. 6 below). Those who lack rational powers are naturally the slaves of those who possess them. The thought in the present passage seems to be that the barbarians are all natural slaves. Thus in their case there is no room for the distinction Aristotle has just made between the relationship of man and wife on the one hand and of master and slave on the other.

meet it is that barbarous peoples should be governed by the Greeks: Euripides, *Iphigeneia in Aulis* 1400. The speaker goes on to remark that barbarians are slaves by nature whereas Greeks are free, but Euripides himself clearly regarded such assumptions as highly questionable.

First house, and wife, and ox to draw the plough: *Works and Days* 405. Assuming that Aristotle read the same text as us, the quotation is not very appropriate since Hesiod makes it clear that the woman is not a wife but a slave who will drive the ox.

1252^b *Charondas . . . Epimenides*: Charondas was the semi-mythical lawgiver of Catana in Sicily. Epimenides was a legendary Cretan religious teacher and wonder-worker.

a colony from a family: the thought seems to be that just as a colony is an offshoot of the mother city so the household grows into the village by producing offshoots when children form households of their own.

Each of them ruleth | Over his children and wives: Odyssey IX. 114–15. The passage refers to the Cyclopes.

the final and perfect association: 'final' and 'perfect' translate a single word, *teleios*. Something is *teleios* if it is itself an end but is not sought for the sake of some further end (*NE* 1097^{a}28–34). So, as Aristotle sees it, other associations exist for the sake of the city, but the city does not exist for the sake of some further association.

the height of full self-sufficiency: this does not mean that the *polis* produces everything that it needs but rather that it has everything necessary for its well-being. Aristotle defines self-sufficiency (*autarkeia*) in *Nicomachean Ethics* I. 7 as 'that which by and of itself makes life desirable and lacking in nothing'. Barker adds 'this may be understood to mean the possession of such material resources and such moral incentives and impulses as make a full human development possible, without any dependence on external help, material or moral'.

while it comes into existence for the sake of mere life, it exists for the sake of a good life: this is one of Aristotle's most distinctive and important claims. While the idea that the city comes into being to provide the necessities of life is relatively uncontroversial, the idea that it has the higher moral aim of bringing about the good life, as Aristotle conceives it, is decidedly questionable.

every city exists by nature: on Aristotle's conception of nature see Introduction, pp. vii–xii. Aristotle's point here is that, although it is the need to secure the necessities of life that brings people together into cities, cities have the higher end of bringing about a good life. A city which fails to achieve this has missed its real goal.

1253^a *man is by nature a political animal (ho anthrōpos phusei politikon zōon)*: this famous phrase does not mean that man naturally engages in political activity, at least as we understand that term. The point appears to be that man's nature is such that only in a *polis* can he achieve fulfilment—his 'final complete and perfect condition'. Against this interpretation it might be argued that Aristotle uses the term 'political animal' to describe other creatures such as ants and bees, which cannot be understood literally as destined for life in the *polis*. Aristotle, in fact, seems to use the term 'political' in different though closely related senses. What makes ants and bees political seems to be the fact that they not only live together but work together for a common goal (see *Historia Animalium* 487^{b}33–488^{a}12). The same also goes for human beings, but they have in addition language and reason. This, as Aristotle makes clear in the lines that follow, means that they are political to a much higher degree, because they can form a common conception of what is good and just. Thus the defining feature of humanity is not so much its political character as its rationality.

Clanless and lawless and heartless is he: *Iliad* IX. 63.

the whole is necessarily prior to the part: the whole is prior to the part in the sense that the part presupposes it; the idea of the whole must be there before the part can be understood, and the whole itself must be there before the part can have or exercise a function (Barker).

a hand, when destroyed, will be no better than a stone 'hand': the point of this odd-sounding sentence seems to be that a hand, once it is disconnected from the body and is thus unable to fulfil its function, ceases to be a real hand.

We thus see that the city exists by nature and that it is prior to the individual: the *polis* is prior to the individual human being in the sense that the human being cannot fulfil his or her true function outside the *polis*. Aristotle can thus draw a parallel between the relation of the individual to the *polis* and that of the hand to the whole human being. But the parallel is misleading to the extent that even though a man without a *polis* may not be fully human, there is a real sense in which human beings can come into existence outside the *polis*. There is no sense in which a hand can come into being apart from the body.

the man who first constructed such an association: this implies that the *polis* is a product of human art. This is not necessarily inconsistent with the claim that the *polis* is natural. See Introduction, p. xi.

1253ᵃ *goodness*: *aretē*. This word is traditionally translated 'virtue' but lacks the exclusively moral overtones of the English word. In the text I have therefore retained Barker's practice of translating it as 'goodness', 'excellence', or 'merit'. The *aretē* of a thing is whatever makes it a good one of its kind. Thus the *aretē* of a knife is the quality that enables a knife to perform well its function of cutting. The *aretē* of man consists in those qualities of mind and character which enable him to live well. In the *Ethics* Aristotle distinguishes 'intellectual virtues' which include practical wisdom (*phronēsis*) and speculative wisdom (*sophia*) from moral virtues such as temperance and courage.

CHAPTER 3

1253ᵇ *the art of acquisition*: this is discussed in Chs. 8–11 below.

as we said in the beginning: Ch. 1, 1252ᵃ7–16.

the distinction of master and slave is due to law or convention; there is no natural difference between them: for the opposition between nature and convention see Introduction, p. viii. It is not known who the critics of slavery to whom Aristotle refers were.

CHAPTER 4

1253ᵇ *Instruments are partly inanimate and partly animate*: Aristotle here introduces his conception of the slave as a living tool or instrument. This highlights very precisely the nature of slavery as an institution which permits one human being to use another purely as a means to his or her own ends. Aristotle finds nothing abhorrent in the institution. Philosophers in the Kantian tradition might argue that slavery is wrong for the very reason that it treats some human beings as means or instruments rather than as ends in themselves.

Of their own motion they entered the conclave of Gods on Olympus: Homer, *Iliad* XVIII. 376.

1254ᵃ *The instruments of which we have just been speaking are instruments of production; but property is an instrument of action*: the distinction between 'production' (*poiēsis*) and 'action' (*praxis*) is based on the idea that 'production' aims at a result beyond the immediate doing, which remains when the doing is over, but 'action', such as the rendering of a service, is complete in itself, and aims at no result beyond the immediate doing. This distinction is explained in the *Nicomachean Ethics* VI. 4, 1140^a1–23; see also VI. 5, 1140^b6–7: 'production has an end other than itself: action cannot have, for good action is itself its own end.'

In this chapter Aristotle (presumably because he is considering the household) ignores the very large numbers of slaves who were employed in manufacturing, farming, and mining. He therefore classifies slaves as instruments of action like garments or beds. They enable us to live well but need not produce anything.

CHAPTER 5

1254^a *We have next to consider whether . . . all slavery is contrary to nature*: in Aristotle's view slavery is justified if and only if there are natural masters and natural slaves. In other words he has to show that there are some human beings who are naturally adapted to command and others who are naturally adapted to obey. In fact he spends most of the chapter arguing that the relationship between an element which naturally rules and one whose nature is to be ruled is to be found throughout nature. He does nothing to demonstrate that there are two different kinds of human being with natural aptitudes differing in this way.

Even with the assumption that there are natural slaves it would be open to Aristotle to criticize the practice of slavery by claiming that those currently held as slaves were not natural slaves. In practice he seems to assume that it is proper for Greeks to have slaves of barbarian origin. This assumption may be to some extent understandable. No doubt those who were born as slaves and non-Greeks who were captured as slaves very quickly acquired servile attitudes. One can see then why a Greek of Aristotle's period might assume that some men are naturally servile. But it is clear that some of Aristotle's contemporaries were more perceptive than he. As becomes apparent in the next chapter, there were those who questioned the legitimacy of slavery.

in a musical harmony: the thought is that in a musical scale there is a leading note which imposes a kind of order on the others.

we must fix our attention . . . on those which are in a natural condition: it is, of course, essential to Aristotle's teleological way of thinking that one discovers something's true nature only by considering how it behaves when it is in a good condition. One discovers the nature of a plant or animal, for example, by looking at a healthy rather than a diseased specimen. But the use of such teleological arguments in connection with slavery brings out their limitations. They can be applied only when we have some independent means of distinguishing the healthy from the unhealthy state. Thus the very cases which Aristotle might see as properly functioning 'healthy' examples of the master–slave relationship might seem to us like perversions of human nature.

1254ª *The soul rules the body . . . a statesman or a monarch*: by associating the rule of the master with the kind of rule which the soul exercises over the body Aristotle assumes, what he argues later in the chapter, that the role of the slave is to provide bodily labour under the master's direction. The slave thus stands to the master as the body does to the soul and the soul may be said to rule the body as a master. This ignores what Aristotle himself concedes, that the slave has a kind of reason—that which is necessary to understand and obey commands.

Some of Aristotle's phrases suggest that the rule of the master over the slave may be more like the rule of the reason over the appetites or emotions. In Aristotle's view the affective or emotional part of the soul is rational in the sense that it can understand and obey reason. But if Aristotle were to adopt this model he would, as the present passage makes clear, be assimilating the rule of a master over slaves to that of the statesman or monarch over free citizens. He would thus be undermining the basis of slavery.

Other animals do not apprehend reason: reading '*logou*', rather than '*logoi*'.

if there were men . . . all would agree that the others should be their slaves: again the strains of harnessing a teleological argument to the defence of slavery are very apparent. If nature had intended that there be masters and slaves, it would, no doubt, have ensured that their bodies differed in appropriate ways. The fact that this is not generally the case would suggest that the master–slave relationship is not natural in Aristotle's sense.

CHAPTER 6

1255ª *an 'indictment of illegality': graphē paranomon*: this was a procedure used in Athens for prosecuting those who introduced proposals contrary to established law. The position under consideration is that purely conventional slavery is just. Aristotle takes it for granted that this position cannot be sustained since brute force does not normally give one right of possession or the right to control others' actions.

the dispute between the two sides thus comes to turn exclusively on the point of justice: the argument of this paragraph is tortuous. Aristotle appears to be saying that both parties agree that those who are superior should rule. The defenders of conventional slavery argue that the victors in battle are superior and are therefore always entitled to rule over those they conquer. Their opponents argue that what counts is not superiority in power but superiority in virtue. Victors in battle need not be superior in virtue and are not therefore entitled to rule. The views thus overlap in that they agree on the right of the superior to rule but disagree about what kind of superiority is relevant.

goodwill: I read *eunoia* with the manuscripts and with Dreizehnter rather than Ross's emendation *anoia* (stupidity). Scholars have had great difficulty in making sense of this sentence on either reading. As the text stands it looks as though the reference to the view that victors are entitled to enslave the vanquished leads Aristotle to make a passing (and not altogether relevant) reference to the contrast between those who see justice as consisting in the rule of the stronger and those who see it as consisting in goodwill.

Theodectes: a tragic poet roughly contemporary with Aristotle.

1255^b *nature wishes but fails to achieve this result*: here, as in Ch. 5, 1254^{b}32, Aristotle is, in effect, obliged to admit that there is no real evidence for his claim that there are natural slaves, and attempts to redeem the situation by arguing that nature does not always achieve its goals. This would be justifiable only if he had some grounds, independent of observation, for supposing that nature really does aim at the goal in question. No doubt Aristotle's conviction that there are natural slaves owes a good deal to his own social prejudices. But he might argue that nature is hierarchically organized, that there is place in the hierarchy for the natural slave and that this place must therefore be filled.

CHAPTER 7

1255^b *it is not the case that all kinds of rule are, . . . identical*: see above, Ch. 1. Barker rightly comments: 'The theme running through the early chapters of the *Politics* (though it sometimes seems to be lost in the ramifications of the argument) is the theme of the peculiar character of the Greek *polis*, and therefore of the peculiar character of the political authority (an authority of freemen over freemen) which is exercised in the *polis*.'

1255^b *Slave may go before slave, and master may go before master*: a quotation from Philemon, a comic poet who was a younger contemporary of Aristotle.

CHAPTER 8

1256^a *the art of acquiring it*: Aristotle suggested in Ch. 3 that the art of acquisition (*chrēmatistikē*) is part of household management. It is not, therefore, surprising that after considering that part of the household which consists in the master–slave relationship he should turn to the art of acquisition. However, he treats this not only in connection with the household but also in connection with the *polis*. So Chs. 8–11 can be regarded as a treatise on domestic and political economy. Karl Marx found anticipations of his own ideas in these chapters and in that light they have been the subject of a good deal of discussion in recent times.

Barker and others have noted that Aristotle's use of the term *chrēmatistikē* (the art of acquisition) varies. (1) Sometimes it indicates the art of acquisition generally. It then covers all forms (sound and unsound) which the acquisition of property might take. (2) Sometimes it is used to indicate only those forms of acquisition which are perverted or unsound in the sense that they are directed merely to selfish monetary gain. (3) Sometimes, but more rarely, it is used to indicate only the sound or natural forms of acquisition which are necessary for the life of the household or state.

Some live by being freebooters: it is curious to find freebooting or piracy regarded as on the same footing with a pastoral or farming life and as a mode of acquisition dependent on the freebooter's own labour. But piracy was a tolerated pursuit in the eastern Mediterranean (on something like the same footing as trade) down to Aristotle's time and even later [Barker].

1256^b *Plants exist for the benefit of animals, and some animals exist for the benefit of others*: this is a rather free translation of the text as punctuated and emended by Dreizehnter. The text of the manuscripts could be rendered 'Plants exist for the sake of animals; other animals exist for the benefit of human beings.'

Solon: the Athenian statesman who effected sweeping political and economic reforms in the early sixth century BC. His poetry has survived only in fragments.

It is thus clear that there is a natural art of acquisition: the main thrust of the present chapter has been that there are forms of acquisition which are natural for man as for animals—they all need to acquire the means for living. This enables Aristotle in the following chapter to contrast these natural kinds of acquisition with kinds which he sees as unnatural.

CHAPTER 9

1256^b *a second form of the art of getting property . . . which it is just to call, 'the art of acquisition'*: Aristotle uses the word *chrēmatistikē* (the art of acquisition) in at least three different senses (see first note to 1256^a). In this chapter, which is of great importance for the understanding of his economic and social theory, he shifts without warning from one sense to another. His main point is to distinguish what he sees as the natural form of the art of acquisition, which consists in acquiring the means of living a good life and is thus an essential part of household management, from a perverted kind whose aim is simply to get as much money as possible. Aristotle disapproves strongly of this latter form of acquisition (i.e. the form which consists in making money for its own sake) and sees it as unnatural. The points he makes remain relevant and have been picked up by modern critics of the capitalist mode of production (notably Marx).

1257^a *All articles of property have two possible uses*: Aristotle is here making the important distinction between the use value and the exchange value of an article.

it was from exchange, as thus practised, that the art of acquisition developed: exchanging one useful thing for another is a natural mode of *chrēmatistikē* (acquisition) which is necessary for the well-being of the household. However, it has an inevitable tendency to develop into forms which Aristotle regards as unnatural. In the first stage people exchange goods for money which they then exchange for more goods. Aristotle does not seem to disapprove of this but it has a tendency to develop into a form of acquisition which is intended purely to make money—money is used to buy goods which are then used to make more money.

the use of a money currency was inevitably instituted: there is a parallel passage concerning the origin and nature of money in *Nicomachean Ethics* v. 5. That passage has been interpreted by some, including Barker, in such a way as to make Aristotle say that it is demand that gives articles their value. What he in fact says is that it is their use which determines their value. It is not clear by what mechanism Aristotle supposed that use value might be translated into monetary value.

1257^b *Midas*: according to the story, he prayed that everything he touched might turn to gold. When his prayer was granted he found that his food turned to gold before he could eat it and even his daughter became a golden statue.

The natural form of the art of acquisition ... is something different: the contrast here is between *chrématistiké* when it means the art of acquisition in its natural form, which is essential for the well-being of households, and *chrēmatistikē* as the art of acquisition in the unnatural sense, which is simply a matter of making money.

the wealth produced by this form of the art of acquisition is unlimited: there is no limit to the amount of money one can accumulate so money-making can go on indefinitely. On the other hand, Aristotle believes that there is a limit to the property a household needs in order for its members to live well. So *chrēmatistikē* in its natural form cannot continue indefinitely.

the end itself constitutes a limit: medicine may seek to produce as much health as possible but the means it uses are limited. For example, the doctor will not give a patient as much as possible of a drug but merely as much as is necessary to restore the patient to health.

The object of the ... quite different: the text of this passage is extremely murky. But the meaning is clear enough. Because there is a substantial overlap between the form of acquisition which is natural and proper and the money-making activities of which Aristotle disapproves, people tend to confuse the two. This leads them to assume that money-making is the only form the art of acquisition can take.

CHAPTER 10

1258^b *currency the son of currency*: the Greek word for 'interest', *tokos*, has the primary meaning of 'breed' or 'offspring'.

CHAPTER 11

1258^b *Lumbering and all mining*: it is not clear why mining, lumbering, and the like should be thought to hold this intermediate position. Perhaps Aristotle assumes that farming generally produces objects for immediate use while mining and the like produce things which will undergo exchange and manufacturing processes before they are of use.

1259ᵃ *Thales of Miletus*: he is said to have predicted an eclipse of the sun in 585 BC and is often regarded as the first of the Greek philosophers or even as the father of natural science. The Greeks also saw him as one of the seven sages (famed for their wisdom in practical matters). In this anecdote both ideas of Thales are neatly combined.

CHAPTER 12

1259ᵇ *like that of a monarch over subjects*: the comparison between the role of the father and that of the king is what one would expect given that Aristotle has already claimed that kingships in early societies were based on paternal authority. See Ch. 2 above, 1252ᵇ19-23. The comparison between the rule of the husband and that of the statesman may seem appropriate to us, if we bear in mind that the statesman is one who rules in a constitutional system over fellow citizens who are free and equal and with whom he alternates the roles of ruling and being ruled. (See above, Chs. 1 and 7.) But, although the wife would be a free citizen, Aristotle clearly does not envisage that she would be equal to her husband in the sense of having an equal say in the direction of the household or that she should alternate roles with her husband. In the *Nicomachean Ethics* (1160ᵇ33, 1161ᵃ23, 1162ᵃ16) Aristotle argues that the relationship between husband and wife is aristocratic because the partner with the highest virtue (the husband!) rules, though he believes that wives should have charge of their own proper sphere.

the saying of Amasis about his foot-pan: Herodotus (I. 172) tells how Amasis king of Egypt was despised because of his humble origins. He had a golden footbath (into which people had spat, urinated, and vomited) broken down and made into a statue of a god. When he saw his subjects venerating this statue with due reverence, he pointed out that his own position was much the same: even though he had once been an ordinary person he should now be revered as a king.

CHAPTER 13

1259ᵇ *such moral qualities*: for Aristotle's conception of goodness or virtue see seventh note to 1253ᵃ. Plato in the *Republic* lists four virtues or forms of goodness: temperance, fortitude, justice, and wisdom. Aristotle here omits any explicit reference to wisdom, presumably because the suggestion that a slave might have wisdom would seem absurd.

1259^b *since they are human beings, with a share in reason*: Aristotle comes close here to admitting the difficulties (some would say contradictions) in his theory of slavery. If slaves are human they must possess reason and be capable of exercising it, but slavery, in Aristotle's understanding, denies this.

1260^a *it is natural . . . for there to be both a ruling element and one that is ruled*: see above, Ch. 5.

master-craftsman: architektōn: one in overall charge of an undertaking who directs the work of his subordinates. In the *Nicomachean Ethics* (I. 1, 1094^a9–14) Aristotle cites strategy (the art of the general) as a master craft which has as one of its subordinate crafts that of horsemanship.

as Socrates held: in the *Meno* 72a–73c Plato makes Socrates insist that there must be a single virtue or goodness common to men, women, children, slaves, etc.

Gorgias: this, too, may be a reference to Plato's *Meno*, where the view that there are different virtues for different kinds of people is ascribed to the sophist Gorgias.

A modest silence is a woman's crown: Sophocles, *Ajax* 293.

1260^b *a limited servitude*: the point seems to be that the artisan who works for a wage is in a position like that of a slave but for only part of his time and for a limited purpose. 'Mechanical' is Barker's translation of *banausos*, a pejorative description of one who demeans himself by working for a wage.

only command should be employed: possibly a reference to Plato, *Laws* 777e, although it is not suggested there that slaves lack reason.

All these are questions which must be treated later in the discourses which deal with constitutions: this passage is puzzling. Naturally these questions, which are concerned with the household, would be treated in Book I, which is a book about the household. Not only so: but the beginning of Ch. 13 seems definitely to promise a treatment of the relations of husband and wife and of parent and child as an integral part of the Book. Why these relations should be postponed is not really clear. Meanwhile the village, which we should expect to be treated somewhere, after what has been said in Ch. 2, has disappeared from view. On the whole it would seem that this course on the household was left incomplete [Barker].

Let us first examine the theories of those who have expressed opinions about the best form of constitution: this passage makes a rather awkward transition from Book I to Book II. It may well be the work of an editor.

BOOK II

CHAPTER 1

1260^b *best for people able so far as possible to live as they would wish*: this sentence embodies a distinction which is of great importance for the understanding of the *Politics*. We may ask either (1) What is the form of constitution which would be best under ideal conditions and is therefore best absolutely, or (2) What is the form of constitution that is best under the conditions that actually prevail? Aristotle here suggests that his primary interest is in the first of these questions, i.e. that he wishes to investigate the form of constitution that would be best absolutely, but that, as a preliminary, he needs to discuss both existing constitutions which are widely admired and the ideal states proposed by his predecessors. His own ideal is described in Books VII and VIII so the present Book seems to lead directly to those. But Aristotle is at least as interested in his second question, What form of constitution would be best under the conditions actually prevailing? This is the main focus of interest in Books IV to VI. See especially IV. 11.

We must therefore consider . . . to have merit: Chs. 2–8 consider the ideal states proposed by earlier thinkers. Chs. 9–12 consider existing states which have the reputation for being well-governed.

It is necessary . . . others not: instead of proceeding directly to discuss the first ideal constitution, that of Plato's *Republic*, Aristotle turns to the question 'How much should the citizens hold in common?' It is important here to remember that the Greek word *koinōnia*, which is translated 'association' means literally 'a sharing' or 'holding in common'. So having defined the city as a political association (*koinōnia politikē*) in Book I, Ch. 1, Aristotle not surprisingly assumes that the citizens must share in something and sees the question 'How much should they hold in common?' as fundamental.

1261ᵃ *'Socrates'*: Aristotle regularly refers to 'Socrates' meaning thereby not the historical Socrates but the figure who appears in Plato's dialogues. I have marked this by using quotation marks (a device unknown to the Greeks).

We are thus faced by the question . . . the Republic: Aristotle's discussion of the *Republic* in this and the next four chapters has caused a good deal of puzzlement. By his account 'Socrates' in the *Republic* assumes that, in order to ensure that the state is a unity, citizens should share as much as possible and should therefore hold wives, children, and property in common. What the *Republic* in fact proposes is that the guardian class should be forbidden to have private property and that they should hold women and children in common. Very little is said about the class of farmers, artisans, and traders but, since the arrangements described for the guardians do not apply to them, most commentators assume that they will have property and families in the usual way. For this reason much of Aristotle's discussion seems to miss the point. On the other hand, it has been pointed out that certain passages in the *Republic* seem to imply that ideally all citizens should have women, children, and property in common. This is particularly so in the passage (*Republic* 462–6) which Aristotle seems chiefly to have in mind. 'Socrates' justifies this claim by arguing that all citizens should so far as possible share the same feelings. So what Aristotle does in Chs. 2–5 is not so much offer a systematic critique of Plato's ideal state but rather use passages in the *Republic* as a starting-point for the discussion of topics which interest him.

CHAPTER 2

1261ᵃ *The object . . . not established by the arguments which he uses*: Aristotle's first line of criticism attacks the assumption attributed to the Platonic Socrates that the city should be made as much of a unity as possible (see *Republic* 422d–423d; 462a–b). This is discussed in the present chapter.

Moreover, the end which he states as necessary for the city (polis) is impracticable: the second line of criticism—that the means 'Socrates' proposes would not achieve his goal—is discussed in Chs. 3–5.

it would be the destruction of the city: Aristotle is, of course, right to argue that the city cannot become a single individual, but since ancient times he has been attacked for confusing different senses of 'unity'. Those who have argued for the unity of the state do not mean that the state should be a single individual but that the individuals who compose it should be bound together by ties of friendship and goodwill. In fact Aristotle's main argument seems to be that one cannot simply assume that unity is the supreme good, especially if this is taken to imply that differences between individual citizens should be abolished. A city depends for its existence and well-being on differentiations of role among the citizens. Proposals for the common ownership of property, women, and children tend to abolish these differences and make everyone alike.

a city cannot be composed of those who are like one another: the argument of the next two paragraphs would constitute a sound criticism of anyone who argued that the citizens should be as alike as possible and should therefore occupy the same roles. But it has no obvious bearing on the ideal state of the *Republic*, which is based on the idea that there should be three classes of citizen each with a clearly defined role.

like the Arcadians: the meaning of this remark is very unclear. The Arcadians had formed a confederacy in the 360s BC. Aristotle's point may be that this confederacy is just an alliance made up of units which do not differ among themselves. It thus differs from a genuine *polis*.

in the Ethics: (*Nicomachean*) *Ethics*, V. 5.

They cannot all rule simultaneously: even in a community of free and equal citizens, there must be a differentiation of roles. So, if no one permanently occupies the role of ruler or subject, citizens must occupy these roles in turns. The idea that a free citizen should 'rule and be ruled' by turns plays a key role in Aristotle's own political theory. See especially III. 4.

1261b *the lesser degree of unity is more desirable than the greater*: again Aristotle's argument may seem to rest on a wilful misunderstanding of those who argue for the unity of the state. Whatever they mean by 'unity' they clearly do not mean that the city should be unified in any sense which would prevent it from being self-sufficient. But Aristotle could again argue that in a city in which everything was common there could be no differen-

tiation of roles and hence there would be no way of carrying out
the myriad functions that are essential for a self-sufficient
community.

CHAPTER 3

1261^b *in the view of 'Socrates'*: *Republic* 462c. 'Socrates' argues that
if all citizens use 'mine' and 'not mine' of the same things, they
will share feelings in the same way that the body as a whole feels
pain when one part of it is injured.

The word 'all' has a double sense: Aristotle is pointing to what
modern logicians call a scope ambiguity. 'All the directors wore
a suit', could mean either that there was a single suit worn by all
the directors, or that each of the directors had a suit of his own.
Similarly 'All the citizens have a son' could mean that there is
one son common to all or that they each have a son of their
own.

they will do so collectively, and not individually: 'mine' has an
individual sense when saying that something is mine implies that
it does not belong to anyone else. It has a collective sense when
what is mine also belongs to others (as, for example, when a
schoolchild says 'my teacher').

'All' and 'both' . . . produce captious arguments: 'both' may
mean 'both together' or 'each separately'; the property of being
even may apply to two numbers (say 3 and 5) when taken together (as making 8) even though each considered in itself is odd.

1262^a *It is better to be someone's own cousin than to be his son after
this fashion*: if the fact that a thousand people all called the same
individual 'my son' meant that they had the same feelings
towards him which someone who says 'my son' now has, then
that might be a good thing. But, Aristotle claims, they would be
using the words in a different sense and would not have the
same feelings.

*some of the citizens might guess who are their brothers, or children,
or fathers, or mothers*: under the system proposed in the *Republic*
the rulers would arrange temporary matings or 'marriages' between male and female members of the guardian class. The
offspring of these unions would be taken from their mothers and
brought up in state nurseries, so that neither parents nor children
could have any knowledge of their biological relationship. Instead the younger guardians would look on all the older members
of the class as their parents and the latter would, correspond-

ingly, look on the younger members as their children. See *Republic* 457c–461e.

Just Return: the mare was called by this name because it produced offspring exactly like their fathers. There may be a play here on the word *tokos* which means both 'offspring' and 'interest [on a loan]'.

CHAPTER 4

1262ᵃ *breaches of natural piety*: Aristotle's objection here takes for granted the contemporary Greek assumption that there is something especially horrendous about assaulting or killing one's parents, even when this is done in ignorance. (Compare the Oedipus legend.) Plato could deny that these biological relationships are of such importance, but in any case his provision that younger guardians should look on older ones as their parents is designed to prevent precisely the kind of occurrence Aristotle fears. See *Republic* 464e–465a.

It is also surprising . . . carnal intercourse: in the *Republic* 403a–b 'Socrates' forbids homosexual intercourse but permits other forms of homosexual love-making. If children and parents did not know one another this would make it possible for there to be homosexual relations between close biological relatives. Aristotle again assumes without argument that there would be something especially wrong about this.

1262ᵇ *The spirit of friendship*: Aristotle shares with Plato the belief that *philia* (friendship or mutual affection) holds the city together. Aristotle argues, against Plato, that community of wives and children will make people less friendly to one another. It would be appropriate therefore only in a population which is to be kept in subjection.

the discourses on love: those in Plato's *Symposium*. The reference is to 191a, and 192d–e.

transferred to the guardian class: the ideal state of the *Republic* has three classes: the guardians or rulers, the auxiliaries or soldiers, and the class of farmers, artisans, and traders. 'Socrates' considers it vital that only those with the appropriate aptitudes should be included in each class. In general, children will resemble their parents but this will not always be the case, so there will have to be arrangements for transferring children from one class to another. Aristotle is right to suggest that if an attempt was made to establish a state along the lines of that described in the *Republic* the arrangements for making such transfers would cause special problems. Indeed some modern critics have seen these as evidence that Plato could not have intended the *Republic*'s ideal state as a practical proposal.

CHAPTER 5

1262^b *The next subject for consideration is property*: this chapter is primarily a discussion of whether property (particularly land) should be held in common. Again it is only loosely connected with Plato's *Republic*. Indeed the first part (down to 1263^{b}9) has no real relevance to that dialogue; it is a discussion of different schemes of landholding, none of which corresponds exactly to anything suggested in the *Republic*. Even those sections which are ostensibly concerned with the *Republic* have been thought by most commentators to involve serious misunderstandings of its proposals. Nevertheless, some of Aristotle's arguments have been much admired by defenders of private property, who see this chapter as a classic statement of their case.

1263^a *Should use and ownership both be common?*: Aristotle distinguishes three possible ways of organizing the ownership of agricultural land and the use of its produce:

(1) land may be held separately but the use of its produce may be common;

(2) the ownership and cultivation of land may be common but the produce may be distributed for separate use;

(3) both ownership of land and the use of its produce may be common.

It is notable that Aristotle does not mention the possibility (4) that both ownership of land and the use of its produce should be private. Perhaps he simply takes this for granted since it is, of course, the system generally prevailing.

None of these systems corresponds to that proposed in the *Republic*, where it seems that land would be owned and worked by the farmers, who would contribute a portion of the produce for the upkeep of the guardians.

We might expect Aristotle to use this classification as a programme for the discussion which follows, but he does not do so. He first discusses possibility (3) that ownership of land and the use of its produce should be common (1263^{a}8–21). He then argues for his own favoured solution (which in some ways resembles possibility (1)), that land should be held privately, but that citizens should be encouraged by education to make its produce generally available (1263^{b}21–9). He then returns to a rather haphazard discussion of the *Republic* (1263^{b}29–1264^{b}25).

Friends' goods are goods in common: this phrase, possibly of Pythagorean origin, is used by Plato to support the abolition of private property for the guardian class (*Republic* 424a). Aristotle uses it in a different sense: to argue that there should be private property but that we should make the use of it available to others.

1263^b *loving oneself in excess*: Plato makes the same point in the *Laws* 731d–e. See also Aristotle's discussion of self-love in *Nicomachean Ethics* IX. 8.

temperance in the matter of sexual relations: this point seems out of place in a discussion of the ownership of property and has little obvious reference to the *Republic*, which certainly does not advocate unlimited licence in these matters. It looks very much as though Aristotle is thinking of wives as their husbands' property.

generosity in the use of property: eleutheriotēs (generosity or liberality) is discussed in *NE* IV. 1 and *EE* III. 4. It is the mean between prodigality and meanness. Valuing generosity implies both that relations between individual citizens are important and that citizens must have some scope for independent action, though it has been questioned whether it requires private property. See Irwin, 'Aristotle's Defense of Private Property'.

are denounced as due to the absence of a system of common property: *Republic* 425c–d, 464c–d.

those who are at variance . . . those who own their property privately: although those who have property in common are more prone to quarrel than are those who own private property, we do not hear much about the quarrels of the former because, as things are at present, there are comparatively few of them.

his incorrect premiss: apparently this refers to the assumption that the unity of the city should be the goal of legislation. See above, Ch. 2.

should none the less think . . . legislation: here again Aristotle may seem unfair to Plato, who would certainly agree that all the educational forces of the state should be geared towards creating a sense of unity. The difference between the two authors is that, while Aristotle believes that education can achieve all the unity that is desirable, Plato in the *Republic* advocates in addition that the guardian class should be without private property and should have women and children in common.

1264ᵃ *Almost everything has been discovered already*: the argument here is unimpressive. Not only does it rule out all real innovation but it is also irrelevant to the matter in hand. It could well be argued that all the elements of Plato's proposals have already existed in some form.

the only peculiar feature of the legislation: again the argument seems unfair to Plato. The originality of the *Republics'* system lies not in the proposal that there should be three classes but in the way in which those classes are distinguished and the roles that are assigned to them. The Spartan system is, in fact, substantially different from that proposed in the *Republic*. The Spartan citizens owned land but used serfs to cultivate it. In the ideal state of the *Republic* the farmers would both own and cultivate the land while the guardians, who rule the state, would own nothing.

their position is left undefined: most interpreters of the *Republic* believe that the farmer/artisan class is intended to have property and a normal family life. If this is right then Aristotle's queries about the way of life of the farmers are misplaced. But, in Aristotle's defence, it could be argued that Plato says very little about this class and does not make it unambiguously clear quite how they are to live.

the character of their association: here, as elsewhere 'association' serves as a translation of *koinōnia*, which means literally 'a sharing' or 'holding in common'. So Aristotle's point is that, on the interpretation he is considering, Plato has not pointed to any sense in which the farmers do share in something that is common. Aristotle indicates some real difficulties in the *Republic*'s ideal state (assuming that it is intended as a practical possibility). It may be significant that 'Socrates' sometimes uses language which, taken literally, would imply that the unity of the state requires the abolition of the family and of private property for all citizens, not just for the guardians.

they will not need a number of regulations: at *Republic* 425c 'Socrates' says that, because of its educational system, his ideal state will have no need for petty regulations. But, as Aristotle rightly points out, the education described in *Republic*, books II and III is for those intended to be guardians. He says nothing about the education of the remaining citizens.

helots, penestae: the names given to serf peoples in Sparta and Thessaly respectively.

1264^b *Animals do not have households to manage*: this is the closest Aristotle comes to considering the *Republic*'s proposal that women should be rulers and receive the same training as men. He simply takes for granted what Plato means to deny, that there must be households and that the domestic duties must be carried out by women. The 'analogy from the animal world' is a reference to *Republic* 451d. There 'Socrates' points out that female dogs are expected to carry out the same tasks (guarding or hunting) as males, and argues that there should therefore be female guardians who carry out the same tasks as their male colleagues.

The 'divine gold': a reference to the 'Myth of the Metals'; see *Republic* 414b–415c.

he deprives his guardians even of happiness: at *Republic* 419a Glaucon is made to object that 'Socrates', by depriving his guardians of all the pleasures most other rulers enjoy, has not made them particularly happy. 'Socrates' replies that it is his aim not to make one class happy but to make the whole city happy. Aristotle, like many other readers, takes this to mean that the happiness of the city is something over and above the happiness of the individual citizens. Others have rejected this interpretation. They take 'Socrates' to mean that he is not concerned with making one class happy to the exclusion of others. On this view the happiness of the city is identified with the happiness of all the citizens (as opposed to a section of them).

CHAPTER 6

1264^b *the Laws*: Aristotle's comments on Plato's *Laws* are, if anything, even more puzzling than those on the *Republic*. Commentators have complained (1) that his remarks are often inaccurate; (2) that he makes no attempt to understand the underlying principles on which Plato is working; and (3) that he criticizes some of Plato's proposals, even though he elsewhere in the *Politics* makes very similar proposals of his own. Some (but not all) of the charges of inaccuracy have been rebutted by Morrow. As with his treatment of the *Republic*, Aristotle concentrates on certain sections of the text and makes little attempt to set them in context. His main concern is to point to what he sees as faults in Plato's treatment rather than to engage in constructive discussion.

1265^a *He says little about the constitution*: this claim is surprising, given the very lengthy description of the city proposed in the *Laws*. Aristotle may here take 'the constitution' in the narrow sense in which it refers only to the organization of offices, rather than in the wider sense in which it refers to the whole way of life of the city, but, even so, his comment seems unfair. The various offices and their modes of election are described in considerable detail.

he gradually brings the form he proposes round again to the other type: this, too, is surprising. While the underlying premisses of the *Laws* may be similar to those of the *Republic*, the political arrangements described in the two dialogues seem very different. Possibly Aristotle's point is that the city of the *Laws* is not significantly more practical than that of the *Republic*.

common meals for women and the number of citizens who bear arms: by implication, at least, the *Republic* suggests that women guardians should join in common meals with the men. Aristotle's point may be that the *Laws* (780d–781d) makes explicit reference to separate common meals for women. *Republic* 423a suggests that the ideal state may have as few as 1,000 soldiers. *Laws* 737e suggests that the state should have 5,040 families.

All the Socratic dialogues are original: this is a surprising remark since Socrates (who is the chief speaker in most of Plato's dialogues) does not appear in the *Laws*. Some scholars have seen this as evidence that Aristotle was using a different version of the *Laws* from the one we have, or else that he had not used much care in reading it.

the territory of the city, and the inhabitants of that territory: Aristotle appears to have in mind the opening pages of *Laws* book IV which raise questions about the territory of the new city (704a ff.) and about its population (707e ff.). The general policy in the *Laws* is to avoid contacts so far as possible with foreigners in order to minimize their corrupting influence. But there is a brief reference to the need for defence against neighbouring peoples (737d).

this way of life: i.e. a life which involves contact with others (what Aristotle has just called 'a political life').

sufficient for a life of temperance and generosity: Plato suggests that the citizens should have enough for a life of temperance and no more (737c–d). As in 1263^{b}11, Aristotle's insistence on the importance of generosity implies a conception of human good which values personal relations and independent activity.

It is strange ... the number of citizens: Aristotle is right that a system in which there is a fixed number of lots cannot guarantee that there will be a lot for each citizen unless the population is controlled. He makes a similar criticism of the proposals of Phaleas (Ch. 7 below). But in the *Laws* 740b–741a Plato suggests a number of measures to deal with this problem.

1265^b *We must leave to a later occasion*: presumably a reference to Aristotle's account of his own best state in the last two books of the *Politics*. Most of the topics mentioned in the chapter are discussed somewhere in Book VII.

like that of warp and woof: *Laws* 734e–735a. This simile implies that there should be a sharp distinction between rulers and ruled but this is not the picture one gets from the rest of the *Laws*.

he allows someone's whole property to be increased fivefold: in the *Laws* (744d–745a) it is proposed that citizens should not be allowed to increase their holdings in land but may hold other property up to four times the value of their lot (making a total estate five times the value of the lot). Plato clearly intends this as a concession to practical demands. The ideal would be a situation in which all citizens were equally wealthy.

He assigns two quite separate plots of land: *Laws* 745c. Aristotle's criticism of the *Laws* on this point is strange since he himself makes a similar proposal. See below, VII. 10, 1330^{a}14–25.

The whole system ... 'constitutional government' (or polity): the Greek word *politeia* which generally means 'constitution', is also used by Aristotle to refer specifically to the moderate form of constitution in which political participation is restricted to those who can afford the arms of a hoplite soldier. In this sense it is often anglicized as 'polity'. Aristotle generally looks on such a constitution with favour. See below, III. 7; IV. 8–9.

of a more aristocratic character: for Aristotle's conception of aristocracy, as government by those citizens who are outstanding for their 'virtue' see below, III. 7; IV. 7. Plato might well reply to this criticism by arguing that in the *Laws* he seeks to ensure that all citizens are virtuous, as Aristotle himself does in his own ideal state.

1266^a *But in the Laws ... the worst of all constitutions*: Aristotle sees tyranny and extreme democracy as deviant constitutions. See below, III. 7. But he is, in any case, unfair to Plato, who argues that the constitution should be a mixture of monarchy (not tyranny) and moderate democracy. See *Laws* 701e, 756e.

1266ª *It is a further objection . . . with a particular inclination towards oligarchy*: Aristotle is right that no one in the constitution of the *Laws* would wield monarchical power. In suggesting that the constitution should combine democracy and monarchy Plato must mean that it should combine liberty with respect for authority. Aristotle himself advocates a constitution which mixes oligarchy and democracy as the best practical possibility. See below, IV. 7–9, 12–13.

the method proposed for appointing officials: the procedures for appointing officials in the *Laws* are very complex and differ for different offices. See especially *Laws* 751a–769e. These procedures, like those for the election of the council, 756b–c, are certainly oligarchical in the sense that they make use of elections, which Aristotle sees as an oligarchical feature. They also make use of the four property classes into which the citizens are divided. But it is not clear that they would give a great preponderance to the wealthier citizens.

CHAPTER 7

1266ª *Phaleas of Chalcedon*: nothing is known about Phaleas apart from the very little that can be gleaned from this chapter. Aristotle is primarily concerned to argue against the idea that property should be equalized. His position is very similar to that taken against the *Republic* in Ch. 5. It is not inequality of property that causes crime but vice. The remedy is thus education rather than a change in property arrangements.

1266ᵇ *Solon's legislation*: Solon was the Athenian statesman and poet who introduced major constitutional and economic reforms around 594 BC. One important element in these was to remove the accumulated burden of debt which had forced many citizens into extreme poverty and debt bondage. See below, II. 12.

the distribution of office is equal: for the importance of different conceptions of equality and their role in causing revolutions see III. 9 and 12; V. 1.

1267ª *Office . . . man: Iliad* IX. 319.

Eubulus: a banker who around 359 BC had become tyrant of the cities of Atarneus and Assos in Asia Minor. Aristotle would of course have been familiar with the history of these cities, since he had himself stayed in them.

1267^b *at first two obols were a sufficient allowance*: the reference is to the practice, scorned by those opposed to democracy, of paying poor Athenian citizens two obols to enable them to attend the theatre.

on the lines ... at Athens: nothing else is known about the schemes mentioned here.

CHAPTER 8

1267^a *Hippodamus*: he is known to have acted as town-planner for the Panhellenic colony of Thurii, in southern Italy, which was founded in 443 BC. We know nothing more than can be gathered from this chapter about his activities in planning the Piraeus (the seaport of Athens) and as a political theorist.

there are only three classes of laws: if Hippodamus really did think there were only these three classes of law he obviously had very limited understanding of the role of law. One suspects that Aristotle has taken out of context a remark which was intended to apply only to disputes between private individuals.

1268^b *the jurymen shall not communicate*: Aristotle's criticisms are based on the assumption that there would be large popular juries in which the members voted without consulting their colleagues. Given the voting arrangements which Hippodamus proposed (see above, 1268^a1–5), this is probably correct.

a plain verdict ... never compels a juryman to violate his oath: one suspects that Aristotle is being pedantic here. If the jurors swore to give a just decision, a requirement that they give an absolute verdict for one party or the other might well mean that they could not, strictly speaking, live up to their oath.

1269^a *actions are concerned with particulars*: the idea that actions are always concerned with particulars plays an important part in Aristotle's ethical theory. (See *Nicomachean Ethics* 1103^b26–1104^a10; 1110^b6–7; 1142^a24–30; 1147^a3.) This is the main reason why he believes that virtuous behaviour requires the judgement of the man of practical wisdom. Circumstances vary so much that one cannot decide what is right in a particular case simply by applying general rules. This would seem to imply not that laws should be easily changed but that courts should be allowed discretion in applying them. See III. 15–16.

CHAPTER 9

1269ª *When we consider . . . any other city*: having discussed forms of constitution proposed by earlier theorists, Aristotle now turns to consider constitutions actually in force in cities considered to be well governed. As he made clear in Ch. 1, his main aim is to show that there are defects in these constitutions and thereby to show that it makes sense for him to propose a new ideal state. Not surprisingly therefore, the chapters which follow catalogue the defects of these states and say little about their merits.

The Spartan constitution and way of life was much admired. Among the reasons for this admiration were (*a*) the thought that what we would call Sparta's social institutions had produced a state of great stability with a military strength far beyond what would be expected for its size, and (*b*) that what we could call its political institutions were based on a mixture of different elements which acted as a check on one another. This was also thought to have contributed to Sparta's strength and stability. As will become evident from this chapter, major elements in the Spartan constitution included:

(*a*) two hereditary kings, chosen from different families;
(*b*) a body of 'ephors' or overseers—officials with considerable power elected for one year;
(*c*) the 'gerousia', an elected council of elders;
(*d*) a citizen assembly.

the second is . . . their constitutions as established: see IV. 1, 1288ᵇ21 ff.

by what mode of organization this leisure is to be secured: Aristotle here broaches a matter which is for him a major problem. The aim of the state is the good life. This requires leisure (see VII. 15 and VIII. 3). If the citizens themselves are to have this leisure they cannot be occupied with agricultural work, manufacturing, or trade (1329ª17, ᵇ36 ff.). They must therefore rely on others to perform these tasks. But the problem how the citizens are to relate to these others is almost insoluble.

1269ᵇ *the Theban invasion*: the Thebans, under Epaminondas, invaded Sparta in 369 BC.

1270ª *Lycurgus*: the supposed founder of the Spartan constitution. It is not clear whether he was a historical personage or merely a mythical figure.

unable to withstand a single blow: Sparta was decisively defeated by the Thebans in 371 BC.

1270ᵇ *the affair at Andros*: it is not certain which event this refers to. Newman suggested an incident in 333. If that is right it would show that this part of the *Politics* was written (or at least revised) at a fairly late stage in Aristotle's career.

If the constitution ... its arrangements: for the idea that a constitution can survive only if there is general consent see IV. 12, 1296ᵇ16, with note.

far too childish: we have no direct information about how the ephors were elected but Plato (*Laws* 692a) describes the power of the ephors as not far removed from a lottery.

1271ª *a childish method of selection*: Plutarch (*Lycurgus* 26) reports that members of the council of elders were elected by acclamation, a process which could be easily manipulated by families with the wealth to marshal a large and noisy claque.

1271ᵇ *Plato in his Laws*: see especially 625c ff.

they are wrong in supposing that these 'goods' are greater than goodness of character: i.e. they see goodness of character as a means rather than as an end. This point is expanded at VII. 14, 1333ᵇ5–25.

CHAPTER 10

1271ᵇ *The Cretan constitution*: this was not the constitution of one particular city. A number of different cities in Crete shared very similar institutions. The Greeks from a very early time recognized that there were close connections between Sparta and Crete. Not only were there marked similarities between their institutions but they also spoke the same Dorian dialect. In both the *Republic* and the *Laws* Plato treats the Cretan and Spartan institutions as though they were essentially similar.

Tradition records: the explanation offered here of the similarity between the Cretan and Spartan constitutions seems to be that the Spartans sent a colony to Crete which adopted the practices of the original inhabitants of the island. Lycurgus visited this colony and took back to Sparta their constitutional ideas. This is unlikely to be a historically accurate account of what happened, though it embodies an element agreed by virtually all the ancient authorities—that the Cretan institutions were more primitive than those of Sparta.

1271b *Minos*: the legendary ruler of an empire centred in Crete. He was also famed as a lawgiver. According to one story he received his laws from Zeus, whom he visited every nine years in a cave on Mount Ida. Plato's *Laws* purports to describe the conversation of a Cretan, a Spartan, and an Athenian as they walk to this cave.

The island seems to be naturally designed: this paragraph is obviously irrelevant to the main theme and could be some kind of interpolation. It uses the geographical situation of Crete to explain how it could have become the centre of an empire. The legend of this empire may represent a folk memory of the pre-Greek culture which we now call the Minoan civilization.

1272a *This makes it possible for all ... to be fed at the public cost*: Aristotle himself proposes that common meals should be supported by the produce of public land (VII. 10, 1330a9–14). It is not clear how the Cretan system could be said to provide food for the whole citizen body, including women and children, unless the adult males who attended the common meals were issued with supplies for the rest of their families.

left for a later occasion: Aristotle does not himself discuss this issue in any surviving work.

1272b *government by clique*: a rather inadequate translation of the Greek *dunasteia*. Although this is the source of the English word 'dynasty', it refers to something rather different—a situation in which a group of individuals (or more likely a group of families) exercise power outside the law. It is, in other words, a kind of collective dictatorship.

laws for the expulsion of aliens: the Spartans, in particular, made a practice of periodically expelling aliens.

it is only lately that foreign forces have penetrated into the island: Aristotle implies that Crete has recently suffered a foreign invasion. There are known to have been incursions into Crete in 346 and 333.

CHAPTER 11

1272b *Carthage*: whereas one would expect Aristotle to discuss constitutions like those of Crete and Sparta which were widely admired in the Greek world, it is remarkable that he also chooses that of Carthage, which was not a Greek state. Aristotle's description of the state is rather vague and we do not have much in the way of other sources against which to check it. He, or rather his source, is clearly translating Carthaginian terms into Greek—a process which may well have led to distortion.

1273ᵃ *Most of the features which may be criticized as deviations*: Aristotle here uses analytical methods which become more prominent in Book III. In effect he compares the Carthaginian system with the moderate constitution he calls 'polity' or 'constitutional government'. He sees it as deviating in some respects towards democracy and in others towards oligarchy.

1273ᵇ *as we have already argued*: the reference is not clear. Aristotle may have in mind references to the division of labour in Ch. 2 of the present book.

CHAPTER 12

1273ᵇ *Some of those who have put forward a view about constitutional matters*: this is a strange chapter which does not fit readily into the programme of Book II. Officially it is concerned to discuss the work of practising politicians who have drawn up legislative codes. The discussion of Solon's work may have some value but the chapter then degenerates to become a catalogue of legislators. Some of these are not known from any other source.

Lycurgus and Solon: see first notes to 1270ᵃ and to 1266ᵇ. Solon's constitution was much admired, particularly by those Athenians who opposed later more democratic developments. The analysis of his constitution as containing democratic, aristocratic, and oligarchic elements is forced. Membership of the Council of the Areopagus was for life and was restricted to those who had held the office of *archōn*, which was itself restricted to members of the higher property classes. So the general effect was to concentrate power in the hands of members of a relatively small number of wealthy families.

1274ᵃ *until the constitution reached its present form*: Aristotle here omits any mention of Cleisthenes, who is normally credited with the introduction of the democratic constitution about 508 BC. Ephialtes and Pericles were responsible for restricting the powers of the Areopagus in 461. Thereafter it simply functioned as a court trying a limited range of cases (notably homicides).

1252^b *He arranged . . . for any office*: the Pentakosiomedimnoi were the wealthiest class with an income over 500 measures of corn; the Hippeis had an income of between 300 and 500 measures; the Zeugitai between 200 and 300, and the Thetes less than 200.

Other legislators: very little is known about most of those mentioned in this and the following paragraph. Zaleucus appears to have been active around 664 BC; Charondas was roughly a century later. Thales of Crete (also known as Thaletas) was active in the mid-seventh century BC. He is not to be confused with the philosopher Thales of Miletus. Nothing is known of Philolaus, but his friend Diocles' Olympic victory can be dated to 728 BC. For Phaleas see above, Ch. 7. Draco codified the laws of Athens in 622–621 BC. His laws were noted for their severity; hence the modern use of 'Draconian'. Pittacus was elected ruler of Mytilene 590/89 BC. He was regarded as one of the seven sages of Greece.

1274^b *Plato's legislation*: this passage, which makes no distinction between the *Republic* and the *Laws*, is particularly inadequate and out of place, especially when Plato's proposals have been discussed at length in Chs. 1–6. For the drinking-parties see the early books of the *Laws*, especially 631e–641d, 645d–650b, 661a–674c. There it is argued at considerable length that properly organized drinking-parties can have a valuable educational effect. For ambidexterity see *Laws* 794d–795d, where it is argued that children should be taught to use both hands so far as possible.

BOOK III
CHAPTER 1

1274^b *we may begin by asking, 'What is the city?'*: Book III is primarily a treatise on constitutions but Aristotle begins by arguing that any discussion of the constitution presupposes some conception of what the *polis* is and that in turn requires an account of the citizen. So the focus of the first five chapters of this book is on citizenship.

It was not the city but the oligarchy or the tyrant: we might make a similar point by saying 'it is not the country that did this but the government'. As becomes clear in Ch. 3, this sort of expression implies that the city is to be identified with its population and/or territory, whereas one might want to argue that the identity of a city (or a modern state) consists not in these alone but in the population and territory with a certain form of political organization, i.e. that the constitution is part of the city's identity.

A city belongs to the order of 'compounds': for Aristotle's notion of a compound see I. 2, 1252ª18 note. There Aristotle analyses the *polis* into simpler forms of association, the family and the village. Now he regards the citizen as the simplest element. While there is no contradiction here, the difference of approach is significant: Aristotle's discussion of the constitution pays no attention to the role which simpler forms of association may play in the state.

we must inquire first about the citizen: one might suppose that one could not know what a citizen is unless one already has some account of the constitution of which he is a member. Aristotle's approach implies that citizenship comes first. The *polis* exists for the sake of the good life. The good life consists in rational activity. This requires participation in decision-making, i.e. active citizenship. So the *polis* exists for citizenship.

1275ª *who should properly be called a citizen and what a citizen really is*: Robinson, in his note on this passage criticizes Aristotle for failing to distinguish the questions 'What are the rights and duties of a citizen?' and 'To whom should they belong?' This is probably unfair to Aristotle. In the present chapter he makes it clear that the citizen is to be defined by reference to the functions he performs. In the next chapter he discusses the criteria (chiefly criteria of birth) which are used in deciding whether any particular individual should be permitted to exercise these functions.

citizens are those who share in the holding of office as so defined: again Aristotle has an important point. We think only of those who exercise special responsibilities as holding office. But in a genuinely participatory constitution all citizens exercise responsibilities and there is no fundamental difference between the office-holders and the rest. It may be noted that Aristotle here ignores women, who in Greece were citizens but had no participation in politics. He takes it for granted that slaves and resident aliens will lack these privileges. This is particularly striking because Aristotle himself spent most of his life as a resident alien in Athens and elsewhere.

We must also notice ... and so on down the series: for the doctrine that things which form an ordered series have nothing (or practically nothing) in common see *Metaphysics* 999ª6–10,

De Anima 414^{b}20–32. Here its function is simply to lay the ground for the idea expounded in the next few sentences that what constitutes a citizen may vary with different kinds of constitution. These may be ranked so that citizens in a democracy are citizens in a full sense while those living under (e.g.) a tyranny are citizens only in a secondary sense.

1275^b *a self-sufficient existence*: see ninth note to 1252^b.

CHAPTER 2

1275^b *by the craftsmen who are Larissaean-makers*: there is an untranslatable pun here on the word *dēmiourgos*, which is derived from two roots meaning 'people' and 'work' and which presumably had the original meaning 'one who works on behalf of the people'. It standardly means a craftsman but in some states was also the title of an important public office. Gorgias is treating it as though it meant 'people-maker'. It appears, too, that 'a Larissaean' could refer to a type of pot as well as to a citizen of Larissa.

Cleisthenes: statesman who reformed the Athenian constitution after the expulsion, in 510 BC, of the tyrants. He is, with some reason, looked on as the founder of democracy.

The question raised . . . is not 'Who is actually a citizen?' but, 'Are they rightly or wrongly such?': here Aristotle, in effect, distinguishes between the questions 'What functions does the citizen perform?' and 'What are the criteria which decide whether an individual ought to be allowed to fulfil those functions?' Since someone can fulfil the citizen's functions without satisfying the appropriate criteria it makes sense to say, in Aristotle's terminology, that someone is a citizen but not justly so. We might make a similar point by distinguishing between those who are citizens *de facto* and those who are citizens *de iure*.

CHAPTER 3

1276^a *a larger question already mentioned*: see the beginning of the first chapter. Barker comments, 'The essence of the larger question is concerned with the nature and identity of the state. Is the nature of the state such that we may identify it with the constitution in force, and therefore with the government in power, at any given time? Or is the nature of the state such that we must distinguish it from the particular constitution which may be in force, and the particular government which may be in power at any given time?' Such questions are obviously of practical importance. Barker referred to the problem of determining whether the communist rulers of Russia after 1917 were bound by obligations undertaken by the Tsars. At the time of writing their successors are facing a similar problem. But these issues are also important philosophically. Just as an animal is not simply a collection of bodily parts and a machine is not simply a pile of cog wheels and the like, so the *polis* cannot be identified with any particular collection of individuals or any particular territory. Its identity consists in its form or, as we might now say, in its functional organization.

the word 'city' is used in different senses: the argument is not clear. Perhaps the thought is that if the territory of a city was divided into two it could remain one city in the sense that the population and institutions remain the same. But the city would not be one in the sense of having a single territory.

to reserve . . . for some other occasion: nowhere in his surviving work does Aristotle take up the theoretical question how large a *polis* can be while still remaining a *polis*. The practical question of how large it is desirable for a *polis* to be is taken up in VII. 4.

1276ᵇ *It is a different question*: Aristotle nowhere answers this question. One might suppose that if a *polis* which has changed its constitution is no longer the same *polis* it cannot be bound by obligations incurred under the previous regime. Barker and others have seen hints of the more moderate view that obligations undertaken for the public good remain binding. But Aristotle does not explicitly endorse such a view and it would not solve all problems. A new government which repudiated obligations on the grounds that they had been undertaken against the public interest might find itself disappointing the legitimate expectations of innocent parties (for example, contractors who had been employed by the previous regime on wasteful public works).

CHAPTER 4

1276ᵇ *whether the excellence of a good man and that of a good citizen are identical or different*: to be a good citizen is presumably to perform well the functions of a citizen. One can perform well the functions of, for example, a sailor without being a good man. So it might also seem that one does not have to be a good man to perform well the functions of a citizen. On the other hand, the purpose of the *polis* as Aristotle conceives it, is to make possible the good life. So it may well seem that, at least in a well-ordered state, someone who functions well as a citizen must also function well as a man, i.e. that the good citizen must be a good man. Aristotle's discussion characteristically shows that this is true in one sense but not in another. In reading this chapter it is vital to remember that for Aristotle the phrase 'the good man' carries quite different connotations from those it has for us. His good man does not embody the Christian ideal of humility, self sacrifice, and the like. Rather he lives a life that is characteristically human, displaying both intellectual excellence and emotional balance.

1276^b *a sailor is a member of an association*: the sailor participates in a common enterprise (a *koinōnia*) in which each member has a different role.

if there are several different kinds of constitution there cannot be a single absolute excellence of the good citizen: Aristotle's argument establishes (*a*) that the goodness of the citizen is relative to the constitution in that what constitutes goodness in a particular case depends on the role one occupies in the constitution. What Aristotle needs to establish is (*b*) that the goodness of a citizen varies from one constitution to another. These points are different. But (*b*) could be said to follow from (*a*) if one makes the not unreasonable assumption that if two constitutions differ the roles they each assign to their citizens must also differ.

we may reach the same conclusion in another way: this paragraph seems to embody two arguments for the distinction between the good man and the good citizen: (1) it is impossible for all to be good men but in the best city all must be good citizens; (2) the excellence required of a citizen varies according to his or her precise role, but the excellence of the good man does not depend on his particular role. These arguments are set out in a compressed and rather obscure way in the first part of the paragraph (1276^b34–1277^a1) and then in a much clearer way in the second part of the paragraph (1277^a1–12).

1277^a *No subtleties for me,* | *But what the city most needs*: from the lost play *Aeolus*. The king is speaking here of the education of his sons.

though it may be so in a particular case: in other words the excellence of the good man and the excellence of the good citizen coincide when the citizen is a ruler.

we can now see the next step which our argument has to take: this sentence appears to be incomplete but the argument is clear enough. Aristotle has identified two distinct claims: (1) that the good man should know how to rule *but not* how to be ruled; (2) that the good citizen knows *both* how to rule *and* how to be ruled. If both of these were true the excellence of the good man and the good citizen could not be the same. But Aristotle is going to solve the problem by distinguishing different senses of 'rule'.

CHAPTER 5

1277ᵃ *mechanics*: *banausoi*. This word originally referred to those, such as smiths, who worked with fire but came to be more generally of non-agricultural manual workers. The suggestion is usually that such work is demeaning. Elsewhere Aristotle argues that it renders both mind and body unfit for the tasks of a citizen. The banausic worker has a kind of limited servitude because he works for another person and would, of course, lack the leisure to spend a great deal of time on politics. It is nevertheless surprising to find Aristotle in this passage taking it for granted without any argument that the *banausoi* are not entitled to hold office. After all he has just argued that 'political offices' include those of serving in the deliberative assembly and on juries, functions which could quite easily be carried out by manual workers (as they regularly were in democracies such as Athens). Barker suggests that the previous chapter with its emphasis on the knowledge required by the ruler may have caused Aristotle to change his mind.

1278ᵃ *all who are necessary to the city's existence*: Aristotle here draws, by implication, a distinction between (1) those members of a *polis* who are 'integral parts' and actively share in its life, thus enjoying the status of a citizen, and (2) those members of the *polis* who are 'necessary conditions' and whose share in its life is not that of active participation in its political activity, but only that of providing the material basis (of housing, food commodities, and services) which is a condition of that activity. This distinction plays an important part in Aristotle's political thought because it implies that the good which the *polis* seeks is not the good of the population as a whole but only that of a privileged group. See below, VII. 8.

1278^a *enough has already been said*: the reference is to Ch. 1 of this Book. There Aristotle argued that constitutions differ and are of different qualities. It follows that citizenship may vary from constitution to constitution. Mechanics and hired labourers may be citizens under one constitution but not under others.

citizenship is confined to those who are of citizen parentage on both sides: the Athenians introduced this requirement at the suggestion of Pericles in 451/50.

like an alien man, without honour: the Homeric phrase is found at *Iliad* IX. 648 and XVI. 59. 'Honour' here translates the Greek *timē*, which could mean both 'office' and 'honour'. Aristotle is using the word primarily in the former sense, though Homer clearly meant it in the latter.

Two conclusions also emerge from our discussion: the conclusions summarized in the final few lines of this chapter are in fact the conclusions of the previous one. It looks as though something may have gone wrong with the order of the text as it has come down to us.

CHAPTER 6

1278^b *A constitution . . . sovereign in all issues*: Aristotle defines a *politeia* (constitution) in a variety of ways: it is 'a way of organizing the inhabitants of a city' (1274^b38); 'an arrangement in regard to the offices of the city' (1290^a7); or most fully 'an organization of offices in a city, by which the method of their distribution is fixed, the sovereign authority is determined, and the nature of the end to be pursued by the association and all its members is prescribed' (1289^a15). In the present context Aristotle focuses on the idea of the constitution as determining who or what is sovereign (*to kurion*) or has ultimate authority in the city. He can thus identify the constitution with the civic body or *politeuma*, the body of persons established in power by the constitution (*politeia*). But Aristotle also recognizes that there needs to be an agreement between a city's constitution and its general way of life, particularly so far as education is concerned (1237^a14 ff.). This is in keeping with a general tendency of the Greeks to include not just the arrangements of offices but the whole organization of the city's communal life within the scope of the *politeia*. Thus at 1295^a40 Aristotle describes a *politeia* as 'the way in which a city lives'.

In democratic cities ... the people (dēmos) is sovereign: *dēmos* often refers to the whole people, rich and poor, but it is also widely used in the sense of 'the populace' or 'the masses' to refer to the poorer citizens, who were, of course, generally in a majority. Thus, as Aristotle makes clear in Ch. 8, democracy (the rule of the *dēmos*) came to mean the rule of the poor rather than the rule of the whole people.

man is a political animal: see I. 2, 1253ᵃ2–3, with note.

works intended for the general public: in the 'exoteric' works, i.e. the lost works which were intended for publication and directed to a wider audience. See Introduction, p. xxxii.

The rule of a master is one kind: see I. 5 and 7.

household management: see I. 12.

1279ᵃ *At any rate ... had considered their interest*: the implication is that the office of ruler is primarily intended for the benefit of the ruled and is therefore a duty to be undertaken by each in turn, though incidentally the ruler shares in the general benefit by being himself a member of the citizen body.

their ardour for office is just what it would be if that were the case: i.e. they seek to get and to hold on to office with the same kind of enthusiasm we would expect sick men to show for a miracle cure.

those constitutions ... perversions of the 'right' forms: the preliminary classification of constitutions into two kinds (the right or normal forms, and the wrong or perverted ones) is based on the principle that political rule is by its nature for the benefit of the ruled. This squares with Aristotle's view that the main end of the *polis* is the common good. The fundamental principle to be followed in a *polis* and embodied in its constitution must therefore be that office is to be held for the common good of all its members.

Such perverted forms are despotic: i.e. they involve the kind of rule that is exercised by a master over his slaves.

CHAPTER 7

1279ᵃ *On this basis ... right constitutions*: Aristotle classifies constitutions by two principles, (*a*) the rightness or wrongness of the constitution and (*b*) the number of rulers. The results may be tabulated as follows:

	Right	Wrong
Rule of one	Monarchy	Tyranny
Rule of a few	Aristocracy	Oligarchy
Rule of many	Constitutional Government (Polity)	Democracy

1279ᵃ 'Constitutional Government': Aristotle uses the word *politeia* both as a general word for 'constitution' and to describe a particular form of constitution—one in which participation is confined to those who can afford the armour of a hoplite soldier. It is customary to translate the word, when used in this latter sense, as 'polity', but that practice can be misleading since it obscures the suggestion, implicit in Aristotle's usage, that the so-called 'polity' has a special claim to be seen as constitutional.

1279ᵇ *What we can expect particularly is the military kind of excellence*: Aristotle takes it for granted that in order to govern in the public interest one must have a proper conception of that interest and must therefore have excellence or goodness of character (*aretē*). It is generally impossible for large numbers to possess this excellence in the full sense but they may possess the more limited excellence to be expected of the hoplite soldier.

CHAPTER 8

1279ᵇ *oligarchy exists ... who are without much property*: at the end of the previous chapter Aristotle indicated that the distinction between oligarchy and democracy really depends on the criterion of economic class rather than on that of number. He now proceeds further along this line: what makes an oligarchy is not so much the fact that a few people rule in their own interest; it is rather the fact that the wealthy rule. Oligarchy is thus really plutocracy (the rule of the rich); while democracy is the rule of the poor. It is only an accident that the poor are generally more numerous than the rich. Aristotle thus recognizes that the political divisions which troubled most Greek cities have an economic basis. But strikingly he does not suggest that they should be dealt with by economic reform.

CHAPTER 9

1280ᵃ *the oligarchical and the democratic conceptions of justice*: Aristotle now approaches the classification of constitutions from a different direction. Each form of constitution has its own distinctive conception of justice—that is its own conception of the way in which offices and honours should be distributed. Oligarchy and democracy, as perversions of right constitutions, have each been shown to rest on a particular social class. Accordingly, they each have a distinctive conception of justice which enables them to justify the predominance of that class.

equality for those who are equal, and not for all: this is the core of Aristotle's account of distributive justice—it consists not in giving everyone exactly the same privileges but in giving equal privileges to those who are equal and unequal privileges to those who are unequal. As Aristotle is well aware, people can be equal in one respect but not in others, so his account of justice yields very different conceptions of the just state, depending on what factors are taken to be relevant in deciding whether particular individuals are to be judged as equal or unequal.

in the Ethics: the reference is to the discussion of distributive justice in (*Nicomachean*) *Ethics* v. 3.

disagreement about what constitutes it in people: although there is general agreement about whether one office or honour is or is not greater than another we tend to disagree about the qualities which entitle people to a larger or smaller share of offices and honours.

the really cardinal factor: i.e. the nature of the end for which the city exists. In Aristotle's view what counts as an equal contribution to the city can be determined only by considering the end for which the city exists. So democrats and oligarchs are, by implication, committed to different views of the city's end. To decide what is truly just we need to know what the end of the city truly is.

happiness: *eudaimonia*, a key term in Aristotle's moral and political philosophy. On this and on Aristotle's view that the city exists for the sake of the good life see Introduction, pp. xii–xiii.

nor does it exist for the purpose of exchange or (commercial) dealing: Aristotle here marks his disagreement with views of the role of the state current in many quarters today, that it exists to primarily provide security and economic well-being. Aristotle argues that the city is concerned with the moral and intellectual well-being of its citizens.

Lycophron: little is known about this man, apart from the fact that he was probably a pupil of Gorgias, and must therefore have been active in the latter part of the fifth century or the early part of the fourth century BC. His view of the state as resting on no more than a contract for mutual self-protection was associated with the sophistic movement and is strongly resisted by Plato as well as Aristotle. See Introduction, pp. viii–ix.

1281ᵃ   *truly valuable life . . . actions valuable in themselves*: in both these phrases the adjective is *kalos*, which is a strong term of approval in Greek but is difficult to translate. It often bears the meaning 'beautiful', in which sense it can be applied to works of art or the human body, but it can also be applied as here to actions and to character. In these contexts it is often translated 'noble' or 'fine' but neither of these terms means very much to us today.

From what has been said it is plain that all sides . . . profess only a partial conception of justice: the fundamental point raised by the different conceptions of justice discussed in this chapter is 'What kinds of equality or inequality are relevant to the distribution of honours?' Aristotle answers such questions by suggesting that we consider them in the light of the end for which the city exists. In a similar way we might argue that who should be appointed to a particular post in an organization such as a commercial firm or university depends ultimately on the purpose for which the organization exists. Aristotle's answer enables him not only to discriminate between different conceptions of justice but also to show that each contains an element of truth. But his solution does, of course, depend on the assumption that we are agreed on the end for which the city exists. This is the main reason why he has devoted so much space in the chapter to the alternative view represented by Lycophron.

CHAPTER 10

1281ᵃ   *all these alternatives appear to involve unpleasant results*: in Ch. 6 above Aristotle began his discussion of constitutions by pointing out that we may classify constitutions by asking who or what is sovereign (i.e. has ultimate authority). Now, having distinguished the different varieties and noted their different conceptions of justice, he argues that there are problems whichever body is sovereign. If any but the best elements in the *polis* become sovereign they will be capable of acting unjustly. If office is confined to the best elements, the others are left without honour. This is true even if law is sovereign because laws can be unjust—by implication Aristotle thus rejects the positivist view that justice is simply what the government decides.

what difference will the sovereignty of law then make in the problems which have just been raised?: as is clear from the following chapter, Aristotle is himself a firm believer in the sovereignty of law. But he recognizes that to guarantee justice in the state laws must themselves be just.

CHAPTER 11

1281ᵃ *for later inquiry*: the questions raised in the previous chapter are all dealt with in the remaining chapters of this Book or in Books IV and VI.

the people at large should be sovereign: this chapter incorporates two arguments which have come to play an important part in democratic theory: (*a*) although each citizen may not be particularly wise, the citizen body as a whole may be wiser than any individual; (*b*) even where it takes an expert to produce a product, non-experts may be as well placed as the expert to judge the quality of the product. These arguments, if they are correct, tend to show that democratic government can be wise government. They therefore differ in kind from arguments which appeal to justice or rights, such as the argument Aristotle attributes to the democrat that it is just for those who are equally free to have an equal share of offices and honour, or the modern democratic argument that the people has the right to make its own decisions. Aristotle's own view on the arguments he discusses here is not altogether clear. It looks as though he would probably accept that they apply to populations which have had the right kind of education but not to any population whatever.

(seem to present problems which): evidently some words have slipped out of the text here. The translation incorporates a guess as to their meaning.

1281ᵇ *What difference, one may ask, is there between some men and the beasts?*: the behaviour of a herd of wild animals is no better guide to what is good or right than that of a single animal. Aristotle does not here explain why an assembly of human beings might be different. He could, however, refer to I. 2, where he argues that language gives human beings the power to form a common conception of the good.

What are the matters over which freemen ... should properly exercise sovereignty?: Aristotle takes the first of these questions,

'What body of persons should be sovereign?', to have been answered. He now goes on to consider the second question, 'Over what matters should the body of free citizens be sovereign?'

1282ᵃ *the function of judging when medical attendance has been properly given should belong . . . to members of the medical profession*: here Aristotle may well have in mind the argument used by Plato in the *Republic* that ruling is a matter for experts. But in his later writings, the *Statesman* and the *Laws*, Plato's position is much closer to Aristotle. He acknowledges that, since expert rulers are not usually available, it makes sense in practice to rely on collective wisdom.

1282ᵇ *Rightly constituted laws should be the final sovereign*: the doctrine that law should be sovereign was not new to Aristotle but he is the main source through which it passed into later political theory. He sees reliance on law as avoiding the arbitrariness which would characterize the rule of a tyrant, an oligarchic clique, or a popular mob, but for the reason given at the end of the previous chapter (the law itself may be biased) he does not see it as a panacea. Aristotle's conception of the sovereignty of law has to be understood in the light of what we know about Greek (particularly Athenian) practice. Law (*nomos*) was seen as a more or less permanent body of standing rules. Although legislative proposals could be initiated in the assembly, it was seen not as a legislative but as a deliberative body. Those who made proposals contrary to the existing law were liable to be prosecuted. Similarly, any citizen could bring a prosecution against an official who had contravened the law.

CHAPTER 12

1282ᵇ *The good in the sphere of politics is justice*: Aristotle is still concerned with the problem of distributive justice. While this chapter covers some of the same ground as Ch. 9, Aristotle is here particularly concerned with the need to recognize that there may be different kinds of contribution to the city, and that a number of different factors thus have to be taken into account in the distribution of offices and honours. This raises the problem of which factors are relevant and how one factor may be weighed against another.

our conclusions on ethics: see above, Ch. 9 and (*Nicomachean*) *Ethics* v. 3.

1283ᵃ *You will begin . . . equally good*: the text of 1283ᵃ3–9 is very obscure and may be corrupt. Dreizehnter's substitution of *sumballetai* for *mallon* in 1283ᵃ4 does not greatly help matters. I have therefore retained Barker's very free interpretation of the manuscript version.

CHAPTER 13

1283ᵃ *culture and goodness*: the claims of virtue or goodness of character were stressed in Ch. 9 above. In IV. 12, 1296ᵇ17–19 Aristotle lists free birth, wealth, culture, and nobility of descent as claims of merit. The claim of culture or education (*paideia*) thus seems to be identified with that of goodness. There is a particular problem about this claim of which Aristotle is certainly aware although he does not address it very explicitly. There is no undisputed criterion by which one can identify who has the requisite kind of goodness. It would therefore be impossible in practice to devise a constitution in which only those with this kind of goodness hold office. In practice one has either to assume that goodness generally accompanies some other characteristic such as noble birth or education or do what Aristotle himself does in Books VII and VIII where he describes a city in which all citizens receive the right kind of education and may all therefore be deemed to be good. But it is doubtful whether a city in which all citizens have a share in office would satisfy Aristotle's definition of aristocracy, which is based on the principle that the better citizens rule over the worse.

in our view the virtue of justice . . . all other forms of goodness: there are two points here: (*a*) the just man necessarily possesses all the other virtues (see (*Nicomachean*) *Ethics* v. 1, 1129ᵇ25–1130ᵇ8); (*b*) it is a shared conception of what is good and just that makes political life possible (see above, I. 2, 1253ᵃ7–18).

1284ᵃ *the words used by the lions*: they asked 'Where are your claws and teeth?' Antisthenes was a follower of Socrates whose works survive only in fragments.

ostracism: a practice introduced at Athens by Cleisthenes, the founder of the democracy. Each year the citizens voted on whether to hold an ostracism. If they decided to do so, each wrote on a potsherd the name of the man he wished to be ostracized. Provided at least 6,000 votes were cast and certain other conditions were satisfied, the individual who received the most such 'votes' was obliged to go into exile for ten years.

1284ᵃ *the advice once given by Periander to Thrasybulus*: Periander was tyrant of Corinth and Thrasybulus tyrant of Miletus. See Herodotus v. 92. Aristotle also refers to this story in v. 10 and 11.

Samos, Chios, and Lesbos: these were all cities which revolted from the Athenian alliance and were subdued by the Athenians: Samos in 440–439, Lesbos in 427, and Chios in 424.

1284ᵇ *claiming to rule over Zeus, according to some division of offices*: Aristotle has in mind a system in which offices rotate, so that lesser beings might find themselves, from time to time, ruling over Zeus.

CHAPTER 14

1285ᵃ *to command death*: Iliad II. 391–3.

Pittacus: he was elected as *aisumnētes* (i.e. he was in effect given dictatorial powers) in about 590 BC. The poet Alcaeus was an active member of the aristocratic faction in Mytilene and went into exile when Pittacus was elected.

CHAPTER 15

1286ᵃ *Is it more advantageous to be ruled by the one best man, or by the best laws?*: there is a clear parallel between the argument of this chapter and the one which follows. Both begin by arguing for the sovereignty of law and against absolute kingship. They then consider the objection that law needs to be supplemented by some power of human decision, but go on to point out that there is a strong case for giving this power to the many rather than to a single individual. It is possible therefore to regard the two chapters as alternative treatments of the same themes but there are important differences in the details of the arguments.

following written rules is therefore foolish in any art whatever: this is the argument of Plato's *Statesman* 294ᵃ ff. But in that dialogue Plato goes on to argue that, where there is no expert ruler, it makes sense to conduct government in accordance with fixed laws.

1286ᵇ *it is now difficult for any form of constitution apart from democracy to exist*: the account here given of the historical succession of constitutions differs from that in IV. 13,

1297^b16–28, which attributes constitutional changes to changes in military practice. Neither of these accounts squares with the criticisms Aristotle makes of Plato's account of constitutional change in the *Republic* (see v. 12, 1315^b40–1316^b25).

CHAPTER 16

1287^a *as has already been noted*: apparently a reference to Ch. 15 above, 1286^a2–5.

law-guardians: there were officials with this title at Athens but they do not appear to have been particularly active or important. In the *Laws* Plato proposes a constitution whose dominant principle is the sovereignty of law and in which a body of 37 guardians of the law would exercise great authority.

'*as justly as in them lies*': the words here apparently reflect those of the Athenian juryman's oath.

the character of the beast: the psychology of this passage and some of its phrasing owes much to Plato's *Republic*. There it is argued that the human soul has three parts: reason, spirit, and appetite (435a–441b), and these are likened respectively to a man, a lion, and a many-headed beast (588b–589b). In that context, as elsewhere, Plato sees law as embodying reason (590e).

1287^b *neutral*: *mesos*, literally 'in the middle' or 'the mean'.

Two men going together: Iliad x. 324.

like unto Nestor: Iliad II. 372.

CHAPTER 17

1287^b *rule of a constitutional type*: this might also mean 'rule by a statesman'—the statesman (*politikos*) is one who rules over his equals under a constitutional arrangement (*politeia*).

1288^a *in an earlier passage*: see above, Ch. 13, 1284^a3–11, 1284^b28–34.

among the wealthy in proportion to merit: following the manuscripts rather than Dreizehnter's rearrangement of the text. This phrase may appear self-contradictory since not all the wealthy have merit and not all those who have merit are wealthy. It may be that by 'the wealthy' Aristotle here means those who are wealthy enough to provide the arms of the hoplite soldier. The constitutional government he describes here would then coincide with the so-called 'polity' in the strict sense—that is, a system where only those who are able to afford arms are full citizens. See above, Ch. 7, 1279ª37–ᵇ4. See also below, IV. 13, 1297ᵇ1–28.

1288ª   *As we said earlier*: see above, Ch. 13, 1284ᵇ28–34.

turn by turn: in Ch. 13 above, 1284ª3–11 Aristotle argued that a man of truly outstanding virtue could not be considered merely as a part of the state. The phrase translated 'turn by turn' in the following sentence means literally 'by parts'. The point then is that, because the man of outstanding virtue is not just one part of state among many, rule by turns is not appropriate for him.

CHAPTER 18

1288ᵇ   *In order to make a proper inquiry into this subject it is necessary*: these words, which do not make much sense on their own, are identical with the opening words of Book VII. For this reason some scholars have argued that Books VII and VIII ought to be placed immediately after Book III and before Book IV.

BOOK IV

CHAPTER 1

1288ᵇ   *it is the task of the same branch of knowledge . . . which sort of civic body*: although there is close correspondence between the functions Aristotle assigns to political knowledge (or as we might say 'political science') and those he assigns to the art of gymnastic training, the order in which he arranges these functions differs in the two cases.

Gymnastics	Politics
A. Which type of training suits which twhich type of physique?	B. Which is the best constitution for the best sort of civic body?
B. Which type of training suits the best type of physique?	A. Which type of constitution suits which type of civic body?

C. Which type of training suits the majority of physiques?

D. Which type of training will suit those who are content with a lower standard of fitness?

D. What is best for a given constitution (i.e. if we take for granted the existence and continuance of a constitution which is not necessarily the best that could be achieved)?

C. Which type of constitution will suit the majority of civic bodies?

It is notable that, although Aristotle (like Plato) is interested in political ideals and has discussed, in Book II, various kinds of utopia, the main focus of his writing in Books IV, V, and VI is on what is practically possible.

A third task is to consider the sort of constitution which depends upon an assumption: although Aristotle's way of expressing himself here may seem tortuous the underlying thought is clear enough. In addition to considering which type of constitution is best absolutely, which is best for a particular kind of people, and which is best in general, the political expert may also offer advice on how to preserve an existing constitution (a constitution which may not be the best in any of the three senses just outlined). He sees this as parallel to the case of someone who has no desire to be a great athlete nor even to achieve the highest level of fitness of which he himself is capable but who wishes to have some training (presumably so that he can survive in reasonable health while so far as possible maintaining his present lifestyle).

matters of practical utility: this phrase (*ta chrēsima*) strikes the general keynote of Books IV, V, and VI which are all occupied with matters of practical utility—in the first instance with what is useful for the preservation of actual constitutions as they stand, and, in the second, with what is useful in the way of practical reform of actual constitutions such as can actually be adopted (Barker).

Aristotle contrasts the methods he means to follow in these books with those of his predecessors who have concentrated on describing ideal states. No doubt he is thinking of Plato, whose major works of political philosophy (the *Republic* and the *Laws*) both consist largely of descriptions of such ideals. But one should not overemphasize the conventional contrast between an idealistically minded Plato and a practically minded Aristotle. Aristotle does not doubt the value of describing ideal states. He has discussed ideal states in Book II and will describe an ideal of his own in Books VII and VIII. He merely insists that the political expert must also consider practicalities. Plato himself would probably have agreed with him on this point.

1289ᵃ *as we said previously*: the reference here is unclear. Aristotle may be thinking of the third task of those described in the previous paragraph.

A constitution is an organization of offices . . . all its members is prescribed: cf. the similar, but briefer definition of 'constitution' in III. 6, 1278ᵇ8–10.

CHAPTER 2

1289ᵃ *In our first discussion of constitutions*: the reference appears to be to III. 14–18.

To consider the best constitution is, in effect, to consider the two constitutions so named: this is a puzzling statement since monarchy and aristocracy are actual constitutions while the ideal constitution should transcend the actual. There may be a reference here to III. 18, 1288ᵃ33–7, where it seems to be claimed that the ideal constitution will be aristocratic or monarchical.

the difference between aristocracy and kingship: this is defined in III. 7, 1279ᵃ32–7; 15, 1286ᵇ3–7; 17, 1288ᵃ6–15. The proper time and place for establishing a kingship is explained in II. 17, 1288ᵃ15–ᵇ2.

It only remains . . . oligarchy, democracy, and tyranny: the relationship between this chapter and the previous one is not clear. Both chapters set out the programme of investigation which Aristotle proposes to follow but they do so in rather different ways. It may be that they were originally alternative introductions to the material which makes up Books IV–VI.

1289ᵇ *One of our predecessors*: apparently a reference to Plato's dialogue the *Statesman*, 303b. The difference seems, in fact, to be largely one of terminology.

tend to produce these results: the programme Aristotle has outlined has five headings:

1. the varieties of the main types of constitutions (especially democracy and oligarchy);
2. the type of constitution which is most generally practicable;
3. which sort of constitution is desirable for which sort of civic body;
4. the methods of establishing constitutions;
5. the causes of the destruction, and the methods of the preservation, of different constitutions.

The difference between this programme and the list of functions ascribed to politics in Ch. 1 (see note to 1286^b above) is not so great as it might seem. Roughly we may say that the first function of politics (that of considering the ideal state) is eliminated; the second function corresponds to the third heading of the new programme; that the third function corresponds to the fourth and fifth headings on the new programme; that the fourth function corresponds to the second heading of the new programme, while a matter only incidentally mentioned in connection with it before (1289^{a}7–11) now becomes the first heading (Barker).

Although all these matters do receive some attention in Books IV–VI, Aristotle does not stick at all closely to his programme. In particular he does not begin describing the different varieties of oligarchy and democracy until the latter part of Ch. 4 (1291^{b}14).

CHAPTER 3

1289^b *The reason why there are many different constitutions is ... that every city has many different parts*: in this chapter Aristotle considers the reasons why there are many different kinds of constitutions. Thus it does not altogether square with the programme outlined at the end of the previous chapter where Aristotle proposed to begin by distinguishing and enumerating the different varieties of constitution. A more serious problem is that the same questions are discussed in a rather different way in Ch. 4. It would appear therefore that these chapters, like Chs. 1 and 2, may have originated in different versions of Aristotle's course on politics.

1290^a *our discussion of aristocracy*: apparently a reference to III. 12, 1283^{a}16–22.

two modes (*the Dorian and the Phrygian*): see VIII. 5.

as has already been suggested: apparently a reference to Ch. 2 of this Book. That chapter and the fuller discussion in III. 7 would imply that there are three 'right' forms of constitution, not just one or two as suggested here. Aristotle rejects what might seem the common-sense view that in classifying constitutions the most fundamental consideration is the number who are allowed to share in political life. His point is presumably that the division into 'right' and 'wrong' forms is at least as important as a division based on numbers.

CHAPTER 4

1290ᵃ *It ought not to be assumed ... number are sovereign*: the structure of this chapter is complicated. It can perhaps most easily be seen as falling into four sections:

(a) 1290ᵃ30–ᵇ20: Aristotle makes once again the point that the distinction between oligarchy and democracy is one of social class rather than numbers. This section largely repeats points made in III. 8.

(b) 1290ᵇ21–37: A parallel is drawn between the classification of constitutions and the classification of animals. If this passage was part of the *Politics* in its original form it would be important because it suggests that Aristotle is prepared to take seriously the idea that Politics is a science like Biology in which systematic knowledge is possible and that the state can be thought of in much the same way as a natural organism. However, as it stands the passage is not closely connected to the context and could be an interpolation.

(c) 1290ᵇ37–1291ᵇ13: The various parts of a state are enumerated. This section is interrupted by a digression (1291ᵃ10–27) in which Aristotle criticizes the account of the parts of the state given in Plato's *Republic*.

(d) 1291ᵇ14–1292ᵃ38: Aristotle proceeds to describe the different varieties of democracy. He thus embarks at last on the programme announced at the end of Ch. 2 where he proposed to begin by giving an account of the different varieties of democracy and oligarchy.

the majority is sovereign: i.e. the majority of those who enjoy full constitutional rights. In an oligarchy this might well be a minority of the citizens.

1290ᵇ *Otherwise*: i.e. if number alone were the essence.

1291ᵃ *The seventh part*: Aristotle has not explicitly identified a sixth part. One might suppose that he has in mind the judicial function which he identified in discussing the *Republic*, but that is mentioned separately below. The service performed by the wealthy is that of undertaking liturgies. Wealthy citizens at Athens and elsewhere were required to finance some public undertaking such as the provision of a fighting ship or a theatrical production.

1291b *what has been previously said*: apparently a reference to the beginning of Ch. 3.

1292a *when popular decrees are sovereign instead of the law*: Aristotle is distinguishing between decrees (*psēphismata*) and laws (*nomoi*). A decree is a decision taken by the assembly. A law is a permanent part of the legal system. Laws are supposed to be superior to decrees and there was at Athens a procedure for prosecuting those who made proposals to the assembly which were contrary to law.

Law should be sovereign on every issue, and the officials and the constitution: the text here makes very little sense. It may well be corrupt.

CHAPTER 5

1292b *A second variety ... choose replacements for any vacancies*: this sentence is very obscure. I take it that Aristotle has in mind a situation where satisfying the property qualification is not in itself sufficient to enable one to take a full part in the constitution: one has also to be elected by those who are already members. Thus this kind of oligarchy differs from the first type in which satisfying the property qualification is enough to guarantee full civic rights. See also below, IV. 6, 1293a24.

a 'dynasty': there is no wholly satisfactory translation of Aristotle's word *dunasteia*, though the sense is clear enough. He has in mind a situation where a small number of families collectively exercise absolute power. See first note to II. 10, 1272b.

CHAPTER 6

1292b *What we have already said ... all these varieties of democracy and oligarchy*: in this chapter Aristotle offers a second or alternative account of the varieties of oligarchy and democracy. This covers much of the same ground as is covered in the latter part of Ch. 4 and Ch. 5. So once again it looks as though two separate versions of the course have been combined in our text.

The main difference between this account and that in Chs. 4 and 5 is that the present chapter emphasizes the importance of leisure. Whether the constitution is oligarchic or democratic citizens will only be able to devote time to politics if their incomes are large enough to permit them to take time off from working. Aristotle undoubtedly has an important point here. In Athens at the end of the fifth century BC. there were sufficient public revenues to permit payments to those who took part in political activities, in particular payment for attending the assembly. Critics of Athenian democracy saw this as a major reason why, as they saw it, Athens descended into demagoguery and mob rule. Admirers of the Athenian system might equally claim that only when all can afford to take part can there be a genuine democracy.

What is not so clear is whether Aristotle is right in assuming that, where participation is limited by lack of funds, law is more likely to be sovereign. There is no obvious reason why a state with mass participation must be relatively lawless. Equally it might be argued that where the majority of those entitled to participate cannot in practice do so, power may tend to fall into the hands of an irresponsible clique.

1292^b *Thus all who have acquired this amount of property have a share*: the text of this passage is corrupt. I have followed Dreizehnter's reconstruction. Aristotle's idea is presumably that, whereas in an oligarchy the right of participation is formally restricted, in democracies the exercise of this right may well be restricted by lack of means.

CHAPTER 7

1293^a *There are still two forms of constitution left, besides democracy and oligarchy*: Aristotle has now completed the first of the tasks described in the programme at the end of Ch. 2, that of outlining the various forms of oligarchy and democracy. We might therefore expect him to proceed to the second task—that of describing the form of constitution that is most generally acceptable—but that is postponed until Ch. 11. Aristotle digresses to discuss three other forms of constitution, aristocracy, 'constitutional government' or polity, and the deviant form tyranny.

One of these is usually reckoned . . . and the form called aristocracy: in III. 7, Aristotle mentioned six constitutions, three right forms (kingship, aristocracy, polity) and three wrong forms (tyranny, oligarchy, and democracy). In speaking here of four constitutions he presumably has in mind a popular classification into kingship, oligarchy, democracy, and aristocracy. He goes on immediately to add 'constitutional government' or polity to this list and presumably sees no need to mention tyranny as it can scarcely claim to be a constitution at all. He has just discussed oligarchy and democracy and goes on to deal with aristocracy, polity, and tyranny. There is no account in this book of kingship, so one might suppose that this is the constitution which is referred to as having already been mentioned. But the phrasing of the Greek makes it more likely that this is a reference to aristocracy.

1293ᵇ *they usually limit themselves, like Plato, to an enumeration of only four forms*: apparently a reference to *Republic* books 8 and 9, where Plato describes four kinds of constitution other than his ideal. But these are not the four just listed.

There are thus these two forms of aristocracy ... which incline particularly to oligarchy: it emerges from this somewhat crabbed passage that there are four different forms of aristocracy—(1) the first and best form, where regard is paid only to goodness; (2) the Carthaginian form, where regard is paid to wealth and numbers as well; (3) the Spartan form, where regard is paid to numbers as well as to goodness; (4) the form presented by those 'mixed' constitutions or polities which pay less regard to numbers than the Spartan constitution does, and thus incline more to oligarchy (Barker).

CHAPTER 8

1293ᵇ *It remains for us to speak of the so-called 'constitutional government' (polity) and of tyranny*: the main aim of this chapter is to distinguish 'constitutional government' or polity from aristocracy. 'Constitutional government', in Aristotle's view, is a mixture of oligarchy and democracy while aristocracy gives power to those who have merit. Because merit is associated in the popular mind with wealth there is a tendency to call those 'constitutional governments' which incline to oligarchy 'aristocracies', leaving the name 'constitutional government' to those which incline to democracy. In Aristotle's view this tendency is to be resisted.

all these constitutions ... the perversions among which they are reckoned are those to which they themselves give rise: the thought is obscure. In III. 7 'constitutional government' and aristocracy were both classified as 'right' forms of government with democracy and oligarchy as their perversions. But both 'constitutional government' and the forms of aristocracy just mentioned fall short of the ideal form of government which would be a genuine aristocracy, rule by men of outstanding merit. There is thus a sense in which they are both perversions. They may therefore be listed as perversions alongside democracy and oligarchy. But if the phrase 'in our first part' is intended to refer to III. 7, Aristotle's implied claim that the so-called aristocracies just mentioned give rise to oligarchy is a bit misleading since in that chapter oligarchy was depicted as a perversion of genuine aristocracy.

1293^b *this is the reason why they are called 'gentlemen' or 'notables'*: the thought seems to be that because the wealthy possess the good things which wrongdoers lack, they must be good men.

1294^a *good government*: *eunomia*, i.e. living under good laws.

CHAPTER 9

1294^a *a token*: the Greek word, *sumbolon*, refers to a coin which contracting parties broke between them as a symbol of their contract. The two parts could, of course, be matched together at some later date.

We may take as an example those about jury service: the Greeks did not have professional judges and political disputes were often fought out in the courts, so the constitution of juries played a key role in determining the political character of Greek states. The measures Aristotle describes as democratic would, of course, ensure that the majority of jurors were drawn from the poorer classes. The measures he describes as oligarchic would have the reverse effect.

1294^b *a majority are in favour of its continuance*: omitting *exōthen*.

CHAPTER 10

1295^a *Kingship has already been discussed in our first part*: III. 14–17.

Two forms of tyranny were distinguished in the course of our discussion: III. 14, 1285^{a}29–^{b}30.

absolute kingship: *pambasileia*. See III. 14, 1285^{a}16–^{b}3, and 16, 1287^{a}8–12.

CHAPTER 11

1295ᵃ *We have now to consider what is the best constitution and the best way of life for the majority of cities and the majority of mankind*: in this chapter, one of the most important in the *Politics*, Aristotle addresses the second question in the programme sketched at the end of Ch. 2: what type of constitution—short of the ideal—is the most generally acceptable, and the most to be preferred? In other words, he is asking what is the best constitution that could be established in the conditions which prevail in the majority of Greek states. It is notable that Aristotle links this question about the best constitution to a question about the best way of life. Although he has defined a constitution as an arrangement of offices, his consistent view is that the state exists for the sake of the good life. As this chapter makes very clear, questions about a state's constitution (the way in which it is organized) are inseparable from questions about the kind of citizens it has and the kind of life that they lead.

If we were right when, in the Ethics . . . a mean of the kind attainable by each individual: this passage summarizes much of Aristotle's ethical theory. For the doctrine that the happy life is one of goodness lived in freedom from impediments see, for example, *Nicomachean Ethics* 1153ᵇ9–12 with 1101ᵃ14. For the doctrine that moral virtue or goodness consists in the mean see 1106ᵇ36–1107ᵃ2. It is noteworthy that in the present passage Aristotle concentrates on moral rather than intellectual virtue, since it would appear that a life of moral virtue would be more readily obtainable for most people. For the relation between Aristotle's account of the good life and his political theory see Introduction, pp. xii–xiv.

the same criteria should determine the goodness or badness of the city and that of the constitution: Aristotle may appear to be arguing that since the best life for an individual is one according to virtue and since virtue lies in the mean, a city which is dominated by its middle class must be best. If this was all he had to say his argument would be fallacious, but the rest of the chapter makes it clear that he believes a city whose constitution is dominated by the middle class and which may therefore be seen as lying in the mean will not only avoid dissension, which would make a good life impossible, but will also avoid the vices that are characteristic of states dominated by the rich or the poor.

1295ᵇ *the third class which forms the mean between these two*: in this passage and elsewhere 'mean' and 'middle' serve to translate the same Greek word, *meson*.

1295^b *they are least prone either to refuse office or to seek it*: reading *phugarchousi*, in place of the manuscripts' *philarchousi*, which makes little sense. The sentence has been rejected by some editors, including Dreizehnter, as a later interpolation.

Phocylides: a poet of the sixth century whose work survives only in fragments.

1296^a *those which approximate to them*: e.g. moderate oligarchies.

We shall explain the reason for this later, when we come to treat of the ways in which constitutions change: Book V is devoted to the ways in which constitutions change, but the precise reference is unclear. At V. 10, 1310^b3 Aristotle argues that tyranny is compounded out of extreme democracy and extreme oligarchy; at V. 8, 1308^b19–24 he explains that this is due to the fact that in such extreme forms of constitution individuals have most power.

Solon . . . and most of the other legislators: for Solon, see I. 8, 1256^b32; II. 7, 1266^b17; II. 12, 1273^b33; and the notes to these passages; for Lycurgus, II. 9; for Charondas, see II. 12.

those who have gained the ascendancy in Greece: the reference is to the Athenians, who, of course, favoured democracy, and the Spartans, who favoured oligarchy.

One man, and one only: extensive scholarly discussion has produced no satisfactory explanation of who the one man who favoured a mixed constitution might be. Whereas a number of Greek statesmen from early times to Aristotle's own day (including, for example, Solon and Theramenes) could be said to have favoured the kind of constitution Aristotle admires, none of these could really be said to have had ascendancy in Greece. Aristotle may have hoped to influence Antipater, whom Alexander left in charge of Greece, to favour such constitutions.

CHAPTER 12

1296^b *The next topic to consider . . . what sort of population*: Aristotle now embarks on the third stage of the programme he outlined in Ch. 2, above, 1295^b12–26—that of investigating what sort of constitution suits what sort of citizen body.

the part of a city which wishes a constitution to continue must be stronger than the part which does not: a key theme for this chapter and the one that follows is that the constitution should be acceptable to whatever element is strongest in the city. This has sometimes been seen as implying the germ of a theory of political consent. But Aristotle's point is very different from modern consent theory. Modern consent theory is a theory of political justification—a government has the right to rule if it has the consent of the majority of its subjects. Aristotle's point is purely prudential. Constitutions will not survive unless they have the support of the most powerful (not necessarily the most numerous) element in the city. So the wise legislator will make sure that his constitution does have that support.

Quality and quantity both go to the making of every city: the contrast between quality and quantity and the suggestion that one may be weighed against the other may sound bizarre. Aristotle's point is that a group may owe its political influence either to its numbers or to some special quality it possesses or to a combination of the two. So a small number of rich men may have more influence than a larger number of poor: A constitution must take into account both kinds of factor.

the proportion just described: i.e. when the number of the poor is more than enough to counterbalance the higher quality of the other side.

If, for example . . . the intermediate forms between these: these types of democracy are distinguished in Ch. 6 above.

CHAPTER 13

1297^a *The devices adopted in constitutions*: in this chapter, as in some other passages, it is not clear whether Aristotle is using the Greek word *politeia* to refer to constitutions in general, or whether he is thinking of the so called 'constitutional government' or polity—the moderate constitution which he admires. The 'devices' Aristotle mentions here would, if successful, discourage the participation of the poorest citizens and thus have a moderating influence, but the general purport of the chapter is that a modest but openly avowed property qualification would be preferable.

to decline office on oath: i.e. an oath to the effect that one's wealth or health is inadequate to the performance of the duties of office.

1297^b *the constitution includes not only those who are actually serving as soldiers, but also those who have previously served*: since those serving in the army had to provide their own arms, confining participation to those who serve in the army has the effect of a modest property qualification.

1297^b *We have now explained*: in this paragraph Aristotle claims, with tolerable justification, to have accomplished the first three parts of the programme set out at the end of Ch. 2 above.

CHAPTER 14

1297^b *There are three elements in every constitution*: it is tempting to assume that the threefold division of powers which Aristotle describes here corresponds to Montesquieu's distinction between the legislative, executive, and judicial powers—a distinction which has been of great importance particularly in American constitutional theory and practice. This would be a mistake. As will be seen from the lines which follow, Aristotle, perhaps because he assumes that laws should be permanent (see above, Ch. 4, 1292^{a}7 with note), leaves no clear place for legislation. His deliberative and official elements combine what might seem to us to be executive and judicial functions. It is also worth remembering that the Greeks did not have professional lawyers or judges, so in speaking of the judicial element Aristotle has in mind the element which constitutes the juries used in important trials.

1298^a *calling them to account*: in Athens and elsewhere the requirement that officials undergo a process of examination or scrutiny (*euthuna*) at the end of their periods of office was an important defence against maladministration and incompetence. The body which was entrusted with conducting these examinations would in practice exercise great power.

there are a number of different ways in which all decisions might be given to them: of the systems Aristotle goes on to describe only the last could be said to entrust all decisions to all citizens. The first three would have the effect of giving all citizens some involvement without bestowing all decision-making powers on the citizen body as a whole.

Telecles of Miletus: nothing else is known of this man—not even whether he was a practising statesman or purely a theorist. The variation in which the boards of officials act as the deliberative element is presumably mentioned here because the citizens were appointed in turns to the different offices, so that all would eventually have served for a time on the deliberative body.

extreme democracy: see above, Ch. 4, 1292^{a}15–23; Ch. 5, 1292^{b}7–10; Ch. 6, 1293^{a}30–4.

1298^b *the system, like the previous one, is oligarchic in character*: the difference between these two kinds of oligarchy is not entirely clear. I take it that in the first kind all who have been judged to satisfy the property qualification take part in deliberation while, in the second kind *some* of those who satisfy this qualification are elected to deliberative office.

with equal numbers from each section: Barker found here the germ of the idea of representation. But there is no suggestion that those selected are chosen by the relevant group to speak on their behalf, or that the representatives thus embody the will of those from whom they were chosen.

In constitutional governments they do the reverse of this: i.e. the officials have a right of veto but cannot pass positive measures on their own account. By contrast, Aristotle recommends that oligarchies should give the people the right of veto but not the power to pass positive measures. The underlying thought is presumably that real power rests with the element that can take positive action but that other elements can be allowed to participate by being given a veto.

CHAPTER 15

1299^a *the classification of offices*: 'office' here, as elsewhere, serves as a rather inadequate translation for the Greek *archē*. An *archē* is the position of one who rules. The question 'What is an *archē*?' is thus very similar to our question 'What distinguishes someone who is part of the government of a state from one who is merely a public servant?' The difference is that for us 'the government' suggests a group of people with some kind of organization and a common programme, whereas in Greece those appointed to the various offices might have no particular connection with each other. They need not represent a particular party or share a common programme.

1299^b *spit-hooks*: *obeliskoluchnia*, apparently a device that could be used both as spit (for roasting meat etc.) and as a lampholder.

which matters need the attention of different offices in different places: Barker found here the germ of the idea of local government (something which had been thought foreign to the Greeks). But the idea that the city might delegate responsibility for particular areas to particular officials is quite different from the idea that the inhabitants of an area might exercise a degree of local autonomy.

1299^b *the ordinary council . . . is democratic*: the *boulē* or council was a relatively large body which had the function of overseeing day-to-day matters and preparing business for the assembly. At Athens it had 500 members and was an essential part of the democratic constitution. It is known that a number of Greek cities appointed officials called *probouloi* or 'preliminary councillors', but little is known about them. Athens appointed some officials of this title, apparently as a temporary expedient, after the defeat at Syracuse. It seems that in some other cities they may have been permanent officials. Evidently they would be few in number and could thus act as a restraint on the democratic assembly.

1300^a *we must now attempt to give a full account of the appointment of public officials*: Aristotle now embarks on the ingenious (though one suspects fundamentally flawed) project of enumerating all possible ways of making appointments to political offices and then associating these with different types of constitution. Textually, however, the passage is one of the murkiest in the *Politics*: there appear to be serious errors in the manuscript tradition, which different editors have repaired in different ways. I have followed Dreizehnter's version.

Although the text is obscure, the method Aristotle follows is reasonably clear. In classifying ways of making appointments he considers three questions: Who makes the appointment? Who is eligible for appointment? and What method is used for making the appointment? He suggests that each of these questions may be answered in two possible ways: appointments may be made either by all the citizens or by a section of the citizens; similarly those eligible for office may be either all the citizens or a section of the citizens; and the method used may be either election or lot.

Aristotle then reflects that it is possible to combine these alternatives. Thus all the citizens may make the appointment to some offices while only some of them make the appointments to others; all the citizens may be eligible for some office while only some may be eligible for others; and appointment to some offices may be by lot and to others by election. If these combined processes were all taken into account there would be in all 27 different ways in which appointments could be made to public office. But in fact the only combination Aristotle includes in his classification is that of election with lot. He thus lists 12 possibilities, which may be set out as follows: in the table opposite.

Who makes the appointment?	Who is eligible?	
	All the citizens	Some of the citizens
All the citizens	1. by election 2. by lot 3. by election and lot	4. by election 5. by lot 6. by election and lot
Some of the citizens	7. by election 8. by lot 9. by election and lot	10. by election 11. by lot 12. by election and lot

This leaves a good many puzzles, of which some may be indicated as follows:

(a) Why does Aristotle leave out of his list the combined processes which consist (i) in some appointments being made by all the citizens and others only by some of them, and (ii) in all citizens being eligible for some offices but only some eligible for others? He clearly did not regard these possibilities as insignificant, since a few lines later he suggests that it is characteristic of polities that all citizens should appoint to some offices from all citizens and to others from a section. It looks as though Aristotle's desire to produce a neat and manageable classification may have clouded his judgement.

(b) Why does he not mention the possibility of combining election and lot in appointments to a single office? The Greeks sometimes used a system which involved electing a larger number of candidates than there were places to be filled and then choosing from among these by lot. This could serve to prevent corrupt electoral practices.

(c) When appointments are made by lot the question who makes the appointment seems insignificant. So processes 2 and 8, 5 and 11 do not seem significantly different.

(d) There are other variations in methods of appointment which seem at least equally significant in determining the character of the constitution. For example, Aristotle himself in this very passage distinguishes systems whereby all the citizens are involved in making appointments at the same time and those in which they take it in turns to do so. He regards the former as characteristic of democracy and the latter as characteristic of constitutional government or polity.

1300ᵃ *Of these methods of making appointments two are democratic*: from this point to 1300ᵇ5 the text is very unreliable. Several attempts have been made to reconstruct this passage. They all require substantial emendations and/or rearrangements and none of them produces a version which makes very good sense. It is likely that the text which has come down to us either combines different versions of what Aristotle wrote or incorporates marginal additions by Aristotle or someone else. I have therefore followed Dreizehnter's suggestion and have deleted lines 1300ᵃ38 to 1300ᵇ1. This produces a reasonably intelligible text.

I mean appointing to some offices by lot and to some by election: at this point the manuscript text continues with a passage which may be translated: 'When a section appoints from all and does so using elections for some offices and using the lot or both methods for others (some by lot and some by election), the arrangement is oligarchic. A more oligarchic method is to choose from both. When a section appoints simultaneously both from all and from a section, or appoints some by election and some by lot, the arrangement is characteristic of a constitutional government [or polity] but one leaning towards aristocracy.' This is bracketed by Dreizehnter and certainly seems out of place as it stands. I suspect a marginal note by Aristotle himself or by someone else has become incorporated in the text.

1300ᵇ *a section appoints from all, or all appoint from a section, by the method of election*: reading *to te*, rather than *tote de*.

BOOK V

CHAPTER 1

1301ᵃ *We have now discussed . . . apart from the following*: Aristotle is referring to the programme laid down at the end of Book IV, Ch. 2. He has discussed four of the subjects in the programme. Books V and VI are devoted to the fifth and last topic—the causes of destruction and the methods of preservation of different constitutions. Book V is, in effect, an important treatise on political change. As usual the structure of Aristotle's treatment is a little complicated. Chapters 1–4 deal with general causes of change which apply to all constitutions. Chapters 5–7 deal with the particular causes of change that affect democracies, oligarchies, and aristocracies. Chapters 8 and 9 deal with general methods of preserving constitutions. Chapters 10–11 deal with the causes which destroy and the methods which preserve monarchies. The final chapter, which seems somewhat out of place, lists those tyrannies which have survived for lengthy periods and then criticizes Plato's account of constitutional change in the *Republic*.

already mentioned: III. 9; and 12, 1282^{b}14–27.

factional conflict: this and other phrases incorporating the word 'faction' are used to translate the Greek *stasis*, a key term in this book. Aristotle has in mind a situation of conflict between political groups of a kind which may (but need not) lead to disorder and violence or revolution. The other key term is *metabolē*, which simply means 'change' and which Aristotle uses to refer to any kind of change, whether peaceful or violent, in the political order.

1301^b *Pausanias*: see below, Ch. 7, 1307^{a}4.

equality proportionate to desert: although Aristotle recognizes the existence of numerical equality, it is proportionate equality which matters from the ethical and political point of view. 'true equality is proportionate equality, or in other words an equality of ratios—i.e. equality of the ratio between A's desert and what he gets with the ratio between B's desert and what he gets' (Barker).

1302^a *the form of constitution based on the middle (group of citizens)*: see IV. 11.

CHAPTER 2

1302^a *that number*: the seven main causes are those which intrinsically and of their own nature lead to faction. There are also, however, four other causes, listed in the last sentence of this chapter, which lead to faction incidentally.

1302^b *arrogant behaviour*: *hubris*, a term which has no precise English equivalent. It refers to arrogance as expressed in thought or deed. In this book Aristotle uses it to describe insulting or abusive behaviour, physical assaults, and in some cases what we should now call sexual abuse.

CHAPTER 3

1302^b *'dynastic' oligarchy*: government by a powerful clique. See II. 10, 1272^{b}3 with note.

ostracism: see III.13, 1284^{a}18 with note. The institution was designed primarily as a precaution against tyranny.

1302^b *were being threatened*: in this book there are many references to events, such as the ones mentioned here, about which little or nothing is known apart from what can be gleaned from Aristotle's own text. Only those about which there is something significant to add will be dealt with in the notes.

Oenophyta: Athens defeated Thebes at Oenophyta in 457 BC.

Gelon became tyrant: Gelon, ruler of Gela, was invited to Syracuse by the aristocratic faction in the city. He ruled there as tyrant from 485 till his death in 478. He was succeeded by his brother Hieron, who died in 468 or 467. His successor Thrasybulus was overthrown shortly after taking up office.

twelve inches: more literal translations of the measures given would be 'four cubits' and 'two spans'.

1303^a *Cleomenes*: he was king of Sparta *circa* 519–487. It is not clear exactly who the men of the Seventh' were. They may have been those who fell in a battle on the seventh day of the month.

1303^b *just mentioned*: i.e. divisions caused by difference of territory.

CHAPTER 4

1304^a *captured the city*: the revolt of Mytilene from the Athenian empire in 428 is covered at length by Thucydides (III. 2–50). Thucydides says nothing about disputes over marriage and makes it clear that the Mytilenians had more serious reasons for revolting. It is possible that the events Aristotle describes played some part. But it is difficult to escape the conclusion that here, as in many other passages of this book, Aristotle overemphasizes relatively trivial occasions as opposed to the more fundamental causes of events. In Aristotle's defence one might argue that he is not offering scientific history but practical advice. It makes sense to warn practising politicians who wish to preserve a constitution to be wary of petty incidents which may spark off a revolt.

strengthen once more the cause of democracy: Aristotle (*Constitution of Athens* 23) claims that the Areopagus—a council composed of those who had held the high office of *archōn*—gained authority during the Persian wars, not by any formal decree but because of the leadership they had shown at the time of the battle of Salamis (480 BC). Among other measures they had offered poorer citizens 8 drachmas to act as oarsmen. But Athens' naval success strengthened the democratic tendencies in the state precisely because it would not have been possible without the efforts of these poorer citizens.

1304ª26 *Mantinea*: 418 BC. The Spartans defeated the Argives. This battle of Mantinea is not to be confused with the one in 362 at which the Thebans under Epaminondas defeated the Spartans.

the war against Athens: the reference is to the overwhelming defeat which the Syracusans inflicted on an Athenian expeditionary force in 413 BC. It is not clear from the account of Thucydides (our main source) why the poorer classes should have claimed special credit for this.

1304ᵇ *the Four Hundred*: see *Constitution of Athens* 29–32. In 411 a group under the leadership of Melobius and Pythodorus claimed that Athens might receive support from the Persians for the war with Sparta if it adopted an oligarchic constitution. On this pretext they were able to introduce the regime of the 400. This lasted only four months.

CHAPTER 5

1304ᵇ *trierarchs*: the trierarchs were wealthy citizens who had the task of equipping a naval vessel. When the sums due to them were withheld they were presumably unable or unwilling to pay the contractors whom they had employed to fit out the ships; the latter brought the lawsuits against them.

Megara: it may be significant that Heraclea (on the Black Sea) was a colony of Megara.

1305ª *party of the Plain*: Peisistratus became tyrant of Athens in 560 BC. According to Aristotle (*Constitution of Athens* 13) and Herodotus (I. 59), the citizens were divided between the wealthy party of the Plain, the moderate party of the Shore, and the party of the Hill, which was composed of poorer citizens and was led by Peisistratus. By a ruse Peisistratus persuaded the citizens to grant him a bodyguard, with whose aid he became tyrant. He was twice expelled but each time recovered his position and retained the tyranny until his death in 527. He was succeeded by his son Hippias, who ruled in association with his brother Hipparchus. Hipparchus was assassinated in 514 and the tyranny was finally overthrown in 510.

Dionysius: Dionysius rose to power in Syracuse by attacking the way in which the governing oligarchy (of which Daphnaeus was a leading member) were conducting the war against Carthage. He ruled as tyrant from 405 to 367 and was succeeded by his son Dionysius II, who was eventually expelled in 357.

CHAPTER 6

1305^b *the Thirty at Athens*: when the Spartans defeated Athens in 404 BC. government was put in the hands of 'the thirty tyrants'. Their regime lasted only a few months.

the Four Hundred: the reference is to the regime of the 400 in 411 BC. See above, Ch. 4, 1304^b12, with note.

1306^a *have already been cited*: Ch. 4, 1303^b37–1304^a17.

CHAPTER 7

1306^b *as we have mentioned*: Ch. 6 1305^b2–22.

Spartan peers: the 'peers', *homoioi*, are the full Spartan citizens. The incidents referred to occurred during the first Messenian war (eighth century BC).

Lysander: Lysander was a Spartan commander in the closing stages of the Peloponnesian War and in the period immediately after it. He proposed to make the position of king at Sparta elective.

1307^a *Good Government*: *eunomia*. For the meaning of this term see IV. 8, 1294^a1 ff. Tyrtaeus, who was in effect the national poet of Sparta, wrote during the seventh century. The reference is to the second Messenian War.

Pausanias: he was a Spartan commander in the war against Persia but was later accused of conspiring treacherously with the Persians. In about 471 he was walled up in a sanctuary where he had taken refuge and died of starvation. It is quite likely that, towards the closing stages of his career, he tried to abolish or limit the power of the Ephors.

(the next stage was the outbreak of civil war): something appears to be missing from the text here. The words in square brackets are a guess as to their likely meaning.

CHAPTER 8

1307^b *the methods for preserving constitutions*: the preceding chapters have dealt quite specifically with factors which have led to the overthrow of oligarchies, democracies, and aristocracies. In this chapter and the one which follows Aristotle discusses in a much more general way the causes which lead to the overthrow of these constitutions and, particularly, suggests general rules by which such constitutions might be preserved. Characteristically he lays stress on the need for moderation and education.

the elements of which it is composed are small: the fallacy is, of course, that of supposing that what holds of each member of a group must also hold of all the members of the group taken together. If each member of the Rugby scrum weighs less than fifteen stone it does not follow that the scrum as a whole weighs less than fifteen stone.

1308ᵃ *We have already explained*: IV. 13, 1297ᵃ14–41.

peers: the Greek *homoioi* means literally 'those who are similar' but the term was used of those, particularly in Sparta, who were members of the hereditary ruling class (see Ch. 7 above). It thus has something in common with the English 'peer', which can mean both 'equal' and 'a member of the House of Lords.'

has already been noticed: Ch. 6, 1305ᵇ22–5.

1308ᵇ *in one case*: i.e. when the amount of money in circulation decreases, but the qualification is left unchanged.

in the other: i.e. when the amount of money in circulation increases, but the qualification remains unaltered.

sent out of the country: presumably by ostracism; see third note to 1302ᵇ.

the remedy: i.e. the remedy for the difficulties which the flourishing of such a section may cause.

CHAPTER 9

1309ᵃ *the quality of justice must also have its corresponding varieties*: for the way in which what is just may vary from one constitution to another see III. 9. For the contrast between the just state of affairs and justice as a virtue of character see I. 2.

how is the choice to be made?: these words are bracketed by Dreizehnter as a gloss.

1309ᵇ *may lack self-control*: see *Nicomachean Ethics* book VII. There Aristotle discusses how it is that we can know what would be the right thing to do but fail to do it (for example, because we are overcome by temptation or fear). The same thing could, of course, happen in the political sphere. One could know what is in the public interest and want to do it but fail because, for example, one lacked the necessary courage.

1309^b *those who do not*: on the need for consent see second note to 1296^b.

the mean: as we saw in IV. 11 and 12, Aristotle believes that the best kind of constitution which is generally attainable is a moderate one in which the middle classes are dominant. Such a constitution will be least prone to faction. Not surprisingly he also argues that other forms of constitution will be less prone to faction the more moderate they are.

not a constitution at all: this passage incorporates two very characteristically Aristotelian patterns of argument: (1) Constitutions, like natural beings and artefacts, exist for the sake of an end. To the extent that they fail to achieve that end they will be deviant constitutions. But if they fail to achieve it at all they will not even count as constitutions. (2) It is generally possible to deviate from the correct standard in either of two opposing directions. Thus the good state lies in a mean. So just as virtue in the individual is a state of choice lying in the mean, so a constitution will be better to the extent that it approximates to the mean.

1310^a *the education of citizens*: for the importance of education see IV. 11, 1295^{b}13–19; VIII.1.

peculiarly democratic: see IV. 14, 1298^{b}13–19, which makes it clear that Aristotle has in mind the kind of 'extreme' democracy in which the will of the people is above the law.

chances to desire: it is not known from which of Euripides' lost plays this comes.

but rather as salvation: here Aristotle, in effect, claims that the democrat slips from a positive conception of liberty as the sovereignty of the masses, to a negative conception in which it is the ability to do as one likes. The founding principle of democracy is that all should be equal and that the population as a whole should be sovereign. This yields one sense of liberty. But, as Aristotle is clearly aware, this is not necessarily consistent with the idea that liberty is the ability to do whatever one wants. The point he stresses is that freedom to do as one wants, far from strengthening the sovereignty of the people, may in fact do the reverse. A similar point has been made from the opposite direction by those who argue that popular sovereignty need not necessarily mean individual liberty since a majority of the population may vote to curtail the liberties of a minority. There is another discussion of these two conceptions of liberty at VI. 2,

1317^a40–^b17, where liberty is linked with the idea of ruling and
being ruled. Barker here raises the question 'What is Aristotle's
own conception of liberty?' and cites with approval the views of
Newman. The latter quotes *Metaphysics* 1075^a18, where Aristotle claims that in a household the freeman has less opportunity
to do what he likes than a slave or a beast, and suggests that
Aristotle would define freedom as obedience to rightly constituted law. But Newman's view may be too heavily influenced by
nineteenth-century political thought. Aristotle's conception of
liberty is bound up with the status of a freeman as opposed to a
slave. The freeman rules and has the rational capacities needed
for ruling. In exercising those capacities he will no doubt be
obeying rightly constituted law but it is his exercise of rational
choice that constitutes his freedom.

CHAPTER 10

1310^a *a monarchy*: a monarchy in Aristotle's usage may be either a
kingship or a tyranny. It is therefore a wider term than 'kingship'.

1310^b *Tyranny is a compound of the extreme forms of oligarchy
and democracy*: the sense in which tyranny is a combination
of oligarchy and democracy is explained below, 1311^a8–21.

'*craftsmen' and 'overseers*': these terms were used to describe the
holders of certain offices in some cities. See III. 2, 1275^b29, with
note.

Codrus: this reference has caused some puzzlement since, according to legend, Codrus was already king of Athens when he saved
the city by sacrificing his own life. Aristotle may be following a
different tradition or he may, rather loosely, be taking Codrus'
self-sacrifice as evidence that the royal family had the capacity
to benefit the citizens.

Cyrus: Cyrus the Great of Persia (d. 530 BC) is credited with
freeing his country from the Medes.

1311^a *the aim of a king is the Good*: the king as aiming for the good: III. 7.

Periander: see III. 13, 1284^a26–33, with note.

Harmodius and Aristogeiton: these were honoured as tyranni-
cides, but, in fact, all they did was to kill Hipparchus the son of
Peisistratus. His brother Hippias remained in power until he was
deposed by the Spartans (a fact the Athenians naturally preferred
to forget).

388

1311ᵇ   *Philip*: the king of Macedon who was assassinated in 336. The reference shows that this part of the *Politics*, at least, was written in the last period of Aristotle's life.

Euripides . . . breath: the Athenian tragic poet spent the last months of his life in Macedon. This incident does not reflect well on his character.

1312ᵃ   *Dion*: the friend of Plato who led an expedition against the younger Dionysius in 356. He succeeded in overthrowing the tyrant but was himself assassinated.

1312ᵇ   *potter quarrels with potter*: Hesiod, *Works and Days* 25; Aristotle's point is that, because extreme democracy and tyranny have similar aims (to rule in their own interest untrammelled by law), they quarrel in the same way that rival craftsmen do.

Gelon: see sixth note to 1302ᵇ.

Peisistratus' family: see above, 1311ᵃ39, with note.

divided tyrannies: i.e. these constitutions are like tyrannies in which power is shared among many individuals.

CHAPTER 11

1313ᵃ   *Theopompus . . . Ephor*: a king of Sparta around the end of the eighth and the beginning of the seventh century BC. For the Ephors see II. 9.

Tyrannies can be preserved in two ways: some readers have been disturbed by what they take to be Aristotle's willingness to give advice on the preservation of tyranny, a form of government which he regards as so deviant that it does not really count as a constitution. But this is the result of over-literal interpretation. The first method he describes is for the tyrant to turn his city into what we would now call a police state. Although this may be a way of preserving tyranny Aristotle clearly does not endorse it. Indeed his remarks have the effect of a powerful condemnation of tyranny. The second method, which presumably Aristotle would endorse, is to moderate the tyranny so that it becomes more like a kingship, i.e. to modify it so that it approximates to one of the 'right' forms of constitution.

the removal of men of spirit: see III. 13, 1284ᵃ26–30, with note.

1313ᵇ   *Hieron*: see above, Ch. 3, 1302ᵇ32, with note.

Cypselus: tyrant of Corinth c.655–c.625, father of Periander.

Polycrates: tyrant of Samos in the second half of the sixth century.

Dionysius: see above, Ch. 5, 1305ª26, with note.

1314ª *almost the very reverse*: the first method is, in effect, to make the subjects incapable of rebelling. The second method is to ensure by exercising a benevolent rule, that they have no desire to do so. Several of the Greek tyrants were, in fact, generally acknowledged to have been good rulers.

1314ᵇ *contributions*: liturgies: see IV. 4, 1291ª34, with note.

1315ª *to pay the price of life*: a slightly inaccurate quotation of Heraclitus fragment 85 (Diels Kranz).

CHAPTER 12

1315ᵇ *Yet no constitutions . . . as oligarchy and tyranny*: this chapter is in the nature of a digression, and it is a curious mixture of criticism of Plato with chronological and other details about tyranny. 'It seems', as Newman says, 'too characteristic of Aristotle not to be his'; but it also seems to contain a number of jottings rather than a sustained argument. On some points of historical fact (e.g. in regard to the change at Syracuse on Gelon's death, and the general constitution of Syracuse) it does not square with statements in other parts of the *Politics*. In any case the abrupt termination of the chapter, almost in the middle of the sentence, suggests that it is unfinished (Barker).

Orthagoras and his descendants: the tyranny at Sicyon was apparently established in the early seventh century.

the family of Cypselus: see second note to 1313ᵇ; for Periander see III. 13, 1284ª26–30, with note.

the family of Peisistratus: see above, Ch. 5, 1305ª24, with note, and Ch. 10, 1311ª39, with note.

Hieron and Gelon: see above, Ch. 3, 1302ᵇ32, with note.

Tyrannies generally have all been quite short-lived: it is curious that this list omits any mention of tyrannies after about 450 BC. Some of these (e.g. that of Dionysius the elder and his son at Syracuse, which Aristotle has referred to several times in earlier chapters) had been quite durable.

1316ª *'Socrates' in the Republic*: in books VIII and IX of the *Republic* Socrates, having described his ideal city, proceeds to describe four inferior forms of constitution: the Spartan and Cretan form, which he calls 'timocracy', oligarchy, democracy, and tyranny. In each case he also describes a corresponding kind of individual. He tells how each of these constitutions develops out of the one before. Aristotle criticizes this account as though it was meant literally to present a historical sequence. But this cannot be what Plato intended for it would have been as obvious to him as it was to Aristotle that constitutions did not necessarily evolve from one another in this order. Plato was clearly using an imaginary historical development as a means of displaying the psychological and moral relationships between the constitutions.

1316ᵃ *in which the root ratio . . . furnishes two harmonical progressions*: *Republic* 546c: according to 'Socrates', the ideal state, although more stable than any other form, eventually declines when the rulers make a mistake in calculating 'the nuptial number' and thus in the mating arrangements of the guardians. As a result inferior offspring are produced. The account of the number is clearly not meant to be taken seriously, but Plato is undoubtedly serious in believing that the universe has a mathematical basis.

all things that come into existence: Aristotle is interpreting in an over-literal sense the remark (*Republic* 456a) that since everything which comes into being must decay, the ideal city must eventually be destroyed. This is clearly not intended to imply that the passing of time in itself causes the city to decline.

from oligarchy to tyranny: in the *Republic*'s account, oligarchy leads to democracy.

1316ᵇ *equal shares in the city*: again Aristotle is being unfair to Plato. According to the *Republic*'s account, timarchy (the Spartan form of constitution) originates when people accumulate private wealth and then pass a law imposing a property qualification for those who would hold office (550e–551b). There is nothing in this inconsistent with Aristotle's own view.

at Carthage, although it is democratically governed, profit-making is common: if the text is sound here the point is presumably that there is no necessary connection between oligarchy and profit-making. But the description of Carthage as democratically governed does not square well with the account in II. 11.

BOOK VI

CHAPTER 1

1316^b *we have discussed*: see IV. 14–16.

the circumstances and causes which lead to the destruction and preservation of the different constitutions: from the problems of the destruction and preservation of constitutions as they stand, Aristotle turns here to the problem of the construction of constitutions in a way that will enable them to stand more securely. He has already discussed, at the end of Book IV, the proper structure of each of the three powers (deliberative, executive, and judicial); and he now promises to discuss the proper structure of the whole constitution, with reference to each type of constitution and the varieties of each type—varieties which have already been described in IV. 4–6. We may add that the general programme stated at the end of IV. 2, which has been followed through the whole of Books IV and V, is now left, and a new programme is started. Book VI may thus be regarded as a separate section or 'method'; and in its course, accordingly, Aristotle more than once refers back to Books IV and V as 'the previous section' (Barker).

1317^a *We have already explained*: the reference is to IV. 12.

already been mentioned: see, in particular, IV. 4, 1291^b13–27; IV. 6, 1292^b22–1293^a10; IV. 12, 1296^b24–34.

as we have already noted: see V. 9, where Aristotle argues that pushing democracy to the extreme tends to destroy it.

CHAPTER 2

1317^b *Liberty in one of its forms consists in the interchange of ruling and being ruled*: Aristotle here distinguishes two different arguments for democracy which involve different ideas of liberty. The first argument starts from the assumption that all should be equal and that everyone should therefore have an equal share of power. It thus leads to the idea that the will of the majority should be sovereign. The second starts from the idea that liberty is the ability to do what one wants. Where this is not possible a situation in which all have an equal share in decision-making is seen as the next best thing. Both arguments, it seems, lead to the democratic conception of liberty as ruling and being ruled. Aristotle makes a similar distinction between conceptions of liberty at V. 9, 1310^a29–35. He there makes clear his own disapproval of the idea of liberty as doing what you want. For the idea of ruling and being ruled see III. 4, 1277^{b}7–30.

1317^b *the Council*: the Council (*Boulē*) at Athens consisted of 500 members chosen by lot and paid for attendance. It prepared business for the assembly, managed the revenues and discharged other executive functions.

the previous section of our inquiry: IV. 15, 1299^{b}36–1300^{a}4; the word translated 'section' is *methodos*.

It may be ... vulgarity: these words seem out of place and are bracketed by Dreizehnter and other editors.

1318^a *There would be ... on a numerical basis*: cf. the (verbally very similar) account of the 'first' form of democracy in IV. 4, 1291^b 29–38.

CHAPTER 3

1318^a *Should the assessed ... equal (voting) power?*: the Greek here is extremely cryptic and makes little sense without some supplementation. However, it is clear that Aristotle is envisaging that the citizens be divided into two sections according to their wealth. In his imaginary example there are 500 citizens in the wealthier section and 1,000 in the poorer. The votes of each block will have equal weight in decision-making. So using the figures from Aristotle's imaginary example, the votes of the 1,000 poorer citizens will have the same collective weight as those of the 500 who are better off, though considered individually the votes of those in the wealthier group will have twice the weight of those in the poorer. It is not clear whether the two blocks will meet together or separately.

Or, alternatively ... given control of the elections and the law-courts?: here again Aristotle envisages a division of the citizens into two blocks according to their property. But, on this system, instead of each of the blocks voting as a whole when decisions are to be taken, they each elect an equal number of representatives. Thus each block will again have equal weight.

as we have already noted: III. 10, 1281^{a}15–17.

In that case we may attribute sovereignty to the will of a majority of those who are also the owners of a majority of property: Aristotle's suggestion differs from the democracy in giving weight to property. But, equally, it differs from oligarchy in taking account of the property of the poor and not simply confining all decision-making powers to those who have more than some fixed quantity of property.

CHAPTER 4

1318ᵇ *in the previous section of our inquiry*: IV. 4, 1291ᵇ29–36; IV. 6, 1292ᵇ24–32; IV. 15, 1299ᵇ32, with note.

do not: Dreizehnter and some other editors have bracketed the negative in this sentence without greatly improving the sense. It is not, however, difficult to see what Aristotle must have in mind. As the passages from IV. 4 and IV. 11 cited in the previous note make clear, the farmers have what they need provided that they work for it. Thus (unlike the rich) they do not have much time for politics, but (unlike the poor) they do not envy the possessions of others.

1319ᵃ *participation in politics*: the point would appear to be that, although ownership of land was an essential condition of participation in politics, the amount of land required was set very low. The amount required was only a fraction of one of the lots into which the territory of the city had originally been divided.

1319ᵇ *a progressively inferior class*: Aristotle expresses himself very curiously. The point is that the lower the qualification is set, the greater the inferiority of those who are excluded.

in the main, described: in Book v, especially Chs. 5 and 9.

CHAPTER 5

1319ᵇ *The maintenance of a constitution is what really matters*: the main theme of Book VI so far has been how to construct democracies and Aristotle goes on, in Chs. 6–8, to discuss the construction of oligarchies. In this chapter he turns aside to discuss the preservation of democracies. The preservation of constitutions was of course one of the main themes of Book v, but, although Chs. 8 and 9 of that book gave general advice about the preservation of constitutions they gave no specific advice about how to preserve democracies or oligarchies.

1320ᵇ *The ideal method . . . in commerce or agriculture*: the idea that the city should provide a living for its poorer citizens by distributing public revenues was accepted by moderates as well as by extreme democrats (Austin and Vidal-Naquet, 119–20). The suggestion that such distributions should be made in such a way as to help those receiving them to become self-supporting was not original: Aristotle ascribes something similar to Peisistratus (*Constitution of Athens* 16). Helping poorer citizens to become farmers would encourage the kind of agricultural democracy which Aristotle prefers.

1320^b *useless public services*: the reference is to 'liturgies', perhaps including ones such as the equipping of choruses at dramatic festivals.

CHAPTER 6

1320^b *each should be compared with the variety of democracy opposed to it*: the point seems to be that oligarchy and democracy both deviate from 'constitutional government' but in opposite directions. So the different forms of oligarchy are, as it were, mirror images of the different forms of democracy. The first and best forms of each are not very different from 'constitutional government' and hence are quite close together. The most extreme forms are farthest from 'constitutional government', but in opposite directions.

CHAPTER 7

1321^a *four kinds of military forces*: this chapter begins as a discussion of the military system proper to oligarchies, but then returns to the theme of the previous chapter—the constitutional method which should be followed in constructing a good form of oligarchy. The connection between the two parts is that military tactics have an important influence on the way in which oligarchies (or indeed other forms of constitution) can be constructed. For the ways in which, so Aristotle believes, military tactics affect constitutional matters, see IV. 3, 1289^b36–9; IV. 13, 1297^b12–28.

CHAPTER 8

1321^b *in a previous passage*: the reference is to IV. 15, which superficially, at least, appears to cover much the same ground as the present chapter, but the approach is very different. In IV. 15 the arrangement of offices is considered in a highly abstract and formal way, whereas this chapter is based on an analysis of existing Greek practice. Most of the offices mentioned here existed at Athens. Their functions and mode of appointment are described in *Constitution of Athens* 43 ff.

1322ᵃ *the custody of prisoners*: prisoners might be held while awaiting trial or sentence but imprisonment as a punishment in itself was not normal in Greece.

the Eleven at Athens: according to *Constitution of Athens* 52, the Eleven were chosen by lot and had the responsibility of looking after the state prison. 'They punish with death the robbers, kidnappers, and thieves who are brought before them, in case they confess; but if they deny the charge they bring them before the lawcourt. If they are acquitted they let them go, and if they are not acquitted, they have them executed.'

1322ᵇ *Preliminary Councillors*: for the nature and functions of the councillors and pre-councillors see IV. 15, 1299ᵇ32, with note.

in others king: in some cities, including Athens, the title of king (*basileus*) was given to an official who carried out public religious functions (presumably those which had been carried out by the king himself in the days of monarchy). See *Constitution of Athens* 55 and 57.

classified on the basis of their various functions: earlier in the chapter Aristotle has classified the various offices in order of importance. He now classifies them into four groups according to the subjects for which they had responsibility.

BOOK VII

CHAPTER 1

1323ᵃ *most to be desired*: the opening words of this book are identical (albeit in a slightly different order) with the fragmentary closing sentence of Book III, 1288ᵇ5–6. See the note on that passage.

for those in their circumstances: it is not clear why the qualification 'in their circumstances' is added here. Elsewhere Aristotle distinguishes between the constitution that is best absolutely and the one that is best given particular conditions. The account of the ideal city which he is about to give presupposed the best possible conditions and would therefore seem to be best absolutely.

in works intended for the general public: literally 'in the exoteric discourses'. Jaeger suggested that the passage which follows was derived from the *Protrepticus*, which was intended to advertise

the advantages of the philosophic life. It certainly has the appro-
priate character, though this does not mean that this part of the
Politics as a whole was composed at the same time as the
Protrepticus (around 351/50).

1323ᵃ *goods of the soul*: the distinction between these three kinds of
good and the superiority of the goods of the soul (which are
taken to consist in the virtues) is a commonplace of Platonic and
Aristotelian philosophy. See *Nicomachean Ethics* 1098ᵇ12–15
and Plato: *Euthydemus* 279a–b, *Philebus* 48e, *Laws* 743e.

courage, temperance, justice, or wisdom: the standard list of
Greek virtues; see e.g. Plato, *Republic* 427e.

coveted without limit: as elsewhere, Aristotle argues that what is
sought as an end has no limit (i.e. that you cannot have too
much of it) whereas there is a limit to what is sought merely as a
means. See, for example, I. 8, 1256ᵇ29–39; I. 8, 1257ᵇ24–30.

1323ᵇ *to predicate 'value'*: the contrast here is between saying that
something is *chrēsimon* (useful) and saying that it is *kalon*. The
latter term is perhaps the strongest term of approval in Greek
but has no real equivalent in English. It is variously translated
'beautiful', 'fine', 'noble', 'good', or 'honourable'. Here the real
contrast is between what is truly valuable in itself and what is
merely useful. See *Eudemian Ethics* 1248ᵇ18–22: '... all goods
have ends that are desirable in and for themselves. Of these all
those are fine (*kalon*) which are laudable as existing for their
own sakes, for these are the ends which are both the motives of
laudable actions and laudable in themselves—justice itself and
its actions, and temperate actions, for temperance is also laudable; but health is not laudable for its effect, nor is vigorous
action laudable, for strength is not—these things are good but
they are not laudable. And similarly induction makes this clear
in the other cases also. Therefore a man is good for whom the
things good by nature are good. For the things men fight about
and think the greatest, honour and wealth and bodily excellences
and pieces of good fortune and powers, are good by nature, but
may possibly be harmful to some men owing to their characters'
(translated by H. Rackham).

the things of which they are states differ: i.e. if A is more valuable
than B then the best state of A is more valuable than the best
state of B.

any external good: Aristotle argues in the *Ethics* that happiness
must be perfect and self-sufficient: i.e. there is nothing more that

the happy man requires and he does not depend on anything outside him for his happiness. The happy man thus approximates to a god-like state, for God, of course, lacks nothing and is not dependent on anything else.

from chance or by chance: for the claim that happiness cannot be a gift of fortune see *Nicomachean Ethics* I. 9 and 10.

To do well is impossible . . . in the absence of goodness and wisdom: this argument is very characteristic of Greek ethics. From our point of view it may look invalid because it seems to rest on an equivocation between two senses of 'doing well', one in which to do well is to be happy and another in which it means to do good deeds. But for Aristotle happiness (*eudaimonia*) is living well and thus consists in virtuous activity: see Introduction, pp.xii–xiii. Thus from Aristotle's point of view the argument is truistic.

CHAPTER 2

1324ᵃ *released from the ties of the political association*: Aristotle does, of course, regard a social life as necessary if a human being is to achieve his greatest good. See, for example, I. 2, 1253ᵃ2– 19; *Nicomachean Ethics* I. 7, 1097ᵇ8–15; VIII. 12, 1162ᵃ16–18; IX. 9.

worthy of a philosopher: this question is addressed in VII. 14, 1333ᵃ 16–30, with note. See also *Nicomachean Ethics* X. 7 and 8.

1324ᵇ *both constitution and laws must conform*: those who favour an active life are thus divided into those who believe happiness consists in the political life (the life of the active citizen) and those who believe happiness consists in exercising despotic rule (the kind of rule a master exercises over slaves). For this distinction see I. 2, 1252ᵃ7–17.

with a general view to war: VII. 14, 1333ᵇ4–1334ᵃ10; VII. 4, 1338ᵇ9–38.

lawful: nomima. Clearly 'lawful' here does not mean 'in accordance with the law currently in force' for then the lawmaker could not act unlawfully. This is thus one of the passages in which Aristotle appears to commit himself to something like a natural law theory.

any attempt to establish control should be confined to the elements meant for control, and not extended to all: a reference to Aristotle's own doctrine of natural slavery: see I. 5.

1325ᵃ *at a later stage*: VII. 13 and 14.

CHAPTER 3

1325ᵃ *Two different schools of opinion have thus to be discussed*:
Aristotle here identifies one of the fundamental problems of
his moral and political theories. Is the good life to be identified
with the life of active virtue (as exemplified by the statesman) or
with the life of intellectual virtue exemplified by the contemplative philosopher? In the rest of the chapter Aristotle seeks to
assimilate the two views by (*a*) distinguishing the life of a
statesman in a constitutional system who in turn is both ruler
and a subject from that of the despotic ruler, and (*b*) arguing
that the philosophic life is active because it involves intellectual
activity. These points do not entirely solve the problem because
it might still be argued that the two lives are incompatible. It
would appear that Aristotle probably means to argue that the
two kinds of activity can be combined in a single life providing
we properly understand their character, but there are those who
hold that Aristotle believed that in the last resort philosophy
and statesmanship are incompatible. See Depew, 'Politics, Music
and Contemplation in Aristotle's Ideal State'.

fine things: the word is *kalon*; see first note to 1323ᵇ.

highest and best: this translates the single word *kallista*, the
superlative of *kalon*.

1325ᵇ *in his transgression*: in other words, the one who domi-
nates others unjustly is not acting in accordance with virtue
(i.e. he is not displaying goodness of character). Hence he
cannot be happy as Aristotle understands happiness.

prime authors: *architektones*. The *architektōn* is literally the
master-craftsman who directs an operation, and whose thought
is embodied in what is done. Aristotle is seeking to diminish the
contrast between the contemplative and the active life by arguing
that it is primarily in thinking that we are active.

CHAPTER 4

1326ᵃ *fineness of form*: *kalon*.

the principle just mentioned: i.e. the principle that good order
requires a limit on size.

1,200 feet long: the measurements are literally 'a span' and 'two
stades'. It would be interesting to know what Aristotle would
make of a modern supertanker.

1326ᵇ *Stentor's voice*: according to Homer (*Iliad* v. 785), Stentor had a voice as loud as fifty men.

undetected among the crowd: this chapter indicates very strikingly some of the major differences between the Greek *polis*, which depended on face-to-face contact and personal knowledge, and modern states. It is notable that Aristotle expects citizens to draw on their personal knowledge of those involved in electing officials and settling legal disputes. Without this kind of personal knowledge constitutional rule as Aristotle understands it is impossible.

CHAPTER 5

1326ᵇ *at a later stage of the argument*: this promise is not fulfilled but the matter is discussed in I. 8, 1256ᵇ26–34 and II. 6, 1265ᵃ 28–38.

CHAPTER 6

1327ᵇ *of active relations with other cities*: literally 'a political life', i.e. a life which involves relations with other states in much the same way in which an individual who lives an active political life must relate to his fellow citizens.

CHAPTER 7

1327ᵇ *what sort of natural endowment they ought to have*: literally 'what sort of people ought they to be by nature'. For the concept of *phusis* or nature, see Introduction, pp.vii–viii.

subjects and slaves: Aristotle is, in effect, attempting a scientific justification for the belief in the superiority of Greeks over barbarians. See I. 2, 1252ᵇ5–9; I. 6, 1255ᵃ32–4.

political unity: there is presumably a reference here to the Macedonian policy of uniting the Greeks under Macedonian leadership for the conquest of Asia. According to Plutarch (*Moralia* 329b), Aristotle advised Alexander to behave towards Greeks as a leader but towards barbarians as a master.

stern to all who are unknown: in the *Republic* 'Socrates' is made to distinguish between three elements in the soul—reason, spirit, and desire. The reference in this passage is to 375a–376b, where he compares guardians' guard-dogs. He says that the dogs are hostile to strangers but does not, in fact, suggest that the guardians should be—once more Aristotle's reading of Plato is, by our standards, careless and unsympathetic.

1328ᵃ *thine own friends*: Archilochus was a poet of the seventh century.

as they have loved: the first of these passages is attributed to Euripides by Plutarch; the author of the second is unknown.

CHAPTER 8

1328ᵃ *as in other natural compounds*: for compounds and wholes see III. 1, 1274ᵇ38-41, with note, and I. 1, 1252ᵃ18-23, with note.

we cannot regard the elements which are necessary for the exist-ence of the city . . . as being 'parts' of the city or of any other such association: for the distinction between parts of the city and necessary conditions of its existence see III. 5, 1278ᵃ2, with note. The distinction is very important for the development of Aristo-tle's ideal since it enables him to leave out of account the large numbers who must inevitably be engaged in what he calls 'banausic' activities.

animate beings: particularly slaves.

1328ᵇ *different constitutions*: as Barker points out, we might here expect Aristotle to argue that since not all men can share in happiness it is not possible for them all to be part of the best state. The conclusion actually drawn is dif-ferent. Arguing that different people share differently in happiness, Aristotle concludes that different peoples must develop different ways of life and must therefore (as a con-stitution is 'a way of life') have different constitutions. This might suggest a line of thought very different from the one Aristotle actually pursues. If different people can achieve their happiness in different ways, one might argue that the ideal state is one in which many different kinds of life are possible and in which everyone in the population has the chance to achieve his or her own form of happiness.

how many elements it must contain: this classification of services or functions to be performed may be compared with the parts of the city listed in IV. 4 as preparation for the discussion of the different types of democracy. The main differences between the two lists are (*a*) that here the deliberative and judicial functions are combined, with nothing being said about the executive, and (*b*) that the list in IV. 4 includes the marketing and labouring elements which are part of the democratic state but not of Aristotle's ideal.

CHAPTER 9

1328^b *as we have noted*: possibly a reference to the immediately preceding passage or to IV. 4, 1291^b3–6.

as we have already stated: cf. VII. 1, 1323^b29–36.

1329^a *to all the citizens*: this passage is, no doubt, intended as a criticism of Plato's *Republic*, where the guardians are forbidden to have property. Aristotle assumes (probably wrongly) that Plato would justify this by saying that there was no need for the citizens to be happy. See II. 5, 1264^b15–24, with note.

CHAPTER 10

1329^b *the projection of Europe*: i.e. what we might think of as the toe of modern Italy.

an indefinite number: cf. II. 5, 1264^a1–5.

1330^a *as friends treat their belongings*: see II. 5, 1263^a26–40.

at a later point: an unfulfilled promise.

each individual receiving a plot in either section: it is notable that Aristotle criticized Plato (in the *Laws*) for making this very proposal; see II. 6, 1265^b24–6.

a matter which we shall discuss later: this promise, too, is not fulfilled.

CHAPTER 11

1330^b *Hippodamus*: see II. 8.

the logic of fact: in the *Laws* 778^d–779^a, Plato had praised the Spartans for refusing to build walls round their city. But Sparta had been unable to resist the Thebans after the battle of Leuctra (371).

CHAPTER 13

1331^b *the constitution itself*: in this context 'the constitution' refers not just to the organization of offices in the city but to its way of life. See III. 6, 1278^b10–11, with note.

1332^a *happiness is 'the complete actualization and practice of goodness, in an absolute rather than a conditional sense'*: Aristotle comes close to this formulation in *Eudemian Ethics* II. 1, 1219^a38–^b2, but the same basic point is made many times in the *Nicomachean Ethics*; see, e.g. I. 6, 1098^a16–17. The meaning of the qualification 'in an absolute sense' is explained in the lines that follow. Some things may be good only in less than ideal circumstances. They are not therefore unconditionally good. See first note to VII. 1, 1323^b.

1332^a *the opposites (of these evils)*: in other words you can only attain absolute goodness (and thus absolute happiness) if you have the requisite health, wealth, etc.

our arguments on ethics: Eudemian Ethics VIII. 15, 1248^{b}26 (quoted in the first note to 1323^b above). See also *Magna Moralia* II. 9, 1207^{b}31 ff.

1332^b *in an earlier chapter*: VII. 7.

CHAPTER 14

1332^b *sufficient in number to overcome all these*: i.e. if the constitution allows one group to rule permanently over another even though they are really of the same quality, the group in the inferior position will join forces with the serfs to overthrow the constitution.

we have already discussed: VII. 9, 1328^{b}40–1329^{a}1–17.

1333^a *in our first part*: III. 4, 1277^{a}26–^{b}6; III. 6, 1278^{b}33–7; VII. 3, 1325^{a}16–30.

It is not the inherent nature of actions, but the end or object for which they are done, which make one action differ from another in the way of honour or dishonour: cf. VIII. 2, 1337^{b}4–22. Elsewhere Aristotle's position seems to be that there are some kinds of activity which are intrinsically demeaning or which cannot be engaged in without harm, so it looks as though the point he makes here is intended to apply to only some actions. See e.g. III. 5. If one recognizes that any action can be honourable if done for the right end one can argue that it is not manual work as such but the condition of slavery or wage labour that is demeaning.

We have said that . . . the same person who begins by being ruled must later be a ruler: III. 4, 1277^{b}7–16.

that which is worse always exists for the sake of that which is better: this, of course, makes sense if one takes for granted Aristotle's teleological view of nature. But one cannot apply this principle unless one has some way of telling what is better and what is worse. In the present passage Aristotle seems simply to assume that the rational element in the soul is better than the irrational and that speculative reason is better than practical reason.

partly practical, partly speculative: in *Nicomachean Ethics* I. 13 Aristotle distinguishes the part of the soul which is intrinsically rational from a part which is not rational in itself but is capable of obeying reason. The virtues of the latter are the moral virtues such as courage and temperance which consist in feeling emotions or passions to the degree that reason would direct. In *Nicomachean Ethics* VI. 1, he divides the intrinsically rational part of the soul into two faculties. The higher of these is that which enables us to contemplate those things whose principles are invariable. With the lower part we contemplate those things whose principles are variable (i.e. we think about the world of change in which we live). Corresponding to this distinction is a division between the activity, on the one hand, of the philosopher, who engages in abstract speculation and that of the man of practical wisdom.

1333^b *rule his own city*: if one assumes (*a*) that whatever way of life is good for the state is also good for the individual and (*b*) that the best life for the state is to rule despotically over other states, it would appear to follow that the best way of life for the individual is one in which he rules despotically over his fellow citizens. See VII. 3, 1325^{a}16–21.

CHAPTER 15

1334^a *work*: I have used 'work' here to translate *ascholia*, which means literally an absence of leisure (*scholē*). It does not necessarily apply to physical work, still less to paid employment, but could apply to any activity which one undertakes as a matter of necessity and as a means to some other goal. Conversely 'leisure' (*scholē*) does not mean inactivity, but rather engaging in an activity that is good for its own sake and is thus an end rather than a means. Both leisure and work can be contrasted with amusement and relaxation, which enable us to rest and prepare for new activities.

1334^b *cultivated*: evidently some words have been lost from the text here. The passage in square brackets represents Newman's conjectural restoration.

natural endowment, habit, and reason: VII. 13, 1332^{a}40–^{b}10.

1334^b *we have already determined*: VII. 7.

CHAPTER 16

1335^a *the response once given by the oracle to the people of Troezen*: 'Plough not the young fallow.'

at 37 or thereabouts: it was normal Greek practice for there to be this kind of discrepancy between the ages of marriage partners. Aristotle justifies it on biological grounds but it would, of course, have the effect of ensuring that the woman was very much the subordinate partner.

1335^b *plants draw on the soil*: Aristotle's view is that the sperm is like the seed of, a plant, while the mother's womb is like the soil in which the plant grows. Thus the child derives its form entirely from its father though the mother provides the matter. Since the mind is form rather than matter Aristotle's eugenics requires that the father's mind be in the best possible condition, whereas the condition of the mother's mind is of no direct importance. Here again Aristotelian biology reinforces the inferiority of women.

render public service: literally 'perform liturgies'.

CHAPTER 17

1336^a *in their Laws*: apparently a reference to Plato, *Laws* 792a.

1336^b *to recline at the common tables*: the Greeks normally reclined on couches while dining but the younger men would be expected to sit on chairs.

indecent speeches: presumably in the theatre. Barker commented that Aristotle moves here from the idea of protecting children to the general idea of censorship for old as well as young and 'takes this in his stride with little or no regard to our modern idea of the artist's freedom or to general freedom of thought'. It is true that Aristotle is not concerned to defend freedom of expression but the restrictions he proposes are in fact very modest and he does not attempt to restrict the freedom of speculative thought.

as well as for themselves: i.e. the wives and children do not need to attend such rites themselves.

iambics: verses in the iambic metre were declaimed at festivals of Dionysus and were thus associated with ribaldry and abuse.

BOOK VIII

CHAPTER 1

1337ª *All would agree that the legislator should make the education of the young his chief and foremost concern*: it is not clear that all would agree with this since, as Aristotle himself admits, many cities treat education as a matter of purely private concern. But it was argued in v. 9, 1310ª12–22 that the right kind of education is needed in order to preserve a constitution. Moreover, Aristotle has defined a constitution not just as an organization of offices but also as prescribing the end which the association pursues, IV. 1, 1289ª15–18, and as the way in which a city lives, IV. 11, 1295ª40. On this conception he, like Plato, can hardly avoid seeing education as a vital part of the constitution.

we must rather regard every citizen as belonging to the city, since each is a part of the city: Aristotle has given two reasons for his claim that education should be a matter of public action: that the city has a common end and that the citizens do not belong to themselves but are part of a larger whole. As Barker points out, this connects his views on education to two of his key doctrines, his doctrine of ends, and his doctrine of wholes. The suggestion that individuals do not belong to themselves but to the city echoes Plato's *Laws* 923a. This passage brings out particularly clearly the conflict between Aristotle's theory and liberal ideas of freedom and individuality.

CHAPTER 2

1337ᵇ *A good deal depends on the purpose for which acts are done or subjects are studied*: Aristotle makes it clear that his objection to banausic activities rests very largely on the idea that they involve working for someone else in a servile or quasi-servile position. Marxists would, of course, argue that the way to solve the problem is not by excluding manual workers from citizenship but by abolishing wage labour.

CHAPTER 3

1337ᵇ *two different points of view*: i.e. they may be seen either as supporting the view that subjects ought to be taught for their usefulness or as supporting the view that the aim ought to be goodness of character. The reference is to the first paragraph of VIII. 2.

1337^b *as we would once more repeat*: see VII. 14 and 15.

1338^a *Sitting in order due*: the first of these lines is not in Homer's poetry as we have it; the second corresponds roughly to *Odyssey* XVII. 385; the third quotation is *Odyssey* IX. 7–8.

further discussion: Aristotle does not take up this discussion again.

1338^b *the high-minded*: megalopsuchos = literally great-souled. In *Nicomachean Ethics* IV. 3 Aristotle describes the great-souled man as one who thinks himself worthy of great things and really is worthy of them, i.e. he is someone whose self-esteem is justifiably high.

CHAPTER 5

1339^a *Some questions concerning music ... to pursue the matter further*: very little Greek music has survived and our knowledge of it, as compared with other Greek art forms, is very limited. In this chapter Aristotle, like Plato in the *Republic* and the *Laws*, takes it for granted that music has great emotional power. Not only can it represent or depict the emotions much more effectively than any other medium but it also tends to create those feelings in the listener. In this way it has the power to shape the characters, particularly of the young. See Plato, *Republic* 398c–400e; *Laws* 664a–671a, 700a–701c.

Euripides says: Bacchae 381.

a cultivated way of living: diagōgē. The word usually means simply 'a way of living or spending one's time', but in this context Aristotle is clearly using it in a more specialized sense to refer to the life of cultivated leisure which he sees as proper for a freeman. Commentators have disagreed about the nature of this cultivated life and the role that music plays in it. Some suppose that the purpose of music is purely to prepare the soul for a life of contemplation. Others see it as an integral part of the cultivated life which Aristotle wants his citizens to pursue. But there is also a disagreement whether this cultivated life is or is not to be identified with the life of contemplation. Some say that Aristotle is admitting that only a few individuals can achieve the contemplative life and is offering the cultivated life as the best possibility for those in charge of cities in the real world. Others believe that the cultivated life in which music plays a part involves the exercise of pure reason and is thus identified by Aristotle with the contemplative life. See Depew, 'Politics, Music and Contemplation in Aristotle's Ideal State'.

1339^b *Musaeus*: a legendary pre-Homeric poet. Collections of verses attributed to him were evidently highly prized.

to achieve our end: i.e. happiness.

1340^a *Olympus*: a semi-legendary Phrygian composer.

in listening to imitative (music): literally 'when listening to imitation'. Barker followed Newman in taking this to refer to 'imitative' sounds (presumably imitations of the sounds of nature). But it is difficult to see how pure sound, without rhythm or melody, could imitate a moral character. The reference is more likely to be to choral performances in which other elements (notably the words) contributed to the representation of emotion and character.

draw some conclusions: the general argument is that since (1) music can give pleasure, and (2) goodness consists in feeling pleasure aright (i.e. in connection with the right sort of acts and the right sort of characters), music of the right character can help in producing goodness, because it can help in producing a feeling of pleasure in acts and characters of the right sort.

everyone shares this sense: while it is easy to see why Aristotle should think that the visual arts can convey emotion only in an indirect and limited way, the relevance of the remark that everyone shares this sense is far from clear.

moral character: Polygnotus was a celebrated painter active in the fifth century BC. His major works were large mural paintings on public buildings in Athens and elsewhere. He was particularly noted for his ability to portray character. Pauso was evidently a painter of lesser stature.

different modes: Greek music was based on a system of modes—different ways of arranging the notes on the scale. Different modes were held to be expressive of different emotions.

1340^b *the attribute of harmony*: the view that the soul is a harmony is ascribed to the Pythagoreans. It is criticized by Socrates in Plato's *Phaedo* (85c–86d, 91c–95a) on the grounds that the soul can be said to have harmony (i.e. the good soul is a harmonious one); it cannot therefore be a harmony.

CHAPTER 6

1340^b *the rattle of Archytas*: Archytas of Tarentum, famous both as a statesman and as a mathematician, was a contemporary of Plato. It is not clear why a child's rattle should bear his name.

1341^a *the effect we have mentioned*: i.e. the objection may apply to some kinds of music but not to all.

that common element in music: i.e. the element of mere (sensual) pleasure.

good listeners: the Greek *akroatēs* means either 'listener' or 'pupil'.

prevents the player from using words: a flute, unlike instruments such as the lyre, makes it impossible to sing as one plays. But the Greek *logos*, 'word', also means 'reason' so there may be a suggestion that the flute is associated with irrationality.

Ecphantides: evidently the flute-player of the chorus.

1341^b *the pēctis, barbitos, the heptagons, triagons, sambukai*: these are all types of plucked string instruments.

a bad standard: their aim is assumed to be the pleasure of their audience.

CHAPTER 7

1341^b *with a view to education*: Aristotle is clearly considering not only what sort of music is appropriate for education but what sorts should be allowed generally.

relaxation from strain: this list of possible purposes differs from those given in VIII. 5 (1339^{a}14–26; 1339^{b}11–14). Here relaxation and amusement are linked with the cultivated way of life (*diagōgē*) and not distinguished from it, and *katharsis* (the release of emotion), which was not mentioned in Ch. 5, is introduced.

1342^a *purging*: *katharsis*, the word earlier translated as 'release of emotion', is here used in its literal sense.

1342^b *he rejected the use of the flute*: *Republic* 399a.

the dithyramb: a song, with music and dancing, originally concerned with the birth and fortunes of the god Dionysus, but afterwards taking a wider range; it was in a lofty but often inflated style, and was always in the Phrygian mode and therefore accompanied by the flute (Barker).

as instruments of education: *Republic* 398e.

and the proper: here the *Politics* ends abruptly. Clearly the account of education is incomplete and there are many other aspects of the ideal city which Aristotle presumably intended to cover—he has made several unfulfilled promises. There is nothing to indicate that the ending of the work has been lost and we must therefore conclude with Barker that this is where Aristotle's notes ended. Barker also points out that almost every section or *methodos* in the *Politics* ends abruptly so it is not surprising that the last 'method' should have a similar ending.

MACEDONIA

Epidamnus

Apollonia

Pella

Amphipolis

Stagira

Olynthus

Aphytis

THESSALY

Larissa

Ambracia

Leucas

Hestiaea/Oreus

Opus

Delphi

Chalcis

Thebes

Eretria

Elis

Sicyon

Corinth

Athens

Salamis

Olympia

Argos

Aegina

Mantinea

ARCADIA

Sparta

The World of the Politics

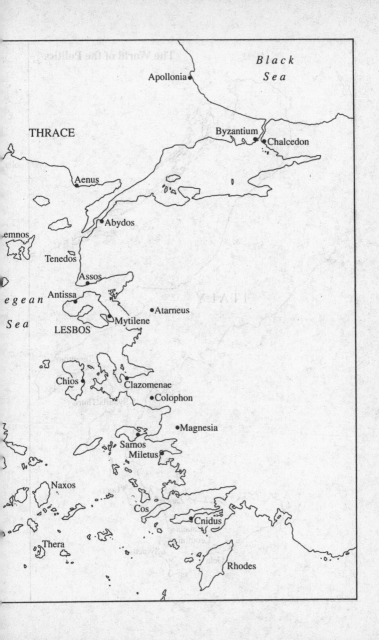

The World of the Politics

ITALY

Tarentum

Sybaris/Thurii

Locri

Zancle

Catana
Leontini
Syracuse
Gela

INDEX

The main purpose of this index is to assist the reader in exploring the political and philosophical concepts which structure Aristotle's thought in *Politics*. It is therefore highly selective. The only proper names included are those of thinkers and legislators whose work Aristotle considers and those of cities whose constitutional arrangements he discusses.

The index is also designed to serve as a glossary. Most entries therefore begin with an English headword followed by one or more Greek equivalents. In each case the Greek terms given are those which Aristotle most commonly uses, but, like every other author, he is capable of using different words to express what is essentially the same idea. Thus the fact that a particular Greek word is given as the equivalent of the headword for an entry does not imply that that particular Greek term occurs in every passage to which a reference is given.

THE WORLD'S CLASSICS

A Select List

HANS ANDERSEN: Fairy Tales
Translated by L. W. Kingsland
Introduction by Naomi Lewis
Illustrated by Vilhelm Pedersen and Lorenz Frølich

ARTHUR J. ARBERRY (Transl.): The Koran

LUDOVICO ARIOSTO: Orlando Furioso
Translated by Guido Waldman

ARISTOTLE: The Nicomachean Ethics
Translated by David Ross

JANE AUSTEN: Emma
Edited by James Kinsley and David Lodge

Mansfield Park
Edited by James Kinsley and John Lucas

Persuasion
Edited by John Davie

HONORÉ DE BALZAC: Père Goriot
Translated and Edited by A. J. Krailsheimer

CHARLES BAUDELAIRE: The Flowers of Evil
Translated by James McGowan
Introduction by Jonathan Culler

WILLIAM BECKFORD: Vathek
Edited by Roger Lonsdale

R. D. BLACKMORE: Lorna Doone
Edited by Sally Shuttleworth

KEITH BOSLEY (Transl.): The Kalevala

JAMES BOSWELL: Life of Johnson
The Hill/Powell edition, revised by David Fleeman
Introduction by Pat Rogers

MARY ELIZABETH BRADDON: Lady Audley's Secret
Edited by David Skilton

GIORGIO VASARI: The Lives of the Artists
Translated and Edited by Julia Conaway Bondanella and Peter Bondanella

JULES VERNE: Journey to the Centre of the Earth
Translated and Edited by William Butcher

IZAAK WALTON and CHARLES COTTON:
The Compleat Angler
Edited by John Buxton
Introduction by John Buchan

OSCAR WILDE: Complete Shorter Fiction
Edited by Isobel Murray

A complete list of Oxford Paperbacks, including The World's Classics, OPUS, Past Masters, Oxford Authors, Oxford Shakespeare, and Oxford Paperback Reference, is available in the UK from the Arts and Reference Publicity Department (BH), Oxford University Press, Walton Street, Oxford OX2 6DP.

In the USA, complete lists are available from the Paperbacks Marketing Manager, Oxford University Press, 200 Madison Avenue, New York, NY 10016.

Oxford Paperbacks are available from all good bookshops. In case of difficulty, customers in the UK can order direct from Oxford University Press Bookshop, Freepost, 116 High Street, Oxford, OX1 4BR, enclosing full payment. Please add 10 per cent of published price for postage and packing.